MEDIUM ÆVUM MONOGRAPHS

SERIES EDITORS
K. P. Clarke, S. Huot, A. J. Lappin,
N. F. Palmer, C. Saunders

MEDIUM ÆVUM MONOGRAPHS
XXIX

HOW TO CORRECT THE *SACRA SCRIPTURA*?

TEXTUAL CRITICISM OF THE LATIN
BIBLE BETWEEN THE TWELFTH AND
FIFTEENTH CENTURY

CORNELIA LINDE

The Society for the Study of Medieval Languages and Literature

OXFORD · MMXII

THE SOCIETY FOR THE STUDY OF
MEDIEVAL LANGUAGES AND LITERATURE

© Cornelia Linde, 2011

British Library Cataloguing in Publication Data

A catalogue record for this book is
available from the British Library

ISBN-13:
978-0-907570-22-6 (hb)
978-0-907570-44-8 (pb)
978-0-907570-54-7 (pdf e-bk)

First published (in hardback) 2012
This reprint first issued 2015

This volume was prepared for publication by A. J. Lappin

for Jorge García de Bustos

CONTENTS

Acknowledgements viii
Editorial Principles xi
A Note on Terminology xi
Abbreviations xii
Bible Editions xii

Part I: Introduction 1
   I.1 Medieval Terminology 7

Part II: The Vulgate and Medieval Editions of the Bible .. 27
   II.1 The Rise of the Vulgate 29
   II.2 Medieval Editions 39
   II.3 Attitudes Towards St Jerome 49

Part III: The Textual Traditions of the Bible and Their
Manuscript Transmission 79
   III.1 Which Version of the Bible Is Contained in the
         Manuscripts? 81
   III.2 Views of the Textual Traditions and Their
         Manuscript Transmission 105

Part IV: Justifications for Interventions 199
   IV.1 *Consuetudo* versus *veritas* 201
   IV.2 The Role of Grammar in Emending the Bible 217

Part V: Conclusion 241

Appendix: Biobibliographical Information 250

Bibliography 267
   Manuscripts 267
   Primary Sources and Secondary Literature 267

ACKNOWLEDGEMENTS

This study is the revised version of my doctoral dissertation, written at the Warburg Institute, University of London. My thanks are due to all the staff, students and fellows at the Warburg Institute who contributed to making my sojourn such a wonderful time and turned the Warburg Institute into much more than an academic institution. Above all, I am deeply grateful to my supervisor, Jill Kraye, who has been more than generous with her time and has contributed greatly to my work with her keen insight and constructive advice. On both an intellectual and a personal level, I could not have wished for a better *Doktormutter*.

Paul Gerhard Schmidt, who sadly passed away before this book was published, has also been an important influence on my career, and I am profoundly indebted to him not only for nourishing my enthusiasm about medieval Latin but also for being an exemplar of scholarly generosity.

Many other colleagues and friends have been crucial to the successful outcome of this project: Guido Giglioni and Magnus Ryan read parts of the dissertation and provided me with valuable feedback; Alastair Hamilton always had time for my questions concerning the biblical tradition; Steffen Egle, Dorian Greenbaum, Ulrike Kern, Saara Leskinen and Jan Loop were and still are good friends, to whose support I often turned, not only when the PhD research got tough. My examiners, David d'Avray and Nigel Palmer, made many useful suggestions and helped greatly in the transformation of the thesis to a book. I am grateful to Anthony John Lappin, the series editor, who made the process of publication easy with his supportive and at times amusing messages. My thanks are also due to Lesley Smith, who peer-reviewed the manuscript, for her constructive comments for improvement.

This study would not have been possible without financial support. I am deeply indebted to the School of Advanced Study, University of London, and the Arts and Humanities Research Council for generously funding my doctoral research from beginning to end. A research trip to Paris was paid for by the Student Travel Fund of the Warburg Institute.

ACKNOWLEDGEMENTS

My research benefited greatly from direct access to manuscripts. For this, I am grateful to the British Library, London, especially the staff in the Manuscripts Reading Room, to the Bibliothèque nationale de France, Paris, and to the Bibliothèque de l'Arsenal, Paris.

I owe special thanks to Clemens Kaiser for many years of friendship and for always being there. Finally, I wish to express my deepest love and gratitude to my family, especially Peter and Renate Eppendorfer, Julius Linde and Jorge García de Bustos, for their love, support and encouragement.

EDITORIAL PRINCIPLES

All translations, with the exception of passages from the Bible, are my own. In transcribing Latin manuscripts and early modern printed books, I have silently expanded abbreviations and occasionally modified capitalization and punctuation for the convenience of the reader. I have not, however, normalised the orthography. Abbreviations in modern editions have been expanded. In my transcriptions, square brackets denote insertions; angle brackets stand for deletions. Further editorial comments are given in curly brackets.

Greek New Testament quotations found in the 1540 edition of Lorenzo Valla's *Annotationes in Novum Testamentum* have not been corrected; in case of deviations from the modern edition, the version as found in the *Novum Testamentum Graece* is given in square brackets.

The anglicized names of medieval and Renaissance authors have been used unless other conventional versions exist (e.g. Hugh of St Cher, but Lorenzo Valla).

A NOTE ON TERMINOLOGY

Throughout this study, some terms have been used more loosely than they usually are nowadays. The term textual critic refers to medieval and early Renaissance scholars who engaged critically with any aspect of the text and transmission of the Latin Bible, even if these scholars were not actively involved in or do not, in their work, focus on the emendation of Scripture. Although their concepts and ideas might at times differ considerably from modern approaches, they should, without doubt, be regarded as precursors, even trailblazers, of modern textual criticism.

The terms emendation and to emend encompass both *emendatio ope codicum* and *emendatio ope ingenii*.

An edition denotes a new recension, deliberately produced by an editor, in contrast to a copy as a transcription produced by a scribe.

ABBREVIATIONS

BNF   Bibliothèque Nationale de France
DBI   *Dizionario biografico degli italiani*, Rome 1960-
LexMA   *Lexikon des Mittelalters*, 9 vols and *Registerband*, Munich 1980-1999
ODNB   *Oxford Dictionary of National Biography. From the Earliest Time to the Year 2000*, 61 vols, ed. H. C. G. Matthew and B. Harrison, Oxford 2004
PL   *Patrologiae cursus completus. Series latina*, 221 vols, ed. J.-P. Migne

Abbreviations for books of the Bible are taken from *The Jerusalem Bible*, ed. A. Jones, London 1966.

BIBLE EDITIONS

Biblia sacra iuxta vulgatam versionem, ed. R. Weber et al., 4th edn, Stuttgart 1994.
Novum Testamentum Graece, ed. E. Nestle et al., 27th edn, Stuttgart 2004.
Septuaginta: id est Vetus Testamentum graece iuxta LXX interpretes, 2 vols, ed. A. Rahlfs, 3rd edn, Stuttgart 1949.
תורה נביאים וכתובים: *Biblia Hebraica Stuttgartensia*, ed. K. Elliger et al., 5th edn, Stuttgart 2007.

All English translations of passages from the Bible are taken from *The Holy Bible. Translated from the Latin Vulgate*, London 2007.

PART I:
INTRODUCTION

INTRODUCTION

In accounts of the Latin Bible in the Middle Ages, it is sometimes assumed that the subject of debate is a specific text – usually identified with the Vulgate – which remained relatively stable and unchanged throughout the centuries. This, however, is far from the truth. In the first place, Jerome's version was by no means the only Latin translation of the Bible in circulation during the Middle Ages. Moreover, every medieval manuscript of the Latin Bible contained corruptions and variants of all kinds. Of course, medieval scholars were aware of this, and often scribes – and sometimes editors – attempted to emend the text. The pursuit of a better text, however, was not merely a practical endeavour: from the twelfth century onwards, we also find theoretical discussions devoted entirely or partly to approaches towards and methods of emendation of the Latin Bible. These texts are the subject of the present study.

Early modern scholars have sought to assemble and evaluate material on the history of the Bible. Ground-breaking work was done in the late seventeenth and early eighteenth centuries by the Frenchman Richard Simon (1638–1712) and the Englishman Humphrey Hody (1659–1707), both of whom collected and presented information on the history and reception of the Bible.[1] Several important studies of the Latin Bible in the Middle Ages were written by Samuel Berger at the turn of the twentieth century.[2] Among the most important contributions by twentieth-century scholars are: Henri de Lubac's monumental work on the

---

[1] Humphrey Hody, *De Bibliorum textibus originalibus, versionibus Græcis et Latina Vulgata*, Oxford 1705. Among Simon's various works, see especially Richard Simon, *Histoire critique des versions du Nouveau Testament...*, Rotterdam 1690; Richard Simon, *Histoire critique des principaux commentateurs du Nouveau Testament...*, Rotterdam 1693; and Richard Simon, *Histoire critique du Vieux Testament. Suivi de Lettre sur l'inspiration*, ed. P. Gibert, Montrouge 2008. For a recent study of Richard Simon, see Sascha Müller, *Richard Simon (1638–1712): Exeget, Theologe, Philosoph und Historiker. Eine Biographie*, Würzburg [2005].

[2] See, e.g., Samuel Berger, *Histoire de la Vulgate pendant les premiers siècles du moyen âge*, Nancy 1893; and Samuel Berger, *Les préfaces jointes aux livres de la Bible dans les manuscrits de la Vulgate*, Paris 1902.

history of medieval exegesis;[3] Bonifatius Fischer's various writings on the transmission and text of the Latin Bible in the Middle Ages;[4] Beryl Smalley's highly influential *The Study of the Bible in the Middle Ages*;[5] and Friedrich Stegmüller's indispensable repertory of medieval Latin literature on the Bible.[6]

The first fundamental piece of modern scholarship which deals explicitly and exclusively with the history of textual criticism of the Latin Bible in the Middle Ages is Heinrich Denifle's 1888 essay 'Die Handschriften der Bibel-Correctorien des 13. Jahrhunderts'. Denifle not only published several important texts for the first time, drawing attention to these pieces, but also made a first attempt at grappling with the still insufficiently explored genre of *correctoria*.[7] This field of research has also found some remarkable proponents in recent times, most notably Gilbert Dahan.[8] Nevertheless, no attempt has yet been made to gather together the available material and to examine the notions and ideas voiced in medieval and early Renaissance works dealing with textual criticism of the Latin Bible. This study will, I hope, start to fill this gap in modern research.

---

[3] Henri de Lubac, *Exégèse médiévale: les quatre sens de l'Écriture*, 4 vols, [Paris] 1959–1964.

[4] See, e.g., Bonifatius Fischer, 'Zur Überlieferung altlateinischer Bibeltexte im Mittelalter', *Nederlands Archief voor Kerkgeschiedenis* 56 (1975), pp. 19–34; and Bonifatius Fischer, 'Bibelausgaben des frühen Mittelalters', in *La Bibbia nell'alto medioevo: 26 aprile – 2 maggio 1962*, Spoleto 1963, pp. 519–600.

[5] Beryl Smalley, *The Study of the Bible in the Middle Ages*, Oxford 1941, 3rd edn Oxford 1983, repr. Oxford 1984.

[6] Friedrich Stegmüller, *Repertorium biblicum medii aevi*, 11 vols, Madrid 1940–1980.

[7] Heinrich Denifle, 'Die Handschriften der Bibel–Correctorien des 13. Jahrhunderts', *Archiv für Literatur- und Kirchengeschichte des Mittelalters* 4 (1888), pp. 263–311 and 471–601. Denifle's essay finishes with the note 'Schluss folgt' (p. 601); but he does not seem to have published the planned final section of his work. For the *correctoria*, see below, pp. 253–255.

[8] See, e.g., Gilbert Dahan, 'La critique textuelle dans les correctoires de la Bible du XIIIe siècle', in *Langages et philosophie: hommage à Jean Jolivet*, ed. A. de Libera, A. Elamrani-Jamal, A. Galonnier, Paris 1997, pp. 365–392. For a bibliography of scholarly literature on the Latin Bible, see Pierre-Maurice Bogaert, 'Bulletin de la Bible latine', most recently VIII, *Revue Bénédictine* 118 (2008), pp. 148–170. Bogaert (*ibid.*, p. 148) provides references to the earlier parts of the 'Bulletin'. See also André Vernet, *La Bible au moyen âge: Bibliographie*, Paris 1989.

My investigation is limited to treatises which either deal exclusively with the emendation of Latin Scripture or focus in part on theoretical considerations regarding the topic. I have not taken into consideration works about orthography, nor have I compared the methods and ideas of textual critics of the Bible with those of textual critics of pagan texts. Other theological writings, such as exegetical works and those dealing with the liturgy, have, with few exceptions, been excluded for reasons of manageability. Most importantly, this study is not concerned with the actual emendations found in biblical manuscripts, the comprehensive examination and evaluation of which would be a vast undertaking, impossible for a single scholar. Instead, the focus rests exclusively on ideas and opinions expressed by medieval and early Renaissance writers about the textual criticism of the Latin Bible. Since this study is devoted to exploring the development of certain text-critical issues in the course of the four centuries examined, the chapters address thematic questions, but within themselves follow chronological order. Part I, in addition to this introduction, is concerned with medieval terminology of various versions of the Bible. In Part II, I give a brief overview of the development of the Latin Bible and its medieval editions. The rise of the cult surrounding St Jerome is discussed and then compared to the views of textual critics about him and his version of the Bible. Part III concerns questions of manuscript transmission. Chapter III.1 is devoted to the question of which version the textual critics thought had come down to them in the manuscripts at their disposal, an issue which has so far been entirely overlooked by modern scholarship. The main section of this study is concerned with the views of medieval and early Renaissance scholars on the textual transmission of the various versions of the Bible and their opinions about the authority and status of these versions. Finally, in Part IV, I examine two ways in which medieval textual critics justified interventions in the biblical text: a discussion of the contrasting principles of *consuetudo* and *veritas* is followed by a chapter investigating the role assigned to grammar in the emendation of the Latin Bible, the results of which challenge the commonly held view in modern scholarship about the relationship between Latin Scripture and grammar in the Middle Ages. After a summary of the main results, the book closes with an appendix containing very brief biographies of the main authors and information on their relevant works.

This study covers the timeframe from the twelfth to the end of the fifteenth century. The starting point corresponds to the emergence of theoretical treatises dealing with textual criticism of the Latin Bible. I conclude before the turbulent times of the sixteenth century because the Reformation and later the Council of Trent gave rise to a different set of issues, parts of which have already been studied in detail.[9]

---

[9] For a study of the early modern history of textual criticism (without any focus on the Bible), see Klara Vanek, *'Ars corrigendi' in der frühen Neuzeit: Studien zur Geschichte der Textkritik*, Berlin 2007. James E. G. Zetzel (*Latin Textual Criticism in Antiquity*, New York 1981) devotes no attention to text-critical problems or discussions of the Latin Bible in late antiquity.

I.1 MEDIEVAL TERMINOLOGY

To the modern reader, medieval terminology can be a thorny issue. Its definitions were, at times, less precise than we would demand of a modern scholar, and this can give rise to the impression that it is inconsistent and variable. The exploration of medieval nomenclature of the different versions of the Bible is fundamental both to our understanding of texts dealing with the history of Scripture and to grasping how the writers themselves understood the issues they discussed. Despite its significance, no survey of medieval terminology of the various versions of the Bible exists.

In order to give an accurate interpretation of the sources consulted, an examination of the Latin terms used to describe the various versions of the Bible is therefore indispensable. In this section, after briefly explaining the terminology that I have adopted, I shall examine the late antique and medieval meaning of the phrases *septuaginta*, *vulgata*, *hebraica veritas* and *graeca veritas*.[1]

Due to the in part considerable discrepancies between their medieval and modern definitions, the phrases *septuaginta*, *vulgata*, *hebraica veritas* and *graeca veritas* cannot be easily translated into English. For instance, as we shall see, the medieval term *vulgata* was used very differently from the modern Vulgate. So, when translating or discussing quotations containing any of these expressions, I shall in most instances leave them in the original Latin.[2] By using the Latin terms, my aim is to embrace the full extent of their medieval meanings, which will be outlined below. In the case of the English terms Vulgate and Septuagint, however, I follow modern usage: the term Vulgate refers exclusively to the Latin version of the Bible commonly ascribed to St Jerome, and

---

[1] For an examination of medieval terminology for the Bible in general, see Monique Duchet-Suchaux and Yves Lefèvre, 'Les noms de la Bible', in *Le Moyen Age et la Bible*, ed. P. Riché and G. Lobrichon, Paris 1984, pp. 13–23.

[2] The phrases *hebraica veritas* and *graeca veritas* are left untranslated by many modern scholars; see, e.g., Eugene F. Rice, *Saint Jerome in the Renaissance*, Baltimore and London 1985, p. 17; Michael Graves, *Jerome's Hebrew Philology: A Study Based on his Commentary on Jeremiah*, Leiden 2007, p. 2; Allan K. Jenkins and Patrick Preston, *Biblical Scholarship and the Church: A Sixteenth-Century Crisis of Authority*, Aldershot 2007, p. 17.

Septuagint to the first Greek version of the entire Old Testament.[3] The phrases Vetus Latina and Old Latin are used interchangeably to denote the first Latin translation(s) of the Bible, pre-dating Jerome's version.[4]

Septuaginta

The Septuagint was the ancient Jewish translation of the Old Testament into Greek. Begun in the third century BCE with the Pentateuch, it was largely finished towards the end of the following century.[5] From the second century BCE onwards, a legend surrounding the origin of the Septuagint came into circulation. It is first found in the so-called Letter of Aristeas, which purports to have been written by a court official of Ptolemy II (309-246 BCE), king of Egypt; in it, it is claimed that seventy-two Jews were sent to Alexandria to translate the Pentateuch from Hebrew into Greek.[6]

---

[3] Pierre-Maurice Bogaert ('La Bible latine des origines au moyen âge: aperçu historique, état des questions', *Revue théologique de Louvain* 19 [1988], pp. 137–159 and 276–314, at p. 289) notes that since the sixteenth century the term *vulgata* has been used for the Latin Bibles containing the text attributed to Jerome. He also stresses (ibid., p. 156) that many modern studies of the language of the Latin Bible mistakenly treat the entire Vulgate as Jerome's translation (for Jerome's actual translations and emendations, see ibid., pp. 139–40, and below, pp. 30–37). Nonetheless, for reasons of manageability and, more importantly, because Jerome was commonly thought to have translated the entire Bible (see below, p. 58), my use of the term Vulgate will include even those books that he left untouched or only emended (but which were usually attributed to him). The term Septuagint technically refers only to the first Greek translation of the Torah. The authors discussed here, however, were not aware of the different stages of translation and summarised the entire first Greek version of the Old Testament under the name *septuaginta*; furthermore, the term Septuagint is to this day commonly applied also to the later translations of the prophetic and hagiographic books. Since I am not dealing with intricacies of the Greek transmission, I shall, for the sake of simplicity, use Septuagint in its broader definition. For the terminological problems concerning the term Septuagint, see David G. Burke, 'The First Versions: the Septuagint, the Targums, and the Latin', in *A History of Bible Translation*, ed. P. A. Noss, Rome 2007, pp. 59–80, at p. 63.

[4] For the Vetus Latina, see also below, pp. 29–30.

[5] See *Septuaginta: id est Vetus Testamentum graece iuxta LXX interpretes*, 2 vols, ed. A. Rahlfs, 3rd edn, Stuttgart 1949, I, p. VI. For a recent short introduction to the Septuagint, see Burke, 'The First Versions', at pp. 61–71.

[6] For an introduction, edition, English translation and commentary, see [Aristeas], *Aristeas to Philocrates (Letter of Aristeas)*, ed. and tr. M. Hadas, New York [1951]. Hadas assumes that the work might have been written around 130 BCE; see ibid., p. 54.

Later writers embellished the story with further details, claiming, for instance, that although the translators occupied separate cells, their translations were all identical, and that they translated not merely the Pentateuch but the entire Old Testament. This extension to include the Old Testament as a whole can be traced back at least to the time of Justin Martyr (d. c. 165 CE).[7]

For medieval scholars, the most influential source of information on earlier translations of the Bible was without doubt Jerome. In his writings, he regularly refers to what he calls the *septuaginta* and to the Greek versions of the Old Testament by the second-century scholars Aquila, Theodotion and Symmachus, discussing the translators and their works, and presenting their renderings of individual words or longer passages.[8] Yet the term *septuaginta* referred not only to the Septuagint but also to its Latin translation. This double meaning, covering what we now call the Septuagint and its Vetus Latina translation, is well attested in Jerome and Augustine (354-430), and, almost certainly through their influence, came to be widely adopted in the medieval Latin West.[9]

Some confusion about the precise meaning of *septuaginta* is apparent in the *Suffraganeus bibliothece* of the twelfth-century Cistercian Nicolò Maniacutia:

> Septuaginta sane translacio ipsa est, ut quibusdam videtur, que Vulgata dicitur, licet Iosephus scribat et Iudei tradant, sicut infert Ieronimus super Micheam et in prologo Hebraicarum questionum, quinque tantum libros Moysi ab eis in grecum translatos et Ptolomeo regi Alexandrie traditos. Sive igitur hii tantum quinque, sive totum

---

[7] See Jean Gribomont, 'Aux origines de la Vulgate', in *La Bibbia 'Vulgata' dalle origini ai nostri giorni: Atti del simposio internazionale in onore di Sisto V, Grottammare, 29–31 agosto 1985*, ed. T. Stramare, Rome and Vatican City 1987, pp. 11–20, at p. 13. The attribution of the entire Old Testament to the Seventy or, more precisely, seventy–two translators is found only in the Christian tradition; see Jenkins and Preston, *Biblical Scholarship*, p. 4. For the history of the legend, see Abraham and David J. Wasserstein, *The Legend of the Septuagint: From Classical Antiquity to Today*, Cambridge 2006.

[8] See, e.g., Jerome, 'Prologus in libro Iob', in *Biblia sacra iuxta vulgatam versionem*, ed. R. Weber et al., 4th edn, Stuttgart 1994, pp. 731–732; here and elsewhere Jerome also provides information on Origen's Hexapla. For a short introduction to Aquila, Theodotion and Symmachus, see Sidney Jellicoe, *The Septuagint and Modern Study*, Oxford 1968, pp. 76–99.

[9] For examples from Jerome and Augustine, see, e.g., below, p. 110, n. 14; and p. 111, n. 17.

vetus fuerit testamentum, quis et hoc, et novum de greco ante Ieronimi tempora verterit in latinum me fateor ignorare.[10]

The *septuaginta* translation, according to some, is the same as the one which is called *vulgata*, even though Josephus writes and the Jews say that, as Jerome relates in his *On Micah* and in the prologue of his *Hebrew Questions*, only the Five Books of Moses were translated into Greek by them and presented to King Ptolemy of Alexandria. I confess that I am at a loss to know if it was only these five, or if it was the entire Old Testament, or who translated both it and the New Testament from Greek into Latin before the time of Jerome.

Admitting that he does not know what exactly *septuaginta* means, Maniacutia mentions the original Greek translation of the Pentateuch and also the entire Greek Old Testament, as well as its Old Latin version. Despite his uncertainty, however, he tacitly accepts the broadest definition of the term. That he includes the Vetus Latina translation of the Old Testament in his understanding of *septuaginta* is more obvious from another passage in the same work. Alluding to a defence found in Jerome's 'In Ionam' of his translation of הקיקיון in Jon 4.6, Maniacutia comments: 'Pro *ciceion* herba quam latinus sermo non habet, lxx interpretes *cucurbitam*, Ieronimus *ederam* transtulit' (For the herb *ciceion*, which does not exist in Latin, the LXX give the translation gourd {*cucurbita*}, Jerome ivy {*hedera*}).[11] Clearly, the reference here is to the Vetus Latina, even though via a quotation from Jerome.

---

[10] Nicolò Maniacutia, [Preface to his *Suffraganeus bibliothece*], in Denifle, 'Die Handschriften', pp. 270-276, at p. 275. The references are to Jerome, 'In Michaeam prophetam', in his *Commentarii in prophetas minores*, 2 vols, in his *Opera*, I: *Opera exegetica*, 6, ed. M. Adriaen, Turnhout 1969–1970, I, pp. 421–524, at pp. 446–447 (I, ii, 9/10); and Jerome, *Hebraicae quaestiones in libro Geneseos*, ed. P. de Lagarde, in his *Opera*, I: *Opera exegetica* 1, Turnhout 1959, pp. 1–56, at p. 2. For biographical information on Maniacutia, see below, pp. 250–252.

[11] Nicolò Maniacutia, *Suffraganeus bibliothece*, in MS Brussels, Bibliothèque royale, 4031-33, ff. 1ʳ–32ᵛ, at f. 29ᵛ. See Jerome, 'In Ionam prophetam', in his *Commentarii in prophetas minores*, I, pp. 377–419, at pp. 414–415 (IV, 6): 'Miror cur mihi non liceat *hederam* transferre pro *cucurbita* ... Pro *cucurbita*, siue *hedera* in Hebraeo legimus *ciceion* ... Latinus sermo hanc speciem arboris non habebat.' The precise meaning of הקיקיון still remains unclear; the basic meaning given in Francis Brown, Samuel R. Driver, and Charles A. Briggs, *A Hebrew and English Lexicon of the Old Testament*, Oxford 1907, repr. 1972, p. 884, is 'a plant', and, with regard to the passage in Jonah, it is suggested that it might mean 'bottle-gourd'.

The use of *septuaginta* to mean both the Septuagint and the Vetus Latina is also attested by other medieval writers. A clear-cut example that *septuaginta* applied to the Vetus Latina is provided by Roger Bacon in his *Opus minus*. He writes: 'Apud Latinos non fuerunt translationes nisi duae, scilicet Septuaginta et Hieronymi' (Among the Latins there were only two translations, namely the *septuaginta* {the Vetus Latina} and Jerome's).[12] Nevertheless, in his *Opus majus*, he applies the same term to the Septuagint:

> In textu sacro inveniuntur falsa, et male translata quamplurima. Nam Hieronymus probat translationem LXX interpretum {*sc. the Septuagint*} et Theodotionis et Aquilae multas habuisse falsitates, quae fuerunt vulgatae per totam Ecclesiam. Et omnes stabant maxime pro translatione LXX, sicut pro vita, et reputabatur Hieronymus falsarius et corruptor scripturarum, donec paulatim claruit veritas Hebraica per solum Hieronymum in Latinum conversa. Ne tamen nimia novita[t]e {*my correction*} deterreret Latinos, ideo, ut ipse scribit, aliquando coaptavit se LXX interpretibus et aliquando Theodotioni, aliquando Aquilae, et ideo multa dimisit, et propter hoc remanserunt plura falsa.[13]

> A very large number of mistakes and bad renderings are found in Scripture. For Jerome shows that the version of the LXX translators, of Theodotion and of Aquila had many errors which were disseminated throughout the entire Church. And everyone stood by the LXX translation, just as they would by their own lives, and Jerome was regarded as a forger and corrupter of Scripture, until gradually the *hebraica veritas* shone forth, rendered into Latin by Jerome alone. But in order not to frighten the Latins with too much novelty, he, for this reason, as he himself writes, accomodated himself at times to the LXX translators, at times to Theodotion, at times to Aquila; and, therefore, he left aside many things, and it is for this reason that many falsities remain.

Here, *LXX* is clearly meant to denote the Septuagint when *LXX* is paralleled with Theodotion and Aquila; its Latin translation might be understood when it is contrasted to Jerome's translation. No distinction, however, is made between the two versions. Instead,

---

[12] See also Roger Bacon, *Opus minus*, in his *Opera quaedam hactenus inedita*, ed. J. S. Brewer, London 1859, pp. 313-389, at p. 336. See below, p. 257, for some biographical information on Roger Bacon.

[13] Roger Bacon, *Opus majus*, ed. J. H. Bridges, 2 vols, Oxford 1897, I, p. 69. Bacon is referring to Jerome, *Commentarius in Ecclesiasten*, ed. M. Adriaen, in his *Opera*, I: *Opera exegetica*, I, Turnhout 1959, pp. 249–361, at p. 249 (*praefatio*).

the Septuagint and the Vetus Latina are subsumed under the name *LXX*.

Gerard of Huy, likewise, includes the Vetus Latina in the term *septuaginta*. In one instance, he writes that the edition of the LXX is contained in the Hexapla – clearly referring to the Septuagint. Yet in another passage he points out how Latin manuscripts of the Bible had been corrupted through the introduction of biblical quotations as found in the Fathers, who used the LXX, that is the Vetus Latina.[14]

This nomenclature persists into the fifteenth century. In his treatise on Jn 21.22, the Byzantine émigré Cardinal Bessarion still treats the term *septuaginta* as including the Vetus Latina:

> Neminem praeterea latere debet, sacros libros Veteris Novique Testamenti ab ipsis Ecclesiae nascentis exordiis apud Latinos tum ex Hebraeo ut veteres, tum e Graeco ut et novos, et veteres per Septuaginta Interpretes editos fuisse longo ante Hieronymum tempore, trecentis scilicet et amplius annis, qua editione sancta Latina Ecclesia tunc utebatur, eamque veteres sanctissimi doctores, Cyprianus, Hilarius, Augustinus, Hieronymo coaetaneus ... exposuere.[15]

> Furthermore, everyone must be aware that from the beginning of the early Church the holy books of the Old and New Testaments were composed for the Latins both from the Hebrew for the Old Testament books and from the Greek for the New Testament; and the Old Testament books were composed by the Seventy translators a long time before Jerome, that is to say, over three hundred years. This edition was then used by the holy Latin Church, and it is this one which the holiest teachers – Cyprian, Hilary, Augustine, the contemporary of Jerome – ... interpreted.

The use of the term *septuaginta* to refer both to the first Greek version of the Old Testament and also to the Latin translation

---

[14] See Gerard of Huy, [Preface to his *correctorium*], ed. Denifle, 'Die Handschriften', pp. 298-310, at p. 301: 'Sciendum autem quod ista editio LXX {sc. the Septuagint} in exaplois contenta', and p. 304: 'Quidam non discernentes, quoniam illud invenerunt in libris doctorum qui editione LXX {sc. the Vetus Latina} utuntur, translationi nostre addendum iudicaverunt.' For some information on Gerard of Huy, see below, pp. 256–257.

[15] Cardinal Bessarion, *In illud Evangelii secundum Joannem:* ἐὰν αὐτὸν θέλω μένειν ἕως ἔρχομαι τί πρὸς σέ; *Si eum volo manere donec veniam, quid ad te?* (*Patrologia Graeca*, ed. J.-P. Migne, CLXI), Paris 1866, cols 623–640, at col. 627C. I have slightly emended the punctuation. For further information on Bessarion, see below, pp. 261–262.

based on it thus survived throughout the Middle Ages and beyond. Moreover, subsuming the Septuagint and the Vetus Latina under one name was not merely a matter of terminology, but also of substance. In the Middle Ages, the Septuagint and the Vetus Latina were apparently seen as essentially the same text: in none of the works examined here was a distinction made between the two versions. Instead, *septuaginta* was perceived as the name of a single work which existed both in Greek and in its Latin translation.[16]

A few further points regarding the use of the term *septuaginta* in the Middle Ages need to be kept in mind. In the first place, some medieval scholars did not employ the term at all in the works examined in this study;[17] so it was neither omnipresent nor indispensable in discussions of biblical textual criticism. Secondly, the notion of *septuaginta* as encompassing both the Septuagint and its Latin translation derived from the Church Fathers, who used the term in this way, and many medieval references to the *septuaginta* were either quotations from Jerome or Augustine, or else based on information supplied by them. This terminology was not, therefore, just a medieval curiosity but instead derived from a concept which was already well defined in the patristic era.

Vulgata

In his writings, Jerome describes certain editions of the Bible as *vulgata*, but he never uses the term in relation to his own new Latin version – only since the Council of Trent in the mid-sixteenth century has it been officially called *Vulgata* or, in English, the Vulgate.[18] Instead, Jerome employs *vulgata* not as a proper name,

---

[16] Further research on the *correctoria* should establish whether *septuaginta* was used to refer to the Vetus Latina New Testament in that genre. For a thirteenth–century distinction between the Old and New Testament of the Vetus Latina, see below, p. 134, n. 86.

[17] For instance, Stephen Harding and Hervaeus of Bourg–Dieu.

[18] I have not been able to find *vulgata* (*editio*) used in reference to a biblical version before Jerome; and even in his own time, he seems to have been an exception. The only other examples I have found are Augustine (*De civitate Dei*, in his *Opera*, XIV, ed. B. Dombaert and A. Kalb [Corpus Christianorum. Series Latina, 47], Turnhout 1955, p. 512 [XVI, 10]) and Rufinus of Aquileia, *Apologia contra Hieronymum*, in his *Opera*, ed. M. Simonetti, Turnhout 1961, pp. 37–123, at p. 75 (I, 40), where, however, he is quoting from Jerome. For the decree made by the Council of Trent, see *Canones et decreta sacrosancti oecumenici Concilii Tridentini sub Paulo III. Iulio III. et Pio IV. pontificibus maximis: cum patrum subscriptionibus*, Leipzig

but rather in its usual sense of widely used, common to all or well known to describe the versions in widespread circulation in his day, above all the *septuaginta*, that is, the Septuagint and its Old Latin rendering. For instance, in his commentary on Isaiah, he writes: 'We have said this in agreement with the Seventy translators whose edition is widely used {*vulgata*} throughout the whole world.'[19] In Jerome's time, it was certainly appropriate to refer to the *septuaginta* as the *editio vulgata*: in the Latin West, the Old Latin version dominated the textual tradition for several centuries after Jerome and, as Sutcliffe has pointed out, even after he had finished his own version, Jerome still regarded the *septuaginta* as the *editio vulgata* and continued to use it in the liturgy.[20] Modern scholars have noted that his use of *vulgata* to designate both the Septuagint and the Vetus Latina means that, at times, it is difficult or even impossible to discern which of the two versions he was referring to.[21] As with *septuaginta*, this inclusive meaning continued throughout the Middle Ages; but, as we shall see, its usage was destined to undergo significant changes.

To complicate matters further, in Jerome's writings, the term *vulgata* is not applied solely to the *septuaginta*. In certain instances,

---

1887, pp. 16–17: 'Insuper eadem sacrosancta synodus considerans, non parum utilitatis accedere posse ecclesiae Dei, si ex omnibus latinis editionibus, quae circumferuntur, sacrorum librorum, quaenam pro authentica habenda sit, innotescat: Statuit et declarat, ut haec ipsa vetus et vulgata editio, quae longo tot saeculorum usu in ipsa ecclesia probata est, in publicis lectionibus, disputationibus, praedicationibus et expositionibus pro authentica habeatur.' On this passage, see Rice, *Saint Jerome*, p. 186, who points out that Jerome is never identified as the translator. Hubert Jedin (*Geschichte des Konzils von Trient*, II: *Die erste Trienter Tagungsperiode 1545/7*, Freiburg i. Br. 1957, pp. 79–81) discusses contemporary reactions to the decree. Rice (*Saint Jerome*, p. 176) states that from around 1520, biblical scholars gradually adopted the term *vulgata* for Jerome's version.

[19] Jerome, *Commentarii in Esaiam*, 2 vols, in his *Opera* I: *Opera exegetica*, 2, ed. M. Adriaen, Turnhout 1963, II, p. 763 (XVIII, lxv, 20): 'Hoc iuxta Septuaginta interpretes diximus, quorum editio toto orbe uulgata est.' See also Edward F. Sutcliffe, 'The Name "Vulgate"', *Biblica* 29 (1948), pp. 345–352, at p. 345.

[20] E. F. Sutcliffe, 'Jerome', in *The Cambridge History of the Bible*, II: *The West from the Fathers to the Reformation*, ed. G. W. H. Lampe, Cambridge 1969, pp. 80–101, at p. 95. Gribomont ('Aux origines', p. 11) assumes that what Jerome means by *vulgata* is the biblical text in use in the liturgy. For the survival of the Vetus Latina, see below, pp. 33–36.

[21] This is the view of Franz Kaulen, *Geschichte der Vulgata*, Mainz 1868, pp. 19–20, and Sutcliffe, 'The Name "Vulgate"', p. 346.

it is employed as a translation of the Greek κοινή, that is, the version of the Septuagint before Origen's Hexapla, which is sometimes explicitly contrasted to the *septuaginta*.²² Jerome, therefore, did not use *vulgata* to indicate a specific edition, but rather to make a statement about the diffusion of a text.²³

In the writings of Jerome's contemporaries, there is no indication that they regarded his version of the Bible as *vulgata*; and even though it had finally asserted itself against the Vetus Latina and had become the most commonly used translation from the Carolingian era onwards, it did not acquire the epithet *vulgata* in the Middle Ages.²⁴ Instead, throughout the medieval centuries, *vulgata* was used almost exclusively to denote the *septuaginta*. In contrast to Jerome's times, however, the implication that the *vulgata* was the translation in common use had become obsolete, so

---

²² See Sutcliffe, 'The Name "Vulgate"', p. 345. Kaulen (*Geschichte*, pp. 18–19) tends to see the use of *vulgata* as a translation of κοινή to be more common. For an example, see, e.g., Jerome, *Commentarii in Esaiam*, II, pp. 642–643 (XVI, prologus): 'Nec esse in septuaginta interpretibus, sed in editione Vulgata, quae Graece κοινή dicitur, et in toto orbe diuersa est.' For a brief comparison of Origen's text of the Septuagint in his Hexapla and the κοινή, see Henry Barclay Swete, *An Introduction to the Old Testament in Greek*, Cambridge 1900, pp. 68–69.

²³ The κοινή was hardly ever mentioned by medieval textual critics; and when it was, it was usually in a quotation from Jerome's letter to Sunnia and Fretela; see Gerard of Huy, [Preface to his *correctorium*], p. 301: 'Sciendum autem quod ista editio LXX in exaplois contenta, quia non fuit publicata, mansit incorrupta; sed illa comunis, que asteriscos et obelos non habuit, vitio scriptorum valde corrupta fuit. Sic enim dicit Ieronimus in epistola ad Sunniam et Fretelam [Jerome, *Epistulae*, 4 vols, ed. I. Hilberg and M. Kamptner, 2ⁿᵈ edn, Vienna 1996, II, p. 249 (CVI, 2)]: "κοινη, hoc est communis editio, ipsa est que et LXX. Sed illa pro locis et temporibus voluntate scriptorum vetus corrupta editio est, ea autem que habetur in exaplois et quam nos vertimus, ipsa est que eruditorum libris incorrupta et immaculata LXX interpretum translatio reservatur."' See also Bacon, *Opus minus*, p. 341, where he adduces the passage from Jerome's *Commentarii in Esaiam* mentioned in the previous footnote to counter the idea that the *vulgata* is not the *septuaginta* but rather the κοινή. For the letter to Sunnia and Fretela, see also below, p. 201 and n. 2.

²⁴ See Sutcliffe, 'The Name "Vulgate"', pp. 347 and 349, where he provides some medieval examples for the use of *vulgata*. For another ninth-century example, see Sedulius Scotus, *Collectaneum in Apostolum*, I: *In epistolam ad Romanos*, ed. H. J. Frede and H. Stanjek, Freiburg i. Br. 1996, p. 88 (III, 10): '"Sicut scriptum est quia non est iustus quisquam" [Rm 3.10] et reliqua: Hi octo uersus neque apud Ebraeos neque apud quenquam reperiuntur interpretum, neque apud ipsos qui LXX editionem habent uulgatam.'

that, as we shall see, *vulgata editio* lost the meaning of widely used version and turned into a proper name.

Various statements made by medieval textual critics confirm this development and also clearly show that the term *vulgata* did not refer to Jerome's version. In the passage cited above concerning the definition of *septuaginta*, Maniacutia states that some people equated the *vulgata* with the *septuaginta*. But he seems insecure about this identification, because in his view, the *vulgata* – here clearly understood to be a particular edition of the Bible – should not consist solely of the Pentateuch, which would be the case if the *septuaginta* were indeed equivalent to the *vulgata* and if the witnesses cited by Jerome were right in claiming that the *septuaginta* comprises only the Five Books of Moses. Since he has no evidence either way, he merely sets out the situation without drawing any definite conclusion.[25] As becomes clear from this passage, *vulgata* was already employed by Maniacutia in the mid-twelfth century, not to indicate that a version was widely diffused, but instead as a proper name designating a particular version.

A similar stance – this time without any hesitation – can be observed roughly a century later in Gerard of Huy's *correctorium*. Gerard was well aware of Jerome's use of *vulgata*: giving a brief overview of the various Greek and Latin translations of the Bible, he explains to the reader that in the time of Jerome and Augustine the *vulgata*, that is, the *septuaginta*, was the version in common use; consequently, there can be no doubt that the *septuaginta* and the *vulgata* – the latter term again used as a proper name – are one and the same edition.[26] He then continues by explaining the origin of

---

[25] See above, pp. 9–10. For an early twelfth-century commentator who had no doubts on this matter, see Rupert of Deutz, *De sancta trinitate et operibus eius*, ed. H. Haacke, 4 vols, Turnhout 1971–1972, I, p. 278 (*In Genesim III, 34*): 'Nam quod apud Lucam euangelistam [Lk 3.34–36] undecimus inuenitur ex uulgata Septuaginta interpretum editione est.'

[26] Gerard of Huy, [Preface to his *correctorium*], pp. 299–300: 'Prima {*sc.* translatio} LXX interpretum, qua utuntur greci doctores ... latini etiam qui fuerunt ante Ieronimum ... et generaliter ante tempora Ieronimi universalis ecclesia, greca scilicet et latina, utebatur editione interpretum LXX. Hec editio indifferenter vel antiqua vel vetus vel vulgata vel LXX interpretum appellabatur ... Cum enim vulgata dicatur manifesta et publica (sicut quod in ore vulgi est, manifestum est et publicum), et nulla alia nisi LXX fuerit publicata ... Ex quo patet quod una et eadem est editio LXX et Vulgata.' An exception is made for the book of Daniel, since, as Jerome had stated (see below, p. 82, n. 4), it was based on Theodotion's version and not on the LXX; see ibid., p. 300: 'In Daniele vero, quia editio Theodotionis legebatur,

readings found in Jerome's Bible edition which differ from those in his commentaries:

> Quidam autem quia aliquando in commentis Ieronimi aliam litteram inveniunt quam contineatur in bibliis nostris, dicunt litteram biblie nostre non esse Ieronimi sed aut vulgatam esse aut alicuius alterius interpretis. Sed quod non sit alterius interpretis patet per beatum Augustinum [*De civitate Dei*, p. 639 (XVIII, 43)], qui dicit quod ecclesia utebatur tantum editione LXX; hec enim sola legebatur, sicut dicit Ieronimus super Isaiam libro VIII° [*Commentarii in Esaiam*, I, p. 361 (IX, xxviii, 9/13)]: 'LXX interpretes qui leguntur in ecclesiis breviter transcurramus.'[27]

Since some people at times find a reading in Jerome's commentaries which is different from the one contained in our Bibles, they say that the reading of our Bible is not that of Jerome but either the *vulgata* or that of some other translator. That it is not the text of another translator, however, is made clear from Augustine, who says that the Church used only the LXX edition. For this edition alone was read, as Jerome says in his commentary on Isaiah, book VIII: 'Let us briefly go through the LXX translators who are read in the churches.'

For Gerard, *vulgata* is thus an alternative proper name for the *septuaginta*. Even though he was aware of the term's original meaning, he does not transfer it to the most widely diffused version of his own day, that is, Jerome's translation. Instead, perhaps believing that the Church Fathers had already used *vulgata* as a proper name for the *septuaginta*, or, at any rate, not wanting to disagree with their terminology, he continues to refer to the *septuaginta* as *vulgata*. Like Gerard, his contemporary Roger Bacon also employs *vulgata* as a synonym for *septuaginta* when he writes that the *vulgata* was composed a good 1500 years before his time.[28]

Some modern scholars have wrongly assumed that, in the thirteenth century, there was a move towards calling Jerome's version *vulgata*.[29] Sutcliffe, however, has pointed out that this is a

---

eiusdem, et non LXX, editio Vulgata vocatur.' For information on the *correctoria* as a genre, see below, pp. 253–255.

[27] Ibid., p. 301.

[28] Bacon, *Opus minus*, p. 343: 'Et sunt circiter mille quingenti anni quod Vulgata editio composita sit.' The chronology clearly indicates that Bacon must be referring to the Septuagint.

[29] See, e.g., Friedrich Stummer, *Einführung in die lateinische Bibel: Ein Handbuch für Vorlesungen und Selbstunterricht*, Paderborn 1928, p. 130; Julius Witte, *Zur Geschichte der Vulgata*, Hanover 1876, p. 20; Kaulen, *Geschichte*, p. 22. According to Hody (*De bibliorum textibus*, p. 547) and,

misconception; and the statements by Gerard and Bacon confirm that, in their eyes, it was the *septuaginta* which should be called *vulgata*.³⁰ A later example, also disproving this assumption, can be cited: towards the end of the fourteenth century, Henry Totting, even though he discussed at length whether Jerome's translation should be preferred to all others, never described it as *vulgata*.³¹

There was, however, another interpretation of the term *vulgata* which had some currency in the Latin Middle Ages. Hugh of St Victor and Peter Comestor, both highly influential writers, claimed that the *vulgata* was not the *septuaginta*, but a different Greek translation: the fifth one after the Septuagint and the versions of Aquila, Theodotion and Symmachus, and usually referred to simply as *quinta*.³² This usage was also taken up, it seems, by the

---

based on Hody, Kaulen (*Geschichte*, p. 300), the view that Jerome was not the translator of the Vulgate was quite widespread in the Middle Ages. Probably, Hody and Kaulen were led astray by the medieval terminology in which *vulgata* is not identical to the Vulgate. In addition, Kaulen claims that Ramon Martí, Peter Comestor and Richard FitzRalph were convinced that Jerome's translation survived only in his commentaries. Yet both Martí and FitzRalph mention Jerome's translation independently of his commentaries; see below, p. 63, n. 54; and p. 95, n. 35. Petrus Comestor identifies, not Jerome's version, but the *quinta* as the *vulgata*, with no implication that this was the version commonly read in his time; see below, p. 18, n. 32.

[30] See Sutcliffe, 'The Name "Vulgate"', pp. 347–348; and, e.g., Bacon, *Opus minus*, p. 336: 'Editio Vulgata, quae fuit Septuaginta interpretum.' For a more elaborate example from Bacon, see below, p. 19. For statements to this effect by Gerard of Huy, see above, p. 16, n. 26.

[31] Henry Totting of Oyta, *Quaestio de Sacra Scriptura*, ed. A. Lang, Münster i. W. 1932.

[32] Hugh of St Victor, *Didascalicon de studio legendi. A Critical Text*, ed. C. H. Buttimer, Washington D.C. 1939, p. 76 (IV, v): 'Quinta {*sc.* interpretatio} est vulgaris, cuius auctor ignoratur'; Peter Comestor, *Scolastica historia: Liber Genesis*, ed. A. Sylwan, Turnhout 2005, p. 33 (16): 'Quinta editio Ierosolimis est inuenta que, quia auctor eius ignoratur, Vulgata dicitur.' This identification had its roots in Isidore of Seville, *Etymologiae*, ed. W. M. Lindsay, 2 vols, Oxford 1911, repr. 1962, VI, iv, 3: '"Fuerunt et alii interpretes, qui ex Hebraea lingua in Graecum sacra eloquia transtulerunt, sicut Aquila, Symmachus et Theodotion, sicut etiam" et vulgaris "illa interpretatio, cuius auctor non apparet et ob hoc sine nomine Quinta Editio nuncupatur."' Isidore quotes from Augustine, *De civitate Dei*, pp. 638–639 (XVIII, 43), but adds the decisive words 'et vulgaris'. Even though the modern editions of Hugh of St Victor and Isidore both read *vulgaris* and not *vulgata*, some manuscripts of the *Didascalicon* must have had the variant reading *vulgata*, as can be seen from the passage by Roger Bacon quoted below, p. 19.

thirteenth-century Dominican Hugh of St Cher in his *Correctio Biblie*.³³ Roger Bacon, however, strongly opposed this identification in his *Opus minus*:

> Dicunt igitur auctores a triginta annis ficti quod quinta editio est, quae Vulgata nominatur. Unde Hugo in Didascalica dicit quod quinta nominatur Vulgata, et Magister Historiarum dicit quod historia {*Hody:* translatio} Vulgata nominatur, quia ejus auctor ignoratur. Et propter hoc fingunt multi novi {*Sutcliffe:* novo?} errore decepti, quod haec editio quae currit his temporibus est Vulgata, scilicet quinta quae successit translationi Septuaginta, propter hoc quod haec quam nunc habemus non est Hieronymi, ut dicunt. Sed istud primo patet esse falsum per auctoritatem Isidori {*see below, p. 35, n. 21*} et exemplaria antiqua de quibus locutus fui. Et praeterea proprias habet conditiones. Cum ergo dicunt pro ratione sui erroris, quod quinta editio dicitur Vulgata, quia ejus auctor ignoratur; ergo pari ratione utraque illarum Vulgata dicitur, quod falsum est. Et ideo haec ratio nulla est. Sed dicitur Vulgata, quae vulgo et publice ab hominibus legebatur, et fuit in usu vulgi, et totius ecclesiae Graecae et Latinae. Et haec fuit sola translatio Septuaginta, quod probatur evidenter.³⁴

> For thirty years, lying authors have been saying that it is the fifth edition which is called *vulgata*. Thus, Hugh in his *Didascalicon* says that the *quinta* is called *vulgata*; and Peter Comestor says that the translation is called *vulgata* because its author is unknown. And because of this, many people, deceived by this new mistake, dream up the idea that the edition which is current in these times is the *vulgata*, that is, the fifth one in succession to the Septuagint, because the one

---

³³ Hugh of St Cher, *Correctio Biblie*, on the Preface to Job (MSS Paris, Bibliothèque de l'Arsenal, 94, fol. 23ᵛᵇ, and Paris, BNF, lat. 3218, fol. 146ᵛᵃ): 'Sex fuerunt translationes scilicet lxx, Aquila, Simachus, Theodotion, Origenes et vulgata cuius auctor ignoratur.' Even though the *vulgata cuius auctor ignoratur* is listed as the sixth translation, and could hence be identified as the *sexta*, the wording of the phrase is so similar to Peter Comestor's, and identical to Hugh of St Victor's that it seems probable that Hugh of St Cher drew on that tradition. For the question of authorship of the *Correctio Biblie*, see below, p. 255

³⁴ Bacon, *Opus minus*, pp. 339–340. Bacon then provides quotations from Augustine and Jerome to prove that the *vulgata* is genuinely the *septuaginta*. Sutcliffe ('The Name "Vulgate"', pp. 348–349) also mentions this passage, but he says that the only author named is Hugh of St Victor. The two emendations I have inserted in the passage come from Sutcliffe (ibid., p. 349, n. 1), who took the first one from Hody, *De bibliorum textibus*, p. 424. Possibly, when Bacon refers to *auctores*, he has in mind Hugh of St Cher, who claimed that the *quinta* was the *vulgata*; see above, p. 19, n. 33. For an example in which *vulgata* is applied by Bacon to the Vetus Latina, see below, p. 87, n. 17.

we have now is not Jerome's, so they say. But that this is wrong is shown, firstly, by the authority of Isidore and by the ancient manuscripts I have mentioned. And, moreover, it has its own particular traits; so, when they say, on the basis of their mistaken argument, that the fifth edition is called *vulgata* since its author is unknown, then, using the same argument, both editions {that is, the *quinta* and the *septuaginta*} are called *vulgata*, which is false. Consequently, this argument is null and void. The version which is called *vulgata* is the one which was commonly and universally read by everyone, and which was in use by the people and by the entire Greek and Latin Church. And this was only the *septuaginta* translation, as is clearly shown.

A similar dismissal of this identification can also be found in Gerard of Huy's *correctorium*.[35] So, both Bacon and Gerard, the two major thirteenth-century advocates of Jerome's translation, as we shall see later on, follow the standard medieval usage of *vulgata*, rejecting the alternative interpretation offered by Hugh of St Victor, Peter Comestor and also Hugh of St Cher. Furthermore, even though aware of the meaning which *vulgata* had in Jerome's writings, they did not transfer it to the version which was, in fact, the most popular in their day, Jerome's translation.

The chronological development of this shift in meaning of *vulgata* from adjective as found in the term *editio vulgata* to proper name still needs further investigation.[36] It is possible that medieval scholars in the Latin West did not have a precise understanding of what the κοινή version — which Jerome had at times described as *vulgata* — was. The *septuaginta*, on the other hand, was familiar to medieval scholars from the long Latin quotations found in the writings of the Fathers, which presented them with a tangible text that they could identify as the *septuaginta*. By contrast, the κοινή was intangible or, at any rate, it was difficult to comprehend which text Jerome was referring to. This may have facilitated the identification of *vulgata* with the *septuaginta*.

---

[35] Gerard of Huy, [Preface to his *correctorium*], pp. 299–300: 'Alia, ut beatus Augustinus scribit in XVIII libro *De civitate Dei* {p. 639 (XVIII, 43)}, fuit interpretatio cuius autor non apparet, et ob hoc sine nomine interpretis *quinta* nuncupatur. Hec, quia eius autor ignoratur, a quibusdam vulgata dicitur. Sed qui hoc dicunt, significationem vocabuli non bene attendunt.'

[36] Kaulen (*Geschichte*, p. 17) assumes that since the time of Gregory the Great, *vulgata* meant nothing more than 'gewöhnlich vorkommend oder allgemein vorhanden'. The passages quoted in this chapter, however, contradict his view.

These terminological considerations are limited solely to the feminine singular *vulgata*. When used in other genders in a relation to biblical texts, *vulgatus/-um* continued to designate a version commonly read at the time. For instance, *textus vulgatus* and *exemplar vulgatum*, when mentioned in the thirteenth century, referred to the Paris Bible.[37]

Medieval scholars made use of yet another term to indicate the widespread diffusion of a biblical edition. In the thirteenth and fourteenth centuries, there are a few examples of a Bible edition being described as *communis*: William de Mara's exasperated response to Hugh of St Cher's *correctorium* – 'He sees to it that the common text {*littera communis*} is destroyed!' – has been interpreted by Denifle as a reference to Jerome's version.[38] In a different passage, William demands that the *littera communis* should be left intact as long as the translation and the original agree in sense.[39] Here, again, *communis* seems to denote the most widely read version, possibly Jerome's: it cannot refer to the Paris Bible, which also had considerable dissemination at the time, since it was not transmitted in ancient manuscripts, a point which is stressed by William.[40]

The use of *communis* becomes more problematic in the fourteenth century. Richard FitzRalph employed *communis* in connection with *translatio* to indicate an edition widely accepted by the Church:

---

[37] For *textus vulgatus*, see Sutcliffe, 'Jerome', p. 99. For Bacon's use of *exemplar vulgatum* to refer to the Paris Bible, see below, p. 146 and n. 131. For problems in thirteenth–century terminology, see below, pp. 124–128.

[38] William de Mara, [*Correctorium Biblie*], on 2 K 5.23 (quoted by Denifle, 'Die Handschriften', p. 295, n. 2): 'Facit destrui litteram communem!'

[39] William de Mara, [Preface to his *Correctorium Biblie*], ed. Dahan, 'La critique textuelle', pp. 387-388, at p. 387: 'Non igitur propter solam litteram hebraicam atque grecam littera communis in antiquis codicibus apostolicarum sedium, ad quos pro ueritate littere recurrendum beatus indicat Augustinus, siue in uoluminibus etiam alias approbatis, est mutanda apud latinos, dum lingue primarie a qua fit translatio sensum uel in summa teneat incorruptum. Cum igitur dicit latinus aliquis, in hiis que translata habemus de hebraico siue greco, hebreus siue grecus hoc uel illud habet aut non est hec littera siue illa, scilicet quia hebreus siue grecus non habet, prius enim probare competit quod non modo uerbis discrepent sed et sensu.'

[40] For the Paris Bible, see below, pp. 42–46. Nor, judging from the complaints regularly voiced about the quality of the Paris Bible, is William likely to have asked for its text to be preserved in its then-current form.

Ob hoc translatio 70 interpretum veridica in omnibus iudicaretur quamvis sic in locis aliquibus diminuta; et quia non repugnat veritati primarie ab ecclesia catholica primaria reputatur et similiter translatio communis.[41]

For this reason, the translation of the Seventy should be deemed to speak the truth in all matters, even though it is impaired in some passages; and since it is not contrary to the original truth, it is held by the Catholic Church to be original; this is also the case for the *translatio communis*.

It is tempting to identify the *translatio communis* with Jerome's version. Yet slightly earlier in the same work, FitzRalph mentions three Latin translations: the *septuaginta*, Jerome's translation and the *translatio communis*;[42] so the *communis* cannot be equated with Jerome's version. FitzRalph might instead be referring to the Paris Bible: as a thirteenth-century example (the *correctorium Sorbonne II*, cited by Dahan) shows, *communis*, here in conjunction with *littera*, did not invariably indicate Jerome's version, but could also refer to the Paris Bible.[43] Possibly, FitzRalph, too, had in mind the Paris Bible when mentioning the *communis* along with the *septuaginta* and Jerome's version.[44]

---

[41] Richard FitzRalph, *Summa ... in Questionibus Armenorum*, ed. J. Sudoris, [Paris] 1512, sig. Ciir (19, 20). I have used the copy London, British Library, shelfmark 4373.k.1.

[42] See below, p. 95, n. 35.

[43] See below, p. 125.

[44] If so, it would provide further proof that the Paris Bible was perceived as a distinct recension. This interpretation of FitzRalph's statement, however, opens up yet more problems: since the Paris Bible was not a new translation, the use of *translatio* to describe it seems unlikely. In addition, FitzRalph, as we shall see, also claimed that the three Latin translations he lists had been officially approved by the Church (see below, p. 64, n. 56). Although this was not the case for any of the Latin versions, several influential authors maintained that the Church had sanctioned either the *septuaginta* or Jerome's version. FitzRalph, however, would be the only one to ascribe this official status to the Paris Bible. Rice, though without adducing any proof, states that FitzRalph's *translatio communis* is, in fact, Jerome's translation and that the *translatio Hieronymi*, also listed by FitzRalph, refers to Jerome's translations as transmitted in his commentaries; see below, p. 64, n. 55. Another explanation might be that FitzRalph regarded the *septuaginta* and the *vulgata*, both of which terms usually referred to the Vetus Latina in his day, as two distinct versions; should this be the case, he might have used *communis* instead of *vulgata*. With the evidence at hand, however, the problem must remain unresolved.

For the period examined here, the only instances I have been able to find of *communis* being used to describe a Bible edition date from the thirteenth and fourteenth centuries. In William de Mara's case, the identification of *communis littera* as Jerome's version, although very likely, is nevertheless speculative;[45] while FitzRalph's use of *translatio communis* remains unclear. As for the *correctorium Sorbonne II*, *littera communis* seems to indicate the Paris Bible. This terminology was therefore neither universally adopted nor consistently applied. In fact, like Jerome's use of *vulgata*, *communis* might simply have indicated that a version was widely diffused.

Hebraica veritas / *graeca veritas*

Two other, very similar, expressions require a brief treatment here: *hebraica veritas* and *graeca veritas*. In Jerome's works, these terms refer to the original versions of the Old and New Testament respectively.[46] Medieval authors followed Jerome in employing *hebraica veritas* to refer to the Hebrew original; and their use of this expression seems to have been very consistent. An example from the early Middle Ages can be found in Bede's *Retractatio*: 'Hieronimus pleraque testimonia veteris instrumenti, ut Hebraica veritas habebat, edocet, nec tamen haec ita in nostris codicibus aut ipse interpretari aut nos emendare voluit' (Jerome expounds many examples from the Old Testament as they are in the *hebraica veritas*; nevertheless, he did not want to translate these passages accordingly in our manuscripts, nor did he want us to correct them).[47] The same usage is later found in both Stephen Harding

---

[45] To resolve this question, further research into the terminology of the *correctoria* needs to be done.

[46] See, e.g., Jerome, *Epistulae*, II, p. 9 (LXXII, 2): 'Et si quidem in his historiis aliter haberent septuaginta interpretes, aliter Hebraica ueritas, confugere poteramus ad solita praesidia et arcem linguae tenere uernaculae'; ibid., III, p. 96 (CXXIV, 1): 'Postulans, ut Graecam ueritatem seruaret Latina translatio'; Jerome, 'Praefatio in Evangelio', in *Biblia sacra*, pp. 1515–1516, at p. 1515: 'Novum opus facere me cogis ex veteri, ut post exemplaria Scripturarum toto orbe dispersa quasi quidam arbiter sedeam et, quia inter se variant, quae sint illa quae cum graeca consentiant veritate decernam.' Sutcliffe ('Jerome', p. 92) confirms that Jerome commonly calls the Hebrew text *hebraica veritas*. For Jerome's use of *graeca veritas* for the Greek original, see also Rice, *Saint Jerome*, p. 12.

[47] The Venerable Bede, *Retractatio in Actus apostolorum*, in *Expositio Actuum apostolorum et Retractatio*, ed. M. L. W. Laistner, Cambridge (Mass.) 1939, pp. 91–146, at p. 93 (*praefatio*).

and Maniacutia;[48] and it is also attested by other twelfth-century writers, including Andrew of St Victor and Rupert of Deutz.[49] In the thirteenth century, various examples of *hebraica veritas* being used to denote the Hebrew original can be seen in Roger Bacon's writings. For instance, he writes in the *Opus majus*: 'The *hebraica veritas* was translated by Jerome alone into Latin.'[50]

Even though these examples provide a very clear indication of how the phrase *hebraica veritas* was used, some modern scholars have been reluctant to accept that it denoted only the Hebrew original. Eugene Rice states that in the Middle Ages the term usually referred to Jerome's translation from the Hebrew rather than to the Hebrew version itself.[51] Gilbert Dahan, likewise, assumes that, when used in texts other than the *correctoria*, *hebraica*

---

[48] Stephen Harding, *Monitum*, in Matthieu Cauwe, 'La Bible d'Étienne Harding: principes de critique textuelle mis en œuvre aux livres de Samuel', *Revue Bénédictine* 103 (1993), pp. 414–44, at p. 416: 'Non modice de dissonantia historiarum turbati sumus, quia hoc plena edocet ratio, ut quod ab uno interprete, videlicet beato Iheronimo, quem ceteris interpretibus omissis, nostrates jamjamque susceperunt, de uno hebraice veritatis fonte translatum est, unum debeat sonare'; Maniacutia, [Preface to his *Suffraganeus bibliothece*], p. 275: 'Ut de ceteris taceam, numquid in psalterio ex hebraica veritate translato poteris invenire "semper" – numquid in Romano vel Gallico "Diapsalma"?'

[49] See, e.g., Andrew of St Victor (d. 1175), *Expositio super heptateuchum*, ed. C. Lohr and R. Berndt, Turnhout 1986, p. 29 (*In Genesim*, 2, 7–8): 'Quem {*sc.* locum} designare uolens scriptura statim adiungit: "Plantaverat autem Dominus Deus paradisum uoluptatis a principio" [Gn 2.8], uel potius, ut hebraica ueritas habet: *Eden ad ortum* siue *ad orientem*.' The Vulgate has '*a principio*'; the Hebrew reads בְּעֵדֶן מִקֶּדֶם. See also Rupert of Deutz, *De sancta trinitate*, I, p. 548 (*In Genesim IX, 16*): 'Quod si quaeritur, cur sanctus Lucas qui supradictae scriptor est historiae in gentes Actuum apostolorum uolumen emittens, non secundum hebraicam ueritatem septuaginta sed septuaginta quinque animas, iuxta Septuaginta interpretum editionem ingressas Aegyptum esse dixerit [Ac 7.14], facilis excusatio est. Non enim debuit contrarium aliquid scribere aduersus eam Scripturam, quae iam fuerat gentilibus diuulgata.'

[50] See above, p. 11, and also below, p. 91, n. 26. See also William de Mara, [Preface to his *correctorium*], p. 387: 'Ieronimo ... attestante [*Epistulae*, II, p. 249 (CVI, 2, 3)]: "Sicut in nouo testamento, si quando apud latinos questio oritur et inter exemplaria uarietas est, recurrimus ad fontem greci sermonis quo nouum scriptum est instrumentum, ita in ueteri testamento, si quando inter grecos latinosque diuersitas est, ad hebraicam confugimus ueritatem".'

[51] Rice, *Saint Jerome*, p. 94.

veritas, as well as *hebreus*, often indicated Jerome's version, especially in relation to the *Psalterium iuxta Hebraeos*.[52]

This assumption is, however, contradicted by statements in various medieval texts. Nicolò Maniacutia, for instance, mentions all three of Jerome's versions of the Psalms; when referring to the version *iuxta Hebraeos*, he describes it as 'translated from the *hebraica veritas*', not as the *hebraica veritas* itself.[53] A very similar instance is found in William Durand's *Rationale*.[54] On the basis of the examples at my disposal, it seems more likely to me that, contrary to the opinion of Rice and Dahan, medieval scholars were, in fact, consistent in their use of *hebraica veritas* to refer solely to the Hebrew original.[55]

The expression *graeca veritas* was used far less often in the Middle Ages than *hebraica veritas*. Indeed, only three of the authors examined in this study employed the phrase. In the preface to his *correctorium*, Gerard of Huy uses *graeca veritas* as the counterpart of *hebraica veritas* to indicate the Greek original.[56] Two centuries later,

---

[52] Dahan, 'La critique textuelle', p. 370, n. 27. Regrettably, Dahan does not provide any examples.

[53] See above, p. 24, n. 48.

[54] William Durand (c. 1230–1296), *Rationale divinorum officiorum*, 3 vols, ed. A. Davril and T. M. Thibodeau, Turnhout 1995–2000, II, p. 132 (VI, 1, 34): 'Tertium {*sc.* psalterium} uero transtulit de hebraica ueritate in latinum.'

[55] There is a passage in Bacon's *Opus minus* which might support Rice's and Dahan's view, but it is not clear-cut: Bacon, *Opus minus*, p. 343: 'Beatus Hieronymus in originalibus super textum ponit aliam literam, quam nos habemus in Bibliis antiquis et novis. Et ideo aliam translationem edisserit et exponit juxta Hebraïcam veritatem, praeter hoc quod simul ponat translationem Septuaginta, quatenus videatur qualiter editio Septuaginta discordet ab Hebraïca veritate, adjungens autem translationes aliorum, ut magis elucescat veritas Hebraïca quam exponit.' In this passage, *hebraica veritas* could mean either the Hebrew original or the Latin translation from the Hebrew.

[56] Gerard of Huy, [Preface to his *correctorium*], p. 307: 'Sed licet recurrendum sit ad hebream et grecam veritatem, non tamen in omnibus sequi debemus lingue earum vel idiomatis proprietatem'; and ibid., p. 308: 'In illis autem in quibus apud veteres est discordia et incerta varietas, consentiendum est illis, quibus concordat hebrea vel greca veritas.' In both quotations, there are echoes of Augustine: *De doctrina christiana*, in his *Opera*, IV, 1, ed. J. Martin (Corpus Christianorum. Series Latina, 32), Turnhout 1962, pp. 1–167, at p. 81 (III, iii, 7), in the first passage, and *Contra Faustum*, in his *Opera*, VI, 1, ed. J. Zycha (Corpus Scriptorum Ecclesiasticorum Latinorum, 25), Prague, Vienna and Leipzig 1891, pp. 251–797, at p. 316 (XI, 2), in the second; however, Augustine does not mention the *graeca veritas* in either passage.

Lorenzo Valla equates *graeca veritas* with the original Greek version of the New Testament.⁵⁷ In the late fifteenth century, Giovanni Crastone refers to the Septuagint translation of the Psalms as *graeca veritas*.⁵⁸

Another term which deserves some discussion in this context is *veritas* on its own. Like *hebraica veritas* and *graeca veritas*, *veritas*, too, implied that a version was authoritative.⁵⁹ For instance, Hervaeus employs *veritas* in relation not only to the original Hebrew and Greek texts of the Bible, but also to Jerome's version; and Bacon applies it, in the *Opus majus*, specifically to the Vulgate; in both cases, the use of *veritas* underlines the special standing of the version.⁶⁰

---

⁵⁷ Lorenzo Valla, *Collatio Novi Testamenti*, ed. A. Perosa, Florence 1970, p. 8: 'Nempe an nostra prorsus cum greco fonte consentiant, id est cum greca veritate – e greco enim omne Testamentum Novum sumus mutuati.'

⁵⁸ See below, p. 184, n. 240.

⁵⁹ The significance of the term *veritas* is also confirmed by Hugh of St Cher, [Preface to his *Correctio Biblie*], ed. Dahan, 'La critique textuelle', pp. 386-387, at p. 386: 'Super omnes scripturas verba sacri eloquii necesse est ut fundamento veritatis firmiter innitantur.' For the conflict between *consuetudo* and *veritas*, see below, pp. 201–216 (Chapter IV.1).

⁶⁰ For Hervaeus, see below, p. 60, n. 45. Bacon, *Opus majus*, I, p. 19: 'Nam sicut prologi beati Hieronymi in bibliam et alia ejus opera probant, ipse vocabatur corruptor scripturae et falsarius et haeresium seminator, et in tempore suo succubuit, nec potuit sua opera in publico promovere; sed tandem post mortem suam veritas suae translationis claruit.'

PART II:

THE VULGATE AND MEDIEVAL EDITIONS OF THE BIBLE

Chapters II.1 and II.2 provide information on the early stages of the development of the Latin Bible in antiquity and its most important medieval editions from the perspective of modern scholarship. This knowledge is fundamental, not only in order to understand the actual intricacies underlying the transmission of the Latin Bible, but also to comprehend the problems that medieval and early Renaissance scholars faced when they sought to reconstruct the history of the text and suggested ways of emending it.

II.1 THE RISE OF THE VULGATE

From the end of the second century AD onwards, the Bible circulated in Latin translation; early references can be found, for instance, in Tertullian's (c. 160-c. 220) *Adversus Marcionem*, written around 207.[1] It was not, however, a single uniform translation, as is clear from evidence provided by Jerome and Augustine, both of whom point out that there was a number of translators.[2] These Latin versions, now commonly referred to in the singular as the Vetus Latina,[3] became the standard biblical text(s)

---

[1] See, e.g., Tertullian, *Adversus Marcionem*, ed. E. Kroymann, in his *Opera*, I, Turnhout 1954, pp. 441–726, at p. 484 (II, ix, 1–2): 'Inprimis tenendum quod Graeca scriptura signauit, *adflatum* [Gn 2.7] nominans, non *spiritum*. Quidam enim de Graeco interpretantes non recogitata differentia nec curata proprietate uerborum pro *adflatu spiritum* ponunt'; ibid., p. 673 (V, iv, 8): 'Haec sunt enim duo testamenta (siue *duae ostensiones* [Ga 4.24], sicut inuenimus interpretatum).' Bogaert ('La Bible latine', p. 143) sees the origin of the Latin Bible in Africa. For a short summary of Greek and pre–Vulgate Latin translations of the Bible, see Alfons Fürst, *Hieronymus: Askese und Wissenschaft in der Spätantike*, Freiburg i. Br. 2003, pp. 91–102. For a study of the Latin Bible in England during the Middle Ages, see Hans Hermann Glunz, *History of the Vulgate in England from Alcuin to Roger Bacon: Being an Inquiry into the Text of Some English Manuscripts of the Vulgate Gospels*, Cambridge 1933. A codicological study of selected manuscripts and printed editions of the Latin Bible from the Church Fathers to the early sixteenth century was conducted by Margaret Gibson, *The Bible in the Latin West*, Notre Dame and London 1993.

[2] See, e.g., Augustine, *De doctrina christiana*, p. 42 (II, xi, 16 – II, xii, 17): 'Qui enim scripturas ex hebraea in graecam uerterunt, numerari possunt, latini autem interpretes nullo modo. Vt enim cuique primis fidei temporibus in manus uenit codex graecus et aliquantum facultatis sibi utriusque linguae habere uidebatur, ausus est interpretari. Quae quidem res plus adiuuit intellegentiam quam impediuit, si modo legentes non sint neglegentes. Nam nonnullas obscuriores sententias plurium codicum saepe manifestauit inspectio'; Jerome, 'Praefatio in Evangelio', p. 1515: 'Cur non ad graecam originem revertentes ea quae vel a vitiosis interpretibus male edita ... corrigimus?' See also Witte, *Zur Geschichte*, pp. 4–5; Fischer, 'Zur Überlieferung', p. 19; Bogaert, 'La Bible latine', p. 146.

[3] For a brief discussion of the theories concerning various geographical versions of the Vetus Latina, see J. K. Elliott, 'The Translations of the New Testament into Latin: The Old Latin and the Vulgate', in *Aufstieg und Niedergang der römischen Welt. Geschichte und Kultur Roms im Spiegel der neueren Forschung*, II, 26, 1, ed. W. Haase, Berlin and New York 1992, pp. 198–245,

and had already held this position for about two hundred years when Jerome undertook the task of producing a new edition of the Bible at the end of the fourth century. Even then, however, the Vetus Latina did not lose its authority and continued to be read for some centuries to come.[4]

Jerome's version of the Latin Bible developed in several stages. In the early 380s, Pope Damasus I (c. 305-384) instructed Jerome to revise the Latin text of the Gospels. This first stage, completed in 384, involved the revision of the Gospels and the Psalms on the basis of the Septuagint – the first of his three versions of the Psalms.[5] Jerome, who is our only source for the pope's request, described this enterprise and the problems it entailed in his 'Praefatio in Evangelio'. He says that Damasus ordered him to produce a new edition of the Gospels by collating the Latin manuscripts with the *graeca veritas*.[6] Jerome admitted that, although this was a pious deed, it might nevertheless be considered presumptuous, especially by those people who were upset to see changes to the sacred text of the Vetus Latina which they had been used to throughout their lives. But since he was acting at the pope's behest, and since he had come to realise that there were as many Latin versions as there were manuscripts, thus diminishing the

---

at pp. 200–202. Elliott argues that it is unlikely that originally there were separate African and European translations of the Vetus Latina.

[4] For the early transmission of the Latin Bible, see Pierre Petitmengin, 'Les plus anciens manuscrits de la Bible latine', in *Le monde latin antique et la Bible*, ed. J. Fontaine and C. Pietri, Paris 1985, pp. 89–127. Bogaert ('La Bible latine', pp. 149–151) lists the sources in which the Vetus Latina survives to this day.

[5] This first version has not come down to us; only the Vetus Latina version of the Psalms, usually known as the *Psalterium Romanum*, survives; see John Norman Davidson Kelly, *Jerome: His Life, Writings and Controversies*, London 1975, p. 89, and Fischer, 'Zur Überlieferung', p. 22. Sutcliffe ('Jerome', pp. 84–85) repeats the view expressed by Alberto Vaccari ('I salteri di s. Girolamo e di s. Agostino', in his *Scritti di erudizione e di filologia*, 2 vols, Rome 1952-1958, I, pp. 207–55, at p. 219) that the Roman Psalter, if it is not Jerome's revision, is certainly the text on which he based his first reworking. For a short summary of the various stages in which the Vulgate was produced, see also *LexMA*, II, cols 91–92.

[6] Jerome, 'Praefatio in Evangelio', p. 1515: 'Novum opus facere me cogis ex veteri, ut post exemplaria Scripturarum toto orbe dispersa quasi quidam arbiter sedeam et, quia inter se variant, quae sint illa quae cum graeca consentiant veritate decernam.' The reason why Jerome added a Preface to his version of the Gospels was certainly self-protection; see Gribomont, 'Aux origines', p. 17.

reliability of the Latin tradition, Jerome agreed to take on the task. With an existing Latin translation already well established, he needed to explain his approach of emending on the basis of the Greek tradition. Why not, he asked, go back to the original to correct what had been corrupted through mistranslation or faulty emendation, or which had simply been changed or added by inattentive scribes?[7] But Jerome was keen to stress that his revision of the Gospels was by no means a new translation, and that it did not diverge very much from the customary text. Indeed, he had corrected only those passages in which the sense seemed to have been altered from what it was in the original Greek; apart from that, he had preserved the accepted Latin version as he found it.[8]

After Damasus's death in December 384, Jerome went to Bethlehem, where, two years later, in 386/387, he commenced work on the second stage of revising the Bible, this time producing another re-working of the Psalms, the so-called *Psalterium Gallicanum*, and several books of the Old Testament. Apart from the *Gallicanum*, which turned out to be his most successful version of the Psalms, hardly any traces of this second phase remain.[9] The

[7] Jerome, 'Praefatio in Evangelio', p. 1515: 'Pius labor, sed periculosa praesumptio, iudicare de ceteris ipsum ab omnibus iudicandum, senis mutare linguam et canescentem mundum ad initia retrahere parvulorum. Quis enim doctus pariter vel indoctus, cum in manus volumen adsumpserit et a saliva quam semel inbibit viderit discrepare quod lectitat, non statim erumpat in vocem, me falsarium me clamans esse sacrilegum, qui audeam aliquid in veteribus libris addere, mutare, corrigere? Adversum quam invidiam duplex causa me consolatur: quod et tu qui summus sacerdos es fieri iubes, et verum non esse quod variat etiam maledicorum testimonio conprobatur. Si enim latinis exemplaribus fides est adhibenda, respondeant quibus; tot sunt paene quot codices. Sin autem veritas est quaerenda de pluribus, cur non ad graecam originem revertentes ea quae vel a vitiosis interpretibus male edita vel a praesumptoribus inperitis emendata perversius vel a librariis dormitantibus aut addita sunt aut mutata corrigimus?'

[8] Ibid., pp. 1515–1516: 'Quae ne multum a lectionis latinae consuetudine discreparent, ita calamo imperavimus ut, his tantum quae sensum videbantur mutare correctis, reliqua manere pateremur ut fuerant.'

[9] The *Gallicanum* was based on a comparison with the Hexapla of Origen. It became part of the Vulgate and the Roman Breviary; see Fischer, 'Zur Überlieferung', p. 22, and Kelly, *Jerome*, pp. 158–59. The reasons for the success of the *Gallicanum* are unclear. It was not until Alcuin's revision of the Bible (see below, pp. 39–41) that the *Psalterium Gallicanum* finally established itself; see Fischer, 'Zur Überlieferung', p. 22. According to Sutcliffe ('Jerome', p. 89), apart from the Psalms, only Jerome's revision of Job and two of his prefaces have survived from the second stage.

result of the third and final stage, which lasted from about 391 to 405/406, was a new rendering of much of the Old Testament, including the *Psalterium iuxta Hebraeos*, a translation of the Psalms made directly from the Hebrew.[10] But even this last version did not comprise the entire Bible: Jerome followed the Hebrew canon, so he left the deutero-canonical works (Baruch, Ecclesiasticus, Wisdom and Maccabees) untouched; these were later introduced into the Vulgate in their Vetus Latina version. Tobit and Judith, however, although not contained in the Hebrew canon, were translated by Jerome, most likely because he was pressurised into doing it.[11]

Jerome's three phases of work on the Vulgate were identified only by modern scholarship and were not mentioned by any of the authors discussed in this study; nor do they appear to have known that certain books had not been translated or revised by Jerome. The text of the Vulgate was, of course, not immune to corruption.[12] An important factor which hampered the accurate

---

[10] Although never used in the liturgy, the *Psalterium iuxta Hebraeos*, finished before 392, circulated in Spain and England and was also incorporated into Theodulf's revision of the Bible; see Fischer, 'Zur Überlieferung', p. 22. For Theodulf, see below, pp. 41–42. For the dating of the third stage, see Kelly, *Jerome*, p. 284.

[11] Ibid., p. 284. For Jerome's change of attitude towards the deutero-canonical books from acceptance to rejection, see Sutcliffe, 'Jerome', pp. 92–93. In the so-called *Prologus galeatus*, Jerome says that these books are not part of the canon; see Jerome, 'Prologus in libro Regum', in *Biblia sacra*, pp. 364–66, at p. 365: 'Hic prologus Scripturarum quasi galeatum principium omnibus libris, quos de hebraeo vertimus in latinum, convenire potest, ut scire valeamus, quicquid extra hos est, inter apocrifa seponendum. Igitur Sapientia, quae vulgo Salomonis inscribitur, et Iesu filii Sirach liber et Iudith et Tobias et Pastor non sunt in canone. Macchabeorum primum librum hebraicum repperi, secundus graecus est, quod et ex ipsa φρασιν probari potest.' In his prefaces to Tobit and Judith, Jerome claims that he had been pressurised to translate these books; see Jerome, 'Prologus Tobiae', in *Biblia sacra*, p. 676: 'Exigitis enim, ut librum chaldeo sermone conscriptum ad latinum stilum traham'; and Jerome, 'Prologus Iudith', in *Biblia sacra*, p. 691: 'Sed quia hunc librum sinodus nicena in numero Sanctarum Scripturarum legitur conputasse, adquievi postulationi vestrae, immo exactioni, et ... huic unam lucubratiunculam dedi, magis sensum ex sensu quam ex verbo verbum transferens.' See also Jenkins and Preston, *Biblical Scholarship*, pp. 21–22.

[12] Texts apparently became corrupt very quickly: Sutcliffe ('Jerome', p. 88) points out that the reason for Jerome's second revision of the Psalms, undertaken only few years after his first version, was that the first had already been corrupted; see also Jerome, 'Praefatio in libro Psalmorum', in *Biblia sacra*, p. 767: 'Psalterium Romae dudum positus emendaram et iuxta Septuaginta

transmission of the Vulgate was that Jerome never produced a complete edition of the books he had edited, let alone of the entire Bible; instead, his revisions and new translations were published as he prepared them over the course of more than twenty years, either as single books or in groups. It was only later that his versions were collected together and compiled into pandects, supplemented by Vetus Latina texts.[13] Later compilations of biblical books consisted of a mixture of the Vulgate and the Vetus Latina. This amalgamation of the two versions was not limited to the juxtaposition of individual books from the different traditions. It was also common for passages or even single readings to be transmitted in the Vetus Latina version, while the rest of the book was in the Vulgate translation. In addition, the introduction of glosses and, of course, scribal errors increased the corruption of the biblical text.[14]

Among the various reasons which led to this conflation of the Vetus Latina and the Vulgate texts, Bonifatius Fischer mentions the fact that, by the time Jerome's re-workings began to circulate, the

interpretes, licet cursim, magna illud ex parte correxeram. Quod quia rursum videtis, o Paula et Eustochium, scriptorum vitio depravatum plusque antiquum errorem quam novam emendationem valere, cogitis ut veluti quodam novali scissum iam arvum exerceam et obliquis sulcis renascentes spinas eradicem, aequum esse dicentes, ut quod crebro male pullulat, crebrius succidatur.' According to Witte (*Zur Geschichte*, p. 21), as early as a century after Jerome's death, the Vulgate had become as corrupt as the Vetus Latina.

[13] Fischer, 'Zur Überlieferung', p. 19. Jerome's translation from the Hebrew created further textual problems in the Latin tradition. For instance, Bogaert ('La Bible latine, p. 295) points out that the original Hebrew and Jerome's translation of 1–2 Samuel (that is, 1–2 Kings) are in some parts shorter than the Vetus Latina version and that the accretions of the Vetus Latina were introduced into the Vulgate. These circumstances might help to explain why Kings was judged to be the most corrupt book of the Bible in the twelfth century (see, e.g., below, p. 121, n. 42); see also Denifle, 'Die Handschriften', p. 471, for the extreme corruption of Kings. Gribomont ('Aux origines', p. 13) notes that in the Septuagint the Hagiographa had been treated with much greater liberty than other books. For Jerome's issuing of his versions in single books or groups, see Fischer, 'Bibelausgaben', p. 523.

[14] See Fischer, 'Zur Überlieferung', p. 33, who adds that further alterations were introduced by scribes who, used to the Vetus Latina and assuming that their Vulgate *Vorlage* contained an error, changed the text to what they considered to be the correct version. A similar point is made by Glunz (*History of the Vulgate in England*, p. 14), who suggests that scribes did not feel compelled to copy Jerome's text faithfully, but instead took the liberty of adjusting it to their needs.

established texts of the Vetus Latina were already in long-standing use by Christian communities, who had become accustomed to them and therefore resisted the introduction of the Vulgate. For such clashes to arise in the first place, as Fischer points out, the communities not only had to be aware of the existence of a new version, but also had to have access to a manuscript containing the text. But even when the Vulgate was available to them, local textual traditions and habits tended to prevail for centuries. Furthermore, throughout late antiquity and the Middle Ages, the Vulgate was never prescribed by the ecclesiastical authorities, not even by Pope Damasus, who had ordered the revision of the Gospels in the first place. In addition, two further circumstances favoured the continued presence of the Vetus Latina: it was the biblical text usually quoted by the Church Fathers – including Jerome – in their works; and it was used in the liturgy.[15]

The few isolated statements found in modern scholarly literature about the Vulgate's transmission in the first centuries of its existence indicate that, in the beginning, its success was very limited. Jerome sent his re-workings of biblical books to friends in Italy, and they spread quickly among the learned; but both Augustine and John Cassian (c. 360-430/435) were not convinced by the new versions, although, as Hugh Houghton argues, Augustine soon started using the Vulgate version of at least certain books.[16] Nevertheless, the Vulgate eventually managed to gain a

---

[15] The information in the above two paragraphs is derived from Fischer, 'Zur Überlieferung', pp. 20–21; Kaulen, *Geschichte*, p. 17; Denifle, 'Die Handschriften', pp. 276–277; Gribomont, 'Aux origines', pp. 17 and 19. Gribomont also maintains that the gradual adoption of the Vulgate for the liturgy was mainly responsible for the textual conflation of the Vulgate and the Vetus Latina; but he does not provide a timeframe or examples to back up his claim. Theodor Klauser (*A Short History of the Western Liturgy*, London, New York and Toronto, 1969, pp. 117–18) points out that only in the sixteenth century, after the Vulgate had become the official Latin version of the Church, did the Council of Trent decree that the liturgy should be based exclusively on the Vulgate. For the elevated status attributed to translations of the Bible on account of their use in the liturgy, see also Jenkins and Preston, *Biblical Scholarship*, p. 25.

[16] Gribomont, 'Aux origines', p. 18; Hugh Houghton (*Augustine's Text of St John*, Oxford 2008, pp. 10-13 and 21) argues that Augustine, although he insisted on the value of the Septuagint, nevertheless used Jerome's version, at least for some books. For Augustine's negative view of producing a new translation from the original, see below, p. 112. Augustine's Bible text is discussed by Pierre-Maurice Bogaert, 'Les bibles d'Augustin', in *Saint*

foothold, and for the two centuries following Jerome's death, the Vetus Latina and the Vulgate were in parallel use.[17] But already in the sixth century there were signs that the balance was slowly shifting: the monastic founder Cassiodorus (c. 485-c. 580), although relying on the Vetus Latina version for his exegetical works, insisted that biblical manuscripts should be corrected orthographically from the Vulgate;[18] and it seems that by around 600 it had become the favoured biblical version in Rome.[19] In the seventh century, the Vulgate's influence spread further, possibly due to the influence of Gregory the Great's (c. 540-604) positive opinion of it. In his time, however, the battle for the Vulgate had not yet been won: in his prefatory letter to the *Moralia in Iob* addressed to Leander of Seville (534-600/601), Gregory acknowledges that both versions were in use at the Holy See, seemingly on an equal footing, and therefore says that he will also refer to both.[20]

From roughly the same time, there is evidence that the Vulgate had gained ground in the Iberian peninsula: Leander's younger brother, Isidore of Seville (c. 560-636), claimed that Jerome's version had been adopted in 'all churches',[21] and most modern

Augustin et la Bible. Actes du colloque de l'université Paul Verlaine–Metz (7–8 Avril 2005), ed. G. Nauroy and M.-A. Vannier, Berne 2008, pp. 17–36.

[17] Witte (*Zur Geschichte*, p. 19) provides a list of the authors who adopted the Vulgate and those who continued to use the Vetus Latina. Popes and councils of the fifth and sixth centuries seem to have wavered between the two versions.

[18] See Raphael Loewe, 'The Medieval History of the Latin Vulgate', in *The Cambridge History of the Bible*, II, pp. 102–154, at pp. 116 and 119–120. Cassiodorus had manuscripts of both the Vulgate and the Vetus Latina prepared for him; see ibid., p. 116.

[19] Gribomont, 'Aux origines', p. 19.

[20] Gregory the Great, *Epistola ad Leandrum*, in his *Moralia in Iob*, ed. M. Adriaen, 3 vols, Turnhout 1979–1985, I, pp. 1–7, at p. 7 (V): 'Nouam uero translationem dissero; sed cum probationis causa me exigit, nunc nouam nunc ueterem per testimonia adsumo, ut, quia sedes apostolica cui Deo auctore praesideo utraque utitur, mei quoque labor studii ex utraque fulciatur.' See also Glunz, *History of the Vulgate in England*, pp. 16–17, and Witte, *Zur Geschichte*, pp. 19–20. Witte stresses that although Gregory in theory preferred the Vulgate, he could not dismiss the Vetus Latina, due to the high esteem in which it was held. Stummer (*Einführung*, p. 126) assumes that in Gregory's time, the Vetus Latina and the Vulgate were of equal status.

[21] Isidore of Seville, *De ecclesiasticis officiis*, ed. C. M. Lawson, Turnhout 1989, p. 13 (I, xii, 8): 'De hebreo autem in latinum eloquium tantummodo Hieronimus presbiter sacras scripturas conuertit; cuius editionem generaliter omnes ecclesiae usquequaque utuntur, pro eo quod ueracior sit in sententiis

scholars assume that no later than the ninth century, after almost half a millennium, Jerome's version finally superseded the Vetus Latina as the standard text of the Bible.[22]

Despite the predominance of the Vulgate from Carolingian times onwards, the text of the Vetus Latina by no means disappeared: it survived and was copied, at least in parts, throughout the Middle Ages. The Vetus Latina versions of Judith and Tobit, for instance, are found in some thirteenth-century manuscripts of what appear to be Paris Bibles. Furthermore, Fischer identifies mixed texts of the Vetus Latina and the Vulgate in Bibles produced in Metz, Salzburg, Italy, Spain and southern France during the twelfth and thirteenth centuries.[23] To some extent, therefore, even after the Vulgate became the standard text of the Bible, the Vetus Latina remained accessible in principle to medieval scholars, either in biblical manuscripts or in quotations from the Church Fathers.

In a passage in his *De viris inlustribus*, Jerome claims: 'I have revised the New Testament according to the Greek and translated the Old according to the Hebrew.'[24] As we have seen, this is not

et clarior in uerbis.' Witte (*Zur Geschichte*, p. 20) interprets '*omnes ecclesiae*' as meaning all Spanish churches. He also claims that the Vulgate was used at the second Council of Seville in 619 and the fourth Council of Toledo in 633. Isidore's statement might have been adapted from Augustine, *De doctrina christiana*, p. 47 (II, xv, 22): 'In ipsis autem interpretationibus, Itala ceteris praeferatur; nam est verborum tenacior cum perspicuitate sententiae.' Elliott ('The Translations', p. 202) points out that it is unclear what Augustine understood by the term Itala.

[22] See, e.g., Kelly, *Jerome*, p. 162. Witte (*Zur Geschichte*, p. 20) sees the break in the eighth century. Stummer (*Einführung*, p. 128) dates the turning point to sometime in the eighth or ninth century. Hermann Josef Frede ('Bibelzitate bei Kirchenvätern. Beobachtungen bei der Herausgabe der *Vetus Latina*', in *La Bible et les Pères. Colloque de Strasbourg [1ᵉʳ – 3 octobre 1969]*, Paris 1971, pp. 79–96, at p. 81) assumes that around 800, the Vulgate had won the battle against the Vetus Latina. Only exceptional authors still quoted from the old version, as, for instance, Sedulius Scotus in the mid-ninth century. Loewe ('The Medieval History', p. 110) assumes that by the seventh century, the Vulgate was in the process of superseding the Vetus Latina.

[23] See Fischer, 'Zur Überlieferung', pp. 32–33, who also provides further examples. Sutcliffe ('The Name "Vulgate", p. 347) likewise stresses that the Vetus Latina continued to be copied.

[24] Jerome, *De viris inlustribus*, ed. W. Herding, Leipzig 1879, p. 66 (CXXXV): 'Novum testamentum graec[a]e fidei reddidi, vetus juxta hebraicam transtuli.' The phrase 'vetus ... transtuli' is not part of the text in the Teubner edition, but was added by the editor in a list of corrigenda; see ibid., p. XLIV. Other editions of the text likewise include the passage; see, e.g., Jerome and Gennadius, *De viris inlustribus*, ed. C. A. Bernoulli, Freiburg i. Br. and

entirely correct in relation to the Old Testament: his re-translation was limited to the books contained in the Hebrew canon, supplemented by Tobit and Judith. His statement is even more misleading with regard to the New Testament: apart from the Gospels, Jerome probably did not emend or re-translate any other New Testament books. Instead, a contemporary – a disciple of Jerome or possibly Rufinus – working around 400 in Rome, completed this task by revising the Vetus Latina versions of Acts, the Epistles and the Apocalypse on the basis of the Greek original.[25] J. N. D. Kelly was no doubt right to interpret Jerome's claim either as a boastful exaggeration or as a reflection of his view that the four Gospels constituted the indispensable core of the New Testament.[26]

When the origin of the Vulgate was discussed at all by medieval and early Renaissance textual critics – which was not often the case – Jerome was almost always treated as the sole translator.[27] His authorship was often mentioned in conjunction with Damasus's order, as described in Jerome's 'Preface to the Gospels', which was generally assumed – although mistakenly – to refer, not to a revision of the existing Latin versions of the Gospels, but instead to a new translation of the entire Bible. It was not until the fifteenth

---

Leipzig 1895, repr. Frankfurt a. M. 1968, p. 57. For a similar claim regarding the New Testament, see also Jerome, *Epistulae*, II, p. 6 (LXXI, 5): 'Nouum testamentum Graecae reddidi auctoritati.'

[25] For the attribution to a disciple, see Gribomont, 'Aux origines', p. 18; on the other hand, Fischer ('Zur Überlieferung', p. 29) and Bogaert ('La Bible latine', p. 159) consider Rufinus a possible candidate. Kelly (*Jerome*, p. 88) does not speculate as to who the revisor might have been. Bonifatius Fischer, in his 1955 review of the 1954 Oxford edition of the Vulgate New Testament, was still in doubt: 'Für die nicht evangelischen Teile des NT stellt sich die Frage, was als Ziel der textkritischen Arbeit anzusehen ist, ob Hieronymus diese Teile überhaupt revidiert hat'; see Bonifatius Fischer, 'Der Vulgata–Text des Neuen Testaments', in his *Beiträge zur Geschichte der lateinischen Bibeltexte*, Freiburg i. Br., 1986, pp. 51–73, at p. 71. For a defence of the possibility that Jerome revised more parts of the New Testament, see Berger, *Les préfaces*, pp. 15–16, and Sutcliffe, 'Jerome', p. 84.

[26] Kelly, *Jerome*, pp. 88–89.

[27] Sutcliffe ('Jerome', pp. 99–100) sums up the content of the Vulgate as containing: Jerome's translation of the Hebrew Bible from the original (except for the Psalms, which were included in the Gallican version), plus his rendering of Tobit and Judith, also from the original. The remaining deutero-canonical books (Wisdom, Ecclesiasticus, Maccabees and Baruch) in the Old Latin version; the New Testament entirely in Jerome's revision (but for doubts about Jerome's revision of the entire New Testament, see above, p. 37 and n. 25).

century that this misconception was challenged: Lorenzo Valla maintained that the account presented in the preface showed that Damasus had merely asked Jerome to revise the Latin translation of the Gospels rather than to make a new translation.[28]

---

[28] Jerry H. Bentley (*Humanists and Holy Writ. New Testament Scholarship in the Renaissance*, Princeton 1983, p. 50) notes that Valla was the first to challenge the ascription of the Vulgate to Jerome; Alastair Hamilton ('Humanists and the Bible', in *The Cambridge Companion to Renaissance Humanism*, ed. J. Kraye, Cambridge 1996, pp. 100–17, at p. 104) points out that Lorenzo Valla seems to be the first to speak about a revision of the New Testament by Jerome rather than about a translation. For Valla, see below, pp. 71–72. Gribomont ('Aux origines', p. 17) also stresses that, as far as can be judged from Jerome's 'Praefatio in Evangelio', Damasus had not granted him a mandate to translate the Old Testament from the Hebrew.

II.2 MEDIEVAL EDITIONS

The Carolingians

During the Middle Ages, numerous efforts to emend the corrupt text of the Latin Bible were made. Among the many scholars involved in this task in the early medieval period were such outstanding figures as Cassiodorus, Isidore of Seville, Alcuin of York (c. 730–804) and Theodulf of Orleans (750/760–821). Although we know that Cassiodorus had three Bibles prepared for him, they apparently had no influence on the development of the text.[1] Not long after Cassiodorus, Isidore of Seville produced an edition of the Bible, which likewise has not come down to us.[2]

The two best-known revisions of the Latin Scriptures in the early Middle Ages were made in the Carolingian period by Alcuin of York and Theodulf of Orleans.[3] Alcuin's revision is distinctive in containing the Vulgate version. Apart from this choice, no special attention seems to have been paid to the quality of the text. It has often been assumed that Alcuin's edition, a copy of which was presented to Charlemagne at Christmas 801, was prescribed as the official version at the emperor's request. Fischer, however, argues that this was not the case; instead, its successful diffusion was due to the productivity of the scribes of Tours, where Alcuin was abbot of the monastery of St Martin.[4] The emperor's role, according to

---

[1] See Fischer, 'Bibelausgaben', pp. 558–559; and Loewe, 'The Medieval History', p. 116. For a summary of Cassiodorus's approach to producing a better text, see ibid., pp. 118–119.

[2] Fischer, 'Bibelausgaben', p. 575.

[3] For a more detailed examination of their work, information on Carolingian Bible manuscripts and further secondary literature, see Bonifatius Fischer, 'Bibeltext und Bibelreform unter Karl dem Großen', in *Karl der Große: Lebenswerk und Nachleben*, II: *Das geistige Leben*, ed. B. Bischoff, Düsseldorf 1965, pp. 156–216.

[4] Fischer, 'Bibelausgaben', pp. 592–593; and Bonifatius Fischer, Die Alkuin–Bibel, Freiburg i. Br. 1957, p. 19. Glunz, however, assumes that Alcuin's edition was based on a mixture of versions; see below, p. 48. For a detailed discussion of whether or not Charlemagne ordered Alcuin to revise the Latin Bible, see Fischer, 'Bibeltext', especially pp. 162–163; Fischer insists that there is no convincing evidence that the emperor issued such an order. Kaulen (Geschichte, pp. 229–30), on the other hand, assumes that Alcuin

Fischer, consisted in preparing the ground for Alcuin's emendational and editorial efforts by encouraging work on the Bible in general.[5]

But what was the extent of Alcuin's emendational activity? The exact meaning of the words *emendare* in the letter accompanying the pandect he presented to Charlemagne and *emendatio* in his letter to Gisla and Rotrud is unclear and could, in theory, range from a simple proof-reading to more advanced interventions in the text. Yet it seems that there was no elaborate philological programme underlying Alcuin's work: he very rarely intervened in the text and employed the term *emendatio* merely to denote the process of selecting the texts for the pandect and making straightforward corrections.[6] Fischer maintains, in his short monograph on the commonly called Alcuin Bibles, that the aim, not only for Alcuin but also for contemporaries of his working on the Bible, was very basic, yet necessary: to provide a text which was free of grammatical blunders and correct with regard to orthography and punctuation. Their interest in variant readings appears to have been minimal.[7]

Even though Alcuin's revision of the Latin Bible was neither the first nor the last of the Carolingian period, it managed to prevail over the other versions and to become the most influential edition for centuries to come.[8] Under Alcuin's successors, the *scriptorium* of Tours flourished and produced numerous copies of the Bible according to his model; these, in turn, were further distributed and copied, so that his edition ultimately achieved a dominant position in the Frankish Empire. This comprehensive success also brought

---

acted at the request of Charlemagne. For a summary of Alcuin's work, see Loewe, 'The Medieval History', pp. 133–40. Fischer (*Die Alkuin–Bibel*, p. 17) sees no hope of rediscovering the presentation copy which Alcuin gave to the emperor.

[5] Fischer, 'Bibeltext', p. 216. Loewe ('Medieval History', pp. 133–134) agrees with this view.

[6] Fischer, 'Bibeltext', pp. 159–160 and 174. The letters have been edited in *Epistolae Karolini Aevi*, II, (*Monumenta Germaniae Historica, Epistolae* IV) ed. E. Dümmler, Berlin 1895, repr. Munich 1978, pp. 322–323 (no. 195 to Gisla and Rotrud) and pp. 418–419 (no. 261 to Charlemagne); Dümmler assumes that Alcuin had sent a manuscript of the Gospels to the emperor; but see the rejection of this assumption by Fischer, 'Bibeltext', p. 159, n. 10.

[7] Fischer, *Die Alkuin–Bibel*, p. 18. Theodulf was an exception to these limited aims; see below, p. 41.

[8] Ibid., p. 6.

an end to much of the earlier production of mixed texts and secured the predominance of the Vulgate.[9]

The other famous Carolingian Bible editor was Theodulf of Orleans. Although, in contrast to Alcuin, Theodulf clearly developed an editorial programme, his work on the Bible was far less influential than that of his slightly older contemporary.[10] Nevertheless, several manuscripts containing his version have come down to us.

A remarkable feature of Theodulf's editorial activity, which is attested in at least one manuscript, is his reporting of variant readings and their sources in the margins. In MS Paris, BNF lat. 9380, containing a Theodulf Bible, there are variants from Alcuin (abbreviated as *a*), from a Spanish manuscript (*s* = Spanus) related to the Toletanus,[11] from both Alcuin and the manuscript related to the Toletanus (*ij*), along with readings formerly contained in the text (*al*) and others from an as yet unidentified source (*r*). Furthermore, the manuscript also records Hebrew collations, which were apparently derived from the commentaries of Hrabanus Maurus (c. 780–856).[12] These marginal notes of variant readings

---

[9] Ibid., p. 19. See also Kaulen, *Geschichte*, pp. 232–33, who maintains, p. 244, that its diffusion was restricted to the Frankish Empire. A remarkable aspect of the Alcuin Bibles was the uniformity of the text throughout the manuscript tradition: see Loewe, 'The Medieval History', p. 137. But see also above, p. 36 and below, p. 48, for the continued presence of mixed manuscripts in later centuries. For a study of the history of the text of the Latin Bible, focusing on the British Isles, see also Hans Glunz, *Britannien und Bibeltext: Der Vulgatatext der Evangelien in seinem Verhältnis zur irisch-angelsächsichen Kultur des Frühmittelalters*, Leipzig 1930.

[10] Fischer, 'Bibeltext', p. 177. Theodulf also added auxiliary texts as tools for a better understanding and handling of the Bible; see ibid., p. 178. In contrast to Alcuin, Theodulf even added Baruch to his Bible; this version then entered the Vulgate; see ibid., p. 182. For a general survey of Theodulf's edition, see Berger, *Histoire de la Vulgate*, pp. 145–184.

[11] MS Madrid, Biblioteca Nacional de España, Vitr. 13-1 (Tol. 2-1); see Fischer, 'Bibelausgaben', pp. 562–563, for a brief history of this important manuscript. Although Fischer ('Bibeltext', p. 179) stated that MS Paris, BNF lat. 9380 contained variants from the Toletanus in the margin, the corrected dating of the Toletanus to the tenth century shows that the annotator of MS BNF lat. 9380 must have drawn on an older, related manuscript. See Fischer, 'Bibelausgaben', pp. 561–575, for more information on Spanish pandects and the Toletanus.

[12] See Berger, *Histoire*, p. 165, who, however, was not able to interpret the abbreviations, and Fischer, 'Bibeltext', p. 179. A few years earlier, Fischer had assumed that Theodulf received help from a converted Jew for the collation

and their sources seem to foreshadow the thirteenth-century *correctoria*.

The Paris Bible

In the thirteenth century, a new type of Latin Bible arose. Almost forty years after its appearance, an account of origins of the Paris Bible was given by Roger Bacon: theologians and stationers who did not care or know about the Bible produced the text of the Paris Bible, which in turn was further corrupted by scribes. When the theologians noticed how bad the text was, Bacon continues, they set themselves to changing it again.[13] Bacon's account is rejected by modern scholarship.[14] Instead, it is generally held that the origins of the Paris Bible probably date back to the twelfth century. It subsequently came to be the most frequently copied type of Latin Bible for centuries.[15] Their identifying characteristics are: the

---

with the Hebrew; see Fischer, 'Bibelausgaben', p. 595. Traces of study of Hebrew in that time are by no means limited to Theodulf's manuscript; several other scholars, including Remigius of Auxerre, tried to learn at least the alphabet; see Smalley, *The Study of the Bible*, p. 43. The manuscript dates to around 800; see Fischer, 'Bibeltext', p. 176, for the dating of some Theodulf Bibles. For the Toletanus, see also Henri Quentin, *Mémoire sur l'établissement du texte de la Vulgate*, I: *Octateuque*, Rome and Paris 1922, pp. 316-23, and esp. 322-23 for the difficulties in dating the manuscript.

[13] Bacon, *Opus minus*, p. 333: 'Nam circa quadraginta annos [sunt] multi theologi infiniti et stationarii Parisius parum videntes hoc proposuerunt exemplar. Qui cum illiterati fuerint et uxorati, non curantes, nec scientes cogitare de veritate Textus Sacri proposuerunt exemplaria vitiosissima et scriptores infiniti addiderunt ad corruptionem multas mutationes. Deinde novi theologi non habuerunt posse examinandi exemplaria; et crediderunt stationariis a principio. Sed postea consideraverunt errores, et defectus, et superflua ibi multa esse: unde iterum proponunt immutare.' The timeframe given by Bacon, his comment on the diffusion (see below, p. 89, n. 23), and, possibly, a reference to the new chapter division (see below, p. 88, n. 18) show that Bacon is referring to what we now call the Paris Bible.

[14] See, e.g., Laura Light, 'Versions et révisions du texte biblique', in *Le Moyen Age et la Bible*, pp. 55–93, at pp. 78 and 93.

[15] Denifle, 'Die Handschriften', pp. 291–292. Laura Light ('French Bibles c. 1200–30: A New Look at the Origin of the Paris Bible', in *The Early Medieval Bible. Its Production, Decoration and Use*, ed. R. Gameson, Cambridge 1994, pp. 155–176, at p. 172) states that the Paris Bible was a revision of a small group of French Bibles written in the beginning of the thirteenth century. According to Dahan ('La critique textuelle', p. 375), it was already in use in the twelfth century. The manuscript used by Johannes Gutenberg for his *editio princeps* of the Bible belonged to the family of the Paris Bible; his text was taken over for many early printed editions of the

presence of specific prologues; the exclusive use of the modern chapter division; the order of the books; and, usually placed after the text of the Bible, the glossary entitled *Interpretationes nominum hebraicorum*, beginning with the words *Aaz apprehendens*.[16] The reason for the unrivalled success of the Paris Bible has been plausibly explained by Martin, who assumes that it was officially endorsed by the University of Paris: before that time, there was no body or authority which could successfully impose the adoption of a specific edition; only with the rise of the faculty of theology at the University of Paris, which produced numerous students, did such regulation become feasible.[17] Although the biblical text contained

Bible; see Heinrich Schneider, *Der Text der Gutenbergbibel zu ihrem 500jährigen Jubiläum untersucht*, Bonn 1954, esp. pp. 109–113. Quentin (*Mémoire*, pp. 485–488) lists some readings he ascribes to Paris Bibles.

[16] See Light, 'French Bibles', p. 156; the modern chapter division was presumably introduced by Stephen Langton before 1206 and is, in essence, still the one in use today, see ibid., p. 171. For the order of the biblical books, see J. P. P. Martin, 'Le texte parisien de la Vulgate latine', [II], *Le Muséon* 9 (1890), pp. 55–70 and 301–316, at p. 302 and n. 3. He assumes that this order, like the chapter division, was based on Stephen Langton. Martin (p. 304) lists the same characteristics for the Paris Bible between 1210 and 1220 as Light, except that he does not mention the prologues. Martin also maintains that the glossary has been wrongly attributed to Remigius of Auxerre and the Venerable Bede and was, in fact, written around 1210; see ibid., p. 67. Amaury d'Esneval ('Le perfectionnement d'un instrument de travail au début du XIIe siècle: les trois glossaires bibliques d'Étienne Langton', in *Culture et travail intellectuel dans l'occident médiéval. Bilan des 'Colloques d'humanisme médiéval' [1960–1980] fondés par le R. P. Hubert, O.P.*, ed. G. Hasenohr and J. Longère, Paris 1981, pp. 163–175, at p. 163) argues that the *Interpretationes nominum hebraicorum* were in great part the work of Stephen Langton. Neil Ripley Ker (*Medieval Manuscripts in British Libraries*, I: *London*, Oxford 1969, pp. 96–97) gives a list of incipits for the prologues and the order of books common to Paris Bibles. For biblical books customarily contained in the Paris Bible, see also Bogaert, 'La Bible latine', p. 298. Lobrichon points out that some of the prefaces considered to be characteristic of Paris Bibles can be traced back to patristic times while others date to 1200–20; see Guy Lobrichon, 'Les éditions de la Bible latine dans les universités du XIIIe siècle', in *La Bibbia del XIII secolo. Storia del testo, storia dell'esegesi. Convegno della Società Internazionale per lo Studio del Medioevo Latino (SISMEL). Firenze, 1-2 giugno 2001*, ed. G. Cremascoli and F. Santi, Florence 2004, pp. 15–34, at pp. 20–21, where he also makes other observations on the Paris Bible.

[17] J. P. P. Martin, 'Le texte parisien de la Vulgate latine', [I], *Le Muséon* 8 (1889), pp. 444–466, at pp. 450–452. For a rejection of the idea that the Paris Bible constituted the edition of the University of Paris, see, e.g., Guy Lobrichon, 'Les traductions médiévales de la Bible dans l'Occident latin', in

in the Paris Bible was notably bad, it was nevertheless rapidly disseminated.[18]

Much research has been done on the defining characteristics of the Paris Bible; nonetheless, scholars still disagree about which textual version forms its basis, if indeed there is base text at all. Stummer saw the Paris Bible as a descendant of Alcuin's text, heavily interpolated with other versions. He claims that the Paris Bible was intended to be based on Jerome's work, but that it failed to achieve its aim because of the inability at this time to distinguish between the texts of the Vulgate and Vetus Latina.[19] Like Stummer, Glunz thought that the Paris Bible was based on Alcuin's recension and that it could therefore claim a close connection to the Vulgate.[20] If that is the case, the question whether the choice of Alcuin's version as a base text was a conscious decision or was, instead, determined by availability remains unanswerable in the current state of our knowledge.

One aspect which undermines the assumption that the editors of the Paris Bible consciously relied on Alcuin's text is the strong influence of Theodulf's edition on the Paris Bible. That Theodulf's version had an impact on the Paris Bible and thus on the milieu in which the *correctoria* were compiled has already been demonstrated: Loewe mentions that the Book of Proverbs in the Paris Bible contains many readings which can be traced back to Theodulf; and Fischer notes that Theodulf's version of the book of Baruch found its way into the Paris Bible.[21] It would be worth investigating the

---

Biblia. Les Bibles en latin au temps des Réformes, ed. M.–C. Gomez–Géraud, Paris 2008, pp. 19–36, at p. 24.

[18] Smalley (*The Study of the Bible*, pp. 334–335) provides a good explanation of why the Paris text was of such poor quality.

[19] Stummer, *Einführung*, p. 151. He gives no references for his assumption that the editors aimed for Jerome's version.

[20] Glunz, *History of the Vulgate in England*, p. 3; however, Glunz and also Laura Light ('The New Thirteenth–Century Bible and the Challenge of Heresy', *Viator* 18 [1987], pp. 275–288, at p. 275) stress that the text of the Paris Bible has never been studied – a remark which holds true to the present day; Glunz also considers Alcuin's version to be a mixed text, which, as a result, would weaken the Paris Bible's link to the Vulgate. Dahan ('La critique textuelle', p. 366) likewise assumes that the text of the Paris Bible was based on Alcuin's version.

[21] See Loewe, 'The Medieval History', p. 123; and Fischer, 'Zur Überlieferung', p. 30. Henri Quentin (*Mémoire*, p. 388), too, confirms the influence of Theodulf's revision on the Paris Bible.

extent of the direct influence of Theodulf's Bibles, not only on the Paris Bible, but also on the *correctoria*. If it emerges, for instance, that the Theodulf Bible MS Paris, BNF lat. 9380 was in Paris in the early thirteenth century and therefore perhaps accessible to Hugh of St Cher or, possibly, his circle working on the first *correctorium*, we might be able to trace the idea for the type of collation found in the *correctoria* back four hundred years to Theodulf of Orleans.[22] Moreover, if the unidentified abbreviation *r* in MS Paris, BNF lat. 9380 stands for readings derived from Hrabanus, which is not impossible – after all, he was probably a source for Theodulf's collation from the Hebrew – this might establish a link between Theodulf and the *correctoria*, in which this same abbreviation is found.[23]

Furthermore, the theory that Alcuin's text was deliberately chosen as a base text for the Paris Bible does not square with the many additions evidently contained in the Paris text. Denifle voices the suspicion that the Paris Bible may have been chosen as a model on account of the sheer quantity of text which it contained.[24] This would help to explain how the immensely corrupt text came about in the first place; moreover, as we shall see, the criterion of quantity seems to have been frequently adopted.[25] Critical remarks about the text of the Paris Bible can already be found in the thirteenth century in some of the *correctoria* and especially in the works of Bacon.[26] Among recent commentators, in opposition of most earlier scholars, Light has queried whether the Paris Bible did, in fact, become the standard text and has even questioned whether it is possible to speak of 'the' text of the Paris Bible.[27] In order to

---

[22] Of course, the influence – if any – might also have derived from another manuscript containing similar notes which does not survive or has not yet been discovered.

[23] See below, p. 133, n. 85. Berger (*Histoire*, p. 174) and, following him, Loewe ('The Medieval History', p. 128) point out that the marginal variants found in MS Paris, BNF lat. 9380 led to further corruption of Theodulf's text.

[24] Denifle, 'Die Handschriften', p. 283.

[25] See below, pp. 120–121.

[26] See, e.g., Gerard of Huy, *Correctorium*, quoted by Denifle, 'Die Handschriften', p. 483: 'In parabolis etiam plures versus de translacione LXX additi sunt in exemplari Parisiensi, qui in hebreo non habentur, nec in antiquis.' For Bacon's remarks on the Paris Bibles, see below, p. 147.

[27] Light, 'French Bibles', p. 156. For a contrary opinion see Martin, 'Le texte parisien', [II], p. 313; he claims (pp. 308–09) that the text of older manuscripts was sometimes updated to that of the Paris Bible. Guy

provide a definitive answer to the question of the text(s) found in the so-called Paris Bibles and whether it was a distinct recension, an examination as comprehensive as possible of the text contained in the manuscripts is still needed.

As Fischer has noted, the best medieval philologists continually tackled the task of emending the text of the Latin Bible. Attempts to emend Scripture were far more common than those aimed at pagan or other Christian works, and they can be found throughout the Middle Ages.[28] Nevertheless, after the flurry of activity in the Carolingian period, primarily due to the efforts of Alcuin and Theodulf, the next two centuries appear to have witnessed far less emendational and editorial work. This conservative phase had the general effect of preserving the textual advances of the Carolingian era. It did not, however, prevent the further corruption of the Latin Bible; and, of course, in these centuries, too, there were attempts to produce a better text.[29] As Kaulen points out, the efforts to edit the Bible from the tenth to the twelfth century were not only the result of the corruption of the text but also one of its causes.[30] This assessment can also be extended backwards to the ninth century, when Theodulf's work unwittingly provided a source of variant readings that were introduced in the text, and forwards to the thirteenth, when Roger Bacon complained that the new Paris Bible was utterly corrupt; indeed, in all likelihood, it reflects the situation

---

Lobrichon (*La Bible au moyen âge*, Paris 2003, p. 176) argues against the textual uniformity of the Paris Bibles. Light ('Versions', pp. 80–82) summarises previous discussions of the Parisian text and suggests that the research done so far is not conclusive. Glunz (*History of the Vulgate in England*, p. 277), on the other hand, assumed that, with the introduction of the Paris Bible, the biblical text became almost uniform. The unresolved questions concerning the text of the Paris Bible are not a problem for this study, since I am dealing only with notions about the text and not with the texts themselves. Medieval scholars seemed to regard the text of the Paris Bible as a proper recension; see, e.g., below, p. 125.

[28] See Fischer, 'Bibelausgaben', p. 600. Fischer ('Bibeltext', p. 216) stresses that in the Carolingian period Alcuin's effort was only one among many.

[29] See Glunz, *History of the Vulgate in England*, pp. 48–49, and Loewe, 'The Medieval History', pp. 140–142. Smalley (*The Study of the Bible*, pp. 44–45) observes a decrease in Bible studies from the early tenth to the mid-eleventh century.

[30] Kaulen, *Geschichte*, p. 236. Among the editors named by Kaulen is Lanfranc of Bec (c. 1010–1089); see ibid., pp. 234–236.

throughout the entire Middle Ages.[31] Additional evidence that editorial work on the Bible introduced further corruption is provided by Glunz, who shows that expressions found in the Church Fathers or glosses to the biblical text aimed at clarifying its meaning – mostly without altering the literal sense – entered the text. According to Glunz, these additions prove that the Bible was seen as a text which needed further information in order to be clearly understood.[32] They also show that scribes were apparently prepared to alter the text for the sake of improving comprehension.

As we have seen, during the Middle Ages, no text of the Bible completely dominated the tradition. Despite its predominance, not even the Vulgate managed to achieve this degree of influence. Lobrichon has insisted that at least until the second quarter of the thirteenth century – and very likely beyond – there was no uniformity in the transmission of the Latin Bible.[33] Although it has been assumed that, with the emergence of the Paris Bible in the thirteenth century, there was finally an edition which provided a uniform (but very corrupt) text that was adopted throughout the Church,[34] it remains unclear what text the Paris Bible actually contained.

Apart from the unsolved problems connected to the text of the Paris Bible, it has to be pointed out that modern discussions of the transmission of Jerome's version and the Vetus Latina are also at times contradictory or sidestep important questions – probably because they cannot be answered. There is widespread agreement that by the ninth century the Vulgate had finally ousted the Vetus Latina from the position of the most commonly available Latin Bible version,[35] largely thanks to the success of Alcuin's edition which is generally thought to be based on a pure text of the

---

[31] For Theodulf, see above, p. 45, n. 23; for Roger Bacon's statement, see below, p. 146, n. 131. Heinrich Joseph Vogels (*Handbuch der neutestamentlichen Textkritik*, Münster i. W. 1923, p. 121) also argues that the *correctoria* increased corruption.

[32] See Glunz, *History of the Vulgate in England*, pp. 88–89. Even though Glunz's study focuses on England, the phenomenon of the introduction of explanatory glosses to the text certainly took place in the entire Latin West and throughout the Middle Ages.

[33] See Lobrichon, *La Bible*, pp. 29–30.

[34] See Glunz, *History of the Vulgate in England*, pp. 267 and 277, and Martin, 'Le texte parisien', [II], p. 313.

[35] See, e.g., Stummer, *Einführung*, p. 144; and also above, p. 36 and n. 22.

Vulgate, though Glunz, for example, assumes that Alcuin's text was, in fact, a mixture of the Vetus Latina and the Vulgate.[36] Broad surveys of the text contained in biblical manuscripts are still lacking, so it is difficult to ascertain which text of the Bible medieval scholars held in their hands. For our purposes, however, it is sufficient to keep two facts in mind: first, that various versions and editions were available and that their texts were often conflated; and second, that the standard text of the medieval Latin Bible did not exist, even if at times certain editions dominated the tradition.

Despite the long history of conflation and contamination and the production of new editions, manuscripts transmitting a pure text managed to survive. Fischer, for instance, maintains that some Bibles written in the twelfth and thirteenth centuries continued to carry a mixed text, but he has also identified certain manuscripts in which the Vulgate text and the Vetus Latina version were copied side by side.[37] In addition to these mixed and pure texts, as well as the various medieval editions, many religious orders no doubt promoted their own editions for the use of their members; and even local textual traditions did not entirely disappear.[38] In the time period covered by this study, a wide array of biblical versions thus remained in circulation.

---

[36] Glunz, *History of the Vulgate in England*, p. 3.

[37] Fischer, 'Zur Überlieferung', p. 33. For the mixed texts, see above, p. 36.

[38] For the Cistercians, see, e.g., Tiburtius Hümpfner, 'Die Bibel des hl. Stephan Harding', *Cistercienser–Chronik* 29 (1917), pp. 73–81, at p. 79; Nicolò Maniacutia, *Libellus de corruptione et correptione Psalmorum et aliarum quarundam scripturarum*, ed. Vittorio Peri, '"Correctores immo corruptores". Un saggio di critica testuale nella Roma del XII secolo', *Italia medioevale e umanistica* 20 (1977), pp. 19-125, pp. 88-125, at p. 105: 'Hoc tamen, sicut et alia plura insueta, nec in translationibus aliis nec in hac ipsa apud alios reperitur, sed apud solos nostri Ordinis patres, qui solent esse aliis cautiores'; and below, p. 139, n. 110; for the Carthusians, see, e.g., below, p. 196; for the Dominicans see below, pp. 137–139. We still do not have comprehensive studies of the biblical versions used by the different religious orders. For the survival of local traditions, see Fischer, 'Zur Überlieferung', p. 33.

II.3 ATTITUDES TOWARDS ST JEROME

The Veneration of Jerome

While Jerome was accepted as a figure of authority throughout the Middle Ages, a decisive shift in his importance took place in the fourteenth century, when he became the object of a powerful cult. Of course, there are earlier examples of this devotion, as, for instance, in the works of Nicolò Maniacutia, who was an ardent admirer and wrote a *vita* of Jerome.[1] Yet despite this and other earlier indications of respect and veneration, it was only in the 1300s that Jerome ascended to a special – indeed, dominant – position among his fellow Church Fathers to become what Berndt Hamm has called a fashion saint (*Modeheiliger*). The cult of Jerome, which arose for a variety of reasons, blossomed in early fourteenth-century Italy, with Germany and the Netherlands soon following suit.[2] In this chapter, I shall provide a brief outline of this new veneration for Jerome. Whether the changing perception which it brought about had any impact on the attitude of textual critics towards Jerome and towards the Vulgate will be discussed in the conclusion to this chapter.[3]

The literary tradition constituted an important foundation for the increasing veneration of Jerome. Three forged letters, dating from the thirteenth century, were to exert an important influence on his cult in the fourteenth century.[4] The pseudepigrapha purport

---

[1] See below, p. 251, n. 7; and Rice, *Saint Jerome*, p. 63. For a comparison between the view of Jerome's translation of the Bible which Maniacutia presents in the *vita* and in his text–critical works, see below, pp. 59–60.

[2] See Berndt Hamm, 'Hieronymus–Begeisterung und Augustinismus vor der Reformation. Beobachtungen zur Beziehung zwischen Humanismus und Frömmigkeitstheologie (am Beispiel Nürnbergs)', in *Augustine, the Harvest, and Theology (1300–1650): Essays Dedicated to Heiko Augustinus Oberman in Honor of his Sixtieth Birthday*, ed. K. Hagen, Leiden, New York, Copenhagen and Cologne 1990, pp. 127–235, at pp. 133 and 147–148. For a good summary of the various aspects of the veneration of Jerome, see also Rice, *Saint Jerome*, pp. 23–83.

[3] See below, pp. 74–77.

[4] Among modern scholars, there is some variation regarding the dating of these letters: Ferdinand Cavallera (*Saint Jérôme: sa vie et son oeuvre*, 2 vols, Louvain and Paris 1922, II, p. 145) dates the forged letter ascribed to Eusebius of

to have been written by three ancient Christian figures: St Eusebius of Cremona (d. after 420); St Augustine writing to St Cyril, bishop of Jerusalem (d. 444); and Cyril replying to Augustine. Most modern scholars agree that in all likelihood the texts were written by a Dominican or by someone who was at least closely associated with the order.[5] In the letters, Jerome's status is exalted, not only by various miracles and the impeccable manner of life attributed to him, but also by the fact that, in the letter to Cyril of Jerusalem, Ps.-Augustine acknowledges Jerome's superiority over other saints.[6] In addition, his learning and especially his version of the Bible are praised in extravagant terms.[7]

Cremona to the twelfth century. This view is now generally rejected. Anna Morisi Guerra ('La leggenda di San Girolamo: temi e problemi tra Umanesimo e Controriforma', *Clio* 23 [1987], pp. 5–33, at p. 7) ascribes them to the late thirteenth or early fourteenth century; Rice (*Saint Jerome*, p. 218, n. 1) argues for the year 1295 as the *terminus post quem*, and 1334 as the *terminus ante quem*. Erika Bauer ('Hieronymus–Briefe', in *Die deutsche Literatur des Mittelalters: Verfasserlexikon*, ed. K. Ruh et al., III, Berlin and New York 1981, cols 1233–1238), however, mentions six manuscripts of the letters dated to the thirteenth century, of which three might also have been written in the twelfth or fourteenth century, respectively.

[5] See Rice, *Saint Jerome*, pp. 49–55 (where Rice also summarises the letters' content and success) and 63. There is some disagreement as to their place of origin: Rice (ibid., p. 63) suggests Rome; Morisi Guerra ('La leggenda', p. 7) assigns them to a Dominican milieu in the Veneto or Romagna. The letters are published in *PL* XXII, Paris 1854, cols 239–282 (Ps.–Eusebius, *De morte Hieronymi*); cols 281–289 (Ps.–Augustine, *De magnificentiis beati Hieronymi*); and cols 289–326 (Ps.–Cyril, *De miraculis Hieronymi*). Another relevant work in this context is the *Translatio corporis S. Hieronymi* (ibid., cols 237–240); for a summary and an account of its impact and of the history of Jerome's relics see Rice, *Saint Jerome*, pp. 55–59.

[6] See, e.g., Ps.-Augustine, *De magnificentiis*, col. 283: 'Si sanctorum singulorum perquirerem vitas, eo (ut puto) majorem neminem invenirem.'

[7] See also Rice, *Saint Jerome*, p. 50; and, e.g., Ps.-Eusebius, *De morte*, col. 241: 'Hic est qui populo Christiano tot librorum volumina ex linguis Hebraica et Graeca in Latinam, non parvo pondere transtulit'; Ps.–Augustine, *De magnificentiis*, col. 283: 'Hic certe gloria virtutis nostrae transferens utrumque Testamentum ex Hebraeorum lingua in Graecam pariter et Latinam'; and ibid., col. 283: 'Hebraicorum, Graecorum, Chaldaeorum, Persarum, et Medorum, Arabicorum, et pene omnium nationum linguas et litteras, tanquam si fuisset in eisdem natus et educatus, scivit.' In the second passage quoted here, a translation of the Bible into Greek is attributed to Jerome; yet it is plausible to assume that there is a corruption in the text. I have double-checked this passage with the version in MS London, British Library, Egerton 839, ff. 159ra–162va, at f. 159va, which is identical to the printed text.

The three Latin letters quickly achieved wide diffusion, first in manuscript – over 100 pre-fifteenth-century copies survive, complemented by another 300 from the fifteenth century – and later in print; and their content was incorporated into the collection of saints' lives in Pietro Calo's (d. 1348) *Legendae de sanctis* (before 1340) and in Pietro de' Natali's (d. c. 1400) widely read *Catalogus sanctorum* (1372). In the fourteenth and fifteenth centuries, the letters were translated into various vernacular languages.[8] The most influential of these versions was probably the German one made around 1370 in Prague by the chancellor of Charles IV, John of Neumarkt (before 1320–80); it was frequently copied and influenced many later texts.[9] In addition, the material in the letters was disseminated in sermons, and artists depicted episodes from them. This swift and widespread diffusion, in different languages and various media, made the attractive portrait of Jerome presented in the letters accessible to a very large audience, both literate and illiterate.[10]

---

[8] See Hamm, 'Hieronymus-Begeisterung', pp. 149–51; and Rice, *Saint Jerome*, p. 49. With the exception of Calo's sections on Dominic (Pietro Calo, *Miracula sancti Dominici mandato magistri Berengarii collecta. Petri Calo legendae sancti Dominici*, ed. S. Tugwell, Rome 1997), there are no modern editions of either text. For Pietro Calo, see also Albert Poncelet, 'Le légendier de Pierre Calo', *Analecta Bollandiana* 29 (1910), pp. 5–116 and Calo, *Miracula sancti Dominici ... Petri Calo legendae sancti Dominici*, esp. pp. 129–44 for Calo's life; and Morisi Guerra, 'La leggenda', p. 8. The fact that the letters were not included in the *Legenda aurea* might be another indication that they were composed in the late thirteenth century. I am grateful to Anthony Lappin for pointing this out to me.

[9] Forty-six manuscript copies and two incunabula of John of Neumarkt's version alone survive; see Hamm, 'Hieronymus–Begeisterung', pp. 150–151. Hamm believes that John of Neumarkt's translation may have prepared the way for the veneration of Jerome in Germany. Joseph Klapper ([John of Neumarkt], *Schriften Johanns von Neumarkt*, II, ed. J. Klapper, Berlin 1932, p. VI) points out that John first revised the Latin letters and then translated them into German from his revision; both versions are published ibid., pp. 3–514. For a list of the Middle High German, Middle Low German and Middle Dutch translations, see Bauer, 'Hieronymus-Briefe', cols 1235–1237. For John's life and works, see Joseph Klapper, *Johann von Neumarkt: Bischof und Hofkanzler. Religiöse Frührenaissance in Böhmen zur Zeit Kaiser Karls IV.*, Leipzig 1964, pp. 5–52.

[10] Rice, *Saint Jerome*, p. 49. For further examples of the veneration of Jerome in the vernacular, see, e.g., the Sicilian *Libru di lu transitu et vita di misser sanctu Iheronimu*, ed. C. di Girolamo, Palermo 1982. The editor (ibid., p. VII) mentions a similar work in Tuscan.

Perhaps the most important person to have been influenced by these letters was Giovanni d'Andrea (1271–1348), a famous teacher of canon law in Bologna, who around 1310 became a devotee of Jerome.[11] He was the single most active and dedicated campaigner for the cult of Jerome, which he promoted in various aspects of religious life and culture.[12] To further his cause, d'Andrea composed the *Hieronymianus*, a compilation of writings by and about Jerome, probably finished in the early 1340s.[13] In it, he repeatedly complains that Italy has all but forgotten Jerome.[14] As in the three pseudepigraphical letters, so, too, in the *Hieronymianus*, Jerome is praised for his translation of the Old and New Testaments. But d'Andrea adds further significant details:

> Quis plus Latinorum profecit ecclesie, quam qui vetus et novum testamentum de Greco et Hebraico et ceteros ipsius libros sicut Danielem de Caldayco sermone, licet hebraicis litteris, et Job de Arabico, premissis in eis suis famosis et utilibus prologis, transtulit in Latinum, quod condoctorum nulli creditum fuisset possibile, cum non legamus illos multiplicis lingue fuisse peritos, quod esse non ambigitur Spiritus sancti donum ... Qui {*sc.* Hieronymus}, quod

---

[11] Hamm, 'Hieronymus–Begeisterung', pp. 147–148. Giovanni d'Andrea does not say what inspired his reverence for Jerome, but Rice (*Saint Jerome*, p. 64) thinks that it might well have been the letters; their impact on the Bolognese canonist is also mentioned by Hamm, 'Hieronymus-Begeisterung', p. 150.

[12] Joseph Klapper ('Aus der Frühzeit des Humanismus. Dichtungen zu Ehren des hl. Hieronymus', in *Bausteine. Festschrift Max Koch zum 70. Geburtstage dargebracht*, ed. E. Boehlich and H. Heckel, Wroclaw 1926, pp. 255–281, at p. 261) lists over a dozen measures undertaken by Giovanni d'Andrea to further the veneration of Jerome.

[13] There is some disagreement about the dating. Rice (*Saint Jerome*, pp. 64 and 224, n. 34) provides evidence that, although Giovanni d'Andrea himself says that he finished the *Hieronymianus* in 1334, he continued working on it until 1346/1347. Klapper ('Aus der Frühzeit', p. 256) gives 1342 as the *terminus ante quem non*. Morisi Guerra ('La leggenda', p. 8) dates the work to around 1342. Justinus Uttenweiler ('Zur Stellung des hl. Hieronymus im Mittelalter', *Benediktinische Monatschrift* 2 [1920], pp. 522–541, at p. 530) claims that it was published in 1346. Millard Meiss ('Scholarship and Penitence in the Early Renaissance: The Image of St. Jerome', *Pantheon* 32 [1974], pp. 134–140, at p. 134) gives the title as *Liber de laudibus S. Hieronymi*.

[14] See Hamm, 'Hieronymus–Begeisterung', p. 148, and Morisi Guerra, 'La leggenda', p. 9.

habemus in divino canone, nobis dedit, quod legimus, scripsit, quod intelligimus, docuit.[15]

Who of the Latin Fathers benefited the Church more than the person who translated the Old and New Testaments from Greek and Hebrew into Latin, and also its remaining books, such as Daniel from the Aramaic tongue – even though written in Hebrew letters – and Job from the Arabic, prefaced by his famous and useful prologues. This would not have been believed possible for any of his fellow Church Fathers, for we do not read that they knew a variety of languages; there is no doubt that this was a gift of the Holy Spirit ... He {Jerome} has given to us what we have in the holy canon, he has written what we read, he has taught what we understand.

Precisely because Jerome was the translator of the Bible, d'Andrea places him above the other Latin Fathers. Furthermore, he repeats a groundbreaking new claim about Jerome's version which was already voiced in the letter by Pseudo-Eusebius: he considers it to be a gift from the Holy Spirit. Attributing divine inspiration to Jerome's translation was an extremely important development in the perception of the Vulgate. In previous centuries, it was almost exclusively the translators of the *septuaginta* who were thought to have received such inspiration.[16] The novel idea that Jerome's version, too, was inspired by the Holy Spirit led in turn to the belief that his text was inviolable. Although, as we shall see, this belief became increasingly popular, it is not – with one exception – found in text-critical writings.[17]

---

[15] Giovanni d'Andrea, *Hieronymianus*, quoted in Klapper, 'Aus der Frühzeit', p. 258. See Jerome, 'Prologus in Danihele propheta', in *Biblia sacra*, pp. 1341–1342, at p. 1341: 'Sciendum quippe Danihelem maxime et Ezram hebraicis quidem litteris, sed chaldaico sermone conscriptos ... Iob quoque cum arabica lingua habere plurimam societatem.' The first commentator to suggest that the Book of Job was actually a translation into Hebrew from another language was Abraham Ibn Ezra (d. 1167); see Marvin H. Pope, *Job*, 3rd edn, Garden City 1973, p. XLIX.

[16] Ps.–Eusebius, *De morte*, col. 239: 'Multifariam multisque modis olim Deus locutus est omnibus nobis per suum dilectissimum filium sanctum Hieronymum, de Scripturis sanctis in virtutibus et prodigiis multis, quae per illum fecit ipse Dominus in medio nostri.' For the alleged divine inspiration of the *septuaginta*, see pp. 8 above and 218 below.

[17] George of Trebizond is the only textual critic to defend the text of the Vulgate with the argument that it was divinely inspired; see below, p. 73. Peter of Ailly, too, puts forward this view (see below, pp. 67–71), but his writings do not deal with textual criticism.

Giovanni d'Andrea's efforts to promote the cult of Jerome were very successful. The *Hieronymianus* was copied numerous times and exerted an influence on the visual arts and other aspects of culture.[18] Together with the three pseudepigraphical letters and their translations, it was the motor that drove the cult of Jerome, which achieved its zenith in the late Middle Ages and the Renaissance.[19] Indeed, in the late fourteenth and fifteenth centuries, various Italian humanists composed works in praise of him. Pier Paolo Vergerio the Elder (1370–1444), for instance, sought to establish Jerome as a patron of humanist studies;[20] and, in a letter dating from the end of the fourteenth century, he tells of his vow to give a speech in honour of Jerome every year on 30

---

[18] See, e.g., Klapper, 'Aus der Frühzeit', pp. 255–256; and Uttenweiler, 'Zur Stellung', p. 530; for information on Giovanni d'Andrea, see *DBI*, LV, pp. 667–672. Rice (*Saint Jerome*, p. 224, n. 34) cites three editions printed between 1482 and 1514, and gives references to secondary literature listing manuscripts of the *Hieronymianus*. For the visual arts, see also below, p. 56. Giovanni d'Andrea's predilection for Jerome was not, however, universally shared; it met with a lack of understanding from no less a figure than Petrarch, who, in two letters to Giovanni d'Andrea, says that he cannot fathom why his correspondent is so devoted to Jerome and admits that he himself much prefers Augustine; see Petrarch, *Le familiari*, I, 1, ed. and tr. U. Dotti, Urbino 1974, pp. 461 and 463 (IV, 15): 'Nempe quod de Ieronimo scribis, te illum sacrorum doctorum ex numero pretulisse, haud novum est michi; vetus est iam et late cognitum hoc iudicium tuum ... Licet de hac re inter amicum tuum clare memorie Lomberiensem epyscopum Iacobum [Jacobus de Colonna, bishop of Lombez 1328–1341] et me crebro disceptatum esse meminerim, illo per vestigia tua semper uno ore Ieronimum, me vero Augustinum inter scriptores catholicos preferente'; and ibid., p. 473 (IV, 16): 'Tu Ieronimum prefers Augustino. Hoc sciebam, sed eam quam affers, iudicii rationem profiteor me non intelligere. Quid enim, queso, sibi vult quod ais, non te illum propterea pretulisse quia sit maior, sed quia fructuosior Ecclesie?'

[19] Basing his judgement on the dissemination of the three pseudepigrapha and their vernacular translations, Hamm ('Hieronymus–Begeisterung', p. 151) comes to the conclusion that the veneration of Jerome increased significantly in the 1400s, culminating at the end of the fifteenth century and the early sixteenth. According to di Girolamo (*Libru di lu transitu*, p. XXIII), the peak was reached in the fourteenth and fifteenth centuries. In addition to the various works about Jerome, his own writings also gained in popularity and were widely translated; see Hamm, 'Hieronymus–Begeisterung', p. 151.

[20] Pier Paolo Vergerio the Elder, *Pierpaolo Vergerio the Elder and Saint Jerome: An Edition and Translation of 'Sermones pro Sancto Hieronymo'*, ed. J. M. McManamon, Tempe 1999, p. 16.

September, the saint's feast day.²¹ As one would expect from a humanist, Vergerio focuses mostly on Jerome's classical erudition, which, he insists, can be applied to biblical studies, in particular to philological criticism of the Bible.²²

Vergerio was not the only humanist to deliver speeches in praise of Jerome. In the first half of the fifteenth century, Niccolò Bonavia da Lucca (fl. early fifteenth century), Isotta Nogarola (1418-1466) and Agostino Dati (1420-1478) also joined the ranks; and others, such as Guarino Veronese (1374-1408) and Giovanni Conversini (1343-1408) likewise revered him.²³ Humanists perceived Jerome as a role model on account of his vast classical and biblical learning, the combination and extent of which set him apart from other Church Fathers.²⁴ He was treated almost as a classical author and praised, among other things, for his rhetorical skill, his knowledge of the biblical languages and his erudition in various fields. In the fifteenth century, he became the patron saint of learned men and institutions.²⁵

The increasing popularity of the cult of Jerome was not limited to the medium of literature. From the second half of the fourteenth century onwards, it can also be observed in devotional practice.²⁶

---

[21] Pier Paolo Vergerio (*Epistolario*, ed. L. Smith, Rome 1934, pp. 91–93) to Santo dei Pellegrini: 'Nichil est quod in presentia magis debeam aut quod iocundius exigere a me possim quam ut et tecum et de sancto Hieronymo dicam. Cum enim quarto iam superiore anno quasi voto quodam constitutum a me fuerit ut in singulos annos die illius festo de laudibus suis sermonem agerem idque triennio hoc sedulo prestiterim solus hic a me annus pretermissus est, non quidem negligentia, quam velim minimum apud me posse, sed quia iter quod in Thusciam estate proxima suscepi minus celeriter quam ratus eram absolvi.' See also John M. McManamon, 'Pier Paolo Vergerio (the Elder) and the Beginnings of the Humanist Cult of Jerome', *The Catholic Historical Review* 71 (1985), pp. 353–71, at p. 353. In addition to ten of these sermons, written between 1390 and 1408, three letters praising Jerome have also come down to us; see ibid., p. 356.

[22] McManamon, 'Pier Paolo Vergerio', pp. 357, 360 and 370–71.

[23] See Rice, *Saint Jerome*, p. 95; and McManamon, 'Pier Paolo Vergerio', pp. 367 and 370. For Isotta Nogarola, see Isotta Nogarola, *In beati Hieronymi laudem oratio*, in her *Opera quae supersunt omnia*, ed. A. Apponyi and E. Abel, 2 vols, Vienna and Budapest 1886, II, pp. 276–289.

[24] See John C. Olin, 'Erasmus and Saint Jerome', *Thought* 54 (1979), pp. 313–321, at p. 319; and Hamm, 'Hieronymus–Begeisterung', pp. 157–158 and 169.

[25] Rice, *Saint Jerome*, pp. 84, 98 and 102; for the veneration of Jerome as a scholar by humanists, see pp. 84–115.

[26] Meiss, 'Scholarship and Penitence', pp. 134–135.

The religious revival which took place in the late fourteenth and early fifteenth centuries brought with it a greater veneration of saints than ever before and the production of a vast amount of hagiographical literature.[27] Perhaps the clearest sign of this heightened veneration of Jerome is the establishment of monastic congregations devoted to him. In the mid-fourteenth century, several houses of the Jeronimites were founded, both in Italy and in Spain, partly out of discontent with the existing orders.[28]

In the visual arts, too, Jerome became an important figure. In the late Middle Ages, depictions of him far outnumber those of other Church Fathers.[29] Moreover, the visual arts and literature often worked in combination: for example, altarpiece paintings dating from 1420 to 1520 often depicted the content of humanist orations;[30] and paintings of Jerome commissioned by Giovanni d'Andrea were provided with explanatory verses written by a Dominus Franciscus Thebaldus, in which, again, Jerome is mentioned as the translator of the Bible.[31]

---

[27] Rice, *Saint Jerome*, p. 81. Apart from hagiographical writings, many hymns also contained praises of Jerome; see, e.g., *De sancti Hieronymo. Ad Vesperas*, in *Analecta hymnica medii aevi*, LII, ed. C. Blume, Leipzig 1909, repr. New York and London 1961, pp. 201–02 (no. 220), at p. 201: 'Omne mandatum vetus et novellum, / quidquid arcani cecinere patres, / quidquid aeternum celebrant latini, / transtulit iste'; the editor (ibid., p. 202) points out that Franciscus Tebaldus might have been the author of this hymn; it may be possible that this is the same Franciscus Thebaldus hired by Giovanni d'Andrea to supply verses for paintings of Jerome (see below, p. 56 and n. 31).

[28] On the early history of the Jeronimites, see J. R. L. Highfield, 'The Jeronimites in Spain, their Patrons and Success, 1373–1516', *The Journal of Ecclesiastical History* 34 (1983), pp. 513–533. On the congregations, their ideas and practices, see Rice, *Saint Jerome*, pp. 68–75. Klapper ('Aus der Frühzeit', pp. 280–81) thinks that there was a connection between the influence of Giovanni d'Andrea and the establishment of the Jeronimites.

[29] Hamm, 'Hieronymus-Begeisterung', pp. 129–130. For the depiction of Jerome in the visual arts, see esp. Renate Jungblut, *Hieronymus: Darstellung und Verehrung eines Kirchenvaters*, Bamberg 1967; she notes changes in the way Jerome was depicted in the fourteenth century compared to the earlier Middle Ages; see pp. 1 and 54.

[30] Rice, *Saint Jerome*, p. 99.

[31] Quoted by Klapper, 'Aus der Frühzeit', p. 265: 'Sacros, Jeronime, libros / transfers.' Klapper, who admits that he has been unable to identify Franciscus Thebaldus, suggests that he might be Teobaldo, bishop of Verona from 1298 until his death in 1331. Bishop Teobaldo or Tebaldo III spent some time in 1309 in Bologna (see Guglielmo Ederle, *Dizionario cronologico bio-bibliografico dei vescovi di Verona. Cenni sulla Chiesa veronese*, Verona 1965,

The popularity of Jerome in literature, devotional practice and art cannot, of course, be attributed entirely to the influence of Giovanni d'Andrea and the three pseudepigrapha. Change was in the air, according to Hamm, and Giovanni d'Andrea facilitated and contributed to the immense success of a phenomenon that was already on the horizon.[32] From the early fourteenth century onwards, there was enough material available for Jerome to become known to a large number of Christians and for a far-reaching and long-lasting cult to develop. In the course of the fourteenth century, this cult took hold, especially in Spain and Italy, but also north of the Alps.[33] Its diffusion, not only in Latin but also in the vernacular, and not only through texts, but also through paintings and sermons, allowed the veneration of Jerome to expand in many different directions.[34]

The Attitude of Textual Critics towards Jerome and the Vulgate

Having briefly surveyed the development of the cult of Jerome from the fourteenth century onwards, I shall now examine how medieval and early Renaissance textual critics perceived his translation of the Bible and to see whether the new veneration of Jerome led to a change in attitude towards his version. Even though

---

p. 55), where he could conceivably have met Giovanni d'Andrea. There is no evidence, however, that the bishop's first name was Franciscus. The *DBI* gives his surname as Fabri or Fabris, but notes that this name is uncertain. In fact, Bishop Teobaldo is most likely Brother Tebaldo, son of Adriano 'Fabris', mentioned in the 1280s in the monastery of S. Eufemia (*DBI*, XLIII, p. 764). A poet named Franciscus Thebaldus is also mentioned as the possible author of at least one hymn praising Jerome (see above, p. 56, n. 27).

[32] Hamm, 'Hieronymus–Begeisterung', p. 148. Klapper ('Aus der Frühzeit', p. 256), for his part, finds the immense success of the *Hieronymianus* incomprehensible: 'Der Hieronymianus ist eine Kompilation ohne irgendwelchen literarischen Wert; man wundert sich heute über den ungeheuren Einfluß, den er in der Literatur und bildenden Kunst der Humanisten haben sollte.' If Giovanni d'Andrea's compilation is genuinely of such low quality – there is as yet no complete critical edition – this might support Hamm's view that Giovanni d'Andrea's efforts, rather than paving the way, fell on fertile ground.

[33] Vergerio, *Pier Paolo Vergerio*, p. 12. For the veneration of Jerome north of the Alps, see above, p. 49.

[34] See Rice, *Saint Jerome*, p. 83. Despite providing evidence of Jerome's widespread popularity, Hamm ('Hieronymus–Begeisterung', p. 134) sees him, not as a saint of the common people, but rather as 'Patron bestimmter spiritueller und intellektueller Eliten'.

Jerome had not translated the entire Bible, already by the time of Charlemagne the Vulgate was considered to be entirely his work, including those books which he had only revised or even left untouched.[35] This conviction that Jerome had translated the complete Bible was perpetuated by medieval textual critics.

Despite the general chorus of praise for Jerome, the Vulgate did not receive official recognition from the Church in the Middle Ages or in the early Renaissance. The authorization of a specific version by the Church would have had a vast impact, since it would have imposed homogeneity on the textual transmission of the Latin Bible. Yet, as Lobrichon insists, no authoritative body, including the Church, ever officially adopted the Vulgate or, for that matter, any other Latin translation of the Bible at any time in the Middle Ages.[36] Neither in antiquity nor in the Middle Ages did textual critics have any authoritative guidelines for deciding which version of the Latin Bible was 'correct'.[37] But even though no official sanction was granted to any Latin translation until the sixteenth century, several authors, both ancient and medieval, refer to the general acceptance and usage of a particular version in churches. Augustine, for instance, mentions the omnipresence of the *septuaginta*; and Isidore of Seville says that Jerome's version was used in all churches.[38] What is most striking, however, is that, contrary to the historical records at our disposal, from the outset of the period covered by this study, textual critics and other scholars regularly claimed that Jerome's version had, in fact, been officially approved by the Church.

---

[35] Fischer, 'Bibeltext', p. 157. For a summary of the books translated by Jerome, see above, p. 37.

[36] Lobrichon, *La Bible*, p. 30. An exception, even though of very limited impact, might be the Bible versions prescribed by religious orders; however, as mentioned above (p. 48, n. 38), no studies of the biblical texts adopted by the different religious orders have been carried out. Should it turn out that the University of Paris had indeed officially adopted the Paris Bible as the standard version, as Martin argued (see above, pp. 43–43), Lobrichon's statement would need to be modified. Even the University of Paris, however, would not have had the power to impose its edition on the entire Latin West.

[37] See Fischer, 'Zur Überlieferung', p. 20. This omission of prescribing one Latin translation for the entire Church has been identified by Lobrichon as a reason why there was so much diversity in the transmission of the Latin Bible; see Lobrichon, *La Bible*, p. 30.

[38] See above, p. 35, n. 21; and below, p. 111, n. 17.

At the beginning of the twelfth century, the Cistercian Stephen Harding noted that the other Latin translations of the Old Testament had been discarded in favour of Jerome's rendering, but without stating that the Church had officially endorsed it.[39] Not much later, however, one of the most influential writers of the twelfth century took a more radical position on the status of Jerome's version. In his *De scripturis et scriptoribus sacris*, Hugh of St Victor, writing about the Vulgate, says that the Church had decreed that 'this [translation] alone is to be read and to be regarded as authoritative'.[40]

Even though Nicolò Maniacutia was strongly influenced by Hugh's works, he did not take up this idea about the official recognition of the Vulgate in his text-critical writings. Maniacutia presents a completely different picture, however, in his *vita* of Jerome. There he writes that the Church did indeed recognise the Vulgate as superior to other versions of the Bible and accepted it as the translation to be read in churches and to be expounded.[41] Furthermore, contrary to his statements in the *Libellus* and in his preface to the *Psalterium Romanum* that Jerome's version does not survive in its original form and that the text in the manuscripts is, in reality, an amalgam of different translations,[42] in the *vita* he claims that the Church has access to Jerome's rendering, which was the result of divine providence. The Vulgate, Maniacutia continues, also superseded the *septuaginta*, the biblical version regarded as inspired by certain Greeks who had applauded its adoption by the Western Church, but whose mockery of the fact that the Latins had to rely on the *septuaginta* had ceased with the arrival of Jerome's version.[43]

[39] See above, p. 24, n. 48.

[40] See below, p. 84, n. 10.

[41] [Nicolò Maniacutia], *S. Eusebii Hieronymi incomparabilis Ecclesiae Christi doctoris, et eximiae sanctitatis viri vita ex ipsius praesertim syngrammatis, e sanctorum item Augustini, Damasi, Gregorii, Gelasii, aliorumque aliquot collecta tractatibus* (*PL*, XXII), Paris 1854, cols 183–202, at col. 197: 'Sane Romana Ecclesia, cujus arbitrio subjacent universa, peritissimi viri non ignorans ingenium, translationem ejus quam vidit aliis veriorem, tam in Ecclesiis legendam, quam etiam exponendam recepit. De qua beatus Gregorius in libro suorum Moralium "novam" inquit "translationem dissero".' For the quotation from Gregory the Great, see above, p. 35, n. 20.

[42] See below, p. 83, n. 6.

[43] Ibid., cols 186–187: 'Quis autem felicem non dixerit fugae hujus eventum, Christique providentia dispensatum, ut scilicet Romana Ecclesia Petri insti-

The precise chronology of Maniacutia's writings which would enable us to position the *vita* within his output has not yet been established.⁴⁴ Nevertheless, it seems clear from the passages discussed above that Maniacutia adapted his position to suit the purpose of each work. So, when writing in praise of Jerome, he attributes the highest honours to the Vulgate, even alleging that it resulted from divine providence – a claim which is not found either in the *Monitum* of his fellow Cistercian, Harding, or in Hugh's *De scripturis*. Yet, in his text-critical works, he does not take up this position, nor does he attempt to reconstruct Jerome's version. Apparently, when dealing with the corruptions of the Bible as a textual critic, he set aside the ideological convictions which he expressed in other contexts.

Hervaeus of Bourg-Dieu presents himself as an avid supporter of Jerome's version of the Bible. This view is certainly influenced by his attribution of the lectionary to Jerome. In *De correctione*, Hervaeus portrays the lectionary as originally free of errors. Any mistakes found in the transmission are blamed on later alterations of the text.⁴⁵ Changing the attribution of a biblical speech in litur-

tuta regimine, omnium etiam veteris et novi Testamenti librorum, desudante Hieronymo, Hebraicam et Graecam habeat certitudinem. Et quia quorumdam Graecorum levitatem {*my emendation from* levitas}, quod cunctas Scripturas sibi divinitus inspiratas Romanos a se acceppisse plaudebant, fecit ab insultatione desistere.' Although Maniacutia here maintains that the Vulgate came about through divine providence, he does not actually explicitly divine inspiration to the act of translation itself or to Jerome.

⁴⁴ Alberto Vaccari ('Le antiche vite di s. Girolamo', in his *Scritti*, II, pp. 31-51, at p. 47) has shown that the *vita* postdates at least the *Suffraganeus bibliothece*.

⁴⁵ Hervaeus of Bourg-Dieu, *De correctione quarundam lectionum*, in Germain Morin, 'Un critique en liturgie au XIIᵉ siècle. Le traité inédit d'Hervé de Bourgdieu *De correctione quarundam lectionum*', *Revue Bénédictine* 24 (1907), pp. 36–61, at p. 50: 'Hieronimianus lectionarius non sinceriter a posteris seruatus est, sed multa continet quae Hieronimus nunquam promulgauit. Vnde et ea quae discrepant a sinceritate ueritatis quam prophete nobis et euangeliste tradiderunt, ac Hieronimus transtulit, non Hieronimo sed uel alicui praesumptori uel aliquibus huiusmodi, sicut praemissum est, deputantur; quippe cum uideamus Hieronimum in cunctis interpretacionibus uel explanacionibus suis hoc prae ceteris elaborasse, ut sincerissima ueritas ita teneatur inuiolabiliter ab ecclesia, quemadmodum ab apostolis et prophetis uel euangelistis est tradita. Quod si quis pertinaciter asserere uoluerit, Hieronimum ista quae inprobamus in lectionario posuisse, respondemus, ut praedictum est, nos id omnino non credere. Non enim credere possumus, tantum uirum sibi ipsi potuisse fieri contrarium, ut contra ea quae senper docuerat, inciperet haec promulgare.' Fernand Cabrol (*Les livres de la liturgie*

gical texts, according to Hervaeus, was a crime against both Jerome, as the translator of the Bible, and the Holy See, since it detracted from their credibility.[46] Here, perhaps for the first time, the Holy See is mentioned in relation to the legitimisation of a sacred text. Previously, it was always the Church in general which was assigned this role. Hervaeus, however, refers specifically to the *sedes apostolica*, though without providing any details as to the part played by the Holy See in the authorization and diffusion of the text of the Bible.

As we shall see, Gerard of Huy and Roger Bacon were among the very few textual critics who maintained that Jerome's version was still in circulation in manuscripts of the Bible.[47] In addition to his firm belief that Jerome's translation was still available, Gerard's statements clearly show that he championed this version. He held the view that, had the Vulgate remained uncorrupted, there would be no need to correct anything in the Latin Bible, thus attributing unrivalled authority to it.[48]

Gerard's more famous contemporary, Roger Bacon, was also an ardent advocate of the Vulgate.[49] Bacon's main reason for giving preference to Jerome's version seems to have been its widespread dissemination throughout the Church. In his *Opus majus*, he goes so far as to claim that the Roman Church had expressly ordered the use of Jerome's version, with the exception of the Psalms. He supports this assertion by quoting Isidore of Seville's statement that

---

latine, [Paris] 1930, pp. 26 and 81) points out that, due to a pseudepigraphical letter from Jerome which prefaced the Roman lectionary, for centuries it was believed that he had composed it.

[46] Hervaeus, *De correctione*, p. 47: 'Auctoritas ergo tantorum sacerdotum apostolicorum ab omnibus est sequenda, ut non Hester sed Mardocheus haec orasse dicatur. Qui autem dicere maluerit, *Orauit Hester*, quid aliud quam non solum librum hunc propheticum et interpretem eius Hieronimum, sed et sedem apostolicam mendacem facere nititur?'

[47] See below, pp. 91 and 131.

[48] Gerard, [Preface to his *correctorium*], pp. 298–299: 'Si enim sancti Ieronymi pura et ut ab eo in latinum versa est edictio permaneret, post tantum ac talem virum aliquid corrigere superfluum esset'; and Gerard, *Triglossos*, quoted by Denifle, 'Die Handschriften', pp. 308–309, n. 4: 'Nec licet antiquam scripturam bibliothece / immutare michi cum littera Ieronimi sit.'

[49] For Bacon's views on Jerome's translation, see below, p. 91. His emphasis on the Vulgate is also noted by Smalley, *The Study of the Bible*, p. 331.

all churches used Jerome's translation.[50] Apparently Isidore's testimony was sufficient proof, not only that the Vulgate had spread throughout the Latin West, but also that the Church had dictated its use. By adding the word *Latinae* to Isidore's phrase *omnes ecclesiae*, he underlines the fact that the Vulgate was embraced by all of Latin Christendom.

In his slightly later *Opus minus*, Bacon takes a more cautious position: rather than maintaining that the use of Jerome's 'first translation', that is, the version found in manuscripts of the Latin Bible, had been prescribed, he writes that it has been received by the Holy Roman Church and has spread throughout all churches – a process in which the Church clearly played a more passive role. Once more, he refers to the famous quotation from Isidore for support.[51]

His reverence for Jerome's translation is further confirmed by a statement from the *Compendium studii philosophiae*. Bacon notices that the text used by Andrew of St Victor in his literal exposition of a biblical passage differs from Jerome's rendering and reproaches him for not interpreting 'our translation'. Andrew's *ad verbum* translation from the Hebrew is criticised for producing a useless text, not only because this partial rendering – instead of constituting a proper translation – is a literal reconstruction of the Hebrew, but, more importantly, because he should have relied on Jerome's authoritative translation. Bacon's judgement on Andrew is harsh, depriving him of any credibility: we must believe the Hebrew text which he is interpreting, says Bacon, but not Andrew.[52]

---

[50] Bacon, *Opus majus*, I, p. 79: 'Nam ipse {*sc.* Isidorus} dicit in libro *de officiis* quod "generaliter omnes ecclesiae Latinae utuntur translatione Hieronymi, pro eo quod veracior sit in sententiis et clarior in verbis"; excepto quod propter nimium usum psallendi in ecclesia solius psalterii translatio scilicet LXX interpretum remansit. Sed antiquitus Romana Ecclesia jussit translationem hanc ubicunque haberi.' For the quotation from Isidore, see above, p. 35, n. 21. For Bacon's opinion on the authorship of the *Gallicanum*, see below, pp. 90–91.

[51] Bacon, *Opus minus*, p. 331: 'In theologia habet translationem illibatam, quam recipit sacrosancta Romana ecclesia, videlicet, per omnes ecclesias derivari, quae est translatio Hieronymi, sicut Isidorus dicit in libro *De Officiis*.' For Bacon's belief that Jerome had prepared two translations of the Bible, see below, p. 91.

[52] Roger Bacon, *Compendium studii philosophiae*, in his *Opera quaedam*, pp. 393–519, at p. 482: 'Veruntamen Andreas quidam qui exponit Bibliam ad literam ponit *herba* in nominativo casu, et literam quamdam ac si nostra esset

Bacon rests his own belief that Jerome's version was present in the manuscripts currently in circulation exclusively on Isidore's statement about the diffusion and general use of the Vulgate, which, in his eyes, carried enough weight to prove that the entire Latin Church had adopted Jerome's translation; and even though Isidore does not mention any official mandate from the Church, Bacon appears to extract this interpretation from the passage, since he does not refer to any other evidence. Yet Bacon did not assume that the Vulgate had been divinely inspired. On the contrary, he admitted that Jerome had made mistakes in his translation – after all, he was only human and therefore prone to error, as he himself had confessed.[53]

A different position from that of Gerard and Bacon was held by the Catalan scholar Ramon Martí (before 1220–1284). He recognised that some of his contemporaries esteemed the Vulgate more highly than other Latin versions. Therefore, when explaining that he was going to provide his own translations from the Hebrew Bible in his anti-Jewish polemics, he noted that it might be considered presumptuous of him not to use Jerome's translation.[54] Yet his awareness of the special position held by Jerome's version did

repetit, cum duplici negatione. Sed omnino utitur litera Latina, secundum quod construitur Hebraeum ad literam, ut superius dixi, et non est nostra translatio. Propter quod nescio de quo intromittit se de hac expositione, quia literam nostram deberet exponere, et non aliam, quae etiam nullius translationis est, sed solius literalis constructionis Hebraei ... Non est ei credendum sed recurrendum est ad Hebraeum de quo loquitur, et si verum dicat, credendum est Hebraeo, sed non ipsi.' Bacon is probably referring to Andrew of St Victor's interpretation of Gn 2.5; see Andrew of St Victor, *Expositio super Heptateuchum*, p. 26 (Gn 2.5).

[53] Bacon, *Opus majus*, I, p. 69: 'Atque scitur manifeste, quod Hieronymus humanum aliquid passus aliquando in translatione sua oberravit, sicut ipsemet pluries confitetur.' I have not been able to identify the reference to Jerome. For Bacon's call for a new edition of the Bible, under the auspices of the pope, see below, p. 152. For Henry Totting's attempt to reconcile mistakes in Jerome's rendering with its divine inspiration, see below, p. 66 and n. 61.

[54] Ramon Martí, *Pugio fidei adversus Mauros et Judaeos*, Leipzig 1687, repr. Farnborough 1967, p. 4: 'Caeterum inducendo authoritatem textus ubicumque ab Hebraico fuerit desumptum, non septuaginta sequar, nec interpretem alium; et quod majoris praesumptionis videbitur, non ipsum etiam in hoc reverebor Hieronymum nec tolerabilem linguae Latinae vitabo improprietatem, ut eorum quae apud Hebraeos sunt, ex verbo in verbum, quotiescumque servari hoc potuit, transferam veritatem.'

not prevent him from ignoring it and producing his own more literal translation of the Hebrew text.

In Richard FitzRalph's *Summa*, FitzRalph, as one of the dialogue's interlocutors, mentions the Church's approval of the Vulgate; but this approval, in his view, also applied to two other Latin versions. According to him, the Church had officially accepted three Latin translations: the *septuaginta*, Jerome's version and the *translatio communis*.[55] The Vulgate did not rank above the other two translations. Moreover, the Roman Church's approval was not based solely on its own discretion; instead, it was the combined verdict of Greek and Hebrew as well as Latin prelates. This endorsement by the Church was the sole criterion of judgement: the truth could not be found in individual manuscripts, which might have been corrupted by scribes, but only in officially sanctioned versions of the Bible.[56] No other scholar examined here mentions the collaboration of Latins, Greeks and Hebrews in determining the authority of biblical translations. Unfortunately, however, FitzRalph does not provide any clue as to where he found this information.

Henry Totting de Oyta, in his *Quaestio*, gathers together, in the usual scholastic manner, various arguments in favour of and against the privileged status of Jerome's version. Like several scholars before him, he puts forward the argument that Jerome's version should be given preference on the grounds that it had been taken up by the Church, an institution with both the power and the discretion to

---

[55] For the three versions, see below, p. 64, n. 56, and p. 95, n. 35. Rice (*Saint Jerome*, p. 175) wrongly claims that FitzRalph thought that Jerome's translation – with the exception of the *iuxta Hebraeos* – was transmitted only in his commentaries and that 'the Latins possessed three whole or partial translations'. FitzRalph, in the passages discussed, nowhere mentions that what he calls Jerome's version survives only in his other writings, nor does he say that any of the Latin translations were partial. For the term *communis*, see also above, pp. 21–23.

[56] FitzRalph, *Summa*, sig. C ii^r (19, 20): 'Sed de contrarietate aut falsitate trium translationum quas ecclesia in communi consilio approbavit ... non ad tuum codicem aut meum qui forte ab indoctis aut negligentibus scriptoribus vitiantur {*emended from* vincilantur; *I am grateful to Paul Gerhard Schmidt for this suggestion*}. Et sicut veritatem credis esse in primaria nostra {*my emendation from* nostre} scriptura, sic pariter eam crede in omni translatione quam ecclesia de communi consilio latinorum grecorum et hebreorum, prelatorum gentium aliarum, cum diligenti examinatione et collectione ad antiquos codices cuiuscunque lingue in qua erat nostra primordialis scriptura recepit et canonica[m] {*my addition*} reputavit et censuit esse tenendam.'

decide on such a weighty matter. The Vulgate is therefore in conformity with the Hebrew text and contains no additions or omissions.[57] Among the reasons which lend credibility to the assumption that the Vulgate has a special status, Totting introduces a line of reasoning which cannot be found in earlier discussions: Jerome's family background and his praiseworthy conduct serve as powerful arguments in support of the Vulgate's exceptional quality. Jerome's Christian heritage – as he himself stressed in his prologue to Job – and his exemplary Christian lifestyle made him superior to other translators; for this reason, Isidore had rightly drawn attention to the Church's preference for Jerome's translation.[58] Furthermore, Totting suggests that Jerome could be regarded as inspired by the Holy Spirit; consequently, his translation contains precisely what it had intended.[59]

[57] Totting, *Quaestio*, p. 19: '2ª conclusio: inter omnes translaciones veteris testamenti translacio beati Jeronimi est simpliciter preferenda. Probatur: Talis translacio suscepta est ab ecclesia, sufficienter instructa per Christum et Apostolos et eorum successores in omnibus veritatibus istius scripture ad novam legem et ecclesie christiane decursum pertinentibus, tanquam conformis Ebrayco textui, nichil falsi et suspecti continens et nichil de pertinentibus et utilibus ecclesie christiane obmittens vel superflui addens.'

[58] Ibid., pp. 19–20: 'Item: Jeronimus erat christianissimus interpres, cui iam constabant perfecte misteria fidei christiane et qui linguam Ebraycam novit et scripturas intellexit et zelum christiane fidei verum et perfectum habuit ad veritatem explanandam et vite sanctitate preclarus fuit, prout notorium est in ecclesia christiana, igitur etc. Unde eciam Ysydorus 6° Ethimologiarum capitulo 4° dicit, quod "eius interpretacio merito ceteris anteferur, quia est et verborum tenacior et perspicacitate sentencie clarior atque utpote christiana interpretacione verior" [Isidore, *Etymologiae*, VI, iv, 5]. Item: ipse de se ipso interprete dicit circa finem prologi super Job: "quod, si apud Grecos post LXXª edicionem, iam Christi evangelio coruscante, Iudeus Aquila et Symmachus, Theodocion, iudaysantes heretici, sunt recepti, qui multa misteria Salvatoris subdola interpretacione celarunt et tamen in exemplo habentur apud ecclesias et exemplantur ab ecclesiasticis viris: quanto magis ego christianus de parentibus christianis natus et vexillum crucis in mea fronte portans cuius studium fuit obmissa repetere, depravata corrigere, sacramenta ecclesie puro et fideli aperire sermone" [Jerome, 'Prologus in libro Iob', p. 732].'

[59] Totting, *Quaestio*, pp. 20–21: 'Translacio Jeronimi complete continet scripturas Ebraycas secundum omnem sensum, ad quem Spiritus S. eas intelligi voluit in toto decursu ecclesie christiane. Probatur: quia ipse transtulit eas sufficienter secundum omnes sensus, quos Christus per se et per suos Apostolos et alios prophetas et doctores ecclesie christiane et eciam ab ipsamet ecclesia in consiliis generalibus aperuit, igitur etc ... Ymo nullum debet esse dubium, quin Spiritu S. dirigente, cuius auxilium non solum per se, sed eciam per alios diligenter imploravit, omnia transtulerit, que ad

In his catalogue of arguments which can be used to refute the special standing of the Vulgate, Totting mentions the assertion that Jerome was by no means divinely inspired, but merely a human translator. After all, Jerome himself had said that a prophet, *vatis*, is not the same as a translator, *interpres*.[60] Furthermore, it could be argued that various Latin translations containing errors and corruptions had been made before the time of Jerome. If the Holy Spirit had permitted this, then surely, Jerome's translation, too, must contain errors.[61] Significantly, Totting states that Jerome's version carries no special weight because, as he rightly asserts, it had not been officially approved by the Church.[62] It could be said, in addition, that the Vulgate was not superior to the *septuaginta*, since

    utilitatem ecclesie christiane quoad eius totum decursum sunt a Deo ordinata.'

[60] Ibid., pp. 27–28: 'Erudicio in lingua Ebrayca quantumlibet perfecta non sufficit humano intellectui ad explicandum misteria novi testamenti, que continentur in obscuritatibus et figuris scripture Ebrayce divinitus revelate. Sed beatus Jeronimus solum secundum exigenciam humane erudicionis in linguis et scienciis sermocinalibus videtur transtulisse scripturas; igitur insufficienter et diminute et forsitan non absque errore. Maior, nota: quia humanum ingenium non sufficit ad intelligendum et per consequens nec ad explicandum omnes tales veritates divinitus revelatas, prout notum est de se et ex questione precedenti. Minor probatur: quia Jeronimus ipsemet dicit in 2° Prologo biblie: "Aliud est esse vatem et interpretem..." [Jerome, 'Prologus in Pentateucho', in *Biblia sacra*, pp. 3–4, at p. 3] Cum igitur ipse interpres fuerit et non vates, sequitur quod non Spiritus S. illustracione, sed humane intelligencie erudicione scripturas transtulit.'

[61] Totting, *Quaestio*, pp. 28–29: 'In primitiva ecclesia fuerunt multa exemplaria indistincte scripta et translata et multipliciter de perversitate vel errore suspecta; igitur non est omnino certum, quin sic sit in exemplaribus translatis a beato Jeronimo. Consequencia tenet: quia tunc, scilicet in primitiva ecclesia, fides fundabatur et erat continua pugna cum hereticis et Iudeis. Si igitur Spiritus Sanctus tunc permisit fieri tales errores scripturarum pro ecclesia: igitur a forciori videtur permisisse errare Jeronimum. Antecedens patet per dictum Ysydori prius allegatum, ubi dicitur [Isidore, *De ecclesiasticis officiis*, p. 13 (I, xii, 7) quoting Augustine, *De doctrina christiana*, p. 42 (II, xi, 16)]: "Si cui primis fidei temporibus ad manus venit quod ex greco [erat] atque aliquantulum sibi utriusque lingue periciam sensit, ausus est statim interpretari". Et Jeronimus in Prologo Josue [Jerome, 'Prologus in libro Iosue', p. 285] dicit quod "apud Latinos fuerunt tot exemplaria quot codices et unusquisque pro arbitrio suo vel addiderit vel subtraxerit. Et utique non possit verum esse quod dissonat" etc.' Totting cites Isidore (quoting Augustine) and Jerome (see above, p. 29, n. 2) to support the existence of various different translations in early Christianity.

[62] Totting, *Quaestio*, p. 29: 'Ecclesia non aprobavit translacionem Jeronimi; igitur non est nobis certitudo etc.'

this was the position of Augustine, who confirmed that the Church also held this view.⁶³

These arguments against the special standing of the Vulgate are then duly disproved by counter-arguments. For instance, Totting writes that it is by no means clear that Jerome was merely an *interpres* and not also a *vatis*: surely the Holy Spirit had provided Jerome with special guidance for this work which was to be the basis and foundation of the entire Church (*quod esse debuit ad tocius ecclesie statum et fundamentum*). Apparent inadequacies in the Latin text compared to the original Hebrew are explained away. The point that the Church had not officially approved the Vulgate is rebutted by the argument that the Church had relied on this version in councils and synods and had thus consistently, although tacitly, sanctioned its use. Augustine's preference for the *septuaginta* over the Vulgate was due to the fact that the Church had not yet examined Jerome's version sufficiently. Although the authenticity of the legend surrounding the *septuaginta* was upheld by Augustine, Jerome, as well as Josephus and Isidore, took the contrary view.⁶⁴ Totting concludes this defence of the Vulgate by stating:

> Tamen quantum ad propositum pertinet, constat per sufficiens examen ecclesie Jeronimum in transferendo non errasse, prout eciam Iudei sibi contestati sunt secundum Augustinum in loco preallegato, scil. 18° De civitate Dei capitulo LIII°.⁶⁵

> as far as our purpose is concerned, it is clear, by means of the Church's adequate appraisal, that Jerome did not err in his translation – accordingly, as reported by Augustine in the place I cited earlier [i.e., *De civitate Dei*, p. 639 (XVIII, 43)], even the Jews appealed to him.

The most outspoken champion of the Vulgate was Peter of Ailly. In two of his early works, he strenuously promoted the privileged status of Jerome's version. In his *Epistola ad novos*

---

⁶³ Ibid., p. 29: 'Translacio Jeronimi non est preferenda translacioni 70ᵃ interpretum, igitur etc. Antecedens patet manifeste per Augustinum XVIII° De civitate Dei capitulo LIII° [Augustine, *De civitate Dei*, p. 639 (XVIII, 43)], ubi dicit quod "Jeronimus, homo doctissimus et omnium linguarum trium peritus, non ex Greco, sed Ebreo in Latinum eloquium convertit scripturas. Sed eius tamen literarum laborem, quamvis Iudei fateantur esse veracem, LXXᵃ vero interpretes in multis errasse contendant: tamen ecclesia tot hominum auctoritati, ab Eleazero tunc pontifice ad hoc tantum opus electorum, neminem judicat preferendum".'

⁶⁴ Totting, *Quaestio*, pp. 30–33.

⁶⁵ Ibid., p. 33. For the passage from Augustine, see below, p. 84, n. 10.

hebraeos, written in 1378, he says that he was angered by 'a certain man of Catholic faith' who claimed that Jerome's translation contained additions and omissions not present in the Hebrew text. This allegation, in his opinion, poses a threat to the Catholic faith.[66] In the dedication to his *Epistola*, Peter writes that the criticisms of Jerome's version which he is trying to refute were made by an English doctor, *doctor anglicanus*. He did not, however, identify his opponent – clearly the 'man of the Catholic faith' who Peter said had angered him – nor did his nineteenth-century editor Tschackert. It was Louis Salembier who, in 1886, named the culprit as Roger Bacon, an unlikely suspect given his strong support for Jerome's version. Yet, in Peter's eyes, Bacon was guilty of excessive fault-finding.[67] Since Jerome was a doctor of the Church and must be considered an authoritative translator, not only was criticism of his version, including any suggestion that he had erred, forbidden, but adherence to it was mandatory.[68] According to Peter, the allegations against Jerome's version were impious: to

---

[66] Peter of Ailly, *Epistola ad novos Hebraeos*, in Paul Tschackert, *Peter von Ailli (Petrus de Alliaco). Zur Geschichte des grossen abendländischen Schisma und der Reformconcilien von Pisa und Constanz*, Gotha 1877, pp. [7]–[12], at p. [7]: 'Vir quidam catholicae professionis ... nuper quendam inveteratum errorem et fere jam penitus suffocatum nisus fuerit noviter suscitare, nedum clam et occulte, sed et palam asserens translationem sancti patris Hieronymi, quam Christianis de hebraeo tradidit in latinum, contra ultra citraque vel praeter hebraicam veritatem in quibusdam passibus aliqua addidisse et in aliis aliqua omisisse nec semper concordasse sententialiter cum eadem. Quae assertio quanti periculi quantive scandali sit in fide arbitratus sum utile esse declarare, ut per hoc et praefato viro via pateat et reditus ab errore, et cuilibet christiano via et aditus deficiat ad errorem.'

[67] Peter of Ailly, *Epistola*, quoted in Louis Salembier, *Petrus ab Alliaco*, Lille 1886, p. 309: 'Magnus liber unius doctoris anglicani qui, inter multa utilia, quaedam sparsim variis in locis continet quae prima facie dictum errorem confirmare ac beati Hieronymi translationem infirmare viderentur, quae hic recolligere et ab eis erroris occasionem excludere utile judicavi.' For the identification of the 'doctor anglicanus' as Bacon, see ibid., pp. 305 and especially 309–10. For Bacon's attitude to Jerome, see above, p. 61.

[68] Peter of Ailly, *Epistola*, p. [11]: 'Negans translationem Hieronymi seu asserens Hieronymum in sua translatione errasse aut aliquid addendo aut aliquid removendo aut aliquid immutando ab hebraica veritate, non potest propter hoc reprehendi de haeresi vel infidelitatis errore; ex hac saltem radice, quod negat autoritatem Hieronymi translatoris, sicut satis apparet ex praemissis ... Certum tamen est quod talis potest ex sola radice praedicta reprehendi de protervia et praesumptione, quia saltem huic translationi propter autoritatem tanti doctoris et tam authentici translatoris debet quilibet probabiliter adhaerere.'

accuse him of producing inaccurate work amounted to temerity.[69] The Church approves Jerome's translation and hands it down as canonical and inspired. Its preference for the Vulgate over other translations was demonstrated by using this version in synods and councils to determine the faith and to confute heresy.[70]

The authority of Jerome's translation is further confirmed by the fact that the Church has formulated its canon according to his guidelines. Consequently, to doubt Jerome's version was equivalent to doubting the Church, which would be blasphemy.[71] For the sake of our salvation, Peter sums up, it is therefore crucial for us to believe in the faithfulness of Jerome's translation – were it not faithful, the Church would not have received and approved it as canonical. As a result, not believing in the Vulgate is a *nefas*, an offence against the divine will.[72]

---

[69] Ibid., p. [11]: 'Primo quia nefas esset dicere tam sanctum doctorem tam arroganter praesumpsisse, ut ad sacrarum scripturarum interpretationem procederet non habita prius plena intelligentia hebraici sermonis et adhibita plena diligentia pro intellectu veritatis ... quare sequitur eos qui Hieronymum in sua translatione reprehendere vel corrigere nituntur merito posse de temeritate culpari.'

[70] Peter of Ailly, *Epistola*, quoted in Salembier, *Petrus ab Alliaco*, p. 308: 'Bibliae Scripturam, ab eo {*sc.* Hieronymo} translatam de hebraeo in latinum, Ecclesia catholica recipit, approbat et tradit tanquam Scripturam canonicam et divinam ... Ecclesia enim eam praeacceptat aliis omnibus versionibus, eam assumit in conciliis, synodis et determinationibus orthodoxis ad veritatum fidei probationem, reprobationem haeresum et confutationem errorum.'

[71] Peter of Ailly, *Epistola*, pp. [11]–[12]: 'Satis ... constat quod diversas et diversorum autorum scripturas veteris testamenti, imo et omnes scripturas novi testamenti ... recipimus tamquam scripturas canonicas seu divinas propter autoritatem ecclesiae catholicae quae eas ita recipit et approbat ... Quare si suspecta vel dubia sit translatio illa Hieronymi, suspecta etiam erit vel dubia ecclesiae probatio et per consequens etiam ejus determinatio, quod dicere est blasphemum ... Propter autoritatem ecclesiae catholicae translatio Hieronymi ... firmiter credenda est de necessitate {*my emendation from* necessitatis} salutis.' Yet Jerome followed the canon of the Hebrew Bible in his translation; see above, p. 32.

[72] Ibid., p. [12]: 'Firmiter de necessitate salutis credendum est beatum Hieronymum in translatione scripturarum non errasse, aliquid in iis vel addendo vel subtrahendo vel immutando a sensu literali hebraicae veritatis. Nam autoritas ecclesiae catholicae dictam translationem nequaquam recepisset, tamquam scripturam canonicam seu divinam nec approbasset tamquam firmiter credendam de necessitate salutis, si ipsa esset tali errore vitiata. Si fas esset de hac translatione dubitare aut eam suspectam habere de errore, pari imo fortiori ratione et de alia data vel dabili translatione quacunque, et ita catholicus nulli translationi quieto animo adhaereret, sed in qualibet anxie

In his *Apologeticus*, Peter put forward yet another robust defence of Jerome's translation. He repeats the view, already voiced in the *Epistola*, that contradicting Jerome's version was equivalent to contradicting the Church and that adherence to the Vulgate was crucial on account of the impregnable authority of the Church.[73] According to Salembier, he also refutes several of Bacon's assumptions about the Vulgate: that it contained many earlier badly translated passages which Jerome had failed to correct; that uncorrupted manuscripts of the Vulgate could be found in monasteries; that the Church had ordered the dissemination of the version contained in these manuscripts; and that Jerome's translation differed in many respects from the corrupt Paris Bible.[74] Peter replies to these allegations by maintaining that, even if there is a grain of truth in them, they need to be toned down.[75]

More than any other scholar of his time, Peter of Ailly insisted on the use of the Vulgate and defended it against any accusations of corruption or conflation with other versions. To him, such assumptions detracted from the authority, not only of Jerome, but also of the Church itself. His view of the transmission of the Latin Bible, at least in the published sections of the *Epistola* and the *Apologeticus*, is rather simplistic: he nowhere considers the possibility that scribes had corrupted the text or that translations of the Latin Bible had become contaminated. He is, in fact, the only author examined here who does not to some extent take these issues into account. This is perhaps because, in contrast to the other

fluctuans dubitaret; sicque nulla posset sumi efficax aut certa probatio ex scripturis, quod consequens quam scandalosum sit et horrendum, qui non percipit caret sensu.'

[73] Peter of Ailly, *Apologeticus*, in Tschackert, *Peter von Ailli*, pp. [50]–[51]: 'Hujusmodi translationi non licet contradicere seu eam reprehendere quasi suspectam de aliqua falsitate; nam hoc esset contradicere autoritati universalis ecclesiae quod non licet ... Translationi Hieronymi adhaerendum est ... propter irrefragabilem autoritatem ecclesiae.'

[74] These points are summarised by Salembier, *Petrus ab Alliaco*, p. 310. For Bacon's statements, see Bacon, *Opus majus*, I, p. 78: 'Sed omnes antiquae Bibliae quae jacent in monasteriis, quae non sunt adhuc glossatae nec tactae, habent veritatem translationis, quam sacrosancta a principio recepit Romana Ecclesia, et jussit per omnes Ecclesias divulgari'; and below, p. 91, n. 26, and p. 93, n. 28.

[75] Peter of Ailly, *Apologeticus*, quoted by Salembier, *Petrus ab Alliaco*, p. 310: 'Praedictas assertiones quas Doctor iste sparsim et diffuse prosequitur, breviter recitavi, quae licet aliqua vera continent, tamen moderatione indigent. Ideo circa eas cursorie aliquas propositiones moderativas explicabo.'

scholars I have been dealing with, he was not writing about textual criticism but instead attempting to safeguard Jerome's version of the Bible from attacks on its authority.

The most detailed and analytical investigation of the legitimacy of the Vulgate is found in the preface to Lorenzo Valla's *Collatio*. Valla critically examines what Jerome said about his work in the 'Preface to the Gospels'. Adopting the point of view of Jerome's opponents,[76] Valla accuses him of wrongly assuming that all manuscripts of the Latin Bible were corrupt. This amounts to suggesting either that Augustine, Hilary and Ambrose did not know they lacked accurate texts of the Bible, or that they knew but did not care; both claims were insulting to these men of authority. Furthermore, it would have been impossible to examine every Latin manuscript then in circulation; so Jerome's assertion that they were all faulty was unwarranted.[77] Valla also blames Jerome for failing to establish which Latin codices agreed with the Greek manuscripts, as Pope Damasus had requested; instead, contrary to his own claims, Jerome had produced a new work, *novum opus*,[78] even though Damasus had not asked him to prepare such a work if it turned out that no good Latin manuscripts were in existence.[79] Were Valla

[76] Valla, *Collatio*, p. 4: 'Sed si vere estimemus, invidiosius tunc fuit illius factum quam est nunc meum, ideoque solicita ei et accurata utendum oratione nec dissimulandum omnes fere sibi reclamaturos, quorum personam, tanquam nunc illud tempus esset, libet mihi paulisper assumere atque ipsorum ore Hieronymum alloqui.' He ends the speech as follows (ibid., p. 5): 'Hec igitur, que fortasse tunc dicebantur, factum Hieronymi invidiosum reddebant.'

[77] Ibid., p. 5: 'Certe potest unum esse in hac diversitate sincerum, quod pro mendoso damnari iniurium est, quanquam qui possis scire de omnibus, qui omnia que sunt in toto orbe non legeris? Ergo de omnibus pronuntiare non licet, presertim cum maximorum virorum contumelia, non modo ipsius summi sacerdotis, sed etiam Hilarii, Ambrosii, Augustini aliorumque plurimorum, quorum neminem vis habere sincerum exemplar, tanquam aut negligant habere aut non habere se nesciant.'

[78] Ibid., p. 4: 'Damasus, inquis, te iussit exemplaria que cum greca veritate consentiant decernere. At id tu non agis, sed dum novum condis opus universa condemnas ... Condemnas universa, quia universa mendosa sunt; condis novum opus, quia id summus sacerdos facere non modo iubet sed etiam cogit.' For the quotation from Jerome's preface to the Gospels, see above, p. 30, n. 6.

[79] Ibid., p. 5: 'Novum opus a Damaso iussus atque coactus es facere. Qua istud fieri ratione potest, ut iusserit ille decerni quenam bona exemplaria sint, tanquam putet aliqua bona esse, et novum fieri opus ex veteri, tanquam putet omnia esse mala? Neque enim dixit "si nulla bona sint, facito novum opus", et si tu forsitan id ab eo dictum interpretaris.'

himself now to find Latin manuscripts which Jerome had not come across and which agreed perfectly with the Greek, Jerome would have to retract his claims about the corrupt state of all Latin biblical manuscripts, which had supposedly forced him to compose a *novum opus*.[80] Valla's implication here is that such a discovery would render the Vulgate obsolete.

With his novel critical approach, Valla does not let Jerome get away with generalising statements intended to exculpate his approach; instead, at least partly to defend his own work as a textual critic, Valla lays bare inaccuracies in Jerome's account, insisting, for instance, that he could not possibly have examined every Latin manuscript of the Bible. Valla's main point is that Damasus had not asked Jerome to prepare a *novum opus*, since the Church already had the *septuaginta*, which was a satisfactory Latin version of the Bible. For Valla, the Vulgate was Jerome's own brainchild and therefore lacked any authoritative footing.[81]

Despite undermining Jerome's claims in the 'Preface to the Gospels', Valla held him in the highest regard.[82] In his works on the New Testament and the related passages in his invectives against Poggio, there were, of course, good reasons for Valla to stress his respect for Jerome. But there is no evidence that this respect was not sincere. Furthermore, he displayed a similarly critical attitude towards another, equally eminent, Church Father, Augustine, noting that his weak knowledge of Greek greatly diminished his authority in matters related to establishing the correct text

---

[80] Ibid., p. 5: 'Nullum e plurimis exemplaribus legeris incorruptum, et omnia non posses toto orbe dispersa legere, ideo te de integro traduxisse et id te interpretari a Damaso fuisse tibi iniunctum, ut ad tuum exemplar codices suos ceteri examinantes vel probarent vel improbarent. Quod siqui nunc codices veritati grece consentanei proferantur, quos tu nullos esse compertum non habes, nonne tibi neganda erunt omnia que dixisti, universos codices esse vitiosos, novum opus te fecisse de veteri, et ut novum opus faceres Damasum coegisse?'

[81] For his view on translations of Scripture, see also below, p. 264, n. 57.

[82] See Lorenzo Valla, *Antidotum primum. La prima apologia contro Poggio Bracciolini*, ed. A. Wesseling, Assen and Amsterdam 1978, p. 118: 'Cernis ... me illud opus condidisse non ut Hieronymum – quod procul absit – reprehenderem.' There is no reason to doubt the truthfulness of this statement. According to Hanna H. Gray ('Valla's *Encomium of St. Thomas Aquinas* and the Humanist Conception of Christian Antiquity', in *Essays in History and Literature Presented by Fellows of the Newberry Library to Stanley Pargellis*, ed. H. Bluhm, Chicago 1965, pp. 37–51, at p. 50), Jerome was the Church Father whom Valla most honoured and respected.

of the Bible, since, in Valla's opinion, this required a good grasp of Greek.[83] Valla was clearly able to combine deep respect with a critical approach to these venerable figures; as Mario Fois has pointed out in relation to Valla's criticism of Augustine, it was a simple matter of recognising the limits of the Fathers and treating the truth, *veritas*, as the ultimate criterion.[84]

The only textual critic of the Bible in the fifteenth century to express the view that the Vulgate had been divinely inspired was George of Trebizond. In his invective against Theodore Gaza, he claims, in a passage which repeats arguments from his first treatise on Jn 21.22, that Jerome was 'filled with the grace of the Holy Spirit which he used especially both in his new translations and emendations of Scripture'.[85]

George's opponent, Cardinal Bessarion, belonged to the group of textual critics who stated that the Church had approved of Jerome's version. In his invective against George, Bessarion writes that the Vulgate had rendered all other translations obsolete;[86] but he does not state that Jerome had been divinely inspired. The status

---

[83] Lorenzo Valla, *Annotationes in Novum Testamentum*, in his *Opera omnia*, I, Basel 1540, reprint Turin 1962, pp. 803-895, at p. 846B: 'Augustinus ne hic quidem graecam ueritatem consulens sperat se inter falsa uerum inuenire ... Ubi de scriptura graeca sine autoritate agitur, ibi Augustinus, magnus alioquin autor, tamen non bene sentiens, neutiquam magnae habendus est autoritatis.'

[84] See Mario Fois, *Il pensiero cristiano di Lorenzo Valla nel quadro storico-culturale del suo ambiente*, Rome 1969, pp. 439–440. For a more detailed discussion of Valla's view of the Church Fathers, see Giovanni di Napoli, *Lorenzo Valla: filosofia e religione nell'umanesimo italiano*, Rome 1971, pp. 123–129.

[85] George of Trebizond, *Adversus Theodorum Gazam in perversionem Problematum Aristotelis*, in Ludwig Mohler, *Kardinal Bessarion als Theologe, Humanist und Staatsmann. Funde und Forschungen*, 3 vols, Paderborn 1923–1942, III: *Aus Bessarions Gelehrtenkreis. Abhandlungen, Reden, Briefe von Bessarion, Theodoros Gazes, Michael Apostolios, Andronikos Kallistos, Georgios Trapezuntios, Niccolò Perotti, Niccolò Capranica*, ed. L. Mohler, repr. Aalen and Paderborn 1967, pp. 277–342, at p. 331 (35, 3): 'Hieronymus certe hunc etiam locum vidit, legit, perpendit. Cumque esset diligentissimus, doctissimus et gratia spiritus sancti plenus, qua maxime usus est tum in transferendis denuo scripturis, tum in emendandis iam translatis, hunc locum ita reliquit, sicut invenit.'

[86] Bessarion, *In illud Evangelii*, cols 627D–628A: 'Ita tamen probata ab omnibus ejus translatio fuit, ut antiqua, vel, ut verius dicam, tot antiquis interpretationibus oblitteratis, Hieronymiana duntaxat traductione catholica utatur Ecclesia.'

which he assigned – or possibly conceded – to the Vulgate as the sole accepted Latin translation did not have any importance for the emendation of the Latin text, since, as we shall see, Bessarion believed that translations had no authority for the establishment of the correct text of the Bible.[87]

In the 1480s, Giovanni Crastone admitted that he had been attacked by contemporary theologians for his emendations of the Psalms. Yet his opponents seem to have condemned interventions in both the *septuaginta* and the Vulgate.[88] Apparently, for them, the two versions were equally authoritative.

As was mentioned above, the Church did not officially sanction any Latin translation of the Bible until the Council of Trent in the sixteenth century. Nevertheless, the importance of ecclesiastical recognition was already appreciated by the time of Augustine, who wrote that he believed in the text of the Gospels because it was endorsed by the Church.[89] This desire for Church accreditation of a biblical version is also reflected in the writings of a number of medieval scholars. Almost all the authors discussed in this chapter maintained that, in some form, the Vulgate held a privileged position based on the Church's consent: either it had tacitly accepted the diffusion of the Vulgate or had expressly promoted it by decreeing that Jerome's version was the translation which should be read. Various scholars – Hugh of St Victor, Roger Bacon, Richard FitzRalph, Peter of Ailly and Cardinal Bessarion – referred to the Church's official endorsement of the Vulgate. With the exception of Bacon, these statements, however, had no direct bearing on textual criticism. Although Hugh, FitzRalph – who

---

[87] See below, p. 176.

[88] Giovanni Crastone, [Dedicatory letter to Ludovico Donato, Bishop of Bergamo, of his edition of the Psalms], in *Praefationes et epistolae editionibus principibus auctorum veterum praepositae*, ed. B. Botfield, Cambridge 1861, pp. 13–16, at p. 13: 'Psalterii quod Graece melos David regis et prophetae inscribitur hanc novam emendationem tuis auspiciis, consultissime antistes, quanvis dubium mihi non erat plerosque criminaturos vel saltem admiraturos aggredi non dubitavi. Compertum nanque mihi est hujus nostrae aetatis theologorum gregem insultaturum subsanaturumque tanquam qui ea quae a divo Hieronymo et ab Septuaginta Interpretibus lucubrata fuerint, attingere ausus sim.'

[89] Augustine, *Contra epistulam quam uocant fundamenti*, in his *Opera*, VI, 1, ed. J. Zycha (Corpus Scriptorum Ecclesiasticorum Latinorum, 25), Prague, Vienna and Leipzig 1891, pp. 193–248, at p. 197 (5): 'Ego uero euangelio non crederem, nisi me catholicae ecclesiae commoueret auctoritas.'

named three translations approved by the Church – and Peter of Ailly were discussing issues related to textual criticism of the Latin Bible, it was not their explicit concern; while for Bessarion it was an irrelevant criterion, since, in his eyes, the Latin tradition had no value for establishing the correct text of the Bible. Bacon, on the other hand, exploited this claim to support his call for the reconstruction of the Vulgate – a call, which, as we shall see, remained unheard.[90] The remaining textual critics of the Bible – such as Harding, Hugh of St Cher and William de Mara – either did not mention the status of Jerome's version or acknowledged that the Church had passively accepted its dissemination. Henry Totting is the only one who raises the argument that there was no official approval from the Church, only to refute this point by insisting on its continuous use of the Vulgate.

The issue of attributing official sanction to the Vulgate was to some extent a question of literary genre. Textual critics had no need to propagate the assumption that the Church had given its approval to the Vulgate, nor perhaps was it in their interest. Since they knew of no official document supporting this assertion, they were not obliged to deal with the matter nor to let it influence their approach to emendation of the biblical text.

In late antiquity and the early Middle Ages, only the *septuaginta* was believed to be divinely inspired. In later centuries, however, a few scholars made this claim for the Vulgate. In the fourteenth century, Henry Totting mentioned divine inspiration as a possible reason for giving preference to the Vulgate; while his contemporary, Peter of Ailly, used this argument in an earnest attempt to defend and exalt Jerome's translation. More than two centuries earlier, Maniacutia had already hinted in the same direction when he referred to divine providence in his *vita* of Jerome.

None of these three works – Maniacutia's *vita*, Totting's *Quaestio* and Peter of Ailly's *Epistola* – was concerned with the emendation of the Latin Bible. Maniacutia's aim was to praise Jerome; Totting's discussion dealt exclusively with the status of the Vulgate and the *septuaginta*; and Peter's *Epistola* was a hyperbolic defence of Jerome's translation. By contrast, with the exception of George of Trebizond's *Adversus Theodorum Gazam*, no text-critical work written between the twelfth and the fifteenth century,

---

[90] For Bacon's call to the pope to set up a team of scholars to reconstruct the Vulgate, see below, p. 152.

including Maniacutia's treatises, contained any reference to the divine inspiration of the Vulgate.[91] Like the belief in the Church's official recognition of the Vulgate, the assumption that Jerome's translation was divinely inspired did not feature in works primarily concerned with the emendation of the Latin Bible.

The emergence of the cult of Jerome might well have had some influence on the fourteenth-century authors examined here. Whereas in twelfth-century text-critical writings only Hervaeus insisted on the special status of the Vulgate – Maniacutia voiced this idea only in his *Vita* of Jerome, not in his philological writings – it became far more prominent in the works of Gerard of Huy and Roger Bacon, culminating, in the fourteenth century, in the writings of Henry Totting and especially Peter of Ailly, neither of whom, it must be stressed, was a textual critic.[92] In the fifteenth century, however, neither Valla nor Manetti refers to the notion that Jerome or the Vulgate held a privileged position; Bessarion's admission of the Church's approval of the Vulgate did not have any impact on his view of its value for establishing the text of the Bible; and Crastone's account of an attack by contemporary theologians included both the *septuaginta* and the Vulgate. It seems, therefore, that fifteenth-century textual critics were not particularly influenced by the cult surrounding the figure of Jerome.

In his monograph on Jerome, Eugene Rice claims that until the sixteenth century, the Vulgate was considered the Church Father's 'greatest gift to the Church'.[93] This was doubtless true for Peter of Ailly and various other writers; but it was not a view which was commonly held by textual critics of the Bible. Most of them did not claim that the Vulgate was superior to other versions, let alone

---

[91] Of course, statements concerning the status of Jerome and the Vulgate appeared in other genres; examining these, however, is beyond the scope of this study. Nevertheless, to give just two random examples: in his *Catena aurea*, Thomas Aquinas took a position opposite to that of Gerard of Huy and Roger Bacon, describing the *septuaginta*, not Jerome's version, as the Church's version (Thomas Aquinas, *Catena aurea in quatuor evangelia*, 2 vols, Turin 1925, I, p. 329 ['In Matthei evangelium', XXI, 1]: 'Non autem ita se habet vel quod Joannes interponit, vel codices ecclesiasticae interpretationis LXX.'); and in the fourteenth century, Petrarch criticised the predilection for Jerome over Augustine; see above, p. 54, n. 18.

[92] It might be worth examining the possible influence of the three pseudepigrapha and Giovanni d'Andrea's *Hieronymianus* on the works of, for instance, Peter of Ailly.

[93] Rice, *Saint Jerome*, p. 173.

that it was divinely inspired. The overall impression one gets is that the vast majority of textual critics treated Jerome's translation in the same way as other Latin versions of the Bible. Likewise, the increasing popularity of the cult of Jerome in the fourteenth and fifteenth centuries seems to have had very little impact on their methods and views, with the exception, perhaps, of Lorenzo Valla. His elaborate refutation of Jerome's 'Preface to the Gospels' might have been formulated in response to the increasing veneration of Jerome and his achievements as a translator of the Bible. The textual critics of the Bible thus seem to form a distinct group, rather sober in their opinions and not given to exaggerated claims about either Jerome or the Vulgate. They tended to hold moderate views which were an advantage for taking an open-minded approach to the text and for justifying their own procedures.

Part III:

The Textual Traditions of the Bible and Their Manuscript Transmission

III.1 WHICH VERSION OF THE BIBLE IS CONTAINED IN THE MANUSCRIPTS?

Modern research has so far neglected to examine the statements made by medieval and early Renaissance scholars about which Latin translation of the Bible they thought they were reading and about the survival of the different Latin versions. Yet these notions need to be considered in order to contextualise and analyse the comments of textual critics concerning their emendational aims and methods. Not surprisingly, their views on these matters often differed from what we now know about the transmission of the Latin Bible; moreover, the variety of opinions which they expressed makes the exploration of these two issues especially interesting.

Ancient and early medieval writers provided some information about the dissemination of both the *septuaginta* and the Vulgate. Jerome and Augustine confirmed the unchallenged supremacy of the *septuaginta* in their day, while later writers often quoted Isidore's testimony about the dominance of Jerome's version throughout the Church. Even though passages from Jerome's prefaces revealed that he did not translate every single book of the Bible and that he merely revised others, most medieval and early Renaissance writers seem to have been convinced that he had, in fact, translated the entire Old and New Testaments.[1] They disagreed, however, about what became of his translation in later centuries.

Nicolò Maniacutia, writing in the mid-twelfth century, made comments in several of his works about the different versions of the Latin Bible and their survival. In the *Suffraganeus bibliothece*, he considered problems of attribution, freely admitting that he did not know whether the Seventy translators had rendered the entire Old Testament into Greek, as was commonly believed, or only the Pentateuch, as Jerome had suggested; nor, he points out, did he know who had translated the Vetus Latina.[2] Although he was unable to

---

[1] For the books left untranslated by Jerome, see above, p. 37; a summary of the stages of his work is given above, pp. 30–37. For the quotation from Isidore, see above, p. 35, n. 21. The remarks of Jerome and Augustine on the elevated status of the *septuaginta* in their day are given below, p. 110, n. 14, and p. 111, n. 17. For the assumption that Jerome had translated the entire Bible, see above, p. 57; but for an exception to this view, see below, p. 85, n. 13.

[2] See above, pp. 9–10.

resolve these matters, he did not pass over them in silence, but instead raised the issues, without attributing too much importance to them.

Regarding other developments in the transmission of the Latin Bible, he displayed more confidence. In his preface to the *Suffraganeus*, he says of the Book of Daniel:

> Horum {*sc.* septuaginta interpretum} quippe translacione usque ad Ieronimi tempora Christi ecclesia utebatur, preter Danielem prophetam, quem secundum Theodocionem ecclesia longe postea frequentavit. Denique et ego, cum ob habunda[n]ciam {*my correction*} mendaciorum mecum singula sollicite perscrutarer, ita Danihelis volumen in quibusdam bibliothecis comprehendi corruptum, ut usque ad id quod ait: 'Et iudicium sedebit ut auferatur potencia' [Dn 7.26], secundum Ieronimum, cetera vero de Theodocionia essent edicione suppleta.[3]

> The Christian Church used their {the Seventy translators'} translation up to the time of Jerome, except for the prophet Daniel, for which the Church, until much later, resorted to the translation of Theodotion. Finally, since I was carefully examining the details, due to the abundance of errors, I learned that in some copies of the Bible the Book of Daniel is so corrupt that up to the passage where it says 'And a judgement shall sit, that his power may be taken away' [Dn 7.26] it follows Jerome, but the rest is completed from Theodotion's edition.

The information in the first part of this passage comes from Jerome, who, in his preface to the Book of Daniel, writes that the *septuaginta* was in common use until his day and who also mentions the use of Theodotion's translation for the Book of Daniel.[4] Maniacutia, however, goes beyond what he took from Jerome. Convinced that he knows the difference between Jerome's translation of Daniel and the Latin version of Theodotion, he gives the precise verse in the Book of Daniel where the change between Jerome's and Theodotion's version takes place.[5]

---

[3] Maniacutia, [Preface to his *Suffraganeus bibliothece*], p. 275. Maniacutia is clearly referring to the Latin translation from Theodotion's version, and not to the original Greek translation. This usage of *edicio Theodocionia* for the Latin translation of Theodotion is similar to the usage of *septuaginta* for both the Septuagint and its Latin translation.

[4] See Jerome, 'Prologus in Danihele propheta', p. 1341: 'Danihelem prophetam iuxta Septuaginta interpretes Domini Salvatoris ecclesiae non legunt, utentes Theodotionis editione, et hoc cur acciderit nescio.'

[5] It is not clear to me why Maniacutia thinks that the change from Jerome's to Theodotion's version occured at Dn 7.26. In Weber's edition of the Vulgate,

Maniacutia's observations reveal a sharp critical insight into the transmission of the Latin Bible. His comment about the combined Latin version of Daniel already foreshadows his later awareness, in both the *Libellus* and his preface to the *Psalterium Romanum*, of the conflation of different Latin translations of the Bible. In the preface to the *Psalterium Romanum*, he accuses scribes of having corrupted Jerome's *Psalterium iuxta Hebraeos* by adding material from other versions. In the *Libellus*, too, he mentions the contamination of translations, this time blaming it on Latin exegetes, who introduce corruption because they try to make the text of the Bible fit their own interpretations by foraging from various versions which were faulty to start with.[6] These defective versions were also partly to blame for the mistakes in Jerome's translation.[7]

This awareness that manuscripts of the Latin Bible contained an amalgam of different versions was by no means limited to Maniacutia. It appears to have been accepted by many theologians throughout the Middle Ages. For example, the confusing mishmash of translations was noted a few decades earlier in the widely read writings of Hugh of St Victor, who had a powerful impact on Maniacutia:

> Dn 3.23 to 3.90 are singled out as translated from Theodotion, followed by the comment: 'Hucusque non habetur in hebraeo et quae posuimus de Theodotionis editione translata sunt'; and after Dn 12 and just before the start of the final passages which do not exist in the Hebrew, there is an insertion: 'Hucusque Danihel in hebraeo volumine legimus cetera quae sequuntur usque ad finem libri de Theodotionis editione translata sunt.' These passages are also present in medieval Latin Bible manuscripts: see, e.g., the 'Floreffe' Bible (MS London, British Library, Add. 17737) from the late twelfth century: f. 249vb for the comment following Dn 3.90; and f. 253rb for the insertion after Dn 12.12. It is possible that Maniacutia had a manuscript at hand in which a similar comment was mistakenly added after Dn 7.26, which induced him to think that the change from Jerome's version to the Latin translation of Theodotion's version occured there.

[6] Maniacutia, [Preface to the *Psalterium Romanum*], ed. Robert Weber, 'Deux préfaces au psautier dues à Nicolas Maniacoria', *Revue Bénédictine* 68 (1953), pp. 3–17, at p. 7: 'Sane psalterium olim a Ieronimo ex hebraica ueritate translatum, sed ammixtione aliarum translationum, scriptorum culpa, ualde corruptum, meo autem labore studiose correctum, illi bibliothece connexui quam ... nuper diligenter transcripsi'; Maniacutia, *Libellus*, p. 97: 'Praeterea multos habuisse leguntur expositores, qui translationes varias commiscentes et ad diversos sensus dicta extorquentes prophetica, addunt ad mendacia translatorum multa imponentes prophetis, quae nunquam venerunt in cor eorum.'

[7] Ibid., p. 117: 'Sic et alia innumera, quae de mendosis translationibus, consuetudine praevalente, editioni Ieronimi videntur annexa.'

> Usu autem pravo invalescente, qui nonnunquam solita magis quam vera appetit, factum est, ut diversas diversis sequentibus translationes ita tandem omnia confusa sint, ut pene nunc cui tribuendum sit ignoretur.[8]
>
> Through increasingly misguided usage, which at times strives for the habitual rather than for the true, it has come about that, with different people following different translations, everything in the end is in such chaos that nowadays one hardly knows what should be attributed to whom.

As these passages show, already in the first half of the twelfth century, scholars had identified one of the main problems in the transmission of the Latin Bible, which helped to explain the lack of uniformity in biblical texts.[9] At the same time, Hugh admitted that it was virtually impossible to separate the various versions. Hugh and Maniacutia mention yet another problem with regard to the textual tradition: both insisted on the existence of biblical translations which were faulty from the start. Unfortunately, neither of them specifies which versions were defective.[10]

One strategy for pinning down the translator of a biblical text found in a given manuscript was to consider the prologues which it

---

[8] Hugh of St Victor, *De scripturis et scriptoribus sacris* (*PL*, CLXXV), Paris 1879, cols 9–28, at col. 18A. It is, of course, possible that Maniacutia knew this passage; his comments are nevertheless more detailed than Hugh's. For another example which indicates that the assumption of contaminated texts was quite common, see below, p. 88, n. 18.

[9] See also above, p. 32–34.

[10] See Hugh of St Victor, *De scripturis*, cols 17D–18A: 'Octavo loco Hieronymus accessit, non jam de hebraeo in graecum sicut priores, sed de hebraeo in latinum transferens sermonem. Cujus translatio, quia hebraicae veritati concordare magis probata est, idcirco Ecclesia Christi per universam latinitatem prae caeteris omnibus translationibus, quas vitiosa interpretatio, sive prima de hebraeo in graecum, sive secunda de graeco in latinum facta, corruperat, hanc solam legendam et in auctoritate habendam constituit.' Since Maniacutia draws upon Hugh's writings regularly, this passage, too, might well have been a source for Maniacutia (see above, p. 83, n. 6). It is possible that Hugh and Maniacutia had in mind the reference by Jerome and Augustine to the countless translators of the Bible into Latin; see above, p. 29, n. 2. A statement from Augustine's *De civitate Dei* might also have shaped this view; see Augustine, *De civitate Dei*, p. 639 (XVIII, 43): 'Sed eius {*sc.* Hieronymi} tam litteratum laborem quamuis Iudaei fateantur esse ueracem, septuaginta uero interpretes in multis errasse contendant: tamen ecclesiae Christi tot hominum auctoritati ab Eleazaro tunc pontifice ad hoc tantum opus electorum neminem iudicant praeferendum.' For another aspect of this passage, see also above, p. 59.

contained. Readers of a Bible manuscript including Jerome's prefaces, in which he introduces himself as the translator or the revisor of individual books, might naturally assume that the Latin version they were holding in their hands was Jerome's. This argument was, in fact, used in the sixteenth century by Agostino Steuco as proof that Jerome was the translator of the version circulating at the time in the manuscripts.[11] There is no evidence, however, that the connection between Jerome's prologues and his version was ever explicitly used by medieval textual critics to argue, as Steuco would later do, that Jerome was the translator of the Bible text contained in manuscripts accompanied by his prefaces.[12] On the contrary, the Dominican Hugh of St Cher warned against this type of reasoning. While he did not doubt that Jerome had translated the Bible, he nevertheless noted that many biblical books, even though prefaced by Jerome's prologues, did not contain his version of the text.[13]

Yet some of Hugh's thirteenth-century contemporaries held that Jerome's version was still to be found in manuscripts of the Bible. Gerard of Huy, for instance, began by citing Isidore's statement that Jerome's translation was in use everywhere. Since, however, quotations from the Bible in the writings of Jerome often differed

[11] See Theobald Freudenberger, *Augustinus Steuchus aus Gubbio, Augustinerchorherr und päpstlicher Bibliothekar (1497–1548) und sein literarisches Lebenswerk*, Münster i. W. 1935, p. 171. Yet for a sixteenth-century rejection of this approach, see below p. 85, n. 13. On the history of the prefaces to the Bible, see Berger, *Les préfaces*.

[12] For Crastone's comment on the use of the prologues to determine the translator, see below, pp. 102–103.

[13] Hugh of St Cher, [*Correctio Biblie*] on 2K 9.11 (quoted in Denifle, 'Die Handschriften', p. 295): 'Unde patet, quod in multis libris, maxime historialibus, non utimur translatione Hieronymi, quamvis eius prologi nostris libris apponantur.' Paul of Middleburg, in the sixteenth century, also held this position; see Rice, *Saint Jerome*, p. 259, n. 15: 'Satis itaque constare arbitror usitatam translationem non esse ipsius Hieronymi, licet eius praefatiunculae in ipsius exordiis sint praemissae.' Jerome, moreover, was not necessarily seen as the translator of all the books of the Old Testament: Hody points out that at the time of Hugh of St Cher in the thirteenth century, the Venerable Bede was considered to be the translator of Proverbs; see Hody, *De bibliorum textibus*, pp. 547–548, and, following him, Kaulen, *Geschichte*, p. 300. Lobrichon (*La Bible*, p. 76) has recently indicated that although Jerome's prefaces are regularly found in manuscripts of the Bible, they are often mixed with other prefaces. This might further weaken the assumption that a text containing Jerome's prefaces must contain his translation, since in such manuscripts his prologues would be less prominent.

from the text found in biblical manuscripts, there were those who argued that the manuscripts contained either the *septuaginta* or a version by some other translator. Gerard points out, in response, that both Jerome and Augustine had stated that only the *septuaginta* was read, which ruled out the possibility that a third Latin version by some other translator could be in circulation; and since biblical quotations from the *septuaginta* in the works of Jerome and Augustine did not match the text found in manuscripts of the Bible, this meant that they did not contain the *septuaginta* either.[14] Gerard thus concludes:

> Cum ergo non sit LXX, qua sola utebatur ecclesia, constat nostram bibliam esse Ieronimi, quam Gregorius in moralibus exponit, et eam novam editionem vocavit, quia novissime post omnes facta fuit; et illa non discrepat a libris nostris.[15]
>
> Since, therefore, it is not the LXX (which the Church used exclusively), it is certain that our Bible is that of Jerome, which Gregory interprets in his *Moralia* and which he called the new edition, since it was made most recently after all the others; and it does not differ from our books.

Despite his insistence that Jerome's version was not only a satisfactory rendering of the Bible but also survived to his day, Gerard did not reject other translations. Instead, he maintains that the eight extant translations – the *septuaginta*, the versions of Aquila, Symmachus and Theodotion, the *quinta*, *sexta* and *septima* and, finally, Jerome's translation – and these alone, were authoritative in their pristine forms. Regrettably for our purpose, Gerard provides no further details about the survival of these other versions. His knowledge of their readings in all likelihood came

---

[14] See above, p. 17, and Gerard of Huy, [Preface to his *correctorium*], pp. 301–302: 'Cum igitur sicut Isidorus dicit omnes ecclesie utantur editione Ieronimi et adhuc exemplaria inveniantur, utpote Gregorii, que erant tempore Isidori et ecclesie tunc utebantur illis, et illa exemplaria non discrepent a nostris bibliis, constat bibliam antiquam qua utimur esse Ieronimi ... In Daniele tamen ecclesia utebatur translatione Theodotionis, ut dicitur in prologo Danielis {*see above, p. 82, n. 4*}. Quod etiam non sit editio vulgata, que et dicitur LXX, patet per litteram qua utitur Augustinus in libris suis, que multum diversificatur a bibliis nostris. Idem patet per litteram LXX, quam ponit Ieronimus in originalibus Prophetarum.' For the quotation from Isidore, see above, p. 35, n. 21.

[15] Ibid., p. 302. For the quotation from Gregory the Great, see above, p. 35, n. 20.

from the works of Jerome, who regularly quoted and translated passages from earlier translations.[16]

Some of the ideas mentioned so far in this chapter were also discussed by Roger Bacon, who did not always support or agree with them – indeed, at times he violently rejected them. Several of his statements confirm that the view expressed by both Hugh of St Victor and Nicolò Maniacutia about the contamination of different versions of the Bible was not uncommon in his time, either, though Bacon's portrayal of the situation is not the same as theirs. In his *Opus majus*, Bacon complains that the Vetus Latina and the Vulgate had been conflated by uncritical readers, who had inserted quotations of the *septuaginta* from the Church Fathers into their manuscripts of the Vulgate.[17]

He elaborates on the contamination of Latin translations of the Bible in his *Opus minus*. According to him, due to the variety of different readings in circulation the rabble of theologians in his day believed that the text in biblical manuscripts was not Jerome's, but rather a mixture of several different versions, compiled from various bits of different translations. They used the assumption that the text was already an amalgam as a licence to introduce yet more

---

[16] Ibid., pp. 302–303: 'Cum ergo sicut dictum est in universo sint octo translationes, non est recipienda littera nisi sit alicuius predictorum interpretum nec credendum est vitiis scriptorum vel imperitorum correctorum vel ut verius dicam, corruptorum.' Earlier in the preface (ibid., pp. 299–301), Gerard lists the eight translations known in the Middle Ages, based mostly on references in the works of the Church Fathers, especially Jerome. For the *quinta*, *sexta* and *septima*, see Jellicoe, *The Septuagint*, pp. 118–124. The three versions are mentioned, for instance, by Jerome, *Die Chronik des Hieronymus. Hieronymi Chronicon*, in Eusebius, *Werke*, VII, ed. R. Helm, Berlin 1956, p. 3.

[17] Bacon, *Opus majus*, I, p. 79: 'Augustinus et alii et ipsemet Hieronymus tempore suo usi sunt sicut Ecclesia translatione antiqua. Et ideo Augustinum quum recitat textum hunc decimo sexto *de Civitate Dei* et exponit oportuit quod uteretur translatione quae fuit vulgata et recepta apud Latinos, nec potuit aliud facere. Omnis vero glossator qui infixit glossas super textum accepit auctoritatem Augustini *de Civitate Dei* et eam posuit infra textum, sed non mutavit eam nec intulit negationem ... inter caeteros hoc fecit. Et sic vulgatus est error horribilis cum contradictorium pro contradictione ponatur.' The verses in the Bible mentioned by Bacon are Gn 8.6–7. I have not been able to locate the passage in *De civitate Dei*; but Augustine refers to these verses in several of his works; see, e.g., Augustine, *Contra Faustum*, p. 348 (XII, 20).

alternative passages and readings.[18] These alterations, which Bacon deplored, are more closely defined later on in the *Opus minus*. Not only did the theologians change whatever they did not understand and insert into the text words found in biblical quotations by the Fathers which they judged to be the most suitable, but borrowings of biblical passages in Josephus's *Antiquitates judaicae* and the liturgy were also adopted.[19] The liturgy, however, as Bacon noted, had been changed in the past to make it more comprehensible, so it was no longer in agreement with the original text of the Bible. This liberty of altering the liturgical text was the privilege of the Roman Church and could not be assumed by anyone without its authorisation.[20]

Much to Bacon's dismay, his contemporaries did not consider the existence of variant readings or passages problematic. On the contrary, they continually introduced new alternative readings. Theologians, he writes, did not think that these readings came from different Latin translations of the entire Bible. Instead, going against the accepted view that there had been two Latin translations of the Bible, the Vetus Latina and the Vulgate,[21] they believed that there had been only one complete translation. Nevertheless, they claimed that two versions were in circulation: a simple one, *simplex*, which was the only complete Latin rendering; and a composite one,

---

[18] Bacon, *Opus minus*, p. 334: 'Praeterea specialis causa erroris est, quod non advertunt qua translatione utitur ecclesia Latinorum. Nam propter hoc quod vident literam diversificatam secundum capita diversorum, credit vulgus theologorum, quod non sit translatio beati Hieronymi, sed alia versio mixta et compilata ex diversis. Et propter hoc cum majori libertate miscentur vocabula quae volunt. Sed istud falsissimum est.'

[19] Ibid., pp. 347–348: 'Illi qui compositam translationem ponunt, illi componunt ut volunt; nam allegant, quod litera Bibliae est composita ex multis. Et ideo ponunt quod volunt, et miscent, et mutant, omnia quae non intelligunt. Et iterum, accipiunt quae volunt a simili translatione et composita, non solum ab illis translationibus recitatis in originalibus sanctorum, sed a Josepho in Antiquitatum libris, qui exponit textum, et ponit sensum historiae sacrae, et mutat verba sicut ei placuit. Unde moderni corrigunt multa, et mutant per eum; cum tamen hoc non deceat fieri aliquando, nisi inveniretur in Bibliis antiquis. Deinde ab officio ecclesiae multa accipiunt et ponunt in textu.'

[20] Ibid., p. 348: 'Sed illi qui statuerunt officium, multa mutaverunt, ut competebat officio propter intellectum planiorem, ad devotionem excitandam. Et ecclesia Romana habet ad hoc auctoritatem, et caeterae per eam.'

[21] For this assumption, see below, p. 93, n. 28.

composita, presumably cobbled together from bits and pieces of the Latin Bible – which they considered to be variants of the same translation – found in other works. They regarded it as unthinkable that the same text had been translated in its entirety more than once. For Bacon, on the other hand, it was unthinkable that a translator could have used different terms to render the same word within a single translation. According to him, therefore, the variant readings found in the Fathers, Josephus and the liturgy belonged to different translations of the Bible.[22]

Many people, Bacon claims, believed that the *composita*, or mixed version, was compiled after Isidore. It was also thought that this version had originally been prepared by an unidentified pope or even by Parisian masters. Bacon regarded the latter theory, in particular, as implausible, since an undertaking of this nature would have required the consent of the Holy See; but there was no evidence that this consent had ever been given. The earlier theory is dismissed on the grounds that no such enterprise was mentioned in any papal documents or registers, nor in any historical works. Both theories were therefore invalid.[23]

---

[22] Ibid., pp. 347–348: 'Sancti, et maxime Hieronymus, recitant omnes translationes ad eandem sententiam propter pleniorem expositionem. Multi vero non considerantes rationem translationum, credunt quod sunt aliae literae ejusdem translationis: et tunc inserunt in textum literam, quam magis intelligunt. Et sic infinitam corruptionem inducunt ... Ex his igitur causis omnes dicunt varias esse literas in textu. Nam dicunt semper quod alia ita est. Et multiplicant istas literas in omni verbo. Et sic se excusant, quia una sententia pluribus sermonibus exprimatur. Nec volunt dicere quod sunt aliae translationes, quia unam volunt confiteri simplicem, aliam compositam; et unum textum esse vulgatum, quia nimis scandalizarent, quod unus textus in uno volumine haberet diversas translationes. Et ideo dicunt quod ejusdem translationis {*my emendation from* translationes} diversae sunt literae. Et non reputant hoc esse per errorem. Sed nunquam accidit, quod unus translator in transferendo posuerit in textu eodem sermones diversos pro eadem sententia. Nam in philosophia nec alibi potest hoc fieri. Translatio enim quaelibet debet habere sua propria verba, sed diversimodae habent diversa verba. Unde istae literae diversae quas allegant, sunt de diversis translationibus, quas sancti recitant in originalibus, quam Josephus recitat, et ecclesia transmutat, et ideo accidit corruptio infinita.'

[23] Ibid., p. 342: 'Sed quia adhuc multi in hac parte dicunt, quod aliqua fuit compilatio facta retroactis temporibus post tempus Isidori ex diversis translationibus ab aliquo papa, vel a magistris Parisiensibus, vulgatum et diffusum nunc ubique, et non translatio Hieronymi. Sed tanta res nec a magistris Parisiensibus, nec ab aliquo, sine sedis Apostolicae auctoritate, fieri potuit, nec decuit, nec etiam rationabile est. Sed vero potest dici quod vel auctoritate papae concessa doctoribus Parisiensibus vel aliis, aut per aliquem

The notions which Bacon ascribes to his contemporaries might appear somewhat strange, but they can be explained if we assume that the *translatio simplex* was Jerome's version. The belief that the composite version was compiled after the time of Isidore would then be based on Isidore's famous statement that in his day only Jerome's translation was read in the churches, implying that until then the *composita* was not in circulation. The fragments of the Latin Bible which did not belong to a full version can be identified as the Latin translations of quotations from Greek versions found in the works of the Latin Fathers, especially Jerome. If the *vulgata* had not been recognised as an independent translation, it might also have been regarded as part of this group. The theory of the existence of a *composita* might have helped medieval scholars to explain those textual discrepancies found in the various Latin manuscripts of the Bible which went beyond mere scribal errors. But although it is possible to explain Bacon's statements about the views of his contemporaries, it is difficult to determine whether what he says is, in fact, reliable. Given the evidence provided by the Church Fathers and by later writers about the circulation of the *septuaginta* and Jerome's translation, it seems hard to imagine that thirteenth-century theologians actually believed that there had been only one complete Latin translation of the Bible. Moreover, no other textual critic of the time mentions this idea.

Bacon's own view of the early history of the Latin Bible differed considerably from what he, rightly or wrongly, ascribed to contemporary theologians. He maintains that until the thirteenth century, the transmission of the Latin Bible in the form of the Vulgate was uncorrupted, apart from unavoidable scribal errors. It was only in Bacon's day that Jerome's translation was contaminated by readings from other Latin versions. He insists that Jerome's translation had been used for a long time by the Church, except for the Psalter, which was read in the *septuaginta* version, that is, the Gallican Psalter. Since the Psalter had been corrected by Jerome, it was generally regarded as his translation; but Bacon disputed this attribution: the only version of the Psalms which could properly be ascribed to Jerome was the *iuxta Hebraeos*, his direct translation from the Hebrew.[24] In Bacon's view, the *septuaginta* version of the

> summum pontificem, facta sit haec compilatio. Sed nulla scriptura, nec registrum papae haec docet, nec chronica, nec historia facit mentionem.'

[24] See ibid., p. 334: 'Nam sola translatione Hieronymi utuntur ecclesiae Latinorum, praeter Psalterium, quod est de translatione Septuaginta

Psalms, that is, the *Psalterium Gallicanum*, which, as he mentions, Jerome had corrected *cum asteriscis et obelis*, had merely been revised by him. Jerome should not, therefore, be treated as the translator: a critical reworking does not justify the attribution of a work to its reviser.[25] In adopting this novel standpoint, supported by sound arguments, Bacon thus challenged the widely held view that the translator of the most popular version of the Psalms was Jerome.

Bacon's assumption that the Latin Bibles circulating in his day – with the exception of the Paris Bibles – still contained the pure text of Jerome's translation posed a different problem for him: if the translation found in the manuscripts of the Bible is Jerome's, even though corrupted by scribes, how can one account for the differences between this version and the biblical quotations in Jerome's commentaries? Bacon's solution was to suggest that Jerome had made not one, but two translations of the Bible. The earlier one is the text found in manuscripts of the Bible; and in it Jerome was still trying not to alter the extant Latin text too much, out of respect for the Church and fear of reproach. The second and later translation is preserved in his other works; and here he finally dared to present his real translation from the original Hebrew, without worrying that he would be prosecuted for producing a new work.[26]

> interpretum, quod ideo remansit, quia modo fuit vulgatum in ecclesia Dei ante quam Hieronymus transtulit eorum translationem in Latinum, et correxit illam cum asteriscis et obelis. Et ideo reputatur quasi translatio Hieronymi; sed non est, quia sua est immediate de Hebraeo ... Quod autem in ecclesiis Latinorum sola translatio Hieronymi sit in usu patet, et quod haec sola sit in omnibus Bibliis Latinorum praeter Psalterium, licet sit multipliciter per scriptores et correctores depravata in exemplari Parisiensi, probatur multipliciter.' This statement is followed by the quotation from Isidore mentioned above, in which he says that Jerome's version is read in 'all churches'; see above, p. 35, n. 21.

[25] For Jerome's three versions of the Psalms, see above, pp. 30–32.

[26] Ibid., pp. 343–44: 'Sed tertio probabiliter potest eligi, et solutione dignum, quod beatus Hieronymus in originalibus super textum ponit aliam literam, quam nos habemus in Bibliis antiquis et novis. Et ideo aliam translationem edisserit et exponit juxta Hebraïcam veritatem, praeter hoc quod simul ponat translationem Septuaginta, quatenus videatur qualiter editio Septuaginta discordet ab Hebraïca veritate, adjungens autem translationes aliorum, ut magis elucescat veritas Hebraïca quam exponit. Ex quo videtur quod cum Hieronymus suam ibi exponat translationem, quae non est illa quam tenemus in Bibliis, id est quod illa editio qua utimur non est Hieronymi; sed ut habeatur vel aliqua compilatio, vel alia translatio, quaecunque sit illa ... Primam ejus translationem, quam vulgo tradidit, habeamus in Bibliis ... Et

This assumption, according to Bacon, is confirmed by the fact that in his commentary on Isaiah, for example, Jerome mentions having changed the translation of two words; since the earlier, incorrect, reading is found in biblical manuscripts, this demonstrated that they contained his first translation.[27]

From Bacon's point of view, the transmission of the Latin Bible offered further support for his conviction that the text found in manuscripts of the Bible is Jerome's first translation. He is certain that no complete copy of the *septuaginta* survives – this earliest Latin translation is transmitted solely through quotations in the works of the Church Fathers. And since only two translations into Latin, the Vetus Latina and the Vulgate, were ever made, the text

> contra, Hebraïcam veritatem juxta quam {*my emendation from* quas} esse visum fuit interpre[ta]tum {*my addition*}, quia haereticus et falsarius reputabatur a multis, et quasi ab omnibus judicabatur in pejorem partem propter novitatem translationis conditae, editione quae fuit ubique vulgata, ipse non expressit meliori modo quo scivit Hebraïcam veritatem et potuit, sed se conformavit translationi Vulgatae, in quibus vitium manifestum non fuit. Et hoc fecit propter pacem ecclesiae et virorum sanctorum ecclesiasticorum qui contradixerunt. Qui cum scivit suam hanc primam editionem non esse sufficientem, ideo veritati et studiosis volens satisfacere, decrevit aliam translationem relinquere in scriptis secretis, scilicet in suis originalibus, quod et fieri potuit sine vulgi scandalo, quia haec secunda editio nunquam fuit adhuc in usu vulgi neque ecclesiae, praesertim cum in omni tempore viri paucissimi usi sunt originalibus sui Hieronymi super textum, ita etiam ut Rabanus et Cassiodorus viri doctores docuerunt se non posse omnia ejus originalia invenire, sicut Rabanus [Hrabanus Maurus, *Expositio super Jeremiam prophetam* (*PL*, CXI), Paris 1852, cols 792-1272, at col. 793B) recitat super Jeremiam in originali.' .

[27] Bacon, *Opus minus*, p. 345: 'Cum igitur in Bibliis nostris omnibus antiquis, et quae fuerunt tempore Isidori, et etiam quae adhuc restant ubique regionum, et in posterioribus Bibliis ad ulla exemplaria transcriptis invenimus in Esaia *refraenantem* [Is 19.15] et *festivitatem* [Is 19.17], quae vocabula se transtulisse Hieronymus memorat, et mutat in originali, patet quod suam correxit translationem quam tenemus, et non aliam.' See Jerome, *In Esaiam*, pp. 196–197 (V, xix, 14.15 and 16.17). Bacon also adduces a quotation from Bede which he interprets as confirming his theory of two translations: *Opus minus*, pp. 346–347 (quoting Bede, *Retractatio*, p. 93 [*praefatio*]): '"Nam et Hieronymus pleraque testimonia veteris instrumenti, ut Hebraïca veritas habet, edocet; nec tamen haec ita in nostris codicibus, aut ipse interpretari, aut nos emendare voluit ... " Haec Beda. Ex quibus sequitur quod aliter Hieronymus primo transtulit, et aliter recitavit cum exposuit in originali, ubi potuit copiosius de veritate translationum disputare.' He does not mention the possibility that the commentaries were not necessarily written after the translation. For a chronological table of Jerome's works, see the verso of the front-cover in Fürst, *Hieronymus*.

now in circulation, with the exception of the Psalms, must be Jerome's. The only reason why the Paris Bible did not appear to contain Jerome's translation was that it was disfigured by corruptions.[28] Furthermore, since Jerome's translation had invalidated the *septuaginta* and also Theodotion's rendering of Daniel, it was only logical that the version now circulating in manuscripts was his.[29] Before Jerome, only the *septuaginta* had been regarded as authentic by the Church, although learned clerics had also read other translations; however, since the *septuaginta* was no longer consulted by theologians, it was clear that the Vulgate was now received by the Church.[30]

In contrast to many other learned men of his time, Bacon was therefore in no doubt that the version of the Latin Bible circulating in manuscripts other than the Paris Bibles was that of Jerome. Since Isidore had said that only this version was in use in his day, all manuscripts from that time must contain Jerome's first translation

---

[28] Bacon, *Opus minus*, pp. 336–337: 'Quoniam igitur apud Latinos non fuerunt translationes nisi duae, scilicet Septuaginta et Hieronymi; et Septuaginta non inveniuntur in aliquo loco apud Latinos, oportet quod haec quae vulgatur apud Latinos sit Hieronymi. Sed cum multipliciter in exemplari Parisiensi depravata sit, [et] ideo non omnibus apparet quod sit Hieronymi, quamvis consideranti omnia alia exemplaria ecclesiae pateat esse Hieronymi, praeterquam in psalterio'; Bacon, *Opus majus*, I, p. 19: 'Post mortem suam veritas suae translationis claruit et sua expositio, et per omnes ecclesias dilatatae sunt, ita ut nullum vestigium translationis antiquae, scilicet LXX interpretum, qua prius usa fuerat ecclesia, valeat reperiri.'

[29] Bacon, *Opus minus*, p. 341: 'Quare cum translatio Hieronymi evacuavit translationem Vulgatam Septuaginta, et similiter Theodotionis, ut certum est omnibus, oportet quod Biblia qua utimur sit translatio Hieronymi.'

[30] Ibid., p. 339: 'Dico quod sola editio Vulgata, quae est Septuaginta interpretum, fuit ecclesiis ante editionem Hieronymi communicata tanquam pro authentica, aliae legebantur a viris ecclesiasticis, ut ex earum collatione magis pateret translatio Septuaginta, et propter studii plenius exercitium, sicut vult Hieronymus ... Cum igitur illa non est in usu Latinorum, nec theologorum, ut omnes sciunt qui theologiam noverunt, manifestum est Hieronymi translationem esse illam quam ecclesia recipit his temporibus.' Bacon considered the Book of Daniel to be an exception to the rule that the entire Latin Old Testament was first translated from the Septuagint, since it had been translated from Theodotion's version as Jerome had noted (see above, p. 82, n. 4); see ibid., p. 336: 'Hae omnes fuerunt de Hebraeo in Graecum transfusae, et una illarum tantum de Graeco in Latinum, scilicet editio Vulgata, quae fuit Septuaginta interpretum, excepto quod Danielis liber juxta translationem Theodotionis in Latinum versus fuit, quia translatione Septuaginta in Daniele ecclesiae Dei non utuntur, ut dicit Hieronymus in prologo Danielis.'

in its original form, apart from scribal errors.³¹ Much to Bacon's annoyance, however, his contemporaries were unaware that Jerome had made two translations of the Bible. Theologians, moreover, did not know that the version they had was Jerome's and, even when told, many still denied or doubted this attribution. Since it was inconceivable to them that Jerome might have translated one way in his first version, and another in his commentaries, they hesitated as to which translation they should adopt. Bacon himself, however, was adamant that Latin manuscripts of the Bible transmitted Jerome's first version.³²

Although convinced that Jerome's second version could be found in his commentaries, Bacon was well aware that not every unattributed biblical quotation contained in them was from this translation. Instead, in some of his commentaries Jerome had expounded the text of the *septuaginta*. Some scholars, Bacon complains, were unaware of this and wrongly believed that the quotations found in these works represented the true text of the Latin Bible. Accordingly, they altered the text in their manuscripts of the Bible to match what they found in these commentaries and vice versa. This textual contamination and corruption was caused by, again, their erroneous belief that Jerome had made only one translation and that, therefore, by replacing the text in Latin Bible

---

³¹ Ibid., p. 335: 'Et innumerabiles aliae Bibliae per diversas regiones, quae fuerunt tempore Isidori et ante eum, adhuc permanent sine corruptione; et in omnibus concordant, nisi sit vitium scriptoris, quo nulla Scriptura carere potest. Quapropter si tempore Isidori usae sunt omnes ecclesiae generaliter translatione Hieronymi, oportet quod adhuc eadem sit translatio in usu, cum eadem exemplaria et similia remanent ubique.' That Jerome's version is universally used is also confirmed in his *Opus tertium*; see Roger Bacon, *Opus tertium*, in his *Opera quaedam*, pp. 3-310, at p. 28: 'Praevaluit post mortem Hieronymi sua translatio, qua nunc tota Christianitas utitur Latinorum.'

³² Bacon, *Opus minus*, p. 347: 'Totum enim Hieronymi quod habemus in antiquis Bibliis, et in originali, haec diversimode hinc inde aliquoties transtulerat. Quapropter concluditur necessario ex his omnibus, quod translatio est Hieronymi quam nos tenemus. Cum igitur vulgus theologorum hoc ignorat, et contradicunt multi, et alii dubitant, quae sit translatio quam sequi debeant, necesse est quemlibet unum recipere pro alio, et improprium pro proprio, et multiplex falsum pro vero. Cum igitur una est translatio in omnibus libris Latinorum, et est illa quam primo Hieronymus transtulit; quia secundam fecit cum expositione sua in originali, translatio quam recepit ecclesia multipliciter depravatur. Quod aliqui non considerant in originalibus sanctorum, quia translatione usi sunt primo.'

manuscripts with readings found in Jerome's commentaries they were restoring his version.[33]

Bacon's theory that Jerome had translated the Bible twice did not attract any followers, as his comments make clear. The view that Jerome had made one translation continued to prevail. Yet the assumption that the biblical quotations found in Jerome's commentaries represented his true translation later crops up in Lorenzo Valla's works, though based on different premises.[34]

In the fourteenth century, Richard FitzRalph had John, one of the interlocutors in his dialogue, say that among the many different Latin translations of the Bible, three were the most important: the *septuaginta*, Jerome's version and the *translatio communis*, the last of which had been more widely used than the others.[35] FitzRalph does not provide any further clues as to the identity of the *translatio communis* – though he may have meant the Paris Bible – so the modern reader is left in the dark.[36]

John brings up another issue concerning the identification of biblical translators. It had already been pointed out in the thirteenth century that the presence of Jerome's prefaces in a manuscript of the Bible did not guarantee that it contained his version. FitzRalph lets John go a step further:

> Certum {*my emendation from* ceterum} etiam non habemus quod translationes iste quibus utimur sunt translationes ipsorum quibus

---

[33] Ibid., pp. 348–349: 'Hieronymus etiam super Genesin, et super Psalterium, et in multis locis, exposuit translationem Septuaginta interpretum, quam vocat nostram, quia tunc omnes ecclesiae usae sunt illa. Non enim transtulerat tunc ex Hebraeo, nec etiam tempore suo fuit ejus translatio recepta communiter. Et ideo viri aestimati valde magni et maximi dicunt, quod litera Bibliae nostrae est quam exponit Hieronymus in talibus Bibliis. Et ideo ponunt eam in textu nostro, et corrumpunt, et magis corrumpunt primam translationem Hieronymi, quae sola est in Bibliis per secundam, quae sola est in originalibus; nam credunt unam esse translationem. Et ideo mutant textum.'

[34] See below, p. 100.

[35] FitzRalph, *Summa*, sig. C iʳ (19, 18): 'Ecce enim nos latini multas translationes habemus et tres praecipuas, scilicet interpretum 70 translationem, sancti Iheronimi et illam quam vocamus communem que magis solebat esse {*corrected from* inesse *by a sixteenth-century hand*} in usu quam cetere.'

[36] For the problems posed by the terms *littera communis* or *translatio communis*, see also above, pp. 21–23 and esp. p. 22, n. 44, for the identification of FitzRalph's *translatio communis* with the Paris Bible.

> ascribuntur, nisi hominum nuda verba qui pro voto suo – ut loquar rusticiter – poterant fabricare mendacia.[37]

> We are not sure that the translations we use are the translations of those to whom they are ascribed, except for the mere words of men who – to speak bluntly – could have made up lies for their oaths.

This statement would even seem to cast doubt on the claim of Jerome to have translated the Scriptures, which no one had previously questioned. John's scepticism does not, however, appear to have been picked up by other scholars, nor did FitzRalph, in the guise of the dialogue partner Richard, reply specifically to this point.[38]

In the fifteenth century, Lorenzo Valla set forth a vast amount of information about his views on the survival of the Vulgate and about which version of the Bible he thought he was reading. Perhaps his most remarkable pronouncements concern his belief that Jerome did not translate all of the New Testament. Valla's observations, limited to the New Testament, added new depth to the considerations of Jerome's contribution to the Latin Bible. Basing himself on statements made by Jerome in his 'Preface to the Gospels', Valla insists that Jerome only corrected those passages which disagreed with the sense of the original Greek. The Latin translation of the Bible attributed to him, therefore, was not entirely his work.[39]

For Valla, there were several other reasons to question the attribution of the Latin text of the Bible in circulation to Jerome. He points out that it is unlikely that all manuscripts were emended according to the new version, so that older versions must still have

---

[37] FitzRalph, *Summa*, sig. C i^r (19, 18).

[38] FitzRalph has Richard insist that the character of the translators had been vetted by an unspecified council; see below, p. 161, and n. 166. The other two fourteenth-century scholars examined in this study, Peter of Ailly and Henry Totting, did not comment on which version they thought was contained in manuscripts of the Bible. Given their preference for the Vulgate, however, it stands to reason that both of them assumed that manuscripts of the Latin Bible contained this version.

[39] Valla, *Collatio*, p. 10: 'Quod sicubi fortassis a translatione Hieronymi dissentio, velim omnes existimant, aut non sic ab eo traductum fuisse sed tempore depravatum, aut certe translationem primam ab eo ita relictam, siquidem non omnia se ille ait emendasse sed que intellectum maxime depravarent'; Valla is, in all likelihood, referring to the passage quoted above, p. 31, n. 8.

remained in circulation.[40] Also, surely after one thousand years the manuscripts of the Bible had become corrupt. Furthermore, although it might be claimed that only Jerome's version survived, there is no evidence to back up this hypothesis.[41] Instead, Valla came up with a different solution to the problem of attributing the Latin translation found in manuscripts of the Bible: he consistently uses the term *interpres* to refer to the translator of the Latin Bible. Valla's belief that the text in circulation either no longer was or never had been Jerome's is reflected in his *Antidotum in Pogium*. Discussing a Latin passage from the New Testament, he writes:

> Non enim veritatis, hoc est Christi, sunt ista verba, sed apostoli 'alter alterius onera portate et sic adimplebitis legem Christi' [Ga 6.2]. Si modo dicenda sunt hec verba apostoli et non potius interpretis nescio cuius.[42]

> Those are certainly not the words of Truth, that is, Christ, but of the Apostle: 'Alter alterius onera portate et sic adimplebitis legem Christi.' [Ga 6.2] – if they are to be called the words of the Apostle at all and not rather the words of some *interpres* or other.

This *interpres*, whom Valla also mentions in his *Collatio* and *Annotationes*, is nowhere further identified. Since Valla's views on Jerome and on the *interpres* have sometimes been misunderstood,[43] this issue deserves careful consideration.

---

[40] Ibid., p. 6: 'At me omni invidia liberat, primum quod credibile est eos codices, qui tum erant, non prorsus ad novi operis formulam omnes fuisse emendatos, utique post summorum virorum super Novum Testamentum commentaria, ut ex quibusdam locis datur intelligi, que hinc repetita secus in libris Hieronymi leguntur.'

[41] Ibid., p. 9: 'Quod si ita non est, confitendum erit aliquod tunc exemplar non fuisse mendosum, quo incolumi, supervacua, ne dicam contumeliosa ac superba, erat recens alia translatio. At, dices, utcunque sit, sola Hieronymi translatio extat, quippe cum unum idemque omnium codicum exemplum sit, quod abs te nunc nefas est impugnari. Esto, ita sit, tam et si hoc tu probare non potes, et ego defensum sane quam impugnatum Hieronymum malo. Verum si post quadringentos solum annos ita turbidus a fonte fluebat rivus, quid mirum si rursus post mille annos – tot enim ab Hieronymo ad hoc evum sunt – hic rivus nunquam repurgatus aliqua in parte limum sordesque contraxit?'

[42] Valla, *Antidotum primum*, p. 110.

[43] See, e.g., Frank Bezner, 'Lorenzo Valla (1407–1457)', in *Lateinische Lehrer Europas: Fünfzehn Portraits von Varro bis Erasmus von Rotterdam*, ed. W. Ax, Cologne, Weimar and Vienna 2005, pp. 353–389, at p. 374, who maintains that Valla attributed many errors in translation to Jerome.

Although Poggio in his *Invectivae* identifies the *interpres* with Jerome and takes Valla's critical statements as an attack on him, this tactic obviously served his polemical purposes since it made Valla look disrespectful to a leading figure of the Church.[44] That Valla was not, in fact, referring to Jerome can be seen from several comments in his works on the New Testament, as well as in his invectives against Poggio. For instance, Valla says that he is not certain that the same person translated the Gospels and the Psalms.[45] Likewise, his statement that either Jerome is not the translator of 1 Corinthians or else his translation has been corrupted shows that the *interpres* and Jerome are not one and the same person, since Valla attributes the error to the *interpres*, but points out that Jerome translated the same phrase correctly elsewhere.[46] The wording of his remarks indicates: firstly, that he is convinced that the text of the Latin Bible in the manuscripts was at most only partly by Jerome; secondly, that he believed there was more than one translator; and, thirdly, that he was unable to identify the additional translator or translators with certainty. When using the term *interpres*, he had in mind the translator(s) and

---

[44] See, e.g., Poggio Bracciolini, *Invectivae in L. Vallam*, in his *Opera omnia*, 4 vols, Basel 1538, repr. Turin 1964–1969, I, pp. 188–251, at p. 189: 'Hieronymum improbat, asserens multa ab eo perperam in sacra scriptura esse in latinum traducta'; ibid., p. 199: 'Scripturam sacram hic homo prophanus adeo contemnit, ut plura in ea non recte scripta asseveret. Notavi pauca e multis: In quibus beatum Hieronymum ut malum interpretem culpat'; ibid., p. 240: 'Theologum se adeo doctrinae opulentum, ut Augustinum, Hieronymum non recte scripturam sacram intellexisse asserat, omnesque malos interpretes fuisse: Hieronymum praesertim, de cuius in traducendo erroribus libellum aediderit impudentissimum.' Even though Poggio's equation of the *interpres* with Jerome clearly aided his invective, it probably also reflected his conviction that the version in circulation was, in fact, Jerome's.

[45] See below, p. 189, n. 256; and Valla, *Annotationes*, p. 813A: 'Haud scio an idem interpres fuerit euangeliorum et psalmorum. Certe et inconstantiae est et infidelis translationis, tam uarie differenterque transferre.'

[46] Ibid., p. 862A: '"Nec in cor hominis ascendit..." [1 Co 2.9]: Interpres non animaduertit uerbum graecum, etsi numeri singularis, tamen fuisse transferendum pluraliter, ut facit Hieronymus in epistola super pentateuchum: *nec in cor hominis ascenderunt*: ut appareat aut non esse hunc interpretem Hieronymum, aut eius interpretationem fuisse corruptam.' See Jerome, 'Prologus in Pentateucho', p. 3.

reviser(s) responsible for the text of the Latin Bible as it stood in his day.[47]

Valla's overall opinion of the *interpres* is inevitably negative: since he only discusses translations with which he disagrees, the *interpres* is constantly questioned and criticised throughout both the *Collatio* and the *Annotationes*. The few statements he makes which are not negative can hardly be considered positive – at best, he attributes an error to a scribe instead of the *interpres*.[48]

Despite his conviction that Jerome had not translated the entire New Testament and that the Latin text of the Bible in circulation was not his, Valla held him in the highest regard. Both in the *Antidotum* and in the *Collatio*, Valla stresses that he would not dare accuse Jerome of falsehood. Nevertheless, Jerome's claim in his 'Preface to the Gospels' that all Latin manuscripts of the Bible were faulty seems absurd to him. Surely the pope, Ambrose, Hilary or Augustine would have had access to correct manuscripts or else would have attempted to rectify the transmission.[49] Had there been a completely accurate manuscript of the earlier Latin translation, Jerome's version would have been superfluous. It might be argued, nonetheless, that only Jerome's translation had survived to Valla's

---

[47] Scribes formed an independent category and were criticised separately from the *interpres*.

[48] See, e.g., Valla, *Collatio*, p. 208: 'Culpa non interpretis fuit, ut reor, sed aut scribentis aut imperiti peritos corrigentis'; and Valla, *Annotationes*, p. 878B [on Ph 1.26]: 'Graece est *gloriatio*, et ita interpres transtulit: sed negligentia librariorum factum est *gratulatio*, καύχημα.' For Salvatore I. Camporeale's view of Valla's relationship to the *interpres*, with which I agree, see his *Lorenzo Valla: umanesimo e teologia*, Florence 1972, pp. 299–302.

[49] Valla, *Collatio*, pp. 8–9: 'Quid ergo? – dicet aliquis. Ista ne errata in Hieronymo probare vis, quem nos sequimur interpretem, cuiusque non magis laudabile opus est, quod ex hebreo Vetus Testamentum quam quod e greco interpretatus est Novum, quod – ut ipse inquit – "tot habebat exemplaria quot codices" {Jerome, 'Praefatio in libro Iosue', in *Biblia sacra*, pp. 285–286, at p. 285}? Equidem nihil ipse adversus Hieronymum non modo dicere sed nec sentire ausim ... sed hoc tamen miror Rome apud summum pontificem, ut sileam de aliis ecclesiis, universa exemplaria fuisse mendosa et, quod non minoris facio, mendosos habuisse codices Ambrosium, quem hic error fallere non poterat, utpote nostri grecique sermonis eruditissimum. Quid dicam de Hilario atque Augustino, qui ambo alter paulo senior, alter vero paulo iunior in eiusdem etatem inciderunt? Hos ac ceteros illius seculi, tanquam religionis nostre luminaria, videtur Hieronymus aut insignis imperitie, quod vitia tanta non deprehenderint, aut nefande negligentie accusare, quod sacros libros a corruptione non vindicaverint.' For the quotation from Jerome's 'Preface to the Gospels', see above, p. 31, n. 7.

times; but after a millennium of manuscript transmission, without proper attempts at emendation, even this version – assuming that it was indeed that of Jerome, as Valla was willing to concede for the sake of argument – must have suffered corruption in every manuscript.[50]

The discrepancies between the biblical quotations in Jerome's commentaries and the Latin text in manuscripts of the Bible further strengthened Valla's theory that Jerome was only partly responsible for the latter. In the *Annotationes*, he points out that the text of Lk 16.2 found in manuscripts differs from a quotation of this passage in the works of Jerome. Valla's explanation is that Jerome had not translated the version found in manuscripts of the Bible. That Jerome might have translated the same passage differently in two separate versions of the Bible, as Bacon argued, was not an option for Valla.[51]

Valla also believed that the Greek Old Testament, like the Latin Bible, existed in various versions which could no longer be disentangled. He asked Poggio to explain to him precisely which rendering should be considered Sacred Scripture, since it was not clear which of the many Greek and Latin versions should be regarded as the one true translation.[52] The New Testament had been rendered into Latin by many translators, as Valla knew from ancient writers; but none of them had provided a faithful translation of the entire Bible. Even in instances when there was a good translation from the Hebrew, as was the case for Jerome's *Psalterium iuxta Hebraeos*, it had not become the commonly read

---

[50] See above, p. 97, n. 41.

[51] Valla, *Annotationes*, p. 837A: '"Redde rationem uillicationis tuae, iam enim amplius non poteris uillicare" [Lk 16.2] … Non fuisse Hieronymum utique qui nouum testamentum ita interpretatus est, uel hinc patet, quod ad Algasiam aliter hunc locum transfert, inquiens: "Redde rationem dispensationis tuae" [Jerome, *Epistulae*, III, p. 22 (CXXI, 7)].' For Bacon, see above, pp. 91–92.

[52] Valla, *Antidotum primum*, p. 112: 'Merito ais me, Pogi, contemnere Scripturam Sacram, qui eam ipse tantopere verearis, cum Herculem, cum Iovem, cum deos omnes testeris. Sed quid est per deos bonos, ut tecum tuis verbis agam, Scriptura Sacra? Omnis ne Veteris Novique Testamenti interpretatio? At ista multiplex est et varia atque hec illi magnopere repugnans. An ignoras ex Hebreo in Grecum primam translationem fuisse septuaginta duorum interpretum, secundam Aquile, tertiam Theodotionis ac deinceps perventum usque ad sextam atque ita apud Grecos Latinosque fuisse incerta omnia? Ubi quid dicas tu esse Sacram Scripturam? Certe nullam nisi veram interpretationem. At hec que sit incertum est.'

version.⁵³ Because there was no satisfactory, let alone inspired, Latin version of Scripture, Valla regarded his emendations as corrections, not of Holy Writ, which would be disrespectful, but rather of its translation, which was an act of piety.⁵⁴

Among fifteenth-century humanists, Valla provides the most detailed comments on the translation and the survival of the Latin Bible. Yet several others also made observations on the transmission of Latin Scripture. In his invective against George of Trebizond, Cardinal Bessarion takes the view that the text of the Bible circulating in manuscripts was Jerome's translation, but in a corrupt state and therefore in need of correction. Like Valla, he absolves Jerome from all responsibility for the mistakes in the Latin Bible; the blame falls instead on scribes.⁵⁵ Bessarion's position that the text of the Latin Bible was Jerome's was probably a concession to his opponent, George of Trebizond. Since, for Bessarion, the only relevant text of the New Testament was the original Greek, it was irrelevant to his argument which Latin translation was circulating in manuscripts of the Bible.

Giannozzo Manetti, in his *Apologeticus*, discusses the previous Latin versions of the Psalms attributed to Jerome. While ascribing to him a version made from the Septuagint – in reality, Jerome's first revision of the Psalms, rather than a translation, as Manetti believed – and the *Psalterium iuxta Hebraeos*, he, like Bacon, did not regard him as the translator of the *Gallicanum*. Many people, he claims, do not know who translated the *Gallicanum*. Even worse, some actually contend that it was Jerome. According to Manetti, however, it was not reasonable to assume that he had made two different translations of the Psalms from the Greek.⁵⁶

---

⁵³ Ibid., p. 112: 'Ita in Testamento Novo, cuius multi fuere interpretes, ut ex veteribus scriptoribus licet cognoscere. At – inquies – Hieronymus utrunque Testamentum postea transtulit. Utinam quidem utrunque sincerum haberemus, si modo eum omnes ecclesie receperunt! Sed cur in multis eum non frequentamus veluti in Psalmis secundum Hebraicam veritatem?' For Augustine and Jerome on the multitude of Latin translators of the Bible, see above, p. 29, n. 2.

⁵⁴ See below, p. 264, n. 57.

⁵⁵ See above, p. 73, n. 86, and Bessarion, *In illud Evangelii*, col. 630C: 'Quod si dissentiat, an id facile potuerit dormitantium librariorum vitio fieri, et an in aliis quoque simile aliquid fieri potuerit factumve sit absque sancti doctoris peritissimique interpretis Hieronymi culpa aut reprehensione.'

⁵⁶ Giannozzo Manetti, *Apologeticus*, ed. A. de Petris, Rome 1981, pp. 55–56 (II, 83–84): 'Patet ergo ex his que dicta et explicata sunt, duas ipsius *Psalterii* esse

Manetti thus attributed to an unknown translator the most successful Latin version of the Psalms, the *Gallicanum*, which was, in reality, Jerome's second reworking of the Vetus Latina Psalter, based on Origen's Hexapla, and which had almost always – Roger Bacon is a notable exception[57] – been assigned to him.

A few decades later, in the 1480s, Giovanni Crastone expressed his doubts about who had translated the Latin Bible and about which version should be attributed to Jerome. In the preface to his bi-lingual edition of the Psalms, he writes:

> Dicant mihi theologi hujus temporis quaenam sit Hieronymi si norunt: interpretatio. Quid irrident? Nonne respondent: Est ea cui ipsius praepositas vides prefationes? Pace vestra O theologi, dixisse velim. Hieronymum ipsi negligentiae aut imperitiae accusatis. Non est ... hujus praefatiunculae enumerare quot loca depravata depraehenderim in utroque testamento: quorum etsi nonnulla librariorum vitio facta sint, multa sane sunt interpretum: quae cum exemplaria quae Hieronymi dicuntur invaserint, quia defendi nequeunt, ego Hieronymi inficior. Quid ergo? Libere fateor nos nescire quae sit Hieronymi interpretatio.[58]

> Let today's theologians tell me which translation is Jerome's, if they know. Why do they laugh? Do they not reply: 'It is the one which you see preceded by his prologues'? Theologians, if only I could have spoken with your conviction! You yourselves are accusing Jerome of negligence and inexperience! It is not the aim of this little preface to list how many corrupt passages I rejected in both Testaments. Even if some of those corruptions were due to the fault of scribes, many are certainly those of the translators. Because these have invaded the manuscripts which are said to contain Jerome's version, I refuse to acknowledge them as Jerome's, since they cannot be defended. What

---

et quidem celeberrimas Hieronymi interpretationes: alteram scilicet de greco quam Septuaginta duorum fuisse constat, alteram de hebreo in latinum sermonem; licet tertia vulgo circunferatur, quam *Gallicanam* dicunt et apud quosdam in usu habetur, sed unde prodierit quisve auctor fuerit, a plerisque ignoratur et presertim ab illis qui id qualecunque sit, a Hieronymo emanasse contendunt et hoc idem sese scire profitentur, haud intelligentes hanc ipsam *Psalterii* interpretationem nisi bifariam, alteram e greco, alteram vero ex hebreo in latinum eloquium traductionem presertim ab eodem interprete probabiliter fieri non potuisse, nisi iam non unam, sed duas *Psalterii* interpretationes ab eo (instar Aquile, quem primam et secundam totius veteris Testamenti traductionem ... edidisse tradunt) factas fuisse allegarent. Quod mihi pluribus de causis non fit verisimile.'

[57] See above, pp. 90–91.
[58] Crastone, [Dedicatory letter], pp. 13–14.

then? I freely admit that we do not know which translation is Jerome's.

Crastone thus rejects the theologians' claim that the text in a biblical manuscript containing Jerome's prefaces must be his version. In addition, he not only assumes that Jerome's translation cannot be re-established but is also convinced that the version circulating in manuscripts of the Bible was translated by an unidentified person or persons.

To sum up: a surprising feature of textual critics' understanding of the transmission of the Latin Bible, which has so far been overlooked in modern scholarship, was the widespread belief that the text which circulated in manuscripts of the Bible was not a corrupt version of Jerome's translation but rather either a mixture of various translations or an unidentified version. Not even Jerome's prefaces induced them to think otherwise, nor, for the period examined here, was the presence of these prefaces in manuscripts of the Bible ever used by textual critics as evidence to prove that the translation they contained was Jerome's. Indeed, Jerome's prefaces were very rarely brought up in the context of identifying Latin translations of the Bible and were expressly discounted by both Hugh of St Cher and Crastone.

It was hardly ever claimed that the text in manuscripts of the Bible could be ascribed to a particular translator or identified with a particular version. Only Gerard of Huy, Roger Bacon – who, as we shall see, was probably heavily influenced by Gerard – and Cardinal Bessarion explicitly stated that the version of the Bible in Latin manuscripts was Jerome's,[59] though all three admitted that the text was extremely corrupt and in need of emendation.

Two scholars discussed Jerome's involvement in the *Gallicanum*, his second reworking of the Psalms, which came to dominate the Latin tradition. Roger Bacon concluded that it was wrong to assume that Jerome was the translator, since the base text was the *septuaginta*; but he did not provide any details as to what role he thought Jerome had played in the making of the *Gallicanum*. Two centuries later, Giannozzo Manetti rejected any claims for Jerome's involvement in the *Gallicanum*.

---

[59] Other fifteenth-century scholars who certainly believed that the translation in Bible manuscripts was Jerome's, but did not explicitly voice their opinion on this matter, are George of Trebizond and Poggio. For the relationship between Bacon and Gerard, see below, pp. 143–146.

Despite questions as to whether Jerome had translated the *Gallicanum* and the widely held view that Bible manuscripts did not transmit his version, no medieval textual critic explicitly doubted that he had translated the entire Bible. The only sceptical voice was that of John in FitzRalph's dialogue, who asserted that, apart from their own statements, there was no proof that those who claimed to have translated the Bible into Latin had actually done so. Yet even John did not name Jerome. It was not until the fifteenth century that Lorenzo Valla pointed out that, according to what Jerome himself had written in his 'Preface to the Gospels', he had not, in fact, translated the complete New Testament but had merely corrected passages which disagreed in sense from the original Greek.[60]

As Rice has noted, several scholars referred to the incongruity between the Latin translation of the Bible cited in Jerome's commentaries and the version which circulated in biblical manuscripts.[61] Yet textual critics devised viable solutions for this apparent problem, whether it was by claiming, as Bacon did, that Jerome had made two translations, or by maintaining, as Valla did, that the version in manuscripts of the Bible was not Jerome's translation.

Medieval and early Renaissance textual critics often presented quite sophisticated notions about the text of the Latin Bible. They were aware that the texts they held in their hands were amalgams of different versions, which had suffered corruption due to inattentive or overly zealous scribes and to the misguided efforts of theologians. Having explored their views on which biblical text they thought they were reading, we shall now examine what they said about the different textual traditions and the manuscript transmission of the Bible.

---

[60] This was noted by Hamilton, 'Humanists and the Bible', p. 104, and Bentley, *Humanists and Holy Writ*, p. 50. Bentley insists that Valla was able to take 'such a critical stand partly because he denied the traditional belief that St Jerome translated the Vulgate New Testament'. For Valla's statement, see above, p. 96, n. 39.

[61] Rice, *Saint Jerome*, p. 175.

III.2 VIEWS OF THE TEXTUAL TRADITIONS AND THEIR MANUSCRIPT TRANSMISSION

As a basic requirement for re-establishing a faithful Latin text of the Bible, textual critics needed to determine which manuscripts should be consulted for its reconstruction. For this, the value of various traditions and versions needed to be assessed. For medieval scholars, the focus of these assessments was almost invariably the Old Testament, for which the status of the original Hebrew, the *septuaginta*, and the Vulgate had to be evaluated. The New Testament played a comparatively minor role in these discussions, but became more prominent among fifteenth-century humanists. In addition, besides the various versions of the Bible, other sources which transmitted the text of the Bible in extracts, such as the works of the Church Fathers, were also taken into consideration.

During the time period examined in this study, several different opinions can be identified. These include: a pronounced preference for manuscripts in the original languages, at one extreme; to an acceptance of Hebrew and Greek readings only if they could also be found in the Latin tradition; and an exclusive reliance on a single, select Latin manuscript, at the other extreme. In this chapter, I shall first give an overview of the statements concerning the authority of different versions of the Bible and the collation of biblical manuscripts made by Jerome and Augustine. The main part of the chapter will be devoted to the views expressed from the twelfth to the fifteenth century about the different textual traditions of the Bible and their manuscript transmission.

Jerome and Augustine

Medieval authors found a number of remarks on the relative authority of the Hebrew, Greek, and Latin traditions of the Bible in the writings of Jerome and Augustine. Jerome, in particular, served as a model for later textual critics. As a biblical translator and editor, he had aimed to produce a new version of Latin Scripture based on the original Hebrew and Greek. In his version of the Old Testament this editorial preference is apparent in his practice of marking verses with obeli and asterisks to indicate omissions and additions with respect to the Hebrew text.¹ To place his work on an even firmer footing, Jerome did not simply rely on a single Hebrew manuscript, but instead collated different Hebrew manuscripts and made judgements on their readings.²

Jerome's reliance on the Hebrew text rather than the Septuagint for his Latin version of the Old Testament was a novelty; and he not only adopted this approach of going back to the original language in his translation but also advocated it in many of his commentaries and letters. He consistently took the view that it was necessary to go beyond the Latin tradition and to consult the original roots of the Bible. One of his main arguments for this approach was that, in contrast to the Septuagint and its Old Latin derivatives, the Hebrew tradition contained a faithful text. For instance, in his 'Prologue to Job', Jerome explains that the Greek version of this book is heavily mutilated; therefore, for his translation, he went back to the original, which has the complete text.³

---

[1] For a comment by Jerome on this practice, see, e.g., his, 'Praefatio in libro Psalmorum', p. 767: 'Commoneo ... ut quae diligenter emendavi, cum cura et diligentia transcribantur. Notet sibi unusquisque vel iacentem lineam vel signa radiantia, id est vel obelos vel asteriscos'; see also below, p. 106, n. 3. Many of the examples from Jerome used in this chapter are derived from Karl Kelchner Hulley, 'Principles of Textual Criticism Known to Jerome', *Harvard Studies in Classical Philology* 55 (1944), pp. 87–109. Other passages have been taken from Jenkins and Preston, *Biblical Scholarship*, pp. 3–26.

[2] See, e.g., Jerome, 'In Abacuc Prophetam', in his *Commentarii in prophetas minores*, II, pp. 579–654, at p. 616 (I, ii, 19.20): 'Praeterea sciendum in quibusdam Hebraicis uoluminibus non esse additum *omnis* sed absolute *spiritum* legi'; Jerome, *Epistulae*, II, p. 257 (CVI, 20): '"Omnia ossa mea dicent: Domine." [Ps 34.10] Pro quo in Graeco bis *domine* inuenisse uos dicitis. Sed sciendum, quod multa sint exemplaria apud Hebraeos, quae ne semel quidem *dominum* habeant.' See also Graves, *Jerome's Hebrew Philology*, p. 54. For the history of the Hebrew text, see Otto Eissfeldt, *Einleitung in das Alte Testament*, 3rd edn, Tübingen 1964, pp. 907–40.

[3] Jerome, 'Prologus in libro Job', p. 729: 'Neque enim fieri potest, ut quos plura intermisisse susceperint, non eosdem etiam in quibusdam errasse fateantur, praecipue in Iob, cui si ea quae sub asteriscis addita sunt subtraxeris, pars maxima detruncabitur. Et hoc dumtaxat apud Graecos. Ceterum apud Latinos ante eam translationem quam sub asteriscis et obelis nuper edidimus, septingenti ferme aut octingenti versus sunt, ut decurtatus et laceratus conrosusque liber foeditatem sui publice legentibus praebeat. Haec autem translatio nullum de veteribus sequitur interpretem, sed ex ipso hebraico arabicoque sermone et interdum syro, nunc verba, nunc sensus, nunc simul utrumque resonabit.' For Jerome's reliance on the original, see also Herman Hailperin, 'The Hebrew Heritage of Mediaeval Christian Biblical Scholarship', *Historia judaica* 5 (1943), pp. 133–154, at p. 137.

In his 'Preface to the Pentateuch', he rails against those who disapproved of his return to the Hebrew. The Hebrew manuscripts, Jerome maintains, contain an intact text, more so than others in circulation. He concedes, however, that the Jews may have tampered with Hebrew manuscripts in passages quoted by the Apostles which refer to Christ and that, consequently, in those instances, the Latin manuscripts would be more correct than the Greek ones, and the Greek more correct than the Hebrew. But in Jerome's eyes that does not diminish the value of the original Hebrew manuscripts in their inviolate state.[4] Even though some passages might have been corrupted by the Jews, Jerome is still convinced of the superiority of the Hebrew tradition. For instance, in his commentary on Galatians, he compares Latin passages of the Old Testament both with the Septuagint and with Hebrew manuscripts. Accusing the Jews of having corrupted their own manuscripts – a futile act, since the correct text was preserved in older textual witnesses in the possession of other peoples – he says that he decided to follow the version found in Hebrew manuscripts owned by Samaritans.[5] The allegation that Jews tampered with their manuscripts often crops up in Jerome's work and would become an important and contentious issue in medieval discussions on the value of Hebrew manuscripts for the establishment of the correct Latin text of the Bible.[6]

In the twelfth century, Jerome's remark in his 'Preface to the Pentateuch' about the superiority of Latin manuscripts in the special case when the original Hebrew had been corrupted was

---

[4] Jerome, 'Prologus in Pentateucho', p. 4: 'Quid livore torqueris? Quid inperitorum animos contra me concitas? Sicubi tibi in translatione videor errare, interroga Hebraeos, diversarum urbium magistros consule: quod illi habent de Christo, tui codices non habent. Aliud est, si contra se postea ab Apostolis usurpata testimonia probaverunt, et emendatiora sunt exemplaria latina quam graeca, graeca quam hebraea! Verum haec contra invidos.'

[5] See Jerome, *Commentarii in Epistulam Pauli Apostoli ad Galatas*, ed. G. Raspanti, Turnhout 2006, pp. 83–84 (II, 3, 10), esp. p. 84: 'Samaritanorum hebraea uolumina relegens inueni "chol" [Dt 27.26], quod interpretatur "omnis" siue "omnibus", scriptum esse et cum Septuaginta interpretibus concordare. Frustra igitur illud tulerunt Iudaei ne uiderentur esse sub maledicto si non possent omnia complere quae scripta sunt, cum antiquiores alterius quoque gentis litterae id positum fuisse testentur.'

[6] For a study of the claims that Jews had falsified their manuscripts, see also Irven M. Resnick, 'The Falsification of Scripture and Medieval Christian and Jewish Polemics', *Medieval Encounters* 2 (1996), pp. 344–380.

taken out of context and interpreted as indicating that he preferred Latin manuscripts to those in the original language in all circumstances.[7] There is no doubt, however, that Jerome was an unwavering advocate of going back to manuscripts in the original language.[8] In fact, his reverence for the original went so far that on occasion, Jerome disregarded the entire Latin manuscript tradition. For instance, even though Latin manuscripts were unanimous in giving the reading *ardeam* in 1 Co 13.3 he noted that the Greek ones had two very similar readings, differing in only one letter: καυθήσομαι (i.e., *ardeam*) and καυχήσομαι (i.e., *glorier*); and, on this basis, he decided to follow the second Greek reading, discounting the Latin tradition.[9]

Jerome was sceptical of the possibility of correcting passages of Scripture by means of quotations found in other biblical books. In his commentary on the prophet Micah, he first juxtaposes his own translation and the Vetus Latina version of Mi 5.2 and then adduces a parallel from Matthew containing an excerpt from the same passage, though with discrepancies. Jerome points out that the quotation in Matthew varies considerably from its source. He,

[7] This can be seen in the decretist tradition on Gratian, *Decretum Magistri Gratiani*, in *Corpus iuris canonici*, I, ed. E. Friedberg, Graz 1959, col. 17 (D. 9, c. 6), where an excerpt from the passage is quoted; for an example, see below, p. 171, n. 190; and J. Cornelia Linde, '"Augustine" versus Jerome: Commentaries on Gratian's *Decretum*, D. 9, c. 6, from Paucapalea to Juan de Torquemada', *Tijdschrift voor Rechtsgeschiedenis* 77 (2009), pp. 367–384. The *Decretum* and the decretists exerted a powerful influence on some of the authors discussed in this study, such as Hervaeus of Bourg-Dieu (see, e.g., below, p. 204, n. 14) and Henry Totting (see below, p. 171).

[8] For other examples of Jerome's support for the original language, see, e.g., Jerome, *Epistulae*, II, p. 6 (LXXI, 5): 'Ut enim ueterum librorum fides de Hebraeis uoluminibus examinanda est, ita nouorum Graeci sermonis normam desiderat'; ibid., II, p. 249 (CVI, 3): 'Sicut autem in nouo testamento, si quando apud Latinos quaestio exoritur et est inter exemplaria uarietas, recurrimus ad fontem Graeci sermonis, quo nouum scriptum est instrumentum, ita et in ueteri testamento, si quando inter Graecos Latinosque diuersitas est, ad Hebraicam confugimus ueritatem, ut, quicquid de fonte proficiscitur, hoc quaeramus in riuulis.'

[9] See Jerome, *Commentarii in Epistulam Pauli*, p. 203 (III, 5, 26): 'Scio in latinis codicibus in eo testimonio quod supra posui, "si tradidero corpus meum ut glorier" [1 Co 13.3], *ardeam* habere pro *glorier*, sed ob similitudinem uerbi, quia apud Graecos *ardeam* et *glorier*, id est καυθήσομαι et καυχήσομαι, una litterae parte distinguitur, apud nostros error inoleuit. Sed et apud ipsos Graecos exemplaria sunt diuersa.' Weber's edition of the Vulgate, however, gives the reading '*ardeam*' in this passage.

therefore, rejects this method of reconstructing the text on the ground that the Evangelists and Apostles could well have quoted from memory without having the actual texts to hand, thus unwittingly introducing errors.[10]

Another important concept regularly expressed in Jerome's writings is that old manuscripts are superior to more recent ones. Justifying his edition of the Gospels, he stresses that it is based on the collation of old Greek manuscripts.[11] As we shall see, this belief in the superiority of old manuscripts persisted throughout the Middle Ages and early Renaissance.

The status of the Septuagint was a matter of dispute between Jerome and Augustine. In Jerome's eyes, the story surrounding the translation's origin was a false legend, and the Septuagint should by no means be considered an inspired text.[12] Furthermore, since the

[10] Jerome, 'In Michaeam', pp. 481–482 (II, v, 2): "'Et tu, Bethleem Ephrata, paruulus es in millibus Iuda; ex te mihi egredietur qui sit dominator in Israel, et egressus eius ab initio a diebus aeternitatis." [Mi 5.2] LXX: *Et tu, Bethleem domus Ephrata, minima es, ut sis in millibus Iuda; ex te mihi egredietur, ut sit in principem Israel, et egressus eius ab initio ex diebus saeculi*. In Euangelio secundum Matthaeum, cum magi de oriente uenissent, et Herodes a scribis quaereret, ubinam Christus Dominus nasceretur, respondisse narratur: *In Bethleem terra Iuda*, qui prophetae testimonium addentes dixerunt: "Et tu, Bethleem terra Iuda, nequaquam minima es in principibus Iuda; ex te enim egredietur dux, qui regat populum meum Israel" [Mt 2.6]. Quod testimonium nec Hebraico, nec Septuaginta interpretibus conuenire, me quoque tacente perspicuum est ... Sunt autem qui asserant, in omnibus pene testimoniis, quae de ueteri testamento sumuntur, istiusmodi esse errorem, ut aut ordo mutetur, aut uerba, et interdum sensus quoque ipse diuersus sit, uel apostolis, uel euangelistis non ex libro carpentibus testimonia, sed memoriae credentibus, quae nonnumquam fallitur.'

[11] Jerome, 'Praefatio in Evangelio', p. 1515: 'Igitur haec praesens praefatiuncula pollicetur quattuor tantum evangelia ... codicum graecorum emendata conlatione sed veterum.' For Jerome's view of old manuscripts, see also Hulley, 'Principles', pp. 92–93. Cassiodorus, likewise, emphasised that he had collated old manuscripts of the Bible; see Cassiodorus, *Institutiones*, ed. R. A. B. Mynors, Oxford 1937, p. 8 (I praefatio 8): 'Quos ego cunctos novem codices auctoritatis divinae ... sub collatione priscorum codicum amicis ante me legentibus sedula lectione transivi.'

[12] Jerome, 'Prologus in Pentateucho', pp. 3–4: 'Nescio quis primus auctor septuaginta cellulas Alexandriae mendacio suo extruxerit, quibus divisi eadem scriptitarint, cum Aristheus eiusdem Ptolomei υπερασπιστης et multo post tempore Iosepphus nihil tale rettulerint, sed in una basilica congregatos contulisse scribant, non prophetasse. Aliud est enim vatem, aliud esse interpretem ... Nisi forte putandus est Tullius Oeconomicum Xenofontis ... afflatus rethorico spiritu transtulisse, aut aliter de hisdem libris per Septuaginta interpretes, aliter per Apostolos Spiritus Sanctus testimonia

Septuagint was translated before the coming of Christ, what had been treated by the Greek translators as hesitant prophecies of Jesus Christ by Jerome's time had become historical events, and this enabled him to provide a more accurate translation.[13] Yet, in a letter to Pammachius, Jerome concedes that despite all the divergences from the Hebrew original, the *septuaginta* was rightly chosen as the authoritative version in the churches. There were two reasons for this choice: first, it was the earliest translation, made before the birth of Jesus Christ; and, secondly, it was the version used by the Apostles.[14]

The presence and general acceptance of the Vetus Latina made it problematic to justify a new Latin version of Scripture. In defending his own translation, Jerome stresses, in his 'Prologue to Job', that his aim was by no means to criticise the previous Latin rendering, based on the Septuagint, but rather to provide a more complete, clear and correct version. Those who wanted to continue reading the *septuaginta* were free to do so and should not feel obliged to use his translation.[15] So, even though he acknowledged the Church's official recognition of the *septuaginta*, Jerome sought

texuit, ut quod illi tacuerunt, hii scriptum esse mentiti sunt.' For the legend of the Septuagint, see above, pp. 8–9.

[13] Ibid., p. 4: 'Illi interpretati sunt ante adventum Christi et quod nesciebant dubiis protulere sententiis, nos post passionem et resurrectionem eius non tam prophetiam quam historiam scribimus; aliter enim audita, aliter visa narrantur: quod melius intellegimus, melius et proferimus.' As we shall see later on, the fact that the Seventy translated the Old Testament before the birth of Christ could also be interpreted as an advantage for the *septuaginta*; see, e.g., below, p. 113.

[14] Jerome, *Epistulae*, I, p. 523 (LVII, 11, 2): 'Porro, quanta dimiserint {*sc.* Septuaginta translatores}, uel asterisci, ut dixi, testes sunt uel nostra interpretatio, si a diligenti lectore translationi ueteri conferatur: et tamen iure Septuaginta editio obtinuit in ecclesiis, uel quia prima est et ante Christi fertur aduentum uel quia ab apostolis, in quibus tamen ab Hebraico non discrepat, usurpata.'

[15] See, e.g., Jerome, 'Prologus in libro Job', p. 730: 'Audiant quapropter canes mei idcirco me in hoc volumine laborasse, non ut interpretationem antiquam reprehenderem sed ut ea quae in illa aut obscura sunt aut omissa aut certe scriptorum vitio depravata, manifestiora nostra interpretatione fierent.... Habeant qui volunt veteres libros'; and Jerome, *Epistulae*, II, p. 390 (CXII, 20, 4): 'Ego enim non tam uetera abolere conatus sum, quae linguae meae hominibus emendata de Graeco in Latinum transtuli, quam ea testimonia, quae a Iudaeis praetermissa sunt uel corrupta, proferre in medium, ut scirent nostri, quid Hebraea ueritas contineret. Si cui legere non placet, nemo conpellit inuitum.'

to reduce the authority of the *Vetus Latina*, with which his own version was in competition, by undermining its claim to be made from an inspired Greek translation. Yet, at least according to his own statements, he did not intend to abolish its use, nor was he in a position to do so.

Augustine held a position contrary to that of Jerome with regard to the *septuaginta*. In *De civitate Dei*, written after 410, he presents a detailed defence of the *septuaginta*. It was his conviction that it was divinely inspired and that the legend surrounding its origin was true.[16] Its authority, which initially derived from the letter of Aristeas, was further enhanced, according to Augustine, by the Greek Church's exclusive use of the Septuagint and the Latin's of the *Vetus Latina*; for even though there were other Greek translations in circulation and even though Jerome had produced a new Latin version from the Hebrew, the Latin churches nevertheless preferred the *septuaginta*.[17]

Although Jerome and his younger contemporary Augustine never met, they exchanged several letters, in which, among other things, they set out their opposing views on the translations of the Bible. Not only, as we have just seen, was Augustine a staunch supporter of the *septuaginta*, but he also expressly opposed Jerome's decision to translate the Old Testament from Hebrew instead of from the Septuagint. In a letter addressed to Jerome, Augustine first

---

[16] See, e.g., Augustine, *De civitate Dei*, p. 638 (XVIII, 42): 'Traditur sane tam mirabilem ac stupendum planeque diuinum in eorum uerbis fuisse consensum, ut, cum ad hoc opus separatim singuli sederint (ita enim eorum fidem Ptolomaeo placuit explorare), in nullo uerbo, quod idem significaret et tantundem ualeret, uel in uerborum ordine alter ab altero discreparet; sed tamquam unus esset interpres, ita quod omnes interpretati sunt unum erat; quoniam re uera spiritus erat unus in omnibus. Et ideo tam mirabile Dei munus acceperant, ut illarum scripturarum non tamquam humanarum, sed, sicut erant, tamquam diuinarum etiam isto modo commendaretur auctoritas, credituris quandoque gentibus profutura, quod iam uidemus effectum.' For a summary of Augustine's opinion of the *septuaginta*, see also Jenkins and Preston, *Biblical Scholarship*, pp. 18–21.

[17] Augustine, *De civitate Dei*, pp. 638–639 (XVIII, 43): 'Nam cum fuerint et alii interpretes, qui ex Hebraea lingua in Graecam sacra illa eloquia transtulerunt ... hanc tamen, quae Septuaginta est, tamquam sola esset, sic recepit ecclesia, eaque utuntur Graeci populi Christiani, quorum plerique utrum alia sit aliqua ignorant. Ex hac Septuaginta interpretatione etiam in Latinam linguam interpretatum est, quod ecclesiae Latinae tenent; quamuis non defuerit temporibus nostris presbyter Hieronymus, homo doctissimus et omnium trium linguarum peritus, qui non ex Graeco, sed ex Hebraeo in Latinum eloquium easdem scripturas conuerterit.'

stated that he did not see the need for Jerome's rendering of Job from the original, and then put forward several objections to this approach. First, Augustine was worried that the divergent texts would lead to disharmony between the Greek and the Latin Churches. Secondly, translating from the Hebrew would entail the problem that no one could check whether or not the rendering was faithful because Christians did not know Hebrew; and if one consulted Jews on this matter, they might provide wrong answers, so that Jerome alone would be capable of defending his version against accusations and false claims. Since Greek was much more widely known, this problem would not exist if Jerome had instead translated from the Septuagint.[18] Moreover, congregations were used to the Vetus Latina; consequently, when a certain bishop attempted to introduce Jerome's translation, his reading of a well-known passage in this new and unaccustomed version provoked such turmoil that he had to renounce his plan in order to preserve his flock. Augustine reprimands Jerome for not taking into account the powerful hold of *consuetudo* on the people.[19]

---

[18] Augustine, *Epistulae*, in his *Opera*, II, 1–5, ed. A. Goldbacher (Corpus Scriptorum Ecclesiasticorum Latinorum, 34; 44; 57; 58), Prague, Vienna and Leipzig 1895–1923, II, p. 252 (71, II, 4): 'Ego sane mallem Graecas potius canonicas te nobis interpretari scripturas, quae septuaginta interpretum perhibentur. Perdurum erit enim, si tua interpretatio per multas ecclesias frequentius coeperit lectitari, quod a Graecis ecclesiis Latinae ecclesiae dissonabunt, maxime quia facile contradictor conuincitur Graeco prolato libro, id est linguae notissimae. Quisquis autem in eo, quod ex Hebraeo translatum est, aliquo insolito permotus fuerit et falsi crimen intenderit, uix aut numquam ad Hebraea testimonia peruenitur, quibus defendatur obiectum. Quod si etiam peruentum fuerit, tot Latinas et Graecas auctoritates damnari quis ferat? Huc accedit, quia etiam consulti Hebraei possunt aliud respondere, ut tu solus necessarius uidearis, qui etiam ipsos possis conuincere, sed tamen, quo iudice, mirum si potueris inuenire.' For Jerome's objections to Augustine's conspiracy theory about the Jews, see his *Epistulae*, II, p. 391 (CXII, 21, 1): 'Dices: "Quid, si Hebraei aut respondere noluerint aut mentiri uoluerint?" Tota frequentia Iudaeorum in mea interpretatione reticebit? Nullus inueniri poterit, qui Hebraeae linguae habeat notitiam, aut omnes imitabuntur illos Iudaeos, quos dicis in Africae repertos oppidulo in meam calumniam conspirasse?'

[19] Augustine, *Epistulae*, II, p. 253 (71, III, 5): 'Quidam frater noster episcopus cum lectitari instituisset in ecclesia, cui praeest, interpretationem tuam, mouit quiddam longe aliter abs te positum apud Ionam prophetam, quam erat omnium sensibus memoriaeque inueteratum et tot aetatum successionibus decantatum. Factus est tantus tumultus in plebe maxime Graecis arguentibus et inflammantibus calumniam falsitatis, ut cogeretur episcopus ... Iudaeorum testimonium flagitare. Utrum autem illi inperitia an

In another letter, Augustine comments on Jerome's project of translating the Old Testament, including passages that allegedly had been left out or corrupted by the Jews. He cautions Jerome and calls on him to consider whether this supposed intervention by Jews took place before the coming of Christ, when, in Augustine's view, there was no reason for them, when translating the Old Testament into Greek, to introduce deliberate errors, or after, when they had good cause to omit or corrupt passages in Greek manuscripts because they were worried that these testimonies might persuade Jews to accept the Christian faith.[20] This standpoint amounts, once more, to a strong defence of the Septuagint, since it had been translated by Jewish scholars from Hebrew into Greek long before the coming of Christ and was therefore free from the suspicion of having been altered.

In *De civitate Dei*, Augustine brings up a similar argument to refute the theory that Jews had corrupted their manuscripts. Discussing the different dates assigned to the death of Methusaleh in the Hebrew original and the Septuagint, he writes that neither the Jews nor the Seventy translators could possibly be accused of having tampered with the text. Although it was commonly believed that the Jews might have unanimously decided to corrupt the text of the Bible, this seems improbable, first, on account of their wide dispersion and, secondly, because there is no reason why they should have wanted to remove the truth from their manuscripts. Looking at the bare facts, Augustine argues, it seems more credible that the Seventy translators, all of whom were Jewish and were translating in the same building at the same time, would have

> malitia hoc esse in Hebraeis codicibus responderunt, quod et Graeci et Latini habebant atque dicebant? ... Coactus est homo uelut mendositatem corrigere uolens post magnum periculum non remanere sine plebe unde etiam nobis uidetur aliquando te quoque in nonnullis falli potuisse et uide, hoc quale sit in eis litteris, quae non possunt conlatis usitatarum linguarum testimoniis emendari.' For Jerome's response to this incident, see his *Epistulae*, II, pp. 391–393 (CXII, 21–22). The important role of *consuetudo* is also discussed below, pp. 201–216.
>
> [20] Augustine, *Epistulae*, II, p. 385 (82, V, 34): 'De interpretatione tua iam mihi persuasisti, qua utilitate scripturas uolueris transferre de Hebraeis, ut scilicet ea, quae a Iudaeis praetermissa uel corrupta sunt, proferres in medium. Sed peto insinuare digneris, a quibus Iudaeis, utrum ab eis ipsis, qui ante aduentum domini interpretati sunt, et, si ita est, quibus uel quonam eorum, an ab istis posterius, qui propterea putari possunt aliqua de codicibus Graecis uel subtraxisse uel in eis corrupisse, ne illis testimoniis de Christiana fide conuincerentur. Illi autem anteriores cur hoc facere uoluerint, non inuenio.'

banded together and corrupted their translation.[21] Both ideas, however, are inconceivable. Instead, it is more likely that the source of the discrepancy was a scribal error which could have occurred when the Septuagint first began to be copied; from there, the mistake was diffused throughout the Greek manuscript tradition.[22] This leads Augustine to conclude that when two texts differ over a matter of established fact, concerning which they cannot both be correct, then the one in the original language is more reliable than the translation.[23]

In the next chapter, he considers readings in the *septuaginta* which differ from the Hebrew text but which cannot be ascribed to scribal error and which are also consistent with the truth, *veritas*. In those instances, he maintains that the disagreements should not be regarded as mistakes, but rather should be interpreted as deliberate departures from the Hebrew by the Seventy translators, acting as divinely inspired prophets.[24] This strengthens the authority of the

---

[21] Augustine, *De civitate Dei*, pp. 467–472 (XV, 11–13).

[22] Ibid., pp. 470–471 (XV, 13): 'Sed absit ut prudens quispiam uel Iudaeos cuiuslibet peruersitatis atque malitiae tantum potuisse credat in codicibus tam multis et tam longe lateque dispersis, uel septuaginta illos memorabiles uiros hoc de inuidenda gentibus ueritate unum communicasse consilium. Credibilius ergo quis dixerit, cum primum de bibliotheca Ptolomaei describi ista coeperunt, tunc aliquid tale fieri potuisse in codice uno, sed primitus inde descripto, unde iam latius emanaret; ubi potuit quidem accidere etiam scriptoris error.'

[23] Ibid., p. 472 (XV, 13): 'Recte fieri nullo modo dubitauerim, ut, cum diuersum aliquid in utrisque codicibus inuenitur, quando quidem ad fidem rerum gestarum utrumque esse non potest uerum, ei linguae potius credatur, unde est in aliam per interpretes facta translatio. Nam in quibusdam etiam codicibus Graecis tribus et uno Latino et uno etiam Syro inter se consentientibus inuentus est Mathusalem sex annis ante diluuium fuisse defunctus.'

[24] Ibid., p. 474 (XV, 14): 'Illa uero numerorum uarietas, quae inter codices Hebraeos inuenitur et nostros, neque de hac antiquorum longaeuitate dissentit, et si quid habet ita diuersum, ut uerum esse utrumque non possit, rerum gestarum fides ab ea lingua repetenda est, ex qua interpretatum est quod habemus. Quae facultas cum uolentibus ubique gentium praesto sit, non tamen uacat, quod septuaginta interpretes in plurimis, quae diuersa dicere uidentur, ex Hebraeis codicibus emendare ausus est nemo. Non enim est illa diuersitas putata mendositas; nec ego ullo modo putandam existimo: Sed ubi non est scriptoris error, aliquid eos diuino spiritu, ubi sensus esset consentaneus ueritati et praedicans ueritatem, non interpretantium munere, sed prophetantium libertate aliter dicere uoluisse credendum est. Vnde merito non solum Hebraeis, uerum etiam ipsis, cum adhibet testimonia de scripturis, uti apostolica inuenitur auctoritas.'

septuaginta without contradicting his earlier statement that in normal circumstances the original is to be preferred to the translation.

Augustine, like Jerome, believed in the usefulness of collation for determining the correct text. After contrasting the innumerable amount of Latin versions of the Bible in circulation with the comparatively small number of Greek translations, he writes in *De doctrina christiana* that 'the inspection of several manuscripts often clarifies obscure passages', thus encouraging the practice of collation.[25] In order to establish which manuscripts should be trusted, Augustine suggests two criteria: either one should follow the text found in the greater number of manuscripts or give preference to older over newer ones. If neither of these criteria resolved the problem, then he recommends that the original text should be consulted.[26]

The writings of Jerome and Augustine provided medieval textual critics with a good deal of material which they could either simply adopt or use as the basis for developing their own opinions on the authority and manuscript transmission of the different textual traditions of the Bible. Both Jerome and Augustine taught them that older manuscripts were superior to more recent ones, a conviction which was embraced throughout the period examined here. Another recurrent point mentioned by both of the Church Fathers was the suggestion that the Jews might have tampered with the text of their own Hebrew manuscripts. This accusation had a strong impact on medieval attitudes towards the authority of Hebrew codices. Augustine, however, explicitly rejected this allegation. He also firmly dismissed the possibility, which he himself had raised, that the Jewish translators of the Septuagint might have intentionally corrupted the later Greek tradition.

As we have seen, Jerome and Augustine presented opposite views on the authority of the Septuagint and its Latin translation and on

---

[25] See above, p. 29, n. 2, for the quotation from Augustine and the statements about the many translators.

[26] Augustine, *Contra Faustum*, pp. 315–316 (XI, 2): 'Itaque si de fide exemplarium quaestio uerteretur, sicut in nonnullis, quae et paucae sunt et sacrarum litterarum studiosis notissimae sententiarum uarietates, uel ex aliarum regionum codicibus, unde ipsa doctrina commeauit, nostra dubitatio diiudicaretur, uel si ibi quoque codices uariarent, plures paucioribus aut uetustiores recentioribus praeferrentur: et si adhuc esset incerta uarietas, praecedens lingua, unde illud interpretatum est, consuleretur.'

the necessity of a new version based on the Hebrew. Augustine followed a more traditionalist path, defending the *septuaginta*, the truthfulness of the legend surrounding it and the Vetus Latina. He also took into account the importance of common believers and their need for a stable text of the Bible, which had been authorised by the Church. Jerome rejected these notions and aimed to produce a new Latin version, based on the original, but without insisting that anyone was obliged to renounce the earlier translation. We shall now explore how these fundamentally different convictions influenced medieval scholars' judgement regarding the value of the different textual traditions of the Bible for the establishment of a faithful Latin text and the complexities of their manuscript transmission.

The Twelfth Century

In the early twelfth century, the Cistercian Stephen Harding described in his *Monitum* the criteria on which he had based his textual decisions for producing a correct Latin manuscript of the Bible. He recounts how he gathered together Latin manuscripts from various churches and then decided to copy from one which offered a more extensive text than all the others at his disposal. On closer inspection, however, he found that the manuscript contained a text which differed considerably from Jerome's translation, which was commonly in use at the time. Since Harding believed that a translation made by a single translator from a single source could not be subject to such wide variation, he was overcome by doubt over the reliability of his chosen manuscript.[27]

In order to shed light on the problem of these divergent texts, Harding consulted Jews learned in Scripture and asked them to go over the passages in which his 'more complete' manuscript differed from the rest of the Latin tradition. The Jews, however, did not

---

[27] Harding, *Monitum*, p. 416: 'Hanc historiam scribere disponentes inter plurimos libros quos de diversis ecclesiis congregavimus, ut veraciorem sequeremur, in quendam fere ab omnibus multum dissonantem impegimus. Et quia illum pleniorem ceteris repperimus, fidem ei accomodantes, hanc historiam secundum quod in eodem libro inveniebamus scripsimus. Qua digesta, non modice de dissonantia historiarum turbati sumus, quia hoc plena edocet ratio, ut quod ab uno interprete, videlicet beato Iheronimo, quem ceteris interpretibus omissis, nostrates jamjamque susceperunt, de uno hebraice veritatis fonte translatum est, unum debeat sonare.'

have these passages in their Hebrew manuscripts.[28] This evidence, combined with the fact that most Latin manuscripts also lacked the additional passages, led Harding to erase them; these erasures could still be seen, he pointed out, in his manuscript, especially in Kings.[29]

Harding's first step was therefore the collection of various Latin manuscripts, followed by the selection of one as his base text. Only when he noticed the substantial differences between Jerome's version and the manuscript which he had chosen on the ground that it transmitted what he thought was a more complete text did he take the next step towards the establishment of the correct text: with the help of local Jews, Harding collated his manuscript against the Hebrew ones. So, even though his knowledge of Hebrew did not suffice to consult the manuscripts himself, he went to some lengths to determine the text in the original language after he discovered that there was considerable and inexplicable disagreement between his manuscript and the rest of the Latin tradition. Instead of relying solely on his own Latin manuscript, the decisive factor for him was that in the original, that is, the Hebrew tradition, the passages in question were absent. When he had established this, he felt that intervention in the text was justified and set about erasing the superfluous passages in his chosen manuscript.[30]

---

[28] Ibid., pp. 416–417: 'Unde nos multum de discordia nostrorum librorum quos ab uno interprete suscepimus ammirantes, Iudeos quosdam in sua scriptura peritos adivimus, ac diligentissime lingua romana ab eis inquisivimus de omnibus illis scripturarum locis, in quibus ille partes et versus habebantur, quos in nostro predicto exemplari inveniebamus, et jam in hoc nostro opere inserebamus, quosque in aliis multis historiis latinis non inveniebamus; qui suos libros plures coram nobis revolventes, et in locis illis ubi eos rogabamus, hebraicam sive chaldaicam scripturam romanis verbis nobis exponentes, partes vel versus pro quibus turbabamur minime reppererunt.'

[29] Ibid., p. 417: 'Quapropter hebraice atque chaldaice veritati et multis libris latinis qui illa non habebant, sed per omnia duabus illis linguis concordabant credentes, omnia illa superflua prorsus abrasimus, veluti in multis huius libri locis apparet, et precipue in libris regum, ubi major pars erroris inveniebatur.' For Kings, see also above, p. 33, n. 13. For further observations on Harding's manuscript, see Samuel Berger, *Quam notitiam linguae hebraicae habuerint Christiani Medii Aevi temporibus in Gallia*, Paris, 1893, pp. 10–11.

[30] Denifle ('Die Handschriften', p. 472) points out that although Harding's preface gives the impression 'als sei Stephan bei Correctur seiner Bibel einseitig dem Hebräischen gefolgt', in the manuscript itself, marginal notes prove that he also consulted earlier Latin manuscripts. 'Sie {that is, the

Roughly three decades later, Nicolò Maniacutia put forward his view on the authority of biblical manuscripts in the *Suffraganeus bibliothece*. Having discovered that there was no such thing as an absolutely correct manuscript of the Latin Bible, he decided that whenever the Latin manuscripts disagreed among each other, he would follow those which were in agreement with the Hebrew, even if these comprised only a small number of manuscripts.[31] At the same time, he imposed some restrictions on this rule. Aware, for instance, that Jews were thought to have corrupted the Bible in passages opposed to their faith, he insisted that he did not have to rely on explanations from Jews in those places.[32] Nor did he delete passages found in all Latin manuscripts that were not in the Hebrew ones, in order to avoid giving the impression that he was setting up a new text instead of merely correcting a corrupt one.[33]

In his later *Libellus*, Maniacutia defended the authority of Hebrew manuscripts in the guise of a short fictive dialogue between himself and an opponent. As in the *Suffraganeus*, Maniacutia again maintains that the truth has to be found in manuscripts in the original language.[34] His opponent, however, brings up the

marginal notes} bilden gewissermassen die Rechtfertigung für die Correcturen und die Adoptirung des thatsächlichen Textes.'

[31] Maniacutia, [Preface to his *Suffraganeus bibliothece*], pp. 271–272: 'Plura itaque lustrans armaria nequibam hoc adipisci, quia et que a doctis viris dicebantur correcta (unoquoque in suo sensu abundante) adeo discordabant, ut pene quot codices tot exemplaria [Jerome, 'Praefatio in libro Iosue', p. 285] reperirem. Diu denique hesitans, hac deliberacione contentus sum, ut, sicubi exemplariorum numerositas discordaret, his pocius crederem, eciam si fore contingeret pauciora, que cum bibliothecis hebraicis concordarent, veras eorum assertiones arbitrans quibus magistra veritas testimonium perhiberet.'

[32] Ibid., p. 272: 'Quod utique faciens, idcirco dissertores hebraicos suspectos nequaquam habui, quia videlicet in aliquo michi non fuit eorum dissercio necessaria, quod iudaicam manifeste perfidiam impugnaret, cuius nimirum gracia et veritatem occultare et litteram depravare dicuntur.' He does not specify which passages these are.

[33] Ibid., p. 272: 'Sciendum ergo est esse quedam in latinis codicibus que non habent hebrei, ut est illud in Genesi: "Dixit Cain ad Abel fratrem suum" [Gn 4.8]. Quod sequitur: "Egrediamur foras" [Gn 4.8] in hebraico non habetur. Sic et alia plurima. Que quidem, sive Jeronimus in aliis reperta translationibus in sua eciam conexuerit, sive ab alio usu pristino prevalente postmodum conexa sint, nescimus, quia nec unum volumen ubi non habeantur potui reperire ne non tam depravata corrigere, quam nova condere volumina denotarer, subtrahere non presumpsi.'

[34] Maniacutia, *Libellus*, p. 92: 'Cum ergo discordantia repereris inter exemplaria, ad linguam recurre unde translata sunt et de variantibus inter se

argument that the Jews might have wilfully corrupted their manuscripts. Explicitly following the advice of the Church Fathers who had maintained that it was necessary to consult the original, Maniacutia unwaveringly continues to defend the authority of Hebrew manuscripts, unless his opponent can provide proof for his claims.[35] Nevertheless, as in the *Suffraganeus*, even though he held Hebrew manuscripts in great esteem, Maniacutia was not prepared to adopt a reading from the Hebrew if none of his Latin manuscripts supported it.[36]

In the prefaces to his Psalter editions, Maniacutia likewise set out his approach to the use of Latin manuscripts: if they did not agree among themselves, he writes in his preface to the *Psalterium Romanum*, he would follow those closest to the Hebrew; but he would not add or omit anything which was not already added or omitted in another Latin Psalter.[37] The unaccustomed readings he introduces from the Hebrew, he points out, are marked with an א in the margin, indicating their source. Maniacutia's decision to emend the *Psalterium Romanum* on the basis of the Hebrew might seem counter-intuitive. He explains, however, that although the Latin version was a translation from the Greek, the original source was, after all, the Hebrew text.[38] For his introduction to the

voluminibus illi crede quem linguae de qua sumptum est invenies concordare.' This is backed up with quotations from both Jerome (see above, p. 108, n. 8) and Augustine (see above, p. 114, n. 23).

[35] Ibid., p. 92: 'Dices autem: "forsan falsati sunt codices Iudaeorum". Respondebo: "pro dubitatione ista tua non negligam sapientium consilium". Adhuc subiunges: "Ego eos credo falsatores esse." Ad quod inquam: "postquam hoc probaveris respondebo; interim a Patrum monitis non recedam".'

[36] Ibid., p. 107: 'Ipsam sane Bibliothecam hac cautela correxi, ut ubicumque Latina exemplaria, quorum plura collegeram, concordarent, etsi aliter haberet Hebraicum, tangere non praesumerem.'

[37] Maniacutia, [Preface to the *Psalterium Romanum*], p. 6: 'Decreui facere, ut in discordia psalteriorum huius translationis id potius sequerer, quod hebraice ueritatis uideretur tramitem imitari, iugemque consuetudinem etiam in corruptionibus formidans transgredi, nichil ascriberem, quod non posset in aliquo psalterio reperiri, et rursus nichil diminuerem, quod non fuisset prius in aliquo diminutum.' Weber ('Deux préfaces', pp. 7–8) notes that this is his usual method.

[38] Maniacutia, [Preface to the *Psalterium Romanum*], pp. 6–7: 'Sicubi in titulis uel psalmorum serie aut etiam in distinctione punctorum, a quorundam abusione uideor discordare, ne fortuitu accidisse, sed serio factum fore noscatur, א alep hebraicum, quod potest interpretari doctrina, in margine annotaui, per hoc edocens sequi me uoluisse, qui uel littera uel sententia

Psalterium iuxta Hebraeos, when he encountered a disagreement among the Latin manuscripts, he asked a Jew to go through the text with him and noted down which of the various readings seemed to be closest to the truth.[39]

At times, it is not entirely clear whether Maniacutia's references to the Hebrew and to variant readings are suggestions for corrections or merely collations for their own sake.[40] If Maniacutia consistently applied his own principle of not introducing readings which were unattested in the Latin tradition, then he might have recorded the variant readings, at least in part, purely out of scholarly interest or, perhaps, he intended them to serve as notes in case any of the readings eventually turned up in Latin manuscripts.

In the beginning of the *Libellus*, Maniacutia tells a story which might well describe the typical approach to the text of the Bible adopted by scribes copying from more than one manuscript. A monk was correcting an old manuscript of the Bible, adding passages from a new manuscript which he thought had been omitted from his text. Maniacutia saw this and asked the monk how he knew that the new manuscript was more reliable than the old one. The monk replied that he assumed it from the fact that the new manuscript had more text. Maniacutia pointed out that one could just as well turn this argument around, maintaining that the new manuscript was less reliable because it contained superfluous text. Then, going through the fuller text, Maniacutia noticed more additions than he had ever seen. The other monks present did not recognise the additional passages either and asked Maniacutia who

---

hebraicum sunt secuti. Ab eo enim fonte auserunt Greci, qui sunt postmodum propinati Latinis; unde et mendosior abseritur latina translatio translationibus aliis, quia tertio deducta gradu ab Hebreis ad Grecos, a Grecis ad nos peruenit.'

[39] Maniacutia, [Preface to the *Psalterium iuxta Hebraeos*], ed. Weber, 'Deux préfaces', pp. 9-14, at p. 10: 'Huius denique ego discordancia reperiens exemplaria, hebraicum nichilominus dissertorem assumpsi et quicquid ille, singulorum subtilissimus indagator, uerius approbabat diligenter studui exarare.' He also mentions the results of discussions with Jews several times in his *Suffraganeus*, both when collating and when discussing exegesis; see, e.g., Maniacutia, *Suffraganeus*, in B, f. 4ʳ: 'Hebreus pro *bdellio* [Gn 2.12] dicit se habere quoddam genus lapidis preciosi.'

[40] See Denifle, 'Die Handschriften', p. 475. For an example, see, e.g., Maniacutia, *Suffraganeus*, in B, f. 4ʳ: 'Hebreus: "*et divisit deus inter lucem et inter tenebras* [Gn 1.4]" ... Item "*et vidit deus quod bonum*". Raro enim in libris hebraicis reperies *est* vel *esset*.'

was to blame for these errors. He replied that it was the fault of those who placed their conjectures above the source of truth; for if these passages had been added by the translators, they would be present in all the manuscripts. Maniacutia then searched for the dubious passages in other manuscripts, but could find them only in new ones or in those old manuscripts which had been changed in accordance with the new ones. He therefore decided to delete the additional passages from the new manuscript of the Bible and to note down the sections where they had been found.[41]

The hapless monk was not alone in believing that he should include as much text as possible in his manuscript of the Bible. As we have seen, Stephen Harding initially fell into this trap; and, before him, this practice was followed by, among others, Theodulf of Orleans. It may also have been the method adopted by the compilers of the Paris Bible.[42]

---

[41] Maniacutia, *Libellus*, pp. 121–122: 'Lustrans nuper cum abbate meo B. officinas monasterii Sancti Martini in Monte, cuius ei visitatio iniuncta erat, cum scriptorium fuissemus ingressi, veterem ibi bibliothecam invenimus, quam ad novum exemplar frater quidam corrigere videbatur. Aggressus igitur eam discutere quam redarguebant mendacii, vix corruptionem reperiebam, nisi in locis illis quae corrigi putabantur. Aio autem scriptori: "Unde scis, frater, novum hunc librum veraciorem veteri?" "Ab eo, ait, quod ibi plura continentur." Cui inquam: "Sicut putas veterem habere minus ea, quae sunt in novo, sic putare potes in novo esse superflua, quae non sunt in veteri." Et investigans adhuc loca, quae dicebantur correpta, tot appositiones repperi quot me numquam recolo repperisse. Intendentes qui aderant transcurrere coeperunt et ipsi, sed ammirantes testabantur se horum plurima amplius non audisse. Loci vero fratres dolere, eo quod cum propria et opera et impensa suum exterminassent volumen. Quaerebant autem a me a quibus mala ista procederent. "A praesumptoribus", inquam: "ipsi faciunt nobis malum hoc grande, qui fonte veritatis postposito ad sui coniecturam arbitrii, vel minuunt vel apponunt. Nam si interpretes hoc fecissent in cunctis exemplaribus haberentur." Ego autem, multa investigans volumina, in novis tantum hec superflua deprehendi, seu etiam in his veteribus quae novorum aemulatio corrupisset. Dixi quoque in corde meo de adiunctionibus istis, ut omnes de tota Bibliotheca exciperem et distinctiones inter quas continentur notarem.'

[42] For Theodulf and others, see Denifle, 'Die Handschriften', p. 276. For the text of the Paris Bible, see above, pp. 44–46. Maniacutia, like Harding, noted that the text of the Books of Kings was particularly corrupt. Even though they were both members of the same order and there are similarities in their accounts, it seems highly improbable that Maniacutia was familiar with Harding's *Monitum*. It is more likely that the introduction of as much text as possible was a common approach; likewise, the immense corruption of Kings (for which see also above, p. 33, n. 13) might have been well known.

In all of his works, Maniacutia consistently took the same approach. Whenever the Latin manuscripts disagreed among each other, he consulted the original Hebrew, usually with help of Jews.[43] Both his insistence that he did not rely on Jewish exegetes for controversial passages and his defence of Hebrew manuscripts in the *Libellus* indicate that there were those at the time who, fearing that the Hebrew tradition had been corrupted by the Jews, opposed this approach. Maniacutia's refusal to correct the biblical text exclusively on the basis of the Hebrew suggests that he gave some credence to these accusations, although he says that he did so because he did not want to produce a new and unfamiliar text. In the end, it seems that Maniacutia, despite his emphasis on the value of the Hebrew tradition, nevertheless gave precedence to the Latin tradition, in contrast to Harding, who considered the original language to be the decisive factor in establishing the correct text of the Bible.

Hervaeus of Bourg-Dieu had a different aim and consequently took a different approach from those of Harding and Maniacutia. Unlike the two Cistercians, he was trying to emend liturgical manuscripts. Nonetheless, Hervaeus's general attitude towards manuscript transmission displays similarities to that of the textual critics of the Bible. For instance, he conforms to that tradition by calling for a return to the sources in order to re-establish the correct text. In his case, however, the sources are not manuscripts in the original language, but rather Jerome's Latin version of the Gospels and Prophets, from which the texts in the lectionary had been

---

[43] Even in his *vita* of Jerome, Maniacutia stressed the importance of manuscripts in the original language by quoting a passage from the Church Father's letters; see Maniacutia, *S. Eusebii Hieronymi ... vita*, cols 196–197: 'Postremo praecavens in futurum si quid forte in novo Testamento vel veteri aliquando corrumpi contingeret, qua cura debeat reformari, scribens ad Lucinum insinuat {*sc.* Hieronymus}, "Ut veterum", inquit, "librorum fides ex Hebraeis voluminibus examinanda est, ita novorum quoque Graeci sermonis normam desiderat" [Jerome, *Epistulae*, II, p. 6 (LXXI, 5)], denique et ego hujus monitis adquiescens, cum inter discordia veteris Testamenti Latina exemplaria fluctuarem, ad hebraicam veritatem, de cujus fonte gustaveram, recursum habui: et inter corrupta et incorrupta, ejus testimonio discrevi, ac sententiam tuli. Cumque sic deprehendissem zizaniorum germina inter triticum divinorum pullulasse voluminum, ea studui ab radice cuncta revellere: consignans etiam per libros loca ad corrumpendum proclivia, et brevi opusculo explicans, quibus maxime occasionibus soleant exemplaria depravari.'

extracted by Jerome himself.[44] Hervaeus was convinced that there could be no error in the source; so, if anything in a liturgical text differed from its *fons*, it was automatically to be considered faulty.[45] It seems that he was true to this principle of strictly following the Latin biblical text: although he does not always give reasons for the emendations he wishes to be made, in some instances he briefly points out that his suggested reading is found in the Latin Bible.[46] Hervaeus also takes into account alternative traditions of the biblical text. He maintains that even if texts are quoted differently in councils from the way they are found in the Gospels, the latter trumps the former; for, in contrast to the Gospels, councils are known on occasion to have erred.[47] Therefore, the decisions made by Church councils held no value for the establishment of the correct text of the lectionary, which should be based solely on the authority of Latin manuscripts of the Bible.

The only other group of texts to which Hervaeus attributes some degree of authority are the writings of the Church Fathers. In one case, he compares a passage not only with Luke's Gospel, but also with patristic works, concluding that a passage as transmitted in the lectionary 'is found neither in the Gospel, nor in the writings of the Holy Fathers, and is only used in a few churches; and therefore it

---

[44] See above, p. 60, n. 45.

[45] Hervaeus, *De correctione*, p. 43: 'Fontem dicimus librum euangelicum uel propheticum; riuulum uero lectionarium inde sumptum, qui in auribus uulgi frequentius legitur. Ad fontem igitur est recurrendum, et quicquid in riuulo corruptum inuenitur est emendandum. In fonte enim nullus error esse potest; in riuulo autem, si a fonte discrepauerit, statim error sine dubio est.' For Hervaeus's preference of the Vulgate, see also above, p. 60.

[46] See, e.g., ibid., p. 55: 'Sic enim habet liber propheticus'; p. 58: 'Nam quod interponitur *secundum legem*, apostolus non hic scripsit.' In these examples, he does not seem to make a distinction between Jerome as translator and the prophets or Apostles as authors.

[47] Ibid., pp. 44–45: 'Si quis opposuerit quia in sinodis legitur: *Dixit Ihesus discipulis suis, Ego sum pastor bonus*, respondemus quia nos in hoc loco non sinodicam sed euangelicam quaerimus auctoritatem, cum non secundum sinodos sed secundum Iohannem [Jn 10.11 and 10.14] pronunciemus lectionem. Non nunquam enim inuenitur falsum quod sinodus recipit uel promulgat; nunquam uero falsum esse potest, quod euangelista recipit uel praedicat. Et ideo quisquis euangelistam sequitur, nunquam errare potest; qui uero sinodum sequitur, non nunquam errare inuentus est.' For Hervaeus, the age of Bible manuscripts is not an issue; his only concern is that they should contain the Vulgate.

should be erased, since it is a gloss'.[48] Yet, like other scholars after him, he does not treat patristic works as an independent source of emendations, but rather believes they should be used in conjunction with manuscripts of the Vulgate.[49]

The Thirteenth Century

Compared to the traditional view that old manuscripts were superior to more recent ones, some authors of *correctoria* established more refined systems for differentiating between Latin codices: for example, in Hugh of St Cher's *Correctio Biblie*, as well as in other *correctoria*, old Latin manuscripts were separated into *antiqui*, *antiquiores* and *antiquissimi*.[50] The terminology employed to designate recent manuscripts, that is, thirteenth-century Bibles and, in particular, the Paris Bible, seems to have varied. In all likelihood, the term *moderni* was used consistently. Even though none of the *correctoria* contains a definition of the term *moderni* – no doubt, because, at the time, the meaning was obvious – it seems that *moderni* can safely be identified with manuscripts containing the Parisian text. Already Martin in 1890 claimed that when the *correctoria* described manuscripts as *moderni*, they were referring exclusively to the Parisian text. In his recent examination of *Sorbonne II* (MS Paris, BNF lat. 15554), a Dominican *correctorium* dating from around 1280, Dahan assumes that the term *moderni* referred to the Paris text, in contrast to *antiqui*, which included all older manuscripts.[51]

Yet *moderni* is not the only term employed to designate the Paris Bible. *Sorbonne II* also contains frequent references to a *Parisiensis*,

---

[48] Ibid., p. 59: 'Quod additum est, *in manibus uestris*, id est *et lucerne ardentes in manibus uestris*, nec in libro euangelii [Lk 12.35], nec in opusculis sanctorum patrum inuenitur, nec nisi in paucis ecclesiis frequentatur; et idcirco debet radi, quia glosa est.'

[49] See, e.g., Roger Bacon, below, p. 149.

[50] See Dahan, 'La critique textuelle', p. 371; for further examples of manuscript groups, see ibid., pp. 369–376.

[51] Gilbert Dahan, '*Sorbonne II*. Un correctoire biblique de la seconde moitié du XIIIe siècle', in *La Bibbia del XIII secolo*, pp. 113–153, at pp. 118–19; 122 and esp. p. 133; for its origin, the Dominican convent of St Jacques in Paris, see p. 150; Martin, 'Le texte parisien', [II], pp. 304–05. *Sorbonne II* is Denifle's *Correctorium F*; see Dahan, '*Sorbonne II*', p. 114, n. 2, and Denifle, 'Die Handschriften', p. 265. For the same assumption of the use of *antiqui* mainly as a contrast to *moderni*, see also Dahan, 'La critique textuelle', p. 371.

which Dahan, by collating samples, identifies in most cases with the 'Bible of St-Jacques', a text in four volumes and including a *correctorium* written in the Dominican convent of St Jacques in Paris. The *Parisiensis* is therefore not to be confused with manuscripts of the Paris Bible, readings from which are attributed in *Sorbonne II* to not only *moderni* but also *exemplaria parisiensia* or *littera communis*.[52] References to a *Biblia Parisiensis* or, more commonly, *Parisius* occur in several other *correctoria*; but Denifle, unlike Dahan, maintains that they allude to the Paris Bible.[53]

The terminology used in *Sorbonne II* raises other knotty issues of identification. The author mentions *falsi codices* and refers to both a *rectus textus* and — distinct from it — a *communis littera*. Dahan reckons that *rectus textus* might refer to Jerome's translation, whereas *communis littera* could be the Paris Bible;[54] but there is no agreed solution to this problem. Furthermore, Dahan's identification of *rectus textus* does not seem to agree with his claim, later in the same essay, that the purpose of Dominican *correctoria*, including *Sorbonne II*, was to collect as many readings as possible in order to establish a clear text, free from ambiguities:[55] if there was a version of the Latin Bible which the author perceived as the correct text, *rectus textus*, it seems odd that he would collate other versions.[56] The terms used in *Sorbonne II* nevertheless show that the

---

[52] Dahan, '*Sorbonne II*', pp. 132–135; Dahan describes the text contained in the Bible of St Jacques as a new recension which differed from that of the Paris Bible. For a short note on the Bible of St Jacques (MSS Paris, BNF, lat. 16719–16722), see Gilbert Dahan, 'La connaissance de l'hébreu dans les correctoires de la Bible du XIIIe siècle: notes préliminaires', *Revue théologique de Louvain* 23 (1992), pp. 178–190, at p. 181.

[53] For examples, see Denifle, 'Die Handschriften', pp. 285–288. It stands to reason that Dahan's *Parisiensis* and Denifle's *Biblia Parisiensis* refer to the same text. Closer examination of the *correctoria* is needed to put assumptions about their terminology on firmer footing.

[54] See Dahan, '*Sorbonne II*', p. 147, where he also inserts the disclaimer that 'on ne rêve en aucune manière à un texte "pur" de saint Jérôme'. I am assuming that Dahan's expression 'recension courante' refers to the Paris Bible. The appellation *communis* might also have been used by FitzRalph to denote the Paris Bible; see above, p. 22.

[55] See Dahan, '*Sorbonne II*', p. 151. He (ibid., p. 119) assumes that *recta littera* is meant to indicate a critical choice and the generic *textus* a reference text. For the purpose of the *correctoria*, see also below, p. 136 and n. 94.

[56] That is, if the *correctoria* were, as Dahan claims (see below, p. 136), aimed at scribes in order to prevent textual corruption. Assuming that Dahan's dating of the text to around 1280 ('*Sorbonne II*', p. 116) is correct, it is unlikely that

author had a clear notion that there was a correct text of the Latin Bible and that other texts, transmitted in *falsi codices*, were wrong.

The terms *LXX* and *greci* were regularly used in the *correctoria* to designate the *septuaginta*;[57] however, in Gerard of Huy's *correctorium*, the Greek translations were referred to by the abbreviations *t* and *o*, the latter standing for the Septuagint and the former for other versions.[58] The compilers of *correctoria* clearly did not limit their collation to the Latin tradition, but also took into consideration readings from Greek and Hebrew manuscripts, which they usually translated into Latin.[59] They also consulted

---

rectus textus referred to the *Correctiones Biblie Senoneses*, by which the Dominican General Chapter in 1236 mandated that manuscripts of the Bible were to be corrected and which were revoked twenty years later (see below, pp. 137–139).

[57] Dahan ('*Sorbonne II*', p. 122, and 'La critique textuelle', pp. 370–371) insists that *LXX* refers, not to the Septuagint, but rather to readings from the Vetus Latina; from a modern perspective, that is certainly the case; but we should perhaps not make such a sharp distinction between the Septuagint and its translation, as is clear from the medieval usage of the term *septuaginta*; see above, pp. 8–13. For the use of the term *greci*, see Dahan, 'La critique textuelle', pp. 371. In *Sorbonne II*, the readings from the Vetus Latina are derived from the works of the Church Fathers; see Dahan, '*Sorbonne II*', pp. 122–23. It seems likely that this is the case for all *correctoria* when they explicitly refer to the Vetus Latina.

[58] See Denifle, 'Die Handschriften', pp. 596–97, n. 2. The abbreviation *o* should probably be understood as referring to the *septuaginta*, not just the Septuagint; but more research needs to be done on this *correctorium*. Gerard of Huy provides a list of abbreviations used in his *correctorium*; see below, p. 133, n. 85.

[59] Dahan ('La connaissance de l'hébreu', p. 186) says that he did not find Hebrew letters in any of the *correctoria* which he examined and that even transliterations were rare. In addition to the passages mentioned by Dahan in Hugh of St Cher's *correctorium* and the *correctorium Sorbonicum*, I can add, as a further example, the *correctorium* notes in the margins of the Bible in MS Paris, BNF, lat. 17; e.g., at f. 18rb (on *aquas calidas* in Gn 36.24), a note in the margin reads: 'Hebreus: *Iammim*'. Greek letters are not used either, although transliterations can be found; see Gilbert Dahan, 'La connaissance du grec dans les correctoires de la Bible du XIIIe siècle', in *Du copiste au collectionneur: Mélanges d'histoire des textes et des bibliothèques en l'honneur d'André Vernet*, ed. D. Nebbiai–dalla Guardia and J.-F. Genest, Turnhout 1998, pp. 89–109, at p. 97. In 'La critique textuelle' (p. 370), Dahan assumed that a distinction was also made between different Hebrew recensions, but later on he revised this notion; see Dahan, '*Sorbonne II*, pp. 129–30. He has not discussed the possibility that the readings from the Hebrew and Greek traditions found in the *correctoria* might derive from the works of the Church Fathers.

biblical quotations from the Church Fathers and medieval commentators.[60]

Although the terminology used in the different *correctoria* remains problematic – in William de Mara's work, for instance, *littera communis* is connected to old manuscripts and therefore, in contrast to *Sorbonne II*, cannot refer to the Paris Bible[61] – it is obvious that their authors, writing in thirteenth-century France, not only had access to a wide range of different manuscripts of the Bible, but were also convinced that they were able to distinguish between the various Latin versions.[62] Even though the classifications employed in the *correctoria* do not correspond to manuscript families as we now think of them, they reveal a serious attempt to grapple with the multitude of manuscripts and with the different textual traditions of the Bible. Conclusions about the use of manuscripts based on the terms found in the *correctoria* need to be made with the utmost caution since, in addition to the uncertainty surrounding the identification of many references, the terminology, as Dahan has pointed out, was neither systematic nor necessarily coherent.[63] Furthermore, in many cases, it is simply unclear, and the best we can do is to make educated guesses. Since modern research has not yet been able to establish precisely which manuscripts were used to compile the *correctoria*, we cannot determine the accuracy of the authors' distinctions and their ability to date manuscripts. The designations of Latin manuscripts apparently differed from one *correctorium* to another; and even within a particular work, their use was not always consistent. Dahan is certain, nevertheless, that the terms *antiqui* and

---

[60] For a list of commentators and the abbreviations used to identify them, see Dahan, 'La critique textuelle', pp. 372–373; see also Dahan, '*Sorbonne II*', pp. 124–25.

[61] For William de Mara's use of *communis littera*, see above, p. 21 and n. 39.

[62] Of course, it is also possible that they derived information from secondary sources rather than directly from manuscripts of the Bible.

[63] Dahan, 'La critique textuelle', p. 374; Dahan ('*Sorbonne II*', p. 118) also mentions *alii* and *aliqui* as generic abbreviations used to classify minority manuscript groups. It is not yet certain which Hebrew tradition the codices used for the *correctoria* belonged to; see Dahan, 'La connaissance de l'hébreu', p. 189.

antiquissimi in Hugh's *correctorium* invariably referred to Jerome's version.⁶⁴

After this short overview of the terminology used in the *correctoria*, we can now examine the statements made in the prefaces to these works about the authority of the different textual traditions of the Bible. In his *Correctio Biblie*, the Dominican Hugh of St Cher explains that, since a faithful text is indispensable for the study of Scripture, he has collated various witnesses – not only different versions of the Latin Bible, but also biblical commentaries and Hebrew manuscripts – for those passages which he thought might be corrupt. He gives special emphasis to the fact that he has consulted very old manuscripts, dating to before the reign of Charlemagne⁶⁵ – in other words, if his claim is true, predating the revisions of the Bible by Alcuin and Theodulf. Hugh therefore exploited a number of sources, though without passing judgement on any of them. The statements in his preface seem to imply that the aim of his work was to serve as an aid to reflection on as many readings as possible. Instead of erasing words and phrases which might be judged to be superfluous, as Stephen Harding had done, Hugh uses dots and lines to signal whether or not portions of text were found in the Hebrew and Greek traditions, the *antiqui* and a variety of biblical commentators.⁶⁶

---

[64] Dahan, 'La critique textuelle', p. 371. Whether this usage was consciously adopted by Hugh is unclear and is not discussed by Dahan, nor does he provide any proof for his assumption. See also below, p. 135.

[65] Hugh of St Cher, [Preface to his *Correctio Biblie*], p. 386: 'Quoniam super omnes scripturas uerba sacri eloquii necesse est ut fundamento ueritatis firmiter innitantur, quatinus super textum littere certioris sanctorum studiorum edificia securius componantur, quantum in breui potuimus ex Glosis beati Ieronimi et aliorum doctorum et ex libris hebreorum et antiquissimis exemplaribus que etiam ante tempora Karoli magni scripta fuerunt, hic in breuissima notula scripsimus ea que ex nouis et diuersis bibliis, propter uarias litteras magis dubia uel superflua credebamus.'

[66] Ibid., pp. 386–387: 'Ubicumque ergo in textu librorum ueteris testamenti, qui in hebreo canone continentur, punctum de minio super aliquam dictionem uel sillabam uel etiam inter duas dictiones uideris, scias illud cum auctoritate multorum expositorum et antiquorum librorum et etiam apud Hebreos sic haberi. Si uero dictio illa uel amplius linea de minio subtracta fuerit, hoc libri expositorum et antiqui non habent et tunc maxime certum est si iuxta Hebreum punctum de minio superpositum habet. In libris uero Sapientie et Ecclesiastici, quos nullus pater exposuit nisi Rabanus, punctum de minio supponit pro Rabano. In libris etiam Machabeorum, quos similiter Hebrei non habent, sed Greci, et in fine Danielis et in toto nouo testamento punctum superpositum notat auctoritatem Grecorum. Quedam tamen sine

This practice of collating for the sake of collation was criticised by some Franciscan scholars. For instance, William de Mara, in the preface to his work, expresses strong disapproval for those who intervene in the text of the Bible merely on account of verbal differences between the Latin and the original Hebrew or Greek:

> The common version {*littera communis*} in old manuscripts of the Apostolic See (to which Augustine suggests we must return for a faithful text) and also in approved manuscripts elsewhere should not be changed in Latin manuscripts because of the Hebrew and Greek text alone, provided that it retains the uncorrupted sense of the original language from which the translation was made. When, therefore, a certain Latin author {*latinus aliquis*} says about a text which we have in translation from the Hebrew or the Greek, 'the Hebrew or the Greek has this or that', or 'this is not the text but rather that', because the Hebrew or Greek versions do not have it, he firstly needs to prove that the texts differ not only in words but also in sense.[67]

The *latinus aliquis* reproached here has been identified by modern scholars as one of the anonymous authors of a Dominican *correctorium* or perhaps even Hugh of St Cher.[68] What William objects to is the indiscriminate collation of Hebrew and Greek variants of passages which, even though they might not be literal translations of the original, have no evident corruption in the sense. William's intention, therefore, was quite different from Hugh's: whereas the Dominican was aiming to provide as many variant readings as possible, the Franciscan believed that one should consult the original only when there was disagreement in content between it and the Latin. Furthermore, even though William quotes several passages from Jerome which support the superiority of manuscripts in the original language, he warns the reader on

linee suppositione sicut erant in textu dimisimus, quia etiam in libris antiquioribus et in ipsis expositorum libris de diuersis confusa translationibus continentur.'

[67] For the quotation, see above, p. 21, n. 39. Gregory the Great's statement (see above, p. 35, n. 20) might shed light on the references made in this and other texts to manuscripts approved by the *sedes apostolica* (see above, p. 61, n. 46, for Hervaeus; p. 89, n. 23, for Roger Bacon), for which no explanation has so far been found: the authors perhaps had this passage in mind when assuming that the Holy See had in the past sanctioned certain manuscripts or had even had the power to approve of certain versions.

[68] Denifle ('Die Handschriften', p. 296, n. 5) identifies the *latinus aliquis* as Hugh of St Cher; Dahan ('La critique textuelle', p. 387, n. 117) assumes that it refers to one of the authors of the Dominican *correctoria*.

several occasions that in order to preserve the text intact one should not attribute too much authority to the Hebrew codices and seems to have been convinced that the Jews had corrupted their own manuscripts.[69] He confirms his preference for Latin manuscripts by demanding that nothing should be changed in them on the grounds of modern Hebrew manuscripts.[70]

William concludes his preface by stressing that interventions based on simple textual differences between the Latin and the original are unacceptable, since they would destroy the established Latin text of the Bible. He says that he himself concentrates on the Latin tradition and, in cases of textual differences, gives preference to the old Latin manuscripts, in which, he claims, the text is preserved intact. But even though he is convinced that there is an inviolate text in old manuscripts, he does not limit himself simply to collating these manuscripts, but also wants to list other variant readings.[71]

It may have been William's preface which induced Denifle to assume that the aim of his work was to re-establish Jerome's version.[72] Denifle's arguments, however, are not entirely persuasive. He interprets William's *communis littera* as referring to the Vulgate; but even though it certainly does not refer to the Paris Bible, as was the case for *Sorbonne II*, it is nowhere identified as Jerome's version.[73] Also, William's proposed method of collation, as we have just seen, is not limited to the inviolate text found in old manuscripts (presumably identified by Denifle as the Vulgate) but

---

[69] William de Mara, [Preface to his *Correctorium biblie*], p. 387. See also Denifle, 'Die Handschriften', p. 296, n. 6, where he quotes several passages from the corpus of the *correctorium* itself to this effect; for instance, William's comment on Ex 5 is: 'Si vis ergo litteram servare incorruptam, non nimis adhereas iudeis.'

[70] William de Mara, *Correctorium biblie* [on Jos 19.48] (quoted by Denifle, 'Die Handschriften', p. 298): 'Propter solum hebreum modernum nullatenus de libris nostris aliquid mutare debemus.'

[71] William de Mara, [Preface to his *Correctorium biblie*], p. 388: 'Noli igitur propter externe lingue idioma canonem destruere latinorum ... Michi ferme in opusculo hoc opere precium est uarias ubi occurrerint litteras recitare atque illam, que in antiquis codicibus ueritate conseruatur illibata, precipue ubi euidens est riuulum a suo fonte procedere, pre ceteris approbare.'

[72] Denifle, 'Die Handschriften', pp. 295 and 297.

[73] For William's use of the term, see above, p. 21 and nn. 38–39. Richard FitzRalph's use of *communis* also remains unclear; see above, p. 21.

also includes other variants as well.[74] Although he insists that it is crucial to focus on the Latin tradition for the emendation of the Latin text of the Bible, he does not specify which Latin text, but merely asserts that it is found in old manuscripts – a common belief already held by the Church Fathers.[75]

From the evidence at our disposal, therefore, we should regard Denifle's notion that William de Mara sought to reconstruct the Vulgate as no more than a speculative, if plausible, hypothesis. William's preference for the Latin tradition over the Hebrew original was not necessarily based on the idea of re-establishing the Vulgate; it derived instead from his fear of corrupt Hebrew manuscripts. In addition, his insistence on not interfering with the Latin text as long as the sense was in agreement with the original version is already found in Jerome and in other writers.[76] William's work can therefore be seen as an attempt to follow certain principles set out by Jerome; but it is by no means certain that it was an attempt to reconstruct or preserve his translation.

Gerard of Huy's *correctorium* appears to be the only work in this genre which explicitly assigns a special status to the Vulgate. In the preface, Gerard writes: 'if St Jerome's version had remained pure and just as he had translated it into Latin, it would be superfluous to correct anything after such a great man.'[77]

Unfortunately, however, Jerome's text had been corrupted; and to remedy these corruptions, Gerard, guided by the principles of the Church Fathers, relied on old Latin manuscripts.[78] After a discourse on the causes of textual corruption, he says that, following Augustine's advice, he collated not only old manuscripts, but also as many versions as possible – the Hebrew, the Greek, the text as it

---

[74] See above, p. 130, n. 71.
[75] See above, pp. 109 and 115.
[76] See Jerome, *Epistulae*, II, p. 255 (CVI, 12, 2): 'Nos emendantes olim psalterium, ubicumque sensus idem est, ueterum interpretum consuetudinem mutare noluimus, ne nimia nouitate lectoris studium terremus'; for a similar view, see the *correctorium* of Gerard of Huy, below, p. 133.
[77] For the quotation, see above, p. 61, n. 48.
[78] Gerard of Huy, [Preface to his *correctorium*], p. 298: 'Non facilem laborem immo vero negotium plenum vigiliarum et sudoris assumpsi, quia veterum codicum biblie diligens investigator sicut et ipso teste Prisciano antiquitatum grammatice studiosus perscrutator studui, ut potui, antiquorum codicum veritate et sacrorum doctorum subnixus auctoritate depravata corrigere, superflua resecare.' On this passage, see also below, p. 222.

appeared in the works of the Fathers – in order to rediscover *veritas*.[79] For this purpose, he did not limit himself to those versions which would be relevant for restoring Jerome's translation, although his statement that the Vetus Latina and 'our' version were different suggests that he had a distinct preference for the Vulgate as far as textual matters were concerned.

For the development of his method, Gerard also relied heavily on views expressed by Augustine. Shortly after the quotation from *De doctrina christiana*, he states that the Paris Bible and its descendants are of no value because they are not only new but also few in number – in fact, they can be traced back to a single *exemplar Parisiense*. This judgement is based on Augustine's pronouncement in *Contra Faustum* that older manuscripts are superior to newer ones, and the greater number to the smaller.[80]

Gerard's attitude towards Hebrew and Greek manuscripts was reserved. In his view, it was only when the old Latin manuscripts – superior to the Paris Bible thanks to their number and age – were in disagreement among themselves that one should go back to the original Hebrew or Greek texts.[81] Further on in the preface, he refines this point: when the old Latin codices are not in agreement, then those manuscripts which conform to the original should be given preference.[82] Manuscripts in the original languages are

---

[79] Gerard of Huy, [Preface to his *correctorium*], p. 306: 'Cum igitur has falsitates et huiusmodi in modernis libris aspicerem, antiquos codices et etiam antiquissimos revolvens contuli cum originalibus et hebreis et grecis, non quia LXX editio, que in grecis continetur, et nostra sit eadem, sed ut ex collatione plurium veritatem elicerem, quia ut dicit Augustinus, in II. libro *De doctrina Christiana*, "nonnullas obscuriores sententias plurium codicum manifestavit inspectio".' For the quotation from Augustine, see above, p. 29, n. 2. Gerard's statement that the *septuaginta* was preserved in the Greek manuscripts gives the impression that he did not have access to a manuscript of the Vetus Latina but assumed that its text could be derived from the Septuagint. He probably took the readings of the Vetus Latina from the works of the Fathers; see also below, p. 134, n. 86.

[80] Ibid., p. 306: 'Ecce quam plane dicit Augustinus, quod plures paucioribus preferrendi sunt. Plures autem sunt antiqui quantum ad exemplar quam moderni, cum ex uno exemplari Parisiensi, quod in multis dissonat ab omnibus aliis, sint conscripti ... Et quod magis est addit "vetustiores recensioribus".' For the quotation from Augustine, see above, p. 115, n. 26.

[81] Ibid., p. 307: 'Si variantur vetusti, tunc recurratur ad hebream linguam que fuit precedens ad omnes translationes hebrei canonis, vel ad grecam linguam quantum ad novum testamentum.'

[82] This is confirmed by the following statement (ibid., p. 308): 'In illis autem in quibus apud veteres est discordia et incerta varietas, consentiendum est illis,

therefore treated as mere props to support readings found in the Latin tradition.

At one point, Gerard gives a brief summary of his approach: 'Utrumque testamentum secundum vetustos codices et originalia et antiquos glosatos et precipue vetus secundum hebreos, novum vero secundum grecos iuxta vires meas correxi' (I have corrected both Testaments, as best I could, by means of old manuscripts, the works of the Church Fathers and old glossed manuscripts – the Old Testament chiefly on the basis of Hebrew manuscripts, the New on the basis of Greek ones).[83] Taking into account what he said earlier about consulting texts in the original languages only when the old Latin manuscripts were in disagreement, his claim to have relied heavily on Hebrew and Greek manuscripts should be understood to apply solely to those passages where there were discrepancies in the Latin ones. Furthermore, Gerard at this point introduces the same reasoning as William de Mara, maintaining that as long as the sense corresponds to the original, one should not interfere at all in the text. Indeed, he takes an even stronger position, insisting that if the correct and approved old Latin manuscripts are in agreement, preference should be given to them and they should not be changed according to the original, even when they differ from it, whether textually or in sense.[84] He thus further diminishes the value of the Hebrew and Greek traditions.

As in other *correctoria*, so, too, in Gerard's, the works of the Church Fathers are collated.[85] But he calls for caution in the

---

quibus concordat hebrea vel greca veritas.' A similar approach can already be found in the works of Maniacutia; see above, p. 119.

[83] Ibid., p. 307. As models for the return to the original language, he quotes from Jerome (*Epistula*, LXXI, 5; see above, p. 108, n. 8) and Augustine (*De doctrina christiana*, p. 48 [II, xv, 22]). The glossed manuscripts he refers to were probably codices containing the Glossa ordinaria. Dahan ('Sorbonne II', p. 129) states that in *Sorbonne II*, the abbreviation *glo.* is used both for the text of the Gloss itself and for the biblical text in glossed manuscripts. This might also be the case for other *correctoria*.

[84] Gerard of Huy, [Preface to his *correctorium*], p. 307: 'Quando igitur consentiunt correcti et approbati codices veteres, quamvis habeant aliquid quod hebreus vel grecus non habent, vel aliter habeant sub eodem sensu, quod forte aliis verbis hebreus et grecus habet, nichil propter hoc in libris antiquis correctis addendum, minuendum vel immutandum est.'

[85] Gerard himself provides a list of abbreviations used throughout his work; see ibid., p. 310: 'Pro hebreo autem ponitur *h*, pro LXX *o*, quia in greco *o* signat numerum LXX, pro greco *t*, pro antiquis *a*, pro modernis *m*, pro Augustino

consultation of biblical passages found in patristic texts: they should not be used to correct the Latin Bible, since they rely on the *septuaginta*.⁸⁶ Nevertheless, as is evident from his preface, he adduced readings from the Church Fathers, not for the purpose of altering the text in conformity with them, but instead to record these variants, possibly out of a kind of scholarly interest or, following Augustine's advice, to elucidate the meaning of obscure passages.⁸⁷

It is clear that, among the *correctoria* which have been examined, there was unanimous agreement that, within the Latin tradition, older manuscripts were more authoritative than more recent ones. Whether, however, the expression 'old manuscripts' should be interpreted as meaning manuscripts containing the Vulgate is difficult to decide in most cases. Only Gerard says that Jerome's version is authoritative and mentions it in direct connection with old manuscripts. For the other *correctoria*, this identification will have to remain mere – if plausible – speculation until we have

aug., pro Ieronimo *ier.*, pro Gregorio *gr.*, pro Beda *B*, pro Rabano *R*, pro glosatis *glo.*'

⁸⁶ Ibid., p. 308: 'Non est autem littera veteris aut novi testamenti iuxta cuncta originalia corrigenda, cum in veteri pleraque originalia sint edita secundum litteram LXX, ut originalia, Ambrosii et Augustini et huiusmodi, et in novo secundum translationem editam antequam Ieronimus transferret suam editionem, qua utemur.' Gerard here makes a distinction between the Vetus Latina translation from the Septuagint and the Vetus Latina translation of the New Testament. This passage again supports the notion that what Gerard was aiming at was a reconstruction of Jerome's translation. Another example that medieval and early Renaissance writers were aware that the Church Fathers had quoted from the Vetus Latina is provided by Petrarch. After citing the translation of Ps 45.11 in Jerome's version and the Vetus Latina, he continues by quoting Augustine, who 'sticks to the old translation'. See Petrarch, *De otio religioso*, in his *Opere latine*, 2 vols, ed. A. Bufano, Turin 1975, I, pp. 568–808, at p. 668: 'Ubi enim ieronimiana translatio habet *Vacate* [Ps 45.11], vetustior habebat *Otium agite*, cui inherens Augustinus ait: "Unum certe querimus, quo nichil est simplicius; ergo simplicitate cordis queramus illud. *Agite otium*, inquit, *et agnoscetis quia ego Dominus*".' See Augustine, *De vera religione*, in his *Opera*, VI, 5, ed. W. Green (Corpus Scriptorum Ecclesiasticorum Latinorum, 77), Vienna 1961, p. 47 (XXXV, 182).

⁸⁷ See above, p. 132, n. 79. For a discussion as to whether Gerard sticks to the precepts set out in his preface in his *correctorium* and his actual method, see Denifle, 'Die Handschriften', pp. 587–592.

detailed studies of the readings attributed to old manuscripts.[88] It is possible that the authors of the *correctoria* – and likewise other textual critics of the Bible – merely took over this belief that old manuscripts were better than new ones from statements made by the Church Fathers, who, of course, were not referring to the Vulgate.[89] Therefore, Dahan's tentative hypothesis that Hugh of St Cher used the terms *antiqui*, *antiquiores* and *antiquissimi* to refer to the Bible editions of Alcuin, Theodulf and those made in pre-Carolingian times respectively, requires further investigation.[90] As for the *moderni* or *novi*, and the Paris Bible in particular, these manuscripts were viewed as offering a text far inferior, both in quality and in authority, to that found in old manuscripts.

Gerard and William appear to have been much more cautious than their Dominican counterpart Hugh with regard to the issue of variant readings.[91] While Hugh says that he marks additions and omissions wherever the text seems corrupt, not just when the sense varies from the original, both William and Gerard oppose intervention solely on the grounds of textual disagreement between the original and the translation. It is difficult to judge, however, whether the Franciscans – assuming that Gerard was a Friar Minor – were simply being conservative or whether they consciously aimed to preserve or restore Jerome's version, which at least was Gerard's aim. Nevertheless, all three authors collated texts not only

---

[88] Gerard is also the only author to note that the *septuaginta* was used by Church Fathers for their commentaries; however, this might well have been general knowledge.

[89] For quotations by Jerome and Augustine on the preferability of old manuscripts, see above, p. 109, n. 11, and p. 115, n. 26. Dahan ('Sorbonne II', p. 119) assumes that the author(s) of *Sorbonne II* used pre-Alcuinian and Alcuinian editions of the Bible.

[90] Dahan, 'La critique textuelle', p. 371. Denifle ('Die Handschriften', p. 276) has noted the numerous additions in Theodulf's text; had Hugh of St Cher been aware of this, he would certainly not have considered it reliable, since it also included as much text as possible. A strong argument in support of the theory that *antiqui* and similar expressions stood for the Vulgate is the absence in the *correctoria* which have so far been studied of a distinct term or abbreviation to denote readings from Jerome's version.

[91] For a similar observation regarding Franciscan and Dominican *correctoria*, see Gilbert Dahan, 'La méthode critique dans l'étude de la Bible (XIIe–XIIIe siècles)', in *La méthode critique au moyen âge*, ed. M. Chazan and G. Dahan, Turnhout 2006, pp. 103–128, at p. 112, who furthermore points out that, in practice, the *correctoria* of the two orders do not differ all that much from each other.

from the Latin tradition, but also from the original Hebrew and Greek, as well as from patristic writings and medieval commentaries.

The exact purpose of the *correctoria* is still unclear. Cardinal Bessarion is the only author discussed in this study who comments on their use. Yet his statement only briefly notes that the *correctoria* served to rid the Bible of errors.[92] While this seems logical judging from the title of the works alone, it is not clear how the *correctoria* were supposed to fulfil this function, and modern scholars have taken different approaches to the texts. Denifle assumed that the aim of Hugh of St Cher and several authors of marginal glosses to *correctoria* was to sift out whatever was not in the original text and to correct the Bible in accordance with manuscripts written in the original language.[93] After the analysis of the prefaces, however, this goal seems unlikely. More recently, Dahan provided a crisp summary of his assumptions about the purpose of the *correctoria*: they were not meant to be preliminary towards a new edition of Jerome's version or even towards a completely new translation. Instead, the authors wanted to guard future scribes against mistakes and prevent them from indulging in textual criticism themselves. Most importantly, they wanted to furnish exegetes with abundant material.[94] Whether these really were the goals of the *correctoria* remains to be proven. Especially the assumption that they were, in part, addressed to scribes seems counterintuitive: particularly in those *correctoria* where a specific version was identified as the correct text, it would appear pointless, even contraproductive, to present other readings instead of just changing the text according to the preferred version. Yet, as we shall see later, Dahan seems to be correct in attributing this purpose to the *correctoria*.[95]

---

[92] See below, p. 254, n. 18.

[93] Denifle, 'Die Handschriften', p. 295.

[94] Dahan, 'La méthode critique', p. 112. Dahan ('*Sorbonne II*', p. 151) states that *Sorbonne II* definitely served the purpose of providing 'la documentation la plus riche possible', on the basis of which a better text could be established. It is odd, however, that this purpose is not mentioned in the prefaces to the *correctoria*.

[95] A comment by Roger Bacon on the reasons why Church Fathers mentioned more than one translation might support Dahan's theory that the main aim of *correctoria* was exegesis: see above, p. 89, n. 22.

The *Acta* of the Dominican General Chapters

From early on, the newly founded Dominican Order made provisions regarding the text of the Bible to be read by its members. In 1236, the General Chapter decreed that Dominican Bibles should be corrected and punctuated according to a particular *correctio*.[96] Fifteen years later, a similar decision was made in relation to liturgical texts: one *Vorlage* of each was to be kept in both Bologna and Paris.[97] In 1256, the mandate for standardised liturgical texts was repeated, and each provincial prior was obliged to pay the prior in Paris for his organisation of this task.[98] In the same year, the General Chapter also forbade the use of what it called the Sens corrections of the Bible, *correctiones biblie Senonenses*.[99]

In the late nineteenth century Denifle maintained that the *correctiones Senonenses* referred to the *correctio* mentioned in the *acta* of 1236; and more recently Dahan has come to the same conclusion.[100] Yet the identification of this text remains problematic. Denifle, while differentiating it from the *correctorium* of Hugh of St Cher and from the manuscripts now known as the Bible of St Jacques, in which some marginal notes derive from the *correctiones Senonenses*, did not identify it with a specific text.[101] Although Dahan originally assumed that the text might not have

---

[96] *Acta capitulorum generalium Ordinis Praedicatorum*, I: *Ab anno 1220 usque ad annum 1303*, ed. B. M. Reichert, Rome 1898, p. 9 (General Chapter of 1236): 'Volumus et mandamus ut secundum correctionem quam faciunt fratres quibus hic iniungitur in provincia [Francie] biblie alie ordinis corrigantur et punctentur.' According to Denifle, it is not known when work on the *correctio* of 1236 started; see *Chartularium Universitatis Parisiensis*, 4 vols, ed. H. Denifle, Paris 1889–1897, repr. Brussels 1964, I, pp. 316–317, n. 3. In 1236, Hugh of St Cher was provincial for the French province; see *LexMA*, V, col. 176.

[97] *Acta capitulorum*, p. 60 (General Chapter of 1251): 'Officium diurnum et nocturnum secundum ultimam correpcionem ab omnibus recipiatur, et unum exemplar Parisius, aliud Bononie reponatur, et secundum eorum formam omnes libri ordinis scribantur vel corrigantur.'

[98] Ibid., pp. 81–82.

[99] Ibid., p. 82 (General Chapter of 1256): 'Correctiones biblie Senoneses non approbamus, nec volumus quod fratres innitantur illi correctioni.'

[100] *Chartularium*, I, pp. 316–317, n. 3. Gilbert Dahan, *L'exégèse chrétienne de la Bible en Occident médiéval: XIIe–XIVe siècle*, Paris 1999, p. 179.

[101] *Chartularium*, I, pp. 316–317, n. 3.

come down to us,[102] in a later work, he changed his mind and suggested that the reference in the 1236 *acta* might be to the *correctorium* of Hugh of St Cher.[103] Yet he provides no evidence for this claim; while we might be able to explain the plural *fratres* in the first mention of the text with the assumption that the *correctorium* ascribed to Hugh was a joint endeavour, at least in the manuscripts which I have consulted, Hugh of St Cher is named as the sole author of his *correctorium*. Nor, finally, does Dahan attempt to establish any connection to Sens. My brief glance at two manuscripts which contain the text of Hugh's *correctorium* did not provide much support for his hypothesis. Even though the title given to the work in one of the manuscripts is *Correctio Biblie*, similar to the wording in the *acta*, there is no indication that the text was ever approved by the Dominican Order nor that it was later rejected; moreover, there is no mention at all of Sens.[104] Nevertheless, I agree with Dahan that the text mentioned in the *acta* is a *correctorium*: the term *correctio* is commonly used at the time to designate *correctoria*, both in manuscripts containing them and also in Bacon's contemporary works.[105] In any case, the text in question cannot as yet be identified with certainty.[106]

A passage in the Dominican *correctorium Sorbonne II* might shed some light on these problems of identification. Commenting on Pr 9.4–5, the author of *Sorbonne II* writes: 'Parisius correctio facit unum versum a *Si quis* usque *venite* [Pr 9.4–5], videtur quod non bene. Sed Senonensis facit duos versus et incipit secundus ibi *Et insipientibus*' (The *correctio* of Paris subsumes [the passage] into one verse, [running] from *Si quis* to *venite*, which does not seem correct. [The *correctio*] of Sens, on the other hand, divides [it] into

[102] See Gilbert Dahan, *Les intellectuels chrétiens et les juifs au moyen âge*, Paris 1990, p. 276.

[103] Dahan, *L'exégèse chrétienne*, pp. 179–180.

[104] See MS Paris, BNF lat. 3218, f. 137ʳᵃ; in another manuscript which contains Hugh's *correctorium*, the title is '*Correpciones Biblie*' (MS Paris, Bibliothèque de l'Arsenal, 94, f. 1ʳ).

[105] For Bacon, see, e.g., below, p. 141, n. 114.

[106] Berger (*Les préfaces*, p. 30) assumed that he had found a copy of the *Correctio Senonensis*, as he called it, in a Bible written in 1434 in MS Vienna, Österreichische Nationalbibliothek, 1217. Modern manuscript catalogues give Bohemia as the place of origin of this Bible; see, e.g., Franz Unterkircher, *Die datierten Handschriften der Österreichischen Nationalbibliothek von 1401 bis 1450*, in *Katalog der datierten Handschriften in lateinischer Schrift in Österreich*, II, 2 vols, Vienna 1971, I, p. 22.

two verses, and the second one starts here: *Et insipientibus)*.¹⁰⁷ This testimony might serve to refute the assumption that the Dominican *Acta* of 1236 and 1256 refer to the same text, possibly Hugh's *correctorium*. Instead, the passage differentiates between two *correctiones*: on the one hand, the *correctio* of Paris, a plausible label for Hugh's *Correctio Biblie*;¹⁰⁸ and, on the other hand, the *correctio* of Sens, not yet identified.

Several further comments on liturgical books are found in the General Chapter's *acta*, but nothing more on the text of the Bible.¹⁰⁹ The decisions as to which biblical *correctiones* should be adopted or rejected by the Dominican Order were, however, noted and ridiculed by Roger Bacon, as we shall see in the next section.¹¹⁰

---

¹⁰⁷ Quoted by Denifle, 'Die Handschriften', p. 536. On the basis of the information contained in this statement, it might be possible at least to narrow down which of the *correctoria* was the *correctiones Senonenses*.

¹⁰⁸ Unfortunately, I have not been able to consult Hugh's *Correctio Biblie* to verify this speculation.

¹⁰⁹ See, e.g., *Acta capitulorum*, p. 88 (General Chapter of 1257): 'Quicumque scripserunt usque hodie aliquid de officio, non dent ad transcribendum aliis, quousque correcta fuerint diligenter, ea que scripserunt ad exemplaria que sunt Parisius, et quicumque amodo scribent, non utantur illis scriptis, quousque per fratres diligenter correcta fuerint scripta illa, nec credatur particularibus correctionibus, quas quidam dicuntur portasse in quaternis et cedulis'; ibid., p. 92 (General Chapter of 1258): 'Apponant fratres curam quod libri de officio qui de novo scribuntur, corrigantur diligenter ad exemplaria prima'; ibid., pp. 98–99 (General Chapter of 1259): 'Procurent priores quod habeant novam correctionem de officio ecclesiastico, et libros de ea bene correctos et illa que certo sciuntur de officio isto esse, amodo dicantur a fratribus, et sciant omnes quod magister ordinis nichil de cetero immutare proponit.'

¹¹⁰ Attempts to standardise liturgical texts are much better documented than attempts to standardise the text of the Bible itself; for the Dominicans, see *Aux origines de la liturgie dominicaine. Le manuscrit Santa Sabina XIV L 1*, ed. L. E. Boyle and P.–M. Gy, Paris and Rome 2004. Between 1173 and 1191 the Cistercians provided a *Vorlage* for liturgical texts (see Alberich Martin Altermatt, '"Id quod magis authenticum...": Die Liturgiereform der ersten Zisterzienser', in *Liturgiereformen. Historische Studien zu einem bleibenden Grundzug des christlichen Gottesdienstes*, I: *Biblische Modelle und Liturgiereformen von der Frühzeit bis zur Aufklärung*, ed. M. Klöckener and B. Kranemann, Münster i. W. 2002, pp. 304–324, at pp. 318–319). For the Cistercian General Chapter's call for uniform liturgical texts from 1134, and their later manuscript *Vorlage*, now MS Dijon, Bibliothèque municipale 114 (82), see Hümpfner, 'Die Bibel', pp. 79–80. A Carthusian prohibition against intereferring in the text of liturgical manuscripts and of the Bible in the *Statuta antiqua* from 1259 also points to the existence of an approved *Vorlage*; see *The Evolution of the Carthusian Statutes from the 'Consuetudines*

Roger Bacon

The *correctoria* of the Dominicans and the provisions which they made in their statutes regarding the text of the Bible encountered an outspoken critic in the Franciscan Roger Bacon. In his works he not only excoriated these efforts on the part of the Dominicans, but also put forward his own views on the transmission of the Bible and the value of the various scriptural traditions. In addition, he suggested ways of restoring the text of the Latin Bible.

Although modern scholarship has devoted some attention to Bacon's remarks, the opinions set out in four of his works – the *Opus majus, Opus minus, Opus tertium* and *Compendium studii philosophiae* – have not yet been considered together, nor have they been examined in detail. I shall first discuss Bacon's relationship to the *correctoria* and analyse his views on them as a genre. I shall then explain his position on various groups of biblical manuscripts of the Bible. Finally, I shall summarise his ideas on the reconstruction of a reliable and accurate Latin text of the Bible.

In the scholarly literature, Roger Bacon is often assumed to be the source of various ideas connected to textual criticism of the Bible which are found in Gerard of Huy's *correctorium*.[111] Bacon certainly must have had a thorough knowledge of the genre, as can be seen on the one hand from his use of the methods applied in the *correctoria*[112] and on the other hand from his scathing remarks about Dominican *correctoria*, in particular, which he regards as unreliable and hastily produced, making them 'the worst corruption of God's Writing'. Using their *correctoria*, he claimed, was worse than reading an uncorrected Paris Bible, considered to be the epitome of a corrupt text of Scripture. His complaints also extended to Franciscan *correctoria* and the attempts at emendation

---

Guigonis' to the 'Tertia Compilatio', 6 vols, ed. J. Hogg, Salzburg 1989–1992, I, p. 61: 'Libros quoque veteris ac novi testamenti eosve cum quibus divina celebrantur officia sine eiusdem capituli consilio nullus emendare presumat, nisi cum exemplariis in ordine nostro emendatis, nisi iudicio prioris et monachorum discretorum error aliquis manifestus appareret.'

[111] See below, p. 144, n. 123, for two scholars who have taken this view. Some of the issues examined in this section have also been raised – but not discussed in detail – by Francis Aidan Gasquet ('Roger Bacon and the Latin Vulgate', in *Roger Bacon: Essays Contributed by Various Writers on the Occasion of the Commemoration of the Seventh Centenary of His Birth*, ed. A. G. Little, Oxford 1914, pp. 89–99).

[112] See below, pp. 141–143.

made by the secular clergy: everyone, he complained, feels qualified and authorised to append 'corrections' to the text of the Bible. The Friars Minor and the Dominicans seemed to be competing with each other to come up with better 'corrections' to Scripture; and this rivalry – which led to numerous variants – produced further confusion. Bacon also accused the Dominican *correctoria* of generating increased insecurity about the correct text of the Latin Bible.[113] He summed up the provisions made in the *acta* of the Dominican General Chapters and noted that a second Dominican *correctio* had been commissioned, which contained even more errors than the first one.[114] With a mixture of harsh words and ridicule, Bacon voiced his contempt for the Dominican's solo effort to set right the corrupt transmission of the Bible.

---

[113] According to Dahan (see above, p. 136 and n. 94), one of the purposes of the *correctoria* was to prevent scribes from introducing variant readings into biblical manuscripts; if Bacon was right, they, in fact, produced the opposite result.

[114] Bacon, *Opus tertium*, pp. 93–94: 'Nam quilibet lector in ordine Minorum corrigit ut vult; et similiter apud Praedicatores; et eodem modo saeculares. Et quilibet mutat quod non intelligit, quod non licet facere in libris poëtarum. Sed Praedicatores maxime intromiserunt se de hac correctione. Et jam sunt viginti anni et plures quod praesumpserunt facere unam correctionem, et redegerunt eam in scriptis. Sed postea fecerunt aliam ad reprobationem illius; et modo vacillant, plus quam alii, nescientes ubi sint. Unde eorum correctio est pessima corruptio et desctructio textus Dei; et longe minus malum est et sine comparatione uti exemplari Parisiensi, non correcto, quam correctione eorum vel aliqua alia.' See also Bacon, *Opus majus*, I, p. 78: 'Sed illi qui nituntur cum omni veritate quantum possint corrigere textum sunt duo ordines Praedicatorum et Minorum. Jam de correctione formaverunt varias scripturas, et plus quam una biblia contineat; contendunt ad invicem, et contradicunt infinities, et non solum ordines ad invicem, sed utriusque ordinis fratres sibi invicem contrariantes plus quam ordines totales; nam omnis dominus alii contradicit, et in eadem correctores sibi invicem succedentes mutuas eradunt positiones cum infinito scandalo et confusione. Unde cum ad viginti annos praedicatores redegerunt correctionem in scripturis, jam venerunt alii, et novam ordinaverunt correctionem, quae continet plus medietate unius bibliae; quantum vix ponatur in tanta scriptura quantum Novum continet Testamentum. Et quia vident se errasse in antiqua correctione, jam fecerunt statuta quod nullus ei adhaereat; et tamen secunda correctio propter horribilem sui quantitatem simul cum veritatibus multis habet sine comparatione plures falsitates quam prima correctio.' Unfortunately, his words do not provide any help in identifying either of the two *correctoria*. For Bacon's view of the Paris Bible, see below, p. 147. Smalley (*The Study of the Bible*, p. 335) thought Bacon's criticism of the Dominicans was not entirely justified.

Yet despite this severe criticism, some passages in Bacon's works dealing with textual problems in the Bible mirror the methods applied in the *correctoria*. For instance, his discussion of Gn 37.28 in the *Opus majus* is based on a collation of groups of manuscripts similar to those mentioned in the *correctoria*: after presenting the text as found in the *exemplar vulgatum*, he cites variant readings not only from old Latin manuscripts but also from other biblical traditions – the Hebrew, the Greek and even the Arabic; he also mentions the readings in Jerome's commentaries and in Josephus's *Antiquities*.[115]

Bacon's methods of collation, therefore, corresponded to those of the *correctoria* but went beyond them in the range of texts which he consulted, including the Arabic version of the Bible and old monastic Psalters, neither of which, judging from the material at my disposal, are mentioned by the *correctoria*.[116] It remains unclear, however, whether Bacon collated all the texts he refers to himself or instead took some readings from *correctoria*.[117] But since he seems

---

[115] Bacon, *Opus majus*, I, p. 80: 'Et exemplum mirabile est de Joseph [Gn 37.28], qui dicitur in exemplari vulgato venditus fuisse triginta argenteis propter exemplum Domini, sed secundum antiquos codices et Hebraeum, et Graecum, et Arabicum, et Hieronymum in originali [Jerome, *Hebraicae quaestiones*, p. 45], et Josephum in Antiquitatum libro [Josephus, *Antiquitates*, ed. F. Blatt in *The Latin Josephus*, I: *Introduction and Text. The Antiquities: Book I–V*, Aarhus 1958, p. 173 (II, 33)] debent esse viginti non triginta.' For Arabic renderings of the Bible, see Georg Graf, *Geschichte der christlichen arabischen Literatur*, 5 vols, Vatican City 1944–53, I: *Die Übersetzungen*, pp. 85–185. Bacon did not, however, endorse the use of medieval glosses; see Bacon, *Opus minus*, p. 353: 'Quapropter illa glossa est falsa; sed quia non est alicujus sancti, sed magisterialis, non est mirum si falsa est, quia multae sunt tales; et ideo qui exponunt secundum glossam errant.' See also Smalley, *The Study of the Bible*, p. 332. For the use of the Gloss and glossed manuscripts of the Bible in the *correctoria*, see above, p. 133, nn. 83 and 85.

[116] For his collation of monastic Psalters, see below, p. 143, n. 118. Of course, it is possible that monastic Psalters, even though not explicitly mentioned, were among the manuscripts collated in the Franciscan *correctoria*; in Bacon's eyes, old manuscripts from monasteries carried special weight (see below, p. 146, n. 132), which is why he might have made a point of stating that the Psalters were monastic. For the omission of the Psalms in the Dominican *correctoria*, see below, p. 255, n. 19.

[117] To resolve this matter, it would be necessary to compare the passages which Bacon collated to the collations in *correctoria*. He may have consulted one or more *correctoria* and then added some collations of his own, say, of Arabic versions. For another example of the similarity between his methods of collation and those used in the *correctoria*, see below, p. 148, n. 135.

to have had detailed knowledge of the *correctoria*, it is likely that he derived at least part of his information from them, even if he adopted only their methods and not the actual readings they contained. Bacon's statement at one point that he 'carefully examined' a passage, *diligenter inspexi*, might imply that he had collated the various texts himself; but it could also mean that he had gleaned his information from other sources such as the *correctoria*.[118] So, despite his criticism of these works, Bacon seems to have adopted ideas and methods found in them.

Apart from methods of collation, there are further similarities between Gerard of Huy's *correctorium*, in particular, and some of the views expressed in Bacon's works. For instance, Bacon's arguments against the Paris Bible are the same as those put forward by Gerard.[119] Also, they both discount the possibility of correcting the Latin Bible by means of quotations from the Church Fathers.[120] Bacon, Gerard and William de Mara as well consider the main problem with the corrupt text currently in circulation not that the translation is too free, but rather that it does not convey the sense of the original.[121] And, finally, both Gerard and Bacon explicitly favour the Vulgate, which they regarded as the authoritative Latin version of the Bible.[122]

On the basis of this evidence, the view of earlier scholars that Bacon's approach closely resembles that of Gerard of Huy seems justified. This similarity has usually been explained by assuming

---

[118] See, e.g., Bacon, *Opus majus*, p. 80: 'Et similiter in Psalterio ad syllabae mutationem mutatur tota dictio cum infinito errore, cum dicitur, "Sitivit anima mea ad Deum fontem vivum" [Ps 41.3]. Nam cum ecclesia in solo Psalterio utatur translatione LXX interpretum, Hieronymus correxit hanc translationem bis, et posuit *fortem* ubi ponimus *fontem* per errorem propter similitudinem dictionis, et propter hoc quod in praecedenti versu fit mentio de fonte; sed ut dixi Hieronymus [*Commentarii in Isaiam*, p. 333 (VIII, xxvi, 7\9); *Epistulae*, II, p. 339 (CVIII, 22) and III, p. 60 (CXXII, 1, 12)] correxit *fortem*, et ita est in Hebraeis bibliis et in psalteriis antiquis monasticis. Nam hoc diligenter inspexi; et omnino certum est quod non est hic error vilissimus propter similitudines praedictas.'

[119] For Bacon's statement, see below, p. 147; for Gerard's position, see above, p. 132.

[120] See below, p. 149, n. 136; for Gerard, see above, p. 134, n. 86.

[121] Bacon, *Opus majus*, p. 77: 'Sexta ratio est propter errorum falsitatum infinitarum correctionem in textu tam theologiae quam philosophiae, non solum in litera, sed in sensu.' For Gerard of Huy and William de Mara on this topic, see above, pp. 129 and 133.

[122] See above, pp. 61–63.

that it was Bacon who influenced Gerard, not the other way around.[123] Yet no proof for this theory has been adduced; and in fact, it seems more likely that the opposite is the case, since Gerard's work is embedded in the *correctoria* tradition, while Bacon, whose aims were more theoretical than practical, took much of his information from these works. Bacon's contemptuous comments about both Franciscan and Dominican *correctoria* also make it appear unlikely that his writings served as an inspiration to compile such a work.[124] In addition, some of Bacon's more unrealistic expectations and ideas – such as his suggestion to set up a commission of correctors under the auspices of the pope and his assumption that Jerome had made two translations of the Bible – do not feature in Gerard's *correctorium*.[125]

Leaving aside the question of influence for a moment, it seems that Bacon regarded one particular *correctorium* as a possible tool for re-establishing the text of the Vulgate. In his *Opus tertium*, he praises a *homo sapientissimus*, who has sometimes been identified as William de Mara, for his outstanding emendational work on the Latin Bible. A few pages later, referring back to the earlier passage, he mentions a *sapiens quem dixi*, with a good knowledge of Hebrew and Greek, who, for almost forty years, had been an unequalled corrector of the biblical text.[126] Since the *homo sapientissimus* and

---

[123] See, e.g., Dahan, 'La méthode critique', p. 107; and Dahan, 'La critique textuelle', pp. 379 and 376, n. 57. Dahan does not provide any arguments in support of his view. Berger (*Quam notitiam*, p. 48) identifies Gerard of Huy as the recipient of some letters written by Roger Bacon.

[124] Berger ('Des essais', p. 65) even reckons that Bacon himself may have compiled a *correctorium*.

[125] For the papal commission, see below, p. 152; for the second translation made by Jerome, see above, pp. 91–92. Concerned with classical texts rather than with the Bible, Coluccio Salutati (1331–1406) suggested the establishment of a committee of learned men for the purpose of textual emendation; see Coluccio Salutati, *De fato et fortuna*, 2, 6, ed. Silvia Rizzo, *Il lessico filologico degli umanisti*, Rome 1973, pp. 342–344, at p. 343.

[126] Bacon, *Opus tertium*, p. 89: 'Sapientissimus homo in studio sacrae Scripturae, qui nunquam habuit parem a tempore sanctorum in litera corrigenda, et expositione sensus literalis'; ibid., p. 94: 'Oportet enim quod homo sciat Graecum et Hebraeum sufficienter et bene grammaticam Latinorum in libris Prisciani; et quod bene consideravit modos corrigendi et vias probationum verae correctionis, ad hoc quod sapienter corrigat; quod nullus unquam fecit nisi ille sapiens quem dixi. Nec mirum cum ipse posuit fere quadraginta annos in literae correctione, et sensu literali exponendo. Omnes sunt idiotae respectu illius, et nihil sciunt in hac parte.' These two passages have been interpreted as referring to William de Mara; see Loewe, 'The Medieval

the *sapiens* are clearly the same person, especially given the very similar references to this wise man as both a corrector and an exegete, and since the *Opus tertium* was written in 1267, he would have had to start working on his corrections around 1230.[127] The year of William's birth is still debated by modern scholars, with the suggested dates ranging from 1210, which would be early enough to make the identification possible, to 1230, which is far too late for William to be the *homo sapientissimus*.[128]

Since the influence of William on Bacon is an unproven hypothesis, another possible identification of the *homo sapientissimus* is Gerard of Huy, particularly when taking into consideration the similarities between his work and Bacon's.[129] Indeed, Denifle, writing in the late 1880s, already suggested that it was more likely that Bacon knew Gerard's *correctorium* than

---

History', p. 150. Smalley, (*The Study of the Bible*, p. 333) does not attempt an identification; her claim (ibid., p. 335, n. 3) that Denifle ('Die Handschriften', pp. 298 and 545) 'tentatively identified' the *homo sapientissimus* as William de Mara is incorrect; in the passages mentioned, Denifle merely points out that this is the view of earlier scholarship. For Denifle's position, see below, p. 146, n. 130.

[127] The expression 'quadraginta annos' should not be taken as an exact period of time but rather as an estimate; see Denifle, 'Die Handschriften', p. 278, n. 3.

[128] For a summary of the discussion about the year of William's birth, see Étienne Anheim, Benoît Grévin and Martin Morard, 'Exégèse judéo–chrétienne, magie et linguistique: un recueil de *notes* inédites attribuées à Roger Bacon', *Archives d'histoire doctrinale et littéraire du moyen âge* 68 (2001), pp. 95–154, at pp. 142–145, who voice tentative doubts about the identification of the *sapientissimus homo* as William and are inclined to opt for a later date, around 1230; but they point out that their considerations are hypothetical. Nor does Bacon's statement that the *sapiens* had good Hebrew and Greek facilitate the identification: both William's and Gerard's knowledge of the two languages are well attested (see, e.g., Denifle, 'Die Handschriften', p. 295; Smalley, *The Study of the Bible*, pp. 336 and 338).

[129] Judging from the considerable similarities between their ideas, it is more likely that Bacon was referring to Gerard of Huy than to William. But since we do not know the dates of Gerard's birth or death, this identification cannot be proven. Moreover, it would also make Berger's assumption that William influenced Gerard untenable (Berger, *Quam notitiam*, p. 46) and would suggest, instead, that William may have been dependent on Gerard, though this speculation, too, cannot be confirmed without more detailed information on Gerard's life. For the assumed influence of Bacon on Gerard, see, e.g., Dahan, *L'exégèse chrétienne*, p. 186; and Berger, *Quam notitiam*, pp. 47–48. Bacon is also thought to have influenced other works of William; see *LexMA*, IX, col. 174.

William's.¹³⁰ Nevertheless, in the current state of research, especially given the lack of biographical information about Gerard, this suggestion must remain in the realm of speculation.

Bacon's opinion of the recent manuscripts of the Latin Bible and of the Paris Bible, in particular, is the same as Gerard of Huy's in his *correctorium*. In several instances, he expresses his disdain for the *exemplar vulgatum*, the term he uses to refer to the Paris Bible, which he describes as infinitely corrupt.¹³¹ He says that he wants to eradicate from it the innumerable textual errors which lead to the falsification of both the literal and the spiritual sense. In order to determine the value of the Paris Bible compared to other editions, Bacon makes use of two principles set out by Augustine, which were also invoked by Gerard of Huy in his evaluation of the Paris Bible: first, old manuscripts are superior to newer ones; and, second, if in doubt, readings found in the greater number of manuscripts should be preferred to those in the minority. Bacon claims that older and therefore superior manuscripts which have not yet been glossed and which preserve an inviolate text can be found in monasteries. Moreover, it is these codices which, in his eyes, contain the faithful Latin version of Jerome's translation, which had been accepted by the Roman Church from the beginning.¹³²

---

[130] The claim made by scholars such as Anheim, Grévin and Morard ('Exégèse judéo–chrétienne', p. 110, n. 34) that Denifle traced the influence of Bacon on William de Mara and on Gerard of Huy's *correctorium* and *Triglossos* is in need of modification; Denifle points out the similarities but comes to the opposite conclusion ('Die Handschriften', p. 311): 'Dies aber dürfen wir schon jetzt aussprechen, dass Bacon eher um E {that is, Gerard's *correctorium*} als um D {William's *correctorium*} wusste. Die Berührungspunkte zwischen Bacon und E sind zu auffallender Art, als dass wir an einen Zufall denken sollten.'

[131] See, e.g., Bacon, *Opus majus*, p. 77: 'Et quoniam violentius et periculosius erratur in textu Dei quam textu philosophiae, ideo convertam linguarum potestatem ad corruptionem textus sacri ut pateat necessitas earum, propter corruptionem infinitam exemplaris vulgati quod est Parisiense.' For the opinion of the authors of the *correctoria* on the Paris Bible, see above, p. 132. For the differing interpretations of the terms *Parisiensis* and *Biblia Parisiensis*, see above, pp. 124–125.

[132] Bacon, *Opus majus*, pp. 77–78: 'Quod autem correctio sit necessaria, probo per corruptionis magnitudinem ... Et Deus novit quod nihil tam valida indigens correptione potest Apostolicae Sedi praesentari sicut haec corruptio infinita. Nam litera ubique in exemplari vulgato falsa est, et si litera sit falsa vel dubia, tunc sensus literalis et spiritualis falsitatem et dubitationem ineffabilem continebit, quod volo nunc ostendere sine contradictione

In the *Opus minus*, Bacon explains in more detail why the Paris Bible should not be considered a reliable text. For this purpose, he again relies on arguments put forward by Augustine:

> Sed unum exemplar est Parisiense, et antiqua exemplaria secundum diversas provincias sunt infinita. Ergo exemplar Parisiense debet cedere antiquis, tum ratione suae novitatis, tum ratione suae singularitatis, quia in veritate singularis fere est quae depravat veritatem totius Scripturae. Antiqui enim libri sunt in omni facultate veraciores.[133]

The Paris Bible is one manuscript, and the old manuscripts, due to their various degrees of kinship, are innumerable. Therefore, the Paris Bible must yield to the old ones, on the grounds both of its novelty and of its singularity, since, in truth, it is usually the singularity which perverts the faithfulness of the entire Bible. To be sure, the old books are in all respects more faithful.

Just as the Paris Bible cannot claim to be an authoritative version, so, too, the *septuaginta* does not have any special status. The fact that only the Pentateuch had been translated by the Seventy leads Bacon to argue that all other Old Testament books transmitted in the *septuaginta* are devoid of authority:

> Sed cum dicitur in aliis libris quam multum distant ab Hebraeo, falsum est, vel omnino dubium an Septuaginta interpretes eos ediderint, quamvis eis totum Testamentum Vetus ascribatur. Sed ab aliis potuit fuisse translatum et additum, propter quod Hieronymus,

---

   possibili. Nam Augustinus contra Faustum dicit, "Si discordia in Latinis codicibus est, recurrendum est ad antiquos et plures. Nam antiqui praeponendi sunt novis, et plures paucioribus praeferuntur." Sed omnes antiquae Bibliae quae jacent in monasteriis, quae non sunt adhuc glossatae nec tactae, habent veritatem translationis, quam sacrosancta a principio recepit Romana Ecclesia, et jussit per omnes Ecclesias divulgari.' Bacon paraphrases the quotation from *Contra Faustum*, for which see above, p. 115, n. 26. For the notion of officially approved manuscripts, see above, p. 61. For Bacon's theory of Jerome's two translations, see above, pp. 91–92. Gerard quotes the passage from *Contra Faustum* in his preface; see Gerard, [Preface to his *correctorium*], p. 306.

[133] Bacon, *Opus minus*, p. 331. J. P. P. Martin ('La Vulgate latine au treizième siècle, d'après Roger Bacon', *Le Muséon* 7 [1888], pp. 88–107; pp. 169–196; pp. 278–291; pp. 381–393, at p. 186) points out that Bacon apparently did not know Theodulf's version, because if he had, he might not have insisted so much on the value of old manuscripts for the re-establishment of Jerome's version. For the meaning of *provincia* as kinship, see Charles du Fresne du Cange, *Glossarium mediae et infimae latinitatis*, [no place] 1883–1887, 10 vols in 5, repr. Graz 1954, VI, p. 546 ('3. *provincia*').

> in prologo libri sui super Esaia [*Commentarii in Isaiam*, p. 641 (XVI, prologus)], dicit 'Apostolos et Evangelistas ea tantum de Septuaginta interpretibus, vel suis vel eorum verbis, ponere testimonia quae cum Hebraïco consonarent; si quae autem ab aliis addita sunt omnino negligere.'[134]

> since it is said in other books how much they {that is, the books other than the Pentateuch} differ from the Hebrew, it is false that – or completely doubtful whether – the Seventy interpreters produced them, even though the entire Old Testament is attributed to them. But it {that is, the text of the other books} could have been translated or added by others; because of this, Jerome says in the prologue to his commentary on Isaiah that 'the Apostles and Evangelists provide only those testimonies from the Seventy interpreters which agree with the Hebrew in their own or the translators' words. But if something was added by others, it has to be entirely dismissed.'

This downgrading of a large portion of the Septuagint also entailed a devaluation of its Latin translation, the Vetus Latina, which in turn strengthened the status of Jerome's version. Bacon dismisses the *septuaginta*: its errors had been pointed out by Jerome 'in innumerable passages', and 'it had already been invalidated from the time of Isidore and before'.[135]

Apart from Bacon's references to well-known passages in Jerome, Augustine and Isidore, in his *Compendium studii philosophiae* he mentions Gregory the Great's interpretation of a verse in Job which, as transmitted in his commentary, contained words that did not exist in Latin. Bacon excuses Gregory by suggesting that he must have had a corrupt text and that, being a busy man, he would not have had the time either to consult more manuscripts or to look at the Greek and Hebrew. Bacon, however, did have the time to do so; and, after establishing the correct Latin text, he not only confirms it on the basis of the Hebrew and Greek,

---

[134] Bacon, *Opus minus*, p. 338. After this passage, Bacon displays his detailed knowledge of Greek Old Testament translations. For problems concerning the term Septuagint, see also above, p. 8, n. 3.

[135] Bacon, *Opus majus*, p. 79: 'De una oratione superflua est exemplum Deuteronomii 27 [presumably Dt 27.20]: "Maledictus qui dormit cum uxore proximi sui, et dicet omnis populus Amen;" quoniam nec antiqui codices, nec Hebraeus, nec Graecus habent versum hunc. De superfluitate dictionis horribile est ac nefandum octavo Genesis [presumably Gn 8.7], cum dicitur quod "Corvus ad arcam non est reversus", et Hebraei et Hieronymus in originali habent affirmativam. Et accepta est negatio a paucis temporibus de alia translatione, scilicet LXX interpretum, cujus falsitatem Hieronymus ostendit locis infinitis, et jam a tempore Isidori et antea evacuata est.'

but even consults a Hebrew gloss on the passage in question. Yet although there was a simple explanation as to why his text of this verse was corrupt, modern theologians were still trying to salvage Gregory's interpretation. Bacon insists, moreover, that there are many other biblical passages in the writings of the Church Fathers which could be emended on the basis of the Hebrew and Greek.[136]

So, for Bacon, attempting to correct the text of the Bible by means of quotations found in the Church Fathers was not a viable option, since their works contained many errors in the biblical quotations. Nevertheless, he seems to have regarded it as legitimate to adduce the works of the Fathers as an additional authority to confirm readings found in manuscripts of the Bible.[137]

---

[136] Bacon, *Compendium studii philosophiae*, pp. 440–441: 'Cum igitur beatus Gregorius, in fine Job [Gregory the Great, *Moralia in Iob*, III, pp. 1803–1804 (XXXV, xvii, 43)], loquens de tertia filia ejus, exposuerit "Cornus tibii", licet videatur ei quod *cornus* non fuisset Latinum nec *tibium* similiter, sed sic inveniens in exemplari suo, non ausus fuit immutare, propter Textus Sacri reverentiam et propter ejus summam humilitatem; cum illi qui modo soliciti sunt de veritate textus Dei, et qui sciunt Graecum et Hebraeum, possunt docere sine contradictione, quod exemplar beati Gregorii fuit corruptum, aut vitiose more antiquo scriptum; ut prima litera hujus dictionis *stibium*, scilicet *s* litera, conjungatur cum ultima hujus dictionis *cornu*; ut dicatur *cornus tibii*, cum tamen deberet dici *cornu stibii*. Multa enim hic sunt adhuc de antiquis qui saepe habent scripturam hujusmodi vitiosam. Et sanctus homo forsan multis occupatus non habuit tempus examinandi plura exemplaria, nec quid in Graeco vel Hebraico scriberetur. Nam in Hebraeo est *cornu stibii*, id est cornu plenum stibio, secundum glossam Hebraicam; ... similiter quia Graecum concordat cum Hebraeo. Sed tamen vulgus modernorum theologorum disputans de his, quae ignorat, nititur salvare expositionem beati Gregorii ... Et sic sunt alia innumerabilia in dictis antiquorum, quae sunt per Graecum et Hebraeum in melius immutanda; et hoc diversis modis, aut scilicet propter falsitatem, aut propter imperfectionem expositionis, aut propter dubitationem minimam, et variis de causis, sicut suis temporibus poterit edoceri.'

[137] See, e.g., Bacon, *Opus minus*, p. 332: 'Item tertia probatio est per Augustinum in libro de concordia evangelistarum. Nam utitur hoc textu: "Qui me confusus fuerit", [Mk 8.38] et illum exponit [Augustine, *De consensu evangelistarum*, in his *Opera*, III, 4, ed. F. Weihrich (Corpus Scriptorum Ecclesiasticorum Latinorum, 43), Vienna and Leipzig 1904, p. 218 (II, lv, 111)]. Similiter idem Augustinus in libro *contra adversarium legis et prophetarum* [Augustine, *Contra adversarium legis et prophetarum*, in his *Opera*, XV, 3, ed. K.-D. Daur, Turnhout 1985, pp. 35–131, at p. 73], et Adimantum, eadem litera utitur. Item Beda [The Venerable Bede, *In Marci evangelium expositio*, in his *Opera*, II, 3, ed. D. Hurst, Turnhout 1960, pp. 431–648, at p. 539 (II, viii, 38)] literatissimus in grammatica et linguis in

Bacon does not limit his collations to manuscripts and secondary sources. He also employs a tool intended to facilitate the location of parallel passages in the Gospels: Eusebius's so-called *canones*, commonly found in Latin manuscripts containing the Gospels. These tables, which list parallel passages in the four Gospels, had already been recommended by Jerome for comparative purposes.[138] Bacon attributed these *canones* to the Fathers in general who, he claims – perhaps drawing on Jerome's statement – used them to correct the text of the Bible; and he, too, relies on them to emend a passage. He reckoned that the *canones* enabled a critic to determine with great certainty that a Gospel text was faulty in those cases when the sense of one parallel passage diverged from that of the others.[139]

To sum up: Bacon rejected the Paris Bible and the manuscripts which he labelled as *moderni*; on the other hand, he was convinced of the authority of the *antiqui*, which he believed contained Jerome's translation, but for which, as Smalley has suggested, he

---

originali utitur hac litera: *Qui me confusus fuerit.*' I have not been able to identify the reference to Adamantius.

[138] Jerome, *Praefatio in Evangelio*, p. 1516: 'Canones quoque, quos Eusebius caesariensis episcopus alexandrinum secutus Ammonium in decem numeros ordinavit ... quo si quis de curiosis voluerit nosse quae in evangeliis vel eadem vel vicina vel sola sint, eorum distinctione cognoscat. Magnus siquidem hic in nostris codicibus error inolevit, dum quod in eadem re alius evangelista plus dixit, in alio quia minus putaverint addiderunt.' The *canones* are on pp. 1516–1526 in *Biblia sacra*; there are a total of thirteen tables in the modern edition. For Eusebius's *canones*, see also Anthony Grafton and Megan Williams, *Christianity and the Transformation of the Book: Origen, Eusebius, and the Library of Caesarea*, Cambridge (Mass.) and London 2006, pp. 195–200. New Testament manuscripts in various cultures and languages contained these tables; see ibid., p. 198.

[139] Bacon, *Opus minus*, pp. 332–333: 'Probatio vero sexta et ultima est certissima, et sola sufficit, et est per canones Evangeliorum. Sancti enim doctores propter certitudinem Evangelicam a principio ordinaverunt quatuordecim canones, in principio concordant omnes, in caeteris tres, et duo secundum combinationes possibiles, in ultimo unus reparatur, qui habet quod alii non habent. Et hi canones Bibliis antiquis ponuntur ante Evangelia, quos pro authenticis habent omnes sancti doctores. Et per hos correxerunt Evangelia. Sed in hoc loco tres Evangelicae concordant, sicut scribitur in illis canonibus, scilicet Marcus, Matthaeus, et Lucas. Sed Lucas habet "qui me erubuerit" [Lk 9.26], quod est contrarium confessioni. Matthaeus vero "qui me negaverit" [Mt 10.33] quod est contradictorium istius literae *Qui me confessus fuerit*. Quapropter damnari debet textus modernorum in loco, et antiquitas revocari.'

did not provide a chronological timeframe.[140] In his preference for old manuscripts, Bacon agreed with what his predecessors, and also his successors, regarded as a crucial criterion for reconstructing the Latin Bible.[141] For Bacon, the decisive factor in support of the *antiqui* – even though they, too, had contained errors since Jerome's day – was that the text in those manuscripts had been officially accepted by the Church and had already been in use for a long time by Isidore's day. Jerome's second, more faithful, translation, which Bacon believed was contained in his commentaries, either had not survived in its entirety or had not yet been discovered. Yet Bacon never suggested that a complete copy of this more faithful translation should be sought out, nor did he demand that the passages which had been preserved in Jerome's commentaries should be used to produce a new edition. Although Jerome's first translation was by no means faultless, Bacon did not reject it; on the contrary, he made it clear that he preferred and endorsed this version, which he believed was contained in manuscripts of the Bible that had been approved by the Church.[142]

Bacon not only criticised the corruption of modern biblical manuscripts, but also devised a plan to remedy the situation. Even though he rarely mentioned Hebrew and Greek manuscripts in the context of correcting Latin Scripture, he nevertheless insisted on the importance of knowing Hebrew, Greek and even Arabic. Precise knowledge of these languages, coupled with an ability to teach them, was, he stressed, almost non-existent in his day. It was, however, crucial for a better understanding not only of theology but also of philosophy and sciences, since the numerous errors found in translations could only be removed by going back to the original.[143] This approach, Bacon pointed out, had already been

---

[140] See Smalley, *The Study of the Bible*, pp. 331–332. Bacon and Gerard were the only textual critics who clearly assumed that old manuscripts contained Jerome's translation.

[141] Whether some of his predecessors also assumed that old manuscripts contained Jerome's version is a different, and possibly unanswerable, question. For some examples of the preference for old manuscripts, see, e.g., above, p. 128 (Hugh of St Cher); p. 130 (William de Mara).

[142] See above, pp. 61–63.

[143] See Bacon, *Opus majus*, p. 77: 'Sexta ratio {*sc. for learning the languages*} est propter errorum falsitatum infinitarum correctionem in textu quam theologiae quam philosophiae, non solum in litera, sed in sensu'; ibid., p. 81: 'Haec exempla volui assumere ut quae probant quod necesse est linguas sciri propter textus Latini corruptionem tam in theologia quam in philosophia.';

promoted by Augustine and Jerome; and all teachers of the Church had demanded a return to the source from which the Latin text of the Bible was derived.[144]

When he developed his new programme for the restoration of the Latin Bible, Bacon may have had in mind the approval which he believed Jerome's translation had received from the Church.[145] In the *Opus minus*, he insists that the Church has to play a leading role in the process and suggests that the pope, at this time Clement IV, should see to the correction of the biblical text, 'for in the Church you have those subordinate to you who have full competence in this matter, even though it is extremely difficult, due to the vastness and immensity of the corruption'.[146] Bacon assumed that the pope, if anyone, not only had the power to put together a team of qualified scholars but also wielded the authority to ensure that the new version was promulgated and accepted. His

---

Bacon, *Opus tertium*, pp. 33–34: 'Multi vero inveniuntur, qui sciunt loqui Graecum, et Arabicum, et Hebraeum, inter Latinos, sed paucissimi sunt qui sciunt rationem grammaticae ipsius, nec sciunt docere eam'; ibid., p. 89: 'Si nesciamus aliquam rationum linguarum, quibus usi sunt sancti et philosophi et poëtae, et omnes sapientes in scriptis suis, etiam pro certo erimus vacui a sapientia sanctorum, et philosophorum et sapientum omnium; quia nec legere nec intelligere poterimus ea quae tractant diffuse. Et hoc probo per exempla sanctorum manifesta, et magni erroris apud vulgus theologorum propter ignorantiam linguarum'; ibid., p. 92: 'Illa quae fuerunt bene translata sunt modo corrupta, propter hoc quod linguas ignoramus, sicut patet per totam Bibliam et philosophiam. Quia nec scimus scribere ea, nec legere, nec proferre; et ideo per consequens perit verus intellectus. Et haec causa habet locum in corruptione textus sacri.' For another passage in which Bacon mentions the importance of manuscripts in the original language, see above, p. 148, n. 135.

[144] Bacon, *Opus minus*, p. 332: 'Deinde aliud est documentum Augustini et omnium doctorum de certificatione textus. Nam ipse libro memorato, et libro *Doctrinae Christianae* secundo, et alibi multipliciter; Hieronymus similiter ubique docet. Et omnes doctores hoc fatentur, quod recurrendum est ad linguam de qua translatus est textus Latinorum, ut videatur veritas in radice.'

[145] See above, p. 61.

[146] Ibid., p. 333: 'Hoc igitur exemplum cum aliis ... per comparationem ad Scripturam sufficiunt modo, donec dignetur vestra celsitudo requirere correctionem totius textus cum certa probatione correctionis. Nam in ecclesia habetis vobis subjectos, qui habent in hac re plenum posse, quamvis gravissima <sint> propter multitudinem et immensitatem falsitatis.'

plea to Clement IV, who died not much later in 1268, came to nothing, however.[147]

Bacon's plan for reconstructing Jerome's translation, even though revolutionary in its call for a universally accepted committee to produce the text, was not entirely thought through. Instead of demanding a collation of Latin Bibles containing, as he believed, the text of Jerome's version, Bacon at times demanded a return to the Hebrew on which this translation was based. He seems to have been unaware that this might not enable him to uncover what he referred to as 'our translation', nor that it would not necessarily help him to decide which variant readings to accept, since, as he himself admitted, there were errors even in Jerome's version. Bacon, furthermore, did not explain how to recognise errors which had been in the Vulgate from the beginning – and which, therefore, belonged to Jerome's first translation – nor did he give advice on how to handle them, that is, whether they should remain in the text or should instead be corrected, either on the basis of readings found in Jerome's commentaries or by making a new translation from the original.

Ramon Martí

Even though Ramon Martí was not a textual critic, his comments on the value of different biblical manuscripts, which vary according to the aim of the work he is writing, are nonetheless relevant to this study. In his *Explanatio simboli Apostolorum*, written in 1256–57, Martí presents a different view of biblical manuscripts, especially Hebrew ones, from what we find in the *Pugio* and the *Capistrum*. In contrast to his later works, he never claims that the Jews had corrupted their manuscripts. He points out that, thanks to the *septuaginta*, even if the Jews had wanted to change anything in their text after the coming of Christ, the original sense would still be preserved among two other peoples, the Greek and Latin Christians.[148] Therefore, any attempt to change the text would have

---

[147] See Martin, 'La Vulgate latine', p. 392.

[148] Ramon Martí, *Explanatio simboli Apostolorum*, ed. Josep M. March, 'En Ramon Martí y la seva "Explanatio simboli Apostolorum"', *Anuari de l'Institut d'Estudis Catalans* 2 (1908), pp. 443–496, at p. 453: 'Et hoc fuit permagnum {*my emendation from* per magnum} tempus ante Christum. Et ista translatio {*sc.* the *septuaginta*} remansit apud grecos. Unde, etiam si voluissent iudei aliquid mutare, nichilominus veritas translationis remansisset apud duas gentes diversas ab ipsis, que ipsos arguere possent de mutatione.'

been futile. He makes a similar argument for transmission in other languages as a guarantee of a sacred text's fidelity and reliability in relation to the New Testament. There can be no doubt, Martí writes, that its original sense has been preserved, because from the very beginning it was preached in different languages. Had anyone dared to alter the text, this would have been noticed by comparing it to versions in other tongues.[149] The faithfulness of the Gospel is also confirmed by the sayings of the prophets, by miracles and by the bravery of Christian martyrs:

> Nostrum quidem Evangelium, non solum a fidelibus testibus conscriptum est, verum multitudine prophetarum veridicorum et concorditer adventum Christi preconizantium roboratur nec non et miraculis quam plurimis supra naturam et martyrum multitudine copiosa, quos nec mors, nec gladius, aut tribulatio quecunque potuit a fide Evangelii separare. Unde, si quis temptasset Evangelium mutare, tam zelo fidelium et devotione, quam librorum collatione, quam diversorum codicum apud diversas nationes attestatione confutaretur.[150]

> Our Gospel was not only written by faithful witnesses, but was also confirmed by a large number of truthful prophets who unanimously heralded the coming of Christ; it was also confirmed by very many supernatural miracles and by the numerous martyrs, whom neither death, nor the sword nor any tribulation whatever could separate from their faith in the Gospel. Therefore, if someone had tried to change the Gospel, he would have been refuted as much by the zeal and devotion of the faithful as by the collation of books and the testimony of diverse manuscripts among the different nations.

In this text addressed to an exclusively Christian audience, Martí defends his belief that the existence of texts of both the Old and the

---

The *duae gentes* are almost certainly the Greek and Latin Christians, since they both were considered to possess the *septuaginta*; for this inclusive use of *septuaginta*, see also above, pp. 8–13.

[149] Ibid., p. 453: 'Postmodum vero tempore apostolorum Christi, cum predicte gentes et alii recepissent fidem Christi receperunt et Evangelium ab ipsis apostolis et ab aliis discipulis, qui predicaverunt eis iuxta mandata Christi, Matthei ultimo [Mk 16.15]: "Euntes in mundum universum predicate Evangelium omni creature"; et hoc in diversis ydiomatibus. Unde iste gentes non possent congregari de finibus mundi ad mutandum Evangelium, cum inter se sint diverse moribus et linguis et sub diversis principibus et regnis, et si factum fuisset, non potuisset latere.'

[150] Ibid., p. 454.

New Testaments in other languages has guaranteed their uncorrupted transmission.

In the *Explanatio*, Martí introduces yet another argument to prove that the text of the Old Testament cannot be corrupt. According to him, the rivalry among Jews and Christians had prevented the corruption of Scripture, since neither group could have interfered in the text without the other one objecting; and since their religious beliefs were strongly at variance, they certainly would not have jointly agreed to alter the texts of the Bible. As a result of this antagonism, the Pentateuch and the prophetic writings cannot be corrupt, since both Jews and Christians agree on these texts.[151] Since, moreover, the Gospels are the fulfilment of the Pentateuch and the prophetic writings and are in harmony with them, they, too, must be transmitted without corruption.[152] Finally, he puts forward his most potent argument: it simply does not make sense to assume that Jews or Christians would corrupt their holy books.[153]

In his *Capistrum Iudeorum*, written in 1267, Martí repeats the common allegation that Jews had for generations tampered with their texts of the Bible by, as he claims, changing letters and vowel points.[154] This conviction even induced him to challenge patristic

---

[151] Ibid., p. 453: 'Item, emulatio est inter christianos et iudeos specialiter de scripturis; et ideo, nec corruptionem iudeorum silerent christiani, nec corruptionem christianorum occultarent iudei. Cum autem sint discordes, circa intellectum scripturarum, constat quod ad corruptionem scripturarum non poterunt concordare. Cum igitur utrique concordent in lege Moysi et prophetis, constat legem Moysi et prophetas non esse corruptos.'

[152] Ibid., pp. 453–454: 'Item, Evangelium est completio legis et prophetarum, et lex et prophete fuerunt figura Evangelii ... Si ergo Evangelium fuisset corruptum discordaret a lege et prophetis, et si lex et prophete corrupti fuissent, similiter ab Evangelio discordarent. Cum ergo perfecte concordent ad in vicem, sicut patet habentibus rectum intellectum scripture; manifestum est, quod tam vetus, quam novum testamentum sine corruptione et mutatione remanserunt.'

[153] Ibid., p. 455: 'Non videtur rationabile, nec verisimile, quod christiani vel iudei corruperint, vel mutaverint libros suos, in quibus est eis tradita a Deo forma vivendi et spes salutis; cum pagani poete non mutaverint libros suos, in quibus fabule et manifesti continentur errores, sicut in eorum libris adhuc hodie invenitur. Unde astutia dyaboli suggestum videtur et hominum etiam malicia hoc firmavit ad fulcimentum sui erroris, ut libros sacros non legerent et corruptos assererent, ne, manifestato errore ipsorum per veritatem sacrorum librorum, a suis erroribus averterentur.'

[154] Ramon Martí, *Capistrum Iudeorum*, 2 vols, ed. A. Robles Sierra, Würzburg 1990–1993, II, p. 156 (II, 3, 29:): 'His modis a veritate quae in ea {sc.

authority. Disputing a statement ascribed to Augustine that Hebrew manuscripts should be used to correct the text of the Latin Old Testament, he maintained that, although it was forbidden by the Talmud, long ago Jewish scholars had altered the Hebrew text in those passages which foretold the passion and death of Christ.[155] Martí suggested two reasons for these interventions: first, the Jews were attempting to avoid confusion over the text among the simple people; and second, they thought they were performing a service to God.[156] He thus made it clear that, in his view, the Hebrew manuscript tradition was corrupt and that, although Hebrew was the original language of the Old Testament, these manuscripts no longer transmitted the original text.

In search of a faithful Latin rendering which was as close to the Hebrew original as possible and which would serve his polemical purpose, Martí discarded the extant Latin translations as unsatisfactory. In the *Pugio fidei* he states that he will use neither the *septuaginta* nor Jerome's translation in his writings against the Jews on the grounds that both differ too much from the Hebrew. Instead, he provides his own literal translations, in order to prevent the Jews from claiming that his arguments are invalid because the Latin text departs from the Hebrew original. Although Martí tells us that some of his contemporaries considered the Vulgate to have

---

sententia} manifeste relucet deviare, et ad suam falsitatem dirivare nituntur, quemadmodum et patres sui, ut infra probabitur, sacrae scripturae pro nobis multa testimonia corrupisse reperti sunt, tam in litteris, quam in punctis.'

[155] Ibid., II, pp. 156 and 158 (II, 3, 29): 'Ideoque illud quod beatus Augustinus ait, in Epistola prima ad Hieronymum, quod "veterum librorum fides", id est veritas Veteris Testamenti, "de Hebraeis voluminibus examinanda est", non quantum ad omnia intelligendum puto, cum ea, suo Talmud testimonium perhibente in locis quam pluribus, sapientes eorum mutaverint antiquitus, ubi, videlicet, Deum moriturum, sive passurum scriptura dicebat.' The statement he refers to comes from Jerome, not Augustine; see Jerome, *Epistulae*, II, p. 6 (71, 5). Martí probably took this misattribution from the decretist tradition or even the *Decretum Gratiani* itself, in which the quotation is mistakenly attributed to Augustine rather than Jerome; see Gratian, *Decretum*, col. 17 (D. 9, c. 6).

[156] Martí, *Capistrum*, II, p. 158 (II, 3, 29): 'Per hoc, intendentes, ut extimo, scandalum auferre simplicibus, quod Iudaei *tiqqûn sopʿrîm*, id est aptationem sapientium vocant, vel etiam cum moderni plurima, ut dictum est, in odium proculdubio nostri corruperint, et corrumpant, putantes miseri per officiosa mendacia Deo magnum obsequium se praestare.' For Martí's reference to *tikkun soferim* (תקון סופרים), see also Resnick, 'The Falsification', pp. 374–376.

a special status, it was clearly not so highly regarded that he felt unable to circumvent it.[157] Martí's recourse to the Hebrew and his provision of a literal translation from the original was, of course, partly dictated by his polemical aims. Yet he also justified his method by arguing that in many instances the truth of the Christian faith was much clearer in the Hebrew than in what he referred to as 'our translation'. This claim might have been interpreted as an attempt to convince his Christian readership of the need for a new, more literal translation of the Bible.[158] So, even though in the *Capistrum* he expressed the belief that the Hebrew manuscripts of the Bible had been corrupted, nevertheless, for the purpose of refuting the Jews in the *Pugio*, he referred to, and translated from, the Hebrew.

We have seen that Martí adjusted his position according to his aims and his readership.[159] When dealing with an exclusively Christian topic, that is, the Creed, he makes very different claims from those he defends in his polemical writings: the affirmation in his *Explanatio* that the Hebrew Bible is uncorrupted stands in sharp contrast to the accusations made in his anti-Jewish writings. Likewise, his view in the *Explanatio* that neither Jews nor Christians would corrupt their sacred texts is contradicted by his claims in the *Capistrum*. His stance on the reliability of Hebrew manuscripts obviously depended on what he was trying to achieve in a given work.

His attitude to the *septuaginta* and the Vulgate in his anti-Jewish writings shows that, in his day, even though there were those who considered the Vulgate to have a special standing – a viewpoint which Martí neither refutes nor endorses – no Latin translation had

---

[157] Martí, *Pugio fidei*, p. 4: 'Per hoc enim Judaeis falsiloquis lata valde spatiosaque subterfugiendi praecludetur via; et minime poterunt dicere, non sic haberi apud eos, ut a nostris contra ipsos, me interprete, veritas inducetur.' For his comments on the special status of the Vulgate, see above, p. 63.

[158] Ibid., p. 5: 'Rursus vero noverint qui ejusmodi sunt, in plurimis valde sacrae Scripturae locis veritatem multo planius atque perfectius haberi pro fide Christiana in litera Hebraica, quam in translatione nostra.' He then illustrates this conviction with an example from Habakkuk. The phrase *nostra translatio* may refer to the Vulgate.

[159] It is also possible that his opinion changed in the course of the decade between the composition of the *Explanatio simboli* and his later anti-Jewish writings. For the Christian readership of the *Explanatio*, see also March, 'En Ramon Martí', p. 447

achieved such an exalted position that it could not be ignored and replaced by a new version.

The Fourteenth Century

Some features of Ramon Martí's works are also present in fourteenth-century writings on the text of the Bible. For instance, like Martí, the Benedictine Hebrew scholar Adam Easton (ca. 1330–97), regarded the composition of a new Latin translation as unproblematic. Although he admitted that his concern over the reliability of Jerome's version was unjustified, it had nevertheless led him to learn Hebrew. Instead of attempting to reconstruct Jerome's version, however, he proudly announced that he had made his own literal rendering from the original.[160] Easton's statements show that at this time it was still possible to make a new translation of Scripture and to discard other Latin versions, including Jerome's.

As we have seen, the particular aim of Martí's writings influenced his statements concerning the authority of different versions and manuscript groups of the Bible. The same might also

---

[160] Adam Easton, *Defensorium ecclesiastice potestatis*, in Leslie John MacFarlane, 'The Life and Writings of Adam Easton, O. S. B.', unpublished PhD thesis, 2 vols, University of London 1955, II, pp. 38–246, at pp. 43–44: 'Sed timens ubi tamen non erat timor in substancia et sentencia translacionis beati Ieronimi monachi presbiteri et abbatis, et finaliter cardinalis precipui patris nostri, in libris veteris testamenti, quod in radicibus et principiis que pro tunc congesseram de eodem, mihi posset impingi propter ignoranciam ebrayce veritatis, sicut in aliis de cessacione legalium alias per Iudeos licet iniuste fuerat michi factum; propositum negocium tunc dimisi, et ad studium ebrayce veritatis in predictis libris continuo me diverti ubi, textum Ieronimi tenens ab una parte, et textum ebraycum ab alia, cum quatuor doctoribus seu expositoribus hebreorum fere duobus annis per Iudeum interpretem quotidie michi lectis super textu ebrayco, verba Ieronimi non sequendo nisi in substanciali sentencia ab ebrayco nullatenus discrepante, translacionem scripseram in latino de verbo in verbum, nichil diminuens neque addens.' The work was presented to Pope Urban VI around 1379–1380; see ibid., I, p. 15. For Easton's dates, see ibid., I, pp. 1 and 32; for his Hebrew scholarship, see ibid., I, pp. 10–11 and 240. See also William A. Pantin, 'The *Defensorium* of Adam Easton', *The English Historical Review* 51 (1936), pp. 675–680, at p. 676. Easton also collated readings from different versions of the Bible; see MacFarlane, 'The Life and Writings', I, e.g., pp. 241–242. Margaret Harvey (*The English in Rome, 1362–1420: Portrait of an Expatriate Community*, Cambridge 1999, pp. 188–237) provides a recent study of Easton. For his works, see also Richard Sharpe, *A Handlist of the Latin Writers of Great Britain and Ireland Before 1540*, Turnhout 1997, pp. 12–14.

be said of Peter of Ailly. In his works defending Jerome's translation, he says nothing about other biblical versions or matters of transmission, since this would not serve his purpose, which was to persuade his readers of the supremacy of the Vulgate. His rigid and preconceived opinion of the value of Jerome's translation differs considerably from that of earlier scholars who had attempted to understand and to evaluate the transmission of the Bible in its various versions.[161]

Other fourteenth-century scholars did, however, devote some effort to studying the textual tradition of the Bible. Richard FitzRalph, in his *Summa*, has the interlocutors, John and Richard, discuss in detail problems concerning the Latin transmission of the Bible. As we have seen, FitzRalph assumed that there were three Latin translations approved by the Church. But since these texts of the three versions at times disagreed with each other, John says:

> Que sibi in multis locis repugnare videntur, in aliis discrepare in sensu, cum tamen non nisi unus fuerit sensus primi auctoris. Et sic omnis translatio continens sensum alium ab illo est falsa translatio ... De ipsis insuper scripturis hebraicis de quibus isti suam translationem acceperint, nihil certum habemus nisi etiam hebreorum verba sola qui {*my emendation from* quos} in prima predicatione legis evangelice tollentes in multis legem suam.[162]

> They {that is, the Latin translations of the Bible} seem to contradict each other in many passages [and] to diverge in sense in others, although only one sense was intended by the original author. And, in this way, every translation containing a different sense from that [original] one is a defective translation ... We, who with the first preaching of the evangelical law made their {that is, the Jews'} Law obsolete in many things, know nothing certain about the very Hebrew writings from which they derived their translation, apart from the sole words of the Jews.

According to John, mistakes in, and contradictions between, the Latin translations provoke doubts about their general reliability. Errors might have been introduced by forgers or through simple carelessness; and, by trusting the words of these corrupt and unfaithful translations, Christians might be forced to believe in

---

[161] For Peter of Ailly's view of the Vulgate, see above, pp. 67–71.

[162] FitzRalph, *Summa*, sig. C i[r] (19, 18). For his belief in the official approval of three translations of the Bible, see above, p. 64, n. 56.

falsehoods.¹⁶³ Yet the contradictions in the Latin versions cannot be resolved by going back to the Hebrew because no one, apart from the Jews, knows Hebrew. But even if Christians had sufficient knowledge of this language, Hebrew manuscripts still could not be used for the emendation of the Latin translations. Jews, John argues, corrupted their text of Scripture in passages assumed to refer to the Christian faith; so, the Latin reader is forced to follow reason rather than Hebrew Scripture in order to determine what the correct text is.¹⁶⁴

John's assumptions are rejected by the other interlocutor, Richard. He tells John that in the case of contradictory or incomprehensible passages there are several possible approaches to the text: comparing different translations; consulting Hebrew and Greek manuscripts; or arming oneself with reason against falsity, since apparently difficult passages sometimes had a clearly understandable meaning if examined closely.¹⁶⁵ Richard's first two suggestions are quite common; however, his third idea, that is, using reason to uncover the deeper sense in the biblical text which

---

¹⁶³ Ibid., sig. Ci^v (19, 18): 'Ex hiis videtur sequi quod in illa parte sit fides adhibenda nostre scripture quoniam in hiis premissis et sibi similibus, ut videtur, non est ei fides adhibenda aut si sic ad errorem et falsitatem ex fide artamur quod non audet dicere christianus. Et per consequens nec in aliis aliquibus est fides adhibenda nostre scripture quoniam equalis auctoritatis affirmatur. Verum si vero quisquam dixerit premissa et alia similia esse a falsariis interserta, sic potest dicere de alia quacunque particula, et consequenter dicere potest rationabiliter nichil in tota scriptura esse autenticum.'

¹⁶⁴ Ibid., sig. Ci^r (19, 18): 'Presumendum est verisimiliter {*my emendation from* virisimiliter} [eos] {*my insertion; sc.* the Jews} suam extra ubi sit sermo de fide nostra corrupisse. Unde, cum ratio dictet certum tenendum, reliquenda sunt incerta; videtur sequi quod nunc omnes tenemur rationem naturalem sequi potius quam scripturam talem cuius veram certitudinem vero habemus.'

¹⁶⁵ Ibid., sig. Cii^r (19, 19): 'Si igitur tibi in aliquibus locis repugnantia seu falsitas videatur in littera, nichilominus tu firmiter tene et nullatenus dubites quod in sensu primario supradictoque nulla contrarietas seu falsitas est omnino et ob hoc iuxta alia loca in quibus non ambigis nec repugnantiam aut falsitatem reperis. Illa loca expone que videntur ambigua aut per inspectionem diversarum translationum, etsi oportuerit per inspectionem diversorum codicum scilicet hebraicorum atque grecorum, aut sensum veracem inquire per solidam rationem cum falsitate scripture. Fateor enim michi sepius apparuisse falsitatem et nonnunquam contrarietatem fuisse in multis locis scripture ubi tamen clara veritas fuerat expressa.' It is not clear whether he thinks that Septuagint manuscripts should be consulted for the Old Testament or whether, instead, his mention of Greek manuscripts refers only to the text of the New Testament.

is hidden at first sight, is more unusual. This third way of discovering the true text of the Bible helped FitzRalph to explain the awkward differences between the three Latin translations which, according to him, had all been officially sanctioned by the Church. Yet the role of reason is not as prominent as it might seem: FitzRalph does not recommend the use of reason to produce new conjectural emendations, but only to determine whether a reading already present in a manuscript is actually correct..

In addition, Richard insists that the focus should be on the original sense of a passage, not on the text as transmitted by manuscripts, especially since the latter may have been altered by ignorant or negligent scribes. To support his exhortation, he explains in detail the grounds on which an unspecified Church council decided to give its official approval to the three Latin versions: according to him, the council must have conducted the necessary checks by verifying each of the three translations. Consequently, its endorsement of a translation was reason and justification enough to trust the text. Furthermore, it was not the identity of the translator which bestowed authority on the versions; instead, the translator's reliability had been officially established and approved by the council, which would have reassured itself not only about the fidelity of the translations but also about the character of the translators. So, for FitzRalph, the ultimate guarantee of the authority and, consequently, the reliability of a Latin translation of the Bible was the official approval given by a Church council. Any corruption in a manuscript containing an approved version must therefore be attributed to the negligence of scribes.[166]

---

[166] Ibid., sig. Cii[r] (19, 20): 'Nec dubit(t)es {*my deletion*} quin in illis consiliis facta fuit fides sufficiens de transferentium personis aut saltem de veritate scripture translate et evidenti convenientia cum suo exemplario {*my emendation from* extrario} primario. Minus enim es providus si translationes tanta diligentia et tanta industria examinatas {*my emendation from* examinatis} de falsitate aut contrarietate audeas infirmare quin potius crederes codicem aliquem quem vidisti scriptoris sui fatuitate {*corrected from* fatuitatem *by a sixteenth–century hand*} esse corruptum – in quo casu habes premissum remedium scilicet ut recurras ad alios codices antiquos correctos et, si oporteat, ad libros lingue alterius – nec dubium quin si(t) {*my deletion*} sic veritatem primariam invenies quarum translationum {*my emendation from* translationem} frustra inquiris auctores propter auctoritatem scripture, que a transferentibus auctoritatem non recipit cum constet de veritate scripture translate et de eius convenientia cum suo exemplari {*my emendation from* exaltari} a quo erat sumpta ipsa translatio, etsi in ipsis primariis translationibus appareat quevis adversitas. Crede potius illud fieri ex penuria

FitzRalph's references to the importance of old manuscripts and to collating Latin manuscripts against Bibles in other languages are commonly found in text-critical writings. Unlike most other scholars, however, he does not limit these languages to the original Hebrew and Greek. In his eyes, *veritas* extended beyond the *hebraica veritas* and the *graeca veritas* to other versions, such as the *Vorlage* of the third officially approved translation. FitzRalph writes about the origin of the three Latin translations, which, even though they might differ in places, were still all to be regarded as authentic:

> Et quia aliqua translatio nostrarum translationum facta est ex hebreo, sicut ea que est Iheronimi, in qua lingua fuit tradita nostra primordialis scriptura veteris testamenti, aliqua fiebat ex greco sicut illa que est 70 interpretum et tertia fortassis ex lingua tertia, ita quod per plures translationes primordialis scripture sensus pervenit illius ad linguam nostram latinam. Non debes reputare absurdum seu mirabile quod in translationibus istis sepius reperiatur discrepantia aliqualis et etiam apparens diversitas cum diversis in cortice litterarum.[167]

> And since one of our translations, that is to say, the version by Jerome, was made from Hebrew, the language in which our original Scripture of the Old Testament was transmitted, [and] another was made from Greek, that is to say, the one which is by the Seventy translators, and the third one probably from a third language – for the sense of original Scripture comes to our Latin language via numerous translations – do not think it absurd or strange that quite often in those translations a few discrepancies and also apparent diversity in the superficial meaning of the letters can be found.

John, in an effort to support his thesis that translations of the Bible are contradictory and unreliable, provides a concrete example. He compares a Latin translation of Dt 32.39, 'ego occidam et vivere faciam' ('I will kill and I will make to live'), with the version found in a Hebrew manuscript written, according to John, by Ezra himself and in the possession of the Dominicans in Bologna. The original Hebrew, John says, does not have the active *occidam*, but instead the passive *occidar*, which, he claims, is a clear reference to

tui ingenii aut exercitii in diversis modis loquendi scripture, aut propter ydiomata diversa exemplariorum {*my emendation from* extrariorum} aut propter equivocationem terminorum in linguis diversis et ex transumptione terminorum qualis fieri potest in una lingua facilius quam in alia quam ex sensu transferentis doctoris cuius sensus ut dixi est totius ecclesie exanimatione diligenti et industria pervigili approbatus.' See also above, p. 64, n. 56.

[167] Ibid., sig. Ciii^r (19, 23).

the passion of Christ. Since the Latin version is harmful to the Christian faith and since he had found a very similar error in many parallel passages, he concludes that the Latin was derived from the Greek, and not from the Hebrew, as it should have been; so, for John, only the Hebrew original constitutes a trustworthy source.[168] In contrast to Richard, therefore, John does not accept contradictions between different versions. Yet instead of subjecting all doubtful passages to the same formula, John demands that every case should be considered on its own merits.[169]

John's mention of a manuscript allegedly written in the hand of Ezra himself underlines the privileged status of this codex, the contents of which were assumed to be correct and uncorrupted.[170]

---

[168] Ibid., sig. Ci^v (19, 18): 'Item Deuteronomii 32. capitulo ubi translatio habet "Ego occidam et vivere faciam percutiam et ego sanabo" [Dt 32.39], littera hebraica scripta manu Esdre prophete, que habetur Bononie a fratribus predicatoribus, pro magno fulcimento fidei christiane de passione domini omnipotentis pro omnibus peccatoribus habet passive *Ego occidar et vivere faciam percutiar et ego sanabo*. Unde translatio illa convincitur non solum esse erronea, sed multum noxia fidei christiane; sic reperio in locis innumeris veteris testamenti et etiam evangelistis et scripturis apostolicis.' Like the Vulgate (*occidam*) and the Septuagint (ἀποκτενῶ), the Hebrew reads 'I will kill' rather than 'I will be killed', אָמִית. For the inscription in the Hebrew manuscript which claimed that it had been written by Ezra, see below, p. 163, n. 170.

[169] Ibid., sig. Ci^v (19, 18): 'Que etiam videntur manifeste contraria et sic in multis similibus que magis expedit suis locis dissolvere quam simul cuncta disserere dum tamen hoc dederis regulam generalem huius omnia dissolvendi.'

[170] Katherine Walsh (*A Fourteenth-Century Scholar and Primate: Richard FitzRalph in Oxford, Avignon and Armagh*, Oxford 1981, p. 159) mentions a different reference to this manuscript of the Pentateuch and to the passage in Dt in the *Summa* (2, 11). There, she writes, FitzRalph states that he had received his information from an unidentified converted Jew (see FitzRalph, *Summa*, sig. biii^v [2, 11]: 'Quod autem littera vera debuit esse passiva dicit michi maximus doctorum hebreorum factus christianus.'). The Hebrew and Latin inscriptions which identified the scribe as Ezra are now missing; see Walsh, *A Fourteenth-Century Scholar*, p. 159, n. 101. Walsh says that the manuscript is the one described by Leonello Modona in his *Catalogo dei codici ebraici della biblioteca della R. Università di Bologna*, in *Cataloghi dei codici orientali di alcune biblioteche d'Italia*, IV, Florence 1889, pp. 323–372, at pp. 323–324 (MS 3569). Modona, who dates the manuscript to the twelfth or thirteenth century (ibid., p. 323), notes that this reference to the hand of Ezra can also be found in other manuscripts of the Hebrew Bible; see ibid., p. 323, n. 3. Bernard de Montfaucon (*Diarium Italicum sive monumentorum veterum, bibliothecarum, musaeorum, et c. notitiae singulares in Itinerario Italico collectae*, Paris 1702) gives both the Latin and the Hebrew

Any reading derived from this manuscript, John seems to imply, must be regarded as authoritative, both because of the scribe and because it was in the possession of the Dominicans in Bologna, which ruled out the possibility that Jews might have interfered with the text.

In replying to John's allegation that the Latin text of Deuteronomy 32.39 was corrupt, Richard attempts to reconcile the different translations by means of interpretation:

> Utriusque dicti unus est sensus ex quo utrunque dictum extat autenticum, sicut in illo apostolico dicto de imitatione et resurrectione: quamvis directe sint contraria, tamen quia utrunque dictum extat autenticum pro eodem sensu, in eodem loco credendum est utrunque scriptum fuisse. Ideo tenendum est quod illud quod alter translator intellexit per imitationem, alius per rationem intelligere {*my emendation from* intellgiere} voluit et sic utriusque littere unus est sensus sic non est contrarietas illa: 'Ego occidar et vivere faciam' et 'ego occidam et vivere faciam' si utrunque intelligatur de eo sicut oportet accipere.[171]

---

inscription which claimed that Ezra was the scribe of the manuscript. The Latin reads (pp. 399–400): 'Hic rotulus legis est quem scripsit Esdras scriba manu sua, quando sub Cyro rege redierunt filii captivitatis in Jerusalem. ... Quod autem sit ille idem numero, habitum est per crebram famam Judaeorum antiquorum qui fuerunt confessi in diversis synagogis, ubi etiam conservabatur. Ab antiquo pro tali habebatur inter Judaeos de generatione in generationem; et pro tali recepit eum reverendus magister ordinis frater Aymericus [Aymeric of Piacenza, OP], cujus est. ... Certus itaque debet haberi et cum reverentia tractari rotulus iste, quia a tanto auctore scriptus, et post combustam legem inspirante sancto Spiritu ordinatus et aliis rotulis pro originali datus, ac tantis temporibus conservatus.' The Hebrew runs as follows (p. 400):

זה ספר תורת משה אשר כתב עזרא הספר ויקרא לפני הקהל מאיש ועד אישה ויעמד על מגדל עץ

('This is the book of the Teaching of Moses which Ezra the Scribe wrote and he called before the congregation from man to woman, and he stood on a pulpit of wood.') Modona (*Catalogo*, p. 323, n. 2) points out the similarities between this passage and Ne 8.1–4. It stands to reason that originally the Hebrew was a reference to the historical figure of Ezra the Scribe and his involvement with the Torah rather than that he was the actual scribe of the manuscript. Ezra's role with regard to the text of the Pentateuch is not clear; see *Encyclopaedia Judaica*, VI, Jerusalem 1971, cols 1104–1107 ('Ezra'), at col. 1105.

[171] FitzRalph, *Summa*, sig. Cii[v] (19, 22). I have not been able to identify the reference to imitation and resurrection.

These two sayings {that is, *occidam* and *occidar*} have one sense by means of which both sayings are authentic, as in that Apostolic saying about imitation and resurrection: although the two are directly contrary, nevertheless, since both expressions are authentic with regard to the same sense, it must be believed that both were written in this passage. Therefore, it must be held that what one translator understood through imitation, the other wanted to understand through reason; and, in this way, there is one sense in both versions, and so there is no contradiction [between] 'I will be killed and I will make to live' and 'I will kill and I will make to live' if both are understood according to this [sense], as it is necessary to interpret.

Richard thus resolves the problem of seemingly contradictory variant readings by attributing to the translators the intention of transmitting the same sense by different means.

John also raises other doubts about the reliability of the Latin translations of the Bible. Any version of Scripture which has omissions or additions to the biblical text cannot be trustworthy, he maintains, and should therefore be regarded as a forgery. Basing his argument on Jerome's 'Preface to the Pentateuch', John claims that many passages in the Vulgate cannot be found in the *septuaginta* – both these translations, according to Richard, were officially approved. Drawing attention to a passage in the Apocalypse in which punishment was threatened for adding anything to or omitting anything from Scripture, he points out a prophecy ascribed to Enoch in Jude [1.14-15] which is nowhere to be found in the Old Testament; so, either Jude should not be regarded as authentic or there is an omission in the Latin translation of the Old Testament and, consequently, it is not authentic.[172]

[172] Ibid., sig. Ci^v (19, 18): 'Isto modo ostendi consequitur nichil esse securum aut certum propter hoc quod asseritur in nostra scriptura et tollitur omnino nostre scripture auctoritas. Item multa inveniuntur in translatione Ieronimi que non habent in translatione 70 interpretum, sicut Ieronimus in 2 prologo Geneseos [presumably Jerome, 'Prologus in Pentateucho', p. 3] satis ostendit. Et illa allegantur in evangeliis et in scripturis apostolicis. Cum ergo diminutio ab aliqua scriptura ita reddat eam falsam sicut adicio unde in apocalipsi in fine equalis comminatio pene sit diminuenti de verbis prophetie libri illius et addanti quicquam [see Rv 22.18–19], ad ea videtur omnino consequi quod nullius sit auctoritatis illa translatio que aliquid de hebraica veritate amitit {*corrected from* admitit *by a sixteenth-century hand*} in qua lingua edita erat nostra scriptura veteris testamenti. Lego insuper epistola Iude apostoli: isto modo prophetavit autem de "hiis septimus ab Adam Enoc dicens: Ecce venit dominus in nubibus suis facere iusticiam contra omnes et arguere omnes impios de omnibus operibus iniquitatis eorum quibus impie egerunt et de

These points, too, are refuted by Richard. He explains to John that just because one version is longer or shorter than the others, this does not mean that they contradict each other as long as the surplus text does not disagree with the shorter version.[173] Differences between the *septuaginta* and the rest of the tradition, for instance, are easily explained: any omissions of references to Christ in the *septuaginta* are understandable, Richard says, because the translators were in fear of Ptolemy, who might have disapproved of their work had they clearly announced the prophecies.[174] Nevertheless, the sense of the approved translations is the same, and they do not disagree with one another. Even a Latin translation which was not made from the original could still be acceptable provided that it contained the approved truth and did not contradict other versions of Scripture.[175]

In the case of 1 Co 9.6 ('Or I only and Barnabas, have not we power to do this?'), which in one Latin translation has an additional negation that is lacking in another, Richard reconciles

omnibus duris que locuti sunt contra dominum peccatores impii." [Jude 1.14–15] Cum tamen nichil tale prophetatum in toto veteri testamento legatur per Enoc qui septimus erat ab Adam et sic aut scriptura Iude non est autentica aut nostra scriptura testamenti veteris diminuta est et ita non est autentica.' Later in the text, Richard not only provides arguments against this claim, he also gives a list of canonical books in which Jude is included; see FitzRalph, *Summa*, sig. Ci^v (19, 19).

[173] Ibid., sig. Cii^r (19, 20): 'Non est enim contrarietas scripturarum si una aliquid plus aut minus habebat quam altera, dum tamen illud amplius non repugnaret alteri.'

[174] Ibid., sig. Cii^r (19, 20): 'Consequens est etiam sicut tu superius intulisti quod ipsorum translatio non est propter eos autentica, quamvis ab ecclesia auctorizetur, ut dixi, verum si ita que ipsi 70 obmiserant non fuissent de Christo secundum aut tertium estimare, sed quia ea que ipsi substraxerunt fuerant prophetie de Christo per quem sicut alia loca sue scripture exprimunt. Eorum lex fuerat immittenda quod ipsi horruerant(ur) {*my deletion*} ideo de Christo [ut] {*my insertion*} illa forsitan tacuerunt, ne a pharaone, qui eorum translationem erat habiturus, eorum lex minus appreciaretur que erat imitanda per Christum. Et forte ob hanc causam in aliis locis de Christo et eius divi[ni]tate {*my addition*} obscurius, non irreprehensibiliter, sunt locuti.'

[175] Ibid., sig. Ciii^r (19, 23): 'Diverse translationes ab ecclesia {*my emendation from* acclesia} comprobate sibi nullatenus adversantur quamvis fortassis altera translatio solum potest argui diminuta sicut in premissis apparet. Sed etiam non esset translatio vera scripture primarie quod tibi nocere non potest dum tamen illud quod ibi asseritur veritatem contineat approbatam modo predicto et nichil contineat alteri translationi aut originali scripture contrarium.'

the discrepancy by pointing out that the passages in both Latin versions have the same perfectly reasonable sense.[176] In the final analysis, he explains, the discrepancies between the three Latin versions are due to issues of translation, such as terminology; but this does not affect their authority nor the truth of their contents.[177] Richard also undermines John's earlier claim that either Jude or the Old Testament is unreliable by arguing that, even though there are many textual parallels between the Old and New Testaments, and the New Testament is confirmed by the Old, there can still be textual differences without implying that either is corrupt.[178]

If the reader is still uncertain about the reliability of a biblical text, FitzRalph gives practical advice on how to approach a potentially corrupt passage in Scripture:

[176] Ibid., sig. Cii^v (19, 22): 'Quod vero allegas litteram unam habere "solus {*emended from* sic lus; *I am grateful to P. G. Schmidt for the suggestion*} ego et Barnabas non habemus potestatem hoc non operandi" [1 Co 9.6] et alia translatio semel habet tantum negationem hoc modo hoc ait *solus ego et Barnabas non habemus potestatem hoc operandi* non oportet contrario modo accipere, quoniam de potestate contradictionis unum infertur ab altero. Qui enim habet potestatem electivam operandi, habet potestatem non operandi et ita e contra et si alter transferens a seipso aut a Spiritu Sancto edoctus illud vellet ostendere negationem addendo ita tamen, ut ex potestate ad non operandum innueret etiam potestatem ad operandum non debet repugnantia reputari; sed si a se illud egit imprudentie forte posset ascribi.' For 1 Co 9.6, the Vulgate has 'solus ego et Barnabas non habemus potestatem hoc operandi'; the original Greek contains the double negation: 'ἐγὼ καὶ Βαρναβᾶς οὐκ ἔχομεν ἐξουσίαν μὴ ἐργάζεσθαι'.

[177] FitzRalph, *Summa*, sig. Ciii^r (19, 23): 'Quam etiam discrepantiam leviter facere potest equivocatio terminorum in linguis diversis ita ut ab uno transferente unus sensus termini equivoci et ab alio alter sensus eius pro ipso ponatur quia sepe terminus equivocus in una lingua non habet sibi correspondens equivocum verbum in alia et etiam terminus transumptibilis a proprio sensu sepe reperitur in uno ydiomate qualis sibi correspondens non reperitur in alio. Non igitur inficitur auctoritas nostre scripture nec veritas contentorum in aliqua translacione ab ecclesia approbata ut tibi videtur etsi in aliquibus locis non sit vera translatio scripture primarie contineat.'

[178] Ibid., sig. Ciii^r (19, 23): 'Cum enim lex antiqua legem approbat, non eius aliquam vel in minimo corruptam eius translationem approbat sed ipsam primariam legem et sensus ipsius sub quacunque lingua et quibuscunque sermonibus exprimatur confirmat'; ibid., sig. Cii^v (19, 22): 'Si enim quisquam hoc diceret contra eum recte inferes scilicet non est ita dicendum scilicet quod inadvertentia et absentia codicis allegati cum sensu modo veridico rationabiliter in casu excusat. Que excusatio non posset in quibuscumque dictis scripture, ut accipis, locum habere sicut enim posset ingenio quoniam non omnis locus scripture alium {*my emendation from* alius} alterius scripture locum allegat.'

> Sicubi vero hesites de primordiali scriptura, ad radices recurre scilicet ut ad originalem linguam in qua scriptura primitus tradebatur scilicet hebraicam et ad codices antiquiores illius non solum [ad] illos {*my emendation from* illis; ad *is my addition*} quos habent iudei sed ad illos si oporteat quos habent christiani in lingua hebraica ne forte, ut obiec[i]sti {*my addition*} superius, esset in hebreis codicibus aliqualis corruptio et ad codices grecos quibus nostram translationem unam accepimus. Et non dubium quin sic errorem si quis fuerit facile deprehendere possis et sensum primordialis scripture valebis extrahere.[179]

> Wherever you are in doubt about the original Scripture, go back to the roots, that is, back to the original language, in which Scripture was first transmitted, that is, to the Hebrew and its older manuscripts, not only to those which the Jews possess, but also to those, if necessary, which the Christians possess in the Hebrew tongue, in case there is perhaps some corruption in the Hebrew manuscripts, as you objected earlier, and go back to the Greek codices, from which we receive one of our translations. And certainly, if there were any error, you could easily detect it and you will be able to extract the sense of original Scripture.

Like his predecessors, FitzRalph confirms the importance of older manuscripts and those in the original Hebrew. To add further security, he suggests consulting, in addition, Greek codices and Hebrew manuscripts owned by Christians, to assuage John's anxiety that the Hebrew ones might have been willfully corrupted by Jews – a notion which Richard neither endorses nor explicitly rejects.

We have seen that the role of John in the dialogue is generally to bring up various – often stereotypical – accusations and doubts about the reliability of the transmission of the biblical text, such as the possible corruption of Hebrew manuscripts and the problems arising from contradictions between the Old and New Testaments, as well as between different translations. The teacher, Richard, however, uses examples and reasoned arguments to refute all of John's claims. The three Latin translations which he believes were sanctioned by the Church – that is, Jerome's version from the Hebrew; the Vetus Latina from the Greek; and another version from an unspecified third language[180] – are all of equal authority due to the official approval which they have received. While

---

[179] Ibid., sig. Ciii^r (19, 23). He gives similar advice above, p. 161, n. 166.

[180] Since he might have thought that the Paris Bible was a separate translation (see above, p. 22 and especially n. 44), it is possible – though not likely – that he identified it with this third translation.

Richard insists that the Church's endorsement does not imply that they are divinely inspired, he does not appear to think that this lessens their authoritative status.[181]

For FitzRalph, any biblical version has to convey the original sense correctly, as do the three approved translations. Of course, the reader might still be faced with a text which he is not able to understand: especially in the prophetic writings, God expressed himself in a way which is difficult to comprehend. But in those instances the reader's lack of insight would be due to his own ignorance.[182] FitzRalph is, in fact, the only author examined in this study to claim that reason could be used to determine a correct reading.[183] This belief also explains his surprising insistence on the importance of good sense when approaching the biblical text and

---

[181] Ibid., sig. Cii[r] (19, 20): 'Unde unum de tribus quo ad 70 interpretes fateri compellimur aut in hoc quod multa obmiserunt graviter deliquerunt aut quod ex causa probabili apud eos sic fecerunt aut quod a deo specialiter moniti erant sic facere quoniam per inadvertentiam sic egerunt non est michi credibile ex quo erant tot prudentes et docti. Si⟨c⟩ {*my deletion*} concesserimus primum, non propter hoc infirmatur nostra scriptura sed sola ipsa translatio et tunc, nisi aliunde approbaretur scilicet per ecclesiam propter veritatem contentorum in ipsa et conformitatem ad codices nostros veraces, esset penitus respuenda. Si autem concesserimus sicut Hebrei dixerunt secundum aut tertium, sicut in secundo prologo Geneseos refert Ieronimus [Jerome, 'Prologus in Pentateucho', p. 3] scilicet ne Tholomeus rex Egipti, qui eos scripturam hebraicam transferre fecerat, estimaret plures deos si plures personas in illis scripturis expressas attenderet quod ob hoc alio interpretes, quando de ministerio trinitatis locus transferendi occurreret, aut expressionem distinctarum personarum {*corrected from* paratarum *by a sixteenth–century hand*} obmiserant aut eam obscurius posuerant. Sed cum de eius causa non constet nec e⟨i⟩tiam {*my deletion*} de amonitione divina consequens est etiam, sicut tu superios intulisti, quod ipsorum translatio non est propter eos autentica quamvis ab ecclesia auctorizetur.' For the possible identification of the third translation with the Paris Bible, see above, p. 22.

[182] Ibid., sig. Ciii[r] (19, 23): 'Quem {*sc.* sensum} tamen clare forte capere non posses dum tamen locus non cerneret fidem nostram sed aliud aliquid in quo error periculosus non esset ambiguitas sensus ibidem tibi in nullo noceret si, ut dixi, nullus sensus ibi expressus esset erroneus. Sed in hoc casu sensum ibi veracem esse deberes supponere, quamvis ad illum sensum exiguitas tui ingenii penetrare non posset. Sic enim ego fateor in multis scripturis propheticis et nonnunquam in aliis quoniam nec deus concedit ut omnibus omnia fiant perspicua, sed ac⟨c⟩errimis {*my deletion*} ingeniis sepe facilima reddit obscura ut non in suo infirmo ingenio, sed in potentissimo domino glorientur qui multa abscondit a sapientibus et revelat ea parvulis suis.'

[183] Bacon (*Opus tertium*, p. 94) and Bessarion (see below, p.176) accept the use of interpretation only to determine whether a reading is incorrect, not whether it is correct.

its manuscript transmission; and it might well have been introduced by him in order to reconcile the three approved Latin translations.

John and Richard are in agreement on the special importance of old manuscripts. Richard's insistence, however, that every version which conveys the true sense of Scripture is of the same value as the original Hebrew – in contrast to John, for whom the Hebrew alone was authoritative – is remarkable. Again, it is possible that he adopted this position in order to defend the equal status of the three approved Latin translations.[184]

The most important aspect of the textual tradition of the Bible, in FitzRalph's view, was the decision of a council, which he never identifies, to give its official approval to three Latin translations. Any doubts about the identity of the translators, contradictions between the different versions and omissions from or additions to the text are brushed aside by pointing to this decision.

In addition to bringing up various arguments for and against maintaining the authoritative position of the Vulgate, Henry Totting de Oyta, in his *Quaestio de Sacra Scriptura*, also discusses the status of the *septuaginta*, as well as general matters concerning the textual transmission and corruption of the Bible.[185] Evaluating Jerome's statement that he had corrected the text of the *septuaginta* against Augustine's claim that this Latin version was divinely inspired, Totting writes: 'Jerome seems to have sinned in those passages in which he wanted to correct them {that is, the Seventy translators}.'[186] For if Augustine's remark was to be taken seriously, then the *septuaginta* must be the authoritative Latin Bible, and

---

[184] Likewise, his insistence on the Church council's vetting of the work and character of the translators (see above, p. 161) might well have served to defend the equal status of the three versions.

[185] For Totting's arguments in support of the Vulgate, see above, pp. 64–67.

[186] Totting, *Quaestio*, pp. 12–13: 'Jeronimus dicit se correxisse 70^a addendo que obmiserunt et delendo superflua, in hoc sequens modum Origenis, prout bene innuit in 2° Prologo biblie [Jerome, 'Prologus in Pentateucho', p. 3]. Et tamen beatus Augustinus 18° De civitate Dei capitulo 53° dicit quod "in eis apparuit signum divinitatis" et quod Spiritu Sancto inspirati scripserunt et quod "ecclesia Christi tot hominum auctoritati ab Eleazaro, tunc pontifice, ad hoc tantum opus electorum neminem iudicat preferendum" [Augustine, *De civitate Dei*, p. 639 (XVIII, 43)]; igitur Jeronimus videtur errasse in illis passibus, ubi eos volebat corrigere.' For the discussion between Jerome and Augustine, see above, pp. 109–113.

Jerome's intervention in the text was tantamount to altering the original text.[187] Augustine's acceptance of the legend surrounding the origin of the Septuagint also favoured the *septuaginta*; however, Jerome held the opposite opinion and rejected the legend.[188] Totting concludes that Jerome and Augustine, both without full knowledge of all details and relying on secondary sources, were simply in disagreement on this point. This was not a matter of great importance, however, since by Totting's time the Vulgate had been sufficiently approved by the Church and could therefore legitimately replace the *septuaginta*.[189]

Like many other scholars, Totting suggested that Jews had corrupted Hebrew manuscripts of the Bible. Yet Henry also mentioned another group which had been accused of falsifying their biblical manuscripts: heretics. His source for this allegation was the commentary tradition to Gratian's *Decretum*, which Henry drew on in several instances. Heretics accused of corrupting Greek manuscripts were named together with Jews by decretists when arguing that both Hebrew and Greek manuscripts of the Bible were unreliable.[190] This might confirm the suggestion made earlier in the

---

[187] Totting, who favours the Vulgate, adduces several arguments against the two preceding points; see above, p. 65, n. 57, and p. 65, n. 59.

[188] Totting, *Quaestio*, p. 29: 'Augustinus ibidem capitulo LII° [*De civitate Dei*, p. 638 (XVIII, 42)] dicit quod singuli de LXX^a separatim sederunt – ita enim eorum fidem Ptholomeo placuit explorare ... Jeronimus vero dicit hoc esse mendacium, ut patet in 2° Prologo biblie ['Prologus in Pentateucho', p. 3]. Quomodo igitur Jeronimo est credendum.' For the legend of the Septuagint, see above pp. 8–9.

[189] Totting, *Quaestio*, p. 33: 'Item dato quod in hac parte discordaverint, non est de hoc magna vis, cum de hoc certitudinem non haberent, nisi ex relatis et veresimilibus coniecturis. Tamen quantum ad propositum pertinet, constat per sufficiens examen ecclesie Jeronimum in transferendo non errasse, prout eciam Iudei sibi contestati sunt secundum Augustinum in loco preallegato, scil. 18° De civitate Dei capitulo LIII° [*De civitate Dei*, p. 639 (XVIII, 43)].'

[190] For the quotation from Totting, see above, p. 66, n. 61. For an example from the decretist tradition, see Rufinus, *Die 'Summa Decretorum' des Magister Rufinus*, ed. H. Singer, Paderborn 1902, p. 23 (referring to Gratian, *Decretum*, col. 17 [D. 9, c. 6]): 'Porro Ieronimus in secundo prologo Bibliothece huic adversarius videtur; ait enim: *Emendatiora sane sunt exemplaria latina quam greca, greca quam hebrea*; propter quod apparet magis de hebraicis ad greca et de grecis ad latina exemplaria recurrendum. Sed sciendum quoniam in tempore primitivo, antequam ecclesia per omnes partes orbis propagaretur, incorrupta erant et integra volumina Hebreorum atque Grecorum, procedente vero tempore, cum admodum Christianus populus cresceret et multorum hereses in ecclesia germinarent, tam ab ipsis Iudeis

Quaestio that Jerome's version could have been based on corrupt manuscripts, since he made his translation at a time when Jews and heretics had already corrupted both Hebrew and Greek manuscripts – his version would therefore be unreliable.[191] Yet Totting discounts this idea: in Jerome's day, not all Hebrew and Greek manuscripts had yet been corrupted.[192]

Totting also mentions possible objections to the assumption that the text of the Gospels and other New Testament writings had been transmitted correctly in its original form. It could be argued, he writes, that they had come down to the present incomplete and corrupt. This might be confirmed by the final verse of John's Gospel [Jn 21.25]: 'But there are also many other things which Jesus did; which, if they were written every one, the world itself, I think, would not be able to contain the books that should be written.' The claim that not all of Christ's deeds are described in

---

ecclesie invidentibus quam ab hereticis hebraica et greca exemplaria corrupta sunt, sed magis hebraica quam greca, magis greca quam latina. Augustinus ergo hic loquitur de antiquis exemplaribus Hebreorum et Grecorum. Ieronimus vero de modernis, que a multis violata fuerunt.' The idea that both Jews and Greek heretics corrupted their manuscripts may derive ultimately from Ac 14.1–5 or Augustine, *Enarrationes in Psalmos*, in his *Opera*, X, 1–3, ed. E. Dekkers and J. Fraipont (Corpus Christianorum. Series Latina, 38–40), Turnhout 1956, II, p. 839 (65, 2): 'Non solum dolete Iudaeos qui gratiam istam gentibus inuidebant, sed plus haereticos plangite', although neither passage mentions the corruption of texts. For another reference to heretics corrupting their manuscripts, see Peter Lombard, *In epistolam ad Romanos* (*PL*, CXCI), Paris 1880, cols 1297–1534, col. 1392A–B (25–26): 'Postquam vero a concordia animis dissidentibus, et haereticis pertu[r]bantibus {*my insertion*} moveri quaestionem coeperunt, multa tam in Graecis quam in Latinis codicibus ab haereticis contentionis studio mutata sunt, qui cum propria auctoritate uti non possunt ad victoriam, verba legis adulterant, ut sensum suum quasi verbis legis asserant, et contradicentibus sibi, quasi auctoritate resistant.'

[191] Totting, *Quaestio*, p. 13: 'Jeronimus transtulit, postquam biblia Ebrayca fuit suspecta de corrupcione a Iudeis et hereticis; igitur sua translacio non videtur secura.'

[192] Ibid., p. 31: '"In primitiva ecclesia" etc., negatur consequencia. Ad probacionem: Concedo quod tunc fides fundabatur etc. Et quando infertur quod "igitur a forciori" etc., negatur consequencia, quia, quando res incipit fieri et crescere, nondum plene separatum est purum ab impuro, sicut cum tritico crescunt zizania, de quo eciam habetur in parabola Salvatoris [Mt 13.24–30].'

the Gospels could be seen as proof that they had been abridged.[193] Totting thus concludes:

> Quia evangelium non est aliud quam ystoria continens doctrinam Christi et acta eius ab eius incarnacione usque ad eius ascensionem, igitur cum quia perfidia Iudeorum et pseudoapostolorum et hereticorum visa est depravare ystorias evangelicas, quam cito perceperunt eas discipulos conscribere, et propter hoc b. Jeronimus in Prologo epistolarum canonicarum dicit "se evangelistas ad veritatis lineam correxisse"; igitur difficile videtur quod ecclesia obtinuerit scripturas originales novi testamenti et per consequens testamenti veteris indepravatas inter tot callidissimorum hominum versucias et insidias.[194]

Since the Gospel is nothing but a story containing the teaching and deeds of Christ from his incarnation to his ascent, therefore, as soon as they realised that the disciples had written them, the perfidy of the Jews, of the pseudo-Apostles and of the heretics was seen to distort the evangelical stories; and for that reason blessed Jerome says in the Prologue to the Catholic Epistles that he 'corrected the evangelists according to the line of truth'. It therefore seems unlikely that the Church received the original texts of the New Testament and,

---

[193] Ibid., pp. 23–24: 'Evangelia et alie scripture novi testamenti nec plene nec absque corrupcione pervenerunt ad ecclesiam, ut videtur, igitur etc. Consequencia patet, tum apercio scripturarum veteris testamenti per novum fuerit propter utilitatem ecclesie. Si ergo ad ecclesiam non integre et perfecte venisset, frustra brevi tempore talis apercio facta fuisset. Sed antecedens probatur: tum quia omnis Christi accio et omnia, que circa ipsum fiebant, nostra fuit instruccio. Sed non omnia Christi facta pervenerunt ad ecclesiam, ut patet Jo ultimo, ubi dicitur [Jn 21.25]: "Sunt autem et alia multa, que fecit Jesus, que si scribantur per singula, nec ipsum arbitror mundum capere eos, qui scribendi sunt, libros." Igitur sequitur quod diminute habeamus evangelium Christi.'

[194] Ibid., p. 24. Jerome did not write a preface to the Catholic Epistles; the preface alluded to here, commonly found in Paris Bibles, is misattributed to him by Totting and also in at least one manuscript of the Paris Bible; see MS London, British Library, Add. 40006, f. 523ᵛ: 'Incipit prohemium VII epistularum canonicarum sancti Jeronimi presbiteri: Non ita est ordo apud grecos qui integre sapiunt fidemque rectam sectantur epistularum septem que canonice nuncupantur, sicut in latinis codicibus invenitur ut quia Petrus est primus in numero apostolorum et prime sunt eius epistule in ordine ceterarum. Sed sicut evangelistas dudum ad veritatis lineam correximus, ita has proprio ordini deo nos iuvante reddidimus.' For an example of a Paris Bible in which the preface is not attributed to Jerome, see MS London, British Library, Add. 39629, f. 545ᵛ. Ker (*Medieval Manuscripts*, pp. 96–97), in his list of incipits of the prologues common to the Paris Bible, gives the preface to the Catholic Epistles under number 63 (ibid., p. 97).

consequently, of the Old Testament, uncorrupted amid the deceitfulness and traps of extremely crafty men.

Having formulated the possible objection that the books of both the Old and the New Testament had come down to the Latin world in a corrupt form, supported by Jerome's statement that he had brought the text of the Gospels into line with *veritas*, Totting then proceeds, in typical scholastic fashion, to argue against these points. For instance, it could be maintained that only those deeds of Christ which were relevant for all times, and not just for a particular moment, were included in the Gospels.[195] It could also be argued that the Holy Spirit induced the Evangelists to write different accounts, so that they would not be accused of having colluded to provide a coherent and fluent storyline of Christ's life. Therefore, the four authors differed in their wording, styles and order, without, however, contradicting each other, since what was omitted by one was taken up by another.[196]

The fourteenth century presents an odd picture: the four authors discussed here, none of whom was a textual critic, offer different approaches to the Bible and to the status of its various versions. They all show a certain respect for the Vulgate, differing in degree from, at one end of the spectrum, Peter of Ailly's complete neglect of all textual traditions other than the Vulgate's, to, at the other end, Adam Easton's readiness to produce a new translation from the Hebrew. Since, moreover, only two of them, FitzRalph and Totting, commented on the textual tradition in any

---

[195] Totting, *Quaestio*, p. 25: 'Non oportuit omnia ista scribi, que pro aliquo certo tempore debebant effectum sortiri, sed ista que ad ecclesie statum pro omni tempore pertinebant.'

[196] Ibid., pp. 25–26: 'Diceres: ex quo Spiritu Sancto dictante, qui est spiritus concordie, conscripta sunt evangelia, quare ergo plurimum discordant in verbis et materia et ordine sentenciarum. Omnimoda enim concordia fuisset manifestum argumentum, quod uno spiritu dictante omnes quatuor scripsissent et uno instinctu. Potest dici quod factum est, ne emuli Christi fidei dicerent, evangelistas inter se fecisse colludium vel fictum esse, si diceretur a christianis quod scripsissent in diversis regionibus et prius super hoc non convenissent; igitur fuit conveniencius, quod eandem veritatem ystoriacam quilibet [de] 4or tangeret, licet aliis et aliis verbis et modo loquendi vario, quandoque et ordine sine tamen contradiccione et quod quandoque unus obmitteret aliqua, que alteri ad supplendum reservabantur. Sic enim manifeste apparet quatuor fuisse et nichilominus eandem intendisse veritatem.'

detail, we should be cautious about assuming that their views are representative of the century as a whole. Their positions are far less radical than Peter of Ailly's, but both of them make it clear that Jerome's version occupies a special position: Totting is unquestionably a supporter of the Vulgate, though a less extreme one than Peter; and, in FitzRalph's dialogue, Richard defends it, together with two other Latin translations, from John's attacks.

FitzRalph and Totting differ from the other authors examined here in one important respect. Even though they held clear opinions on the questions discussed, both put forward detailed arguments for and against the various issues at stake; in each case, this procedure can be explained by the genre in which they wrote. Totting composed a *quaestio*, in which arguments *pro* and *contra* certain propositions were aired; and FitzRalph chose the dialogue format, in which the interlocutors presented opposing views.

The Fifteenth Century

In his treatise on Jn 21.22, Cardinal Bessarion recounts a discussion that took place on the feast of St John about the passage, noting that there were those who maintained that the Latin reading *sic* was better or, at any rate, no worse than the Greek ἐάν, translated by Bessarion as *si*.[197] He, on the other hand, insists that the Greek version has greater authority than the Latin, since Greek was the language in which John had written his Gospel. To him, it is obvious that a translation has to be in agreement with the original, otherwise it is faulty.[198] So, whenever there is a mistake or a doubtful passage in the translation, it is necessary to go back to the original text.[199] He therefore strongly supports the view that Greek manuscripts of the New Testament are more authoritative than

---

[197] Bessarion, *In illud Evangelii*, col. 623: 'Cum nuper sacrum Evangelium Joannis Evangelistae in eius festivitate legeretur.' The feast of St John is on 24 June. Bessarion does not specify where the discussion was held or who was present. Ibid., col. 625AB: 'Tum alii quidam ex his qui aderant, contradicere, non *si* sed *sic* legi debere asseverantes beneque se habere Latinum sermonem dicentes, et aut rectiorem esse Graeco, aut illo non minus rectum.'

[198] Ibid., cols 629D–630A: 'Cum sacrum Joannis Evangelium Joannes ipse apostolus et Evangelista, Spiritus sancti gratia plenus, Graeco sermone scripserit, nulli dubium esse debet, quamlibet translationem originali litterae minime respondentem, non rectam esse, sed vitiatam atque mendosam.'

[199] Ibid., col. 630A: 'Si quis in interpretis opere error animadvertitur, si qua dubitatio oritur, profecto eo recurrendum est, unde facta est translatio.'

Latin ones, a position which, given his background, is hardly surprising.

Bessarion says that those defending the reading *sic* invoke Jerome and Augustine, who both cited the passage with the reading *sic* rather than *si*.[200] In their eyes, this must be the right reading, because neither of these Fathers would have hidden the truth, and both of them knew Latin and Greek very well.[201] The fact that Augustine interpreted Jn 21.22 with the reading *sic* is not enough, however, to convince Bessarion that it must be accepted, and he proceeds to rule out the authority of exegetes in establishing the text of the Latin Bible. Just because it is possible to interpret a passage with certain readings, this does not mean that the text is necessarily correct, since incorrect texts have been interpreted in the past.[202]

To support his position, Bessarion, too, relies on the Latin Fathers. He repeatedly points out that the Latin version should yield to the Greek when it comes to establishing the true text, since this has been recommended by the Fathers, above all Jerome and Augustine. First, he quotes Jerome's recommendation to go back to the Greek original whenever the true text has to be identified from among many possible versions. This is better than trying to correct

[200] Apart from the Vulgate, I have not been able to find any further citation of this passage in Jerome's works. For passages in which Augustine uses *sic*, see below, p. 178, n. 209.

[201] Ibid., col. 625C: 'Primo enim id auctoritate Hieronymi et Augustini et aliorum Latinorum doctorum confirmant, quos eo in loco non *si*, sed *sic* scripsisse et ita eam partem exposuisse constat. Hos enim non est verisimile et veritatem latuisse, qui et sapientiores nobis fuere et non modo Latinae, sed etiam Graecae linguae doctiores, quando praesertim ante ipsorum quoque aetatem non *si*, sed *sic* apud Latinos scriptum fuisse animadvertitur.'

[202] Ibid., col. 634AB: 'Ad haec dicimus non esse sufficiens veritatis testimonium, quod aliqui doctores ita eum locum exposuerunt, siquidem pleraque alia in hujusmodi translationibus invenies, vel per librarios corrupta, vel per interpretes non recte translata, quae tamen sancti doctores, litteram quam repererunt, secuti, iuxta eamdem litteram conati sunt exponere, et ita exposuerunt, ut aliquando, quamvis litterae veritatem non fuerint assecuti, veram tamen sententiam cum summa sapientia, excerpserint, nonnunquam etiam, si aliam ediderint sententiam, quam auctoris exstiterit, ita tamen acutam et gravem et luculentam ediderint, ut ipsa et non alia videatur esse debere. Equidem fateor Augustinum, virum sublimis ingenii, per *sic* hunc locum exposuisse, et quidem gravissimis acutissimisque rationibus, hoc autem non satis esse ad persuadendum ita debere scribi.' This and the other arguments which Bessarion is attempting to refute may well have been used by George in his first, unpublished, treatise.

a translation which has been badly rendered, incompetently corrected or to which additions or changes have been made by malignant scribes.[203] Next, he cites Augustine, who stressed the necessity of knowing Greek and Hebrew, so that one might be able to return to the source in cases where the Latin translation raised doubts.[204] If the Latin disagrees with the Greek original – Bessarion explicitly rejects any censure of Jerome, blaming instead careless scribes or suchlike for any errors – then the Greek has full authority and has to be endorsed and confirmed.[205] His conviction of the superiority of Greek over Latin leads him to assert that, when it comes to interpreting the text of the New Testament, the Greek Fathers are more authoritative than the Latin ones, since Greek was their native language.[206]

Bessarion's opponent, George of Trebizond, does not devote a great deal of attention to the authority of Greek and Latin manuscripts for the emendation of Latin Scripture. Instead, George draws a clear line between the author, on the one hand, and the translator, on the other hand. For him, the translation is no longer

---

[203] Bessarion quotes Jerome's 'Praefatio in Evangelio' (p. 1515) in *In illud Evangelii*, col. 630A: '"Si veritas", inquit, "est quaerenda de pluribus, cur non ad Graecam originem recurrentes, ea quae vel a vitiosis interpretibus male dicta, vel a praesumptoribus imperitis emendata perversius, vel a librariis dormitantibus aut addita sunt, aut mutata corrigimus?"'

[204] Ibid., col. 630B, citing Augustine (Augustine, *De doctrina christiana*, p. 42 [II, xi, 16]): '"Latinae quidem linguae homines quos nunc instruendos suscepimus, duabus aliis ad Scripturarum divinarum cognitionem opus habent, Hebraea scilicet et Graeca, ut ad exemplaria praecedentia recurratur, si quam dubitationem attulerit Latinorum interpretum infinita varietas."' For further examples, see Bessarion, *In illud Evangelii*, col. 630BC (quoting Augustine, *De doctrina christiana*, p. 48 [II, XV, 22]); and Bessarion, *In illud Evangelii*, col. 633BC (quoting Jerome, 'Praefatio in Evangelio', p. 1515; and Augustine, *De doctrina christiana*, p. 42 [II, xi, 16]).

[205] Bessarion, *In illud Evangelii*, col. 630CD: 'Videndum itaque primo, quomodo se habeat in Graeca atque originali lingua, haec, de qua quaerimus, Evangelii auctoritas, et an sermo Latinus Graeco consentiat; quod si dissentiat, an id facile potuerit dormitantium librariorum vitio fieri, et an in aliis quoque simile aliquid fieri potuerit factumve sit absque sancti doctoris peritissimique interpretis Hieronymi culpa aut reprehensione.'

[206] Ibid., col. 634A: 'Quod principio doctorum Latinorum auctoritatem adducunt, et nos quidem Graecorum auctoritatem opponimus, quibus certe, cum de his quae in eorum lingua scripta sunt loquantur, et alioquin nec sanctitate vitae, nec doctrina habeantur inferiores, credendum potius esse fatendum est.'

the work of the original author but rather that of the translator.[207] In this way, he liberates Latin manuscripts from the Greek tradition and strengthens their autonomous authority. Already in the summary of his earlier treatise which appeared in his invective against Theodore Gaza, he had asked why we remain in doubt about this reading, given that we have the testimony of Augustine, with whom no one has so far disagreed.[208] In his later *In expositionem*, George once again points to the Western Fathers as authorities who had cited and interpreted the passage in Jn 21.22 in the usual Latin way with the reading *sic*.[209] He thus remains true

---

[207] George of Trebizond, *In expositionem illius textus evangelii 'Sic volo eum manere, etc' et quod S. Joannes Evangelista nondum sit mortuus ad Sixtum IV pontificem maximum* (*Patrologia Graeca*, ed. J.–P. Migne, CLXI), Paris 1866, cols 867–882, at col. 880CD: '"Oportet te iterum prophetare populis, gentibus, linguis et multis regibus" [Rv 10.11]. Id certe non potest de Evangelio dici, licet posteaquam Apocalypsis scriptum ab eo sit. Nam nec Evangelium prophetiam ullus unquam appellabit nec multis scriptum est linguis, sed Graece solum. Nec refert si per traductionem ad multas pervenerit linguas. Traductiones enim non sunt auctorum, sed translatorum. Ipse autem prophetaturus multis populis, gentibus, regibus per multas dicitur linguas.'

[208] George of Trebizond, *Adversus Theodorum Gazam*, p. 331 (35, 3–4): 'Testis est ipse Augustinus, qui cum super evangelium Iohannis scriberet, non "si eum volo manere", sed "sic eum volo manere" saepius repetit. Hieronymus certe hunc etiam locum vidit, legit, perpendit ... Quare si Augustinus clamat et ceteri assentiuntur tacentes, quid nos quaerimus? Quid volumus? Quid contendimus? Graecamne linguam aut latinam melius quam illi tenere arbitramur? His rationibus ego mihi iam diu persuasi sequenda esse vestigia patrum, qui et ingenio et studio et doctrina non erant nobis inferiores. Sanctitate vero non praestantiores illi nobis, sed illi praestantes. Nos autem vermes, et non homines terrena solum sapimus. Ac ideo ad sapientiam et gratiam quam illi habebant, vix respicere possumus.'

[209] George of Trebizond, *In expositionem*, col. 871D: 'Non *si* sed *sic* Patres interpretati sunt'. Ambrose has *si sic* once (Ambrose, *Expositio Psalmi CXVIII*, in his *Opera*, V, ed. M. Petschenig, Vienna and Leipzig 1913, repr. New York and London 1962, p. 451 [20, 12]), and *si* once (Ambrose, *Expositio Evangelii secundum Lucam*, ed. M. Adriaen, in his *Opera*, IV, Turnhout 1957, pp. 1–400, at p. 215 [VII, 3]). All medieval Latin authors seem to have *sic*; see, e.g., the Venerable Bede, *Homeliarum Evangelii libri II*, in his *Opera*, III–IV, ed. D. Hurst, Turnhout 1955, p. 63 l. 100 [I, 9]); Bernard of Clairvaux (*Sermo de festivitatibus sancti Stephani, sancti Ioannis et sanctorum Innocentium*, in his *Opera*, IV: *Sermones*, I, ed. J. Leclercq and H. Rochais, Rome 1966, pp. 270–273, at p. 271) and Thomas Aquinas (*Summa theologiae*, II, ed. B. de Rubeis, C.–R. Billuart and X. Faucher, Turin 1950, p. 846 [q. 182, art. II, 2]. George might be referring solely to Augustine, who quotes Jn 21.22 about a dozen times, always using *sic*; see, e.g., Augustine, *In Iohannis evangelium tractatus CXXIV*, ed. R. Willems (Corpus

to his own method, ignoring Bessarion's claim that exegetical writings have no value for establishing the text of the Bible.

Unlike Bessarion and George of Trebizond, Lorenzo Valla, in the two redactions of his work on the New Testament, does not quote any Church Fathers in support of his attitude towards the authority of Greek and Latin manuscripts, possibly because he did not feel the need to justify his approach with quotations from Jerome or Augustine. In the *Collatio*, Valla makes very few clear pronouncements as to his preference for Greek or Latin manuscripts. Mostly, he limits himself to simple statements such as: 'This is missing in some manuscripts' or 'Some manuscripts have *x*.'[210] It seems that, for him, the supremacy of Greek manuscripts over Latin ones is so obvious that it is not worth mentioning, let alone a matter of discussion – he refers, for instance, to the 'rule of *graeca veritas*'.[211] We might therefore assume that statements such as 'In Greek, it is *x*' can be understood as having authority for the establishment of the Latin text. But Valla did not, in fact, regard the Greek version as the unquestionable truth. So, for example, he says at one point that he thinks the Greek is more correct; he does not say that it actually is.[212] At times – although very rarely – he goes even further and endorses a translation despite the fact that it differs from the Greek original.[213]

In addition to Greek manuscripts, Valla also attributes authority to very old Latin manuscripts, and in one case he even puts them side by side with Greek ones.[214] He also distinguishes between

---

Christianorum. Series Latina, 36), Turnhout 1964, p. 680 (CXXIV, 1); Augustine, *Sermones* (*PL*, XXXVIII), Paris 1865, col. 1181 (CCLIII, IV, 5); and Augustine, *De consensu evangelistarum*, p. 382 (III, xxv, 78).

[210] See, e.g., Valla, *Collatio*, p. 24: 'Deest in quibusdam codicibus *eis* seu *ipsis*'; ibid., p. 63: 'Quidam codices non habent *fortasse* et recte'; ibid., p. 96: 'Melius habent ii codices, ubi legimus...'

[211] Ibid., p. 140: 'Emendatius et ad legem grece veritatis in quibusdam codicibus legitur...'.

[212] Ibid., p. 253: 'Aliter grece legitur et, ut arbitror rectius, sic: ...'. At first glance, this example might not seem convincing; however, Valla very rarely inserts expressions such as 'I believe', which leads me to suspect that he was doubtful about this case.

[213] Ibid., p. 238: 'Melius ii codices qui habent *quod operatur* [1 Th 2.13], licet grece sit *qui*.' In fact, the Greek New Testament reads ὃς καὶ ἐνεργεῖται.

[214] Ibid., p. 147: 'Male conantur emendare quidam hunc locum pro *quia* dicentes *qui connumeratus est* [Ac 1.17], nam ut Greci, ita nostri vetustissimi codices habent *quia*.'

several Latin versions of the New Testament in his *Collatio*,[215] without, however, specifying which versions he means.

As in the *Collatio*, so, too, in his *Annotationes* most references to manuscripts are limited to statements along the lines of 'These manuscripts have the better text, in which one reads *x*', or 'In Greek, it is *x*'.[216] And, as before, Valla regards Greek manuscripts as more authoritative than Latin ones.[217] Often, he simply gives Greek quotations to confirm a reading he supports.[218] He explicitly says in one instance that '*suae* is not in the Greek, therefore it must not be in the Latin either',[219] making it clear that the Latin version has to conform to the Greek text. Unlike his procedure in the *Collatio*, he now seems – though infrequently – to distinguish and classify Greek readings.[220] In another instance, he defends one of his stylistic emendations and explains why he felt the need to add a justification, leaving no doubt that for him the Greek reading is the only thing that matters: 'I said this on account of those who are obstinate, although the Greek authority should suffice.'[221] He often

---

[215] See, e.g., ibid., p. 262 [on 1 P 1.13]: 'Melius in iis codicibus, in quibus scriptum est *sobrii perfecte sperate*; tamen grece est *fertur* non *offertur*, ut in omnibus editionibus latinis invenitur'; ibid., p. 264 [on 1 P 3.19]: 'In quibusdam editionibus est *spiritualiter veniens*, grece est *spiritibus*.'

[216] See, e.g., Valla, *Annotationes*, p. 807A: 'Melius ij codices habent, in quibus legitur...'; ibid., p. 821B: 'Graece est...'.

[217] See, e.g., ibid., p. 818A: '"Accedens autem ad alterum dixit similiter. At ille respondens ait: eo domine, et non iuit [Mt 21.30]". Quia sequitur *et non ivit*, mutaverunt temerarij corruptores *ego* in *eo*, non intelligentes non satisfacere hanc responsionem filii iussionis patris... Sed quid argumentor cum ueritas graeca habeat ἐγὼ κύριε [*Novum Testamentum Graece:* ἐγώ κύριε].'

[218] Ibid., p. 868B: '"Et gratia eius in me uacua non fuit" [1 Co 15.10]: Graece est *et gratia eius quae est in me*, ἡ εἰς ἐμὲ [*Novum Testamentum Graece:* ἡ εἰς ἐμέ].' In contrast to the *Collatio*, where Valla gives only Latin translations of the readings he has found in Greek manuscripts, he now cites the Greek version in the original. There is, however, an apparatus with Greek readings in the margins of both manuscripts of the *Collatio*; see Valla, *Collatio*, p. LV.

[219] Valla, *Annotationes*, p. 830B: '"Suscepit Israël puerum suum, recordatus misericordiae suae": Verius illi codices, in quibus legitur *memorari misericordiae suae*, quanquam graece non est *suae*, ergo nec latine debet esse.'

[220] Ibid., p. 864B: 'Optimi graecorum codices non habent illud, *magno*'; ibid., p. 892B (on 3 Jn 4): 'Etiam *his* non *horum* dicendum fuit: quidam tamen graeci codices habent genitiuum singularem, id est non τούτων sed ταύτης. In quibus, si recte scribitur, legendum est, *maius hoc gaudium*, sive *maiorem hanc laetitiam*.'

[221] Ibid., p. 847B: 'Haec dixi propter pertinaces, cum satis esse deberet autoritas graeca'; see also ibid., 829B: 'Neque est graece *ueritatem* [Lk 1.4], sed ut sic

quotes the Greek version to prove his point;[222] and in one case – when discussing the name of Simon – he even gives the Hebrew original.[223]

His attitude towards Latin manuscripts in the *Annotationes* is the same as in the *Collatio*: although he does not explicitly say that older codices are to be preferred to more recent ones, he draws attention to their antiquity when he accepts their readings.[224] He continues to distinguish between different Latin versions.[225] And, as in the earlier treatise, there are a few instances when he goes against what is dictated by the authority of the Greek text.[226] This, however, can be explained by his goal, in both the *Collatio* and the *Annotationes*, of presenting a better Latin translation.[227]

Valla's move to Rome, where he worked on the *Annotationes* until his death, gave him increased access to manuscripts of the New Testament.[228] Some modern scholars have argued that this had an impact on his view of their importance.[229] Yet the examples given here do not suggest that Valla's move to Rome changed his approach to, or his classification of, manuscripts. The only

---

dicam, *certitudinem*, ἀσφάλειαν.' For the role of *graeca veritas* for Valla, see also Fois, *Il pensiero cristiano*, pp. 410–411.

[222] See, e.g., ibid., p. 825B: '"Gerasenorum" [Mk 5.1]: *Gadarenorum* legendum est γαδαρηνῶν.' In fact, the *Novum Testamentum Graece* reads Γερασηνῶν in the main text and gives γαδαρηνῶν as a variant reading in the apparatus.

[223] Ibid., p. 851B: '"Respondit Iacobus, dicens: Viri fratres audite me, Simon narrauit" [Ac 15.13–14]: Graece non est *Simon*, sed *Symeon*. De Petro enim Iacobus loquebatur. Ergo ut Paulus graece uocabatur Saulus, hebraice Saul, graece Simon, hebraice Symeon, שמעון.'

[224] Ibid., p. 826B: '"Bene omnia fecit, surdos fecit audire ... " [Mk 7.37]: Graece legitur *et surdos* et ita in quibusdam uetustis apud nos exemplaribus translatum legimus'; ibid., p. 846A: '"Et illa nocte nihil prendiderunt" [Jn 21.3] et iterum: "afferte de piscibus quos prendidistis" [Jn 21.10]. Alij codices melius habent *ceperunt* et *cepistis*. Alij optime, et quidem uetustiores, *prehenderunt* et *prehendistis*.'

[225] See, e.g., ibid., p. 842B: 'Melius in ijs aeditionibus legitur ubi scriptum ...'; ibid., p. 869A: 'Melius in nonnullis aeditionibus legitur.'

[226] Ibid., p. 875B (on Ga 3.3): 'Legendum est *consummemini*, quanquam graece est *consummamini*.'

[227] See below, p. 264 and especially n. 57.

[228] See, e.g., Robert Stupperich, 'Schriftauslegung und Textkritik bei Laurentius Valla', in *Text – Wort – Glaube: Studien zur Überlieferung, Interpretation und Autorisierung biblischer Texte. Kurt Aland gewidmet*, ed. M. Brecht, Berlin and New York 1980, pp. 220–233, at p. 222; and see below, p. 263.

[229] See, e.g., Valla, *Collatio*, pp. XLIX–L.

detectable alterations are a slight tendency to differentiate between Greek manuscripts and the incorporation of Greek quotations from the Bible into the main text.[230]

Valla has at times been criticised for having a one-dimensional, uncritical approach to Greek manuscripts, since he does not take into account problems within the Greek tradition.[231] He does not, however, follow the Greek manuscripts blindly. In the first place, he distinguishes between Greek variants in his collations,[232] indicating an awareness of differences within the Greek tradition. Secondly, on rare occasions he is prepared to accept deviations from the Greek if otherwise the text could not be translated precisely into Latin or if, in order to mirror the Greek original, it would be necessary to distort the Latin translation.[233]

In the *Antidotum Primum*, when forced to defend his work against Poggio, Valla expresses his view that the Latin version of the Bible ranks well below the original Hebrew or Greek – indeed, is of no sacred value whatever.[234] For him, the Latin version is nothing

---

[230] Stupperich ('Schriftauslegung', p. 227) claims that in the *Annotationes* Valla thought that certain Greek exemplars were not good and therefore should not be consulted for the sake of clarifying the text, which is why he tried to find better readings. I have found no evidence of this in the treatise.

[231] See, e.g., ibid., p. 227.

[232] See, e.g., Valla, *Annotationes*, p. 836A: '"Sic est qui sibi thesaurizat, et non est in deum diues dixitque ad discipulos suos" [Lk 12.21–22]. Deest hoc apud nos: *Haec dicens clamabat, qui habet aures ad audiendum audiat*, tum sequitur *dixit autem ad discipulos suos*, ταῦτα λέγων ἐφώνει, ὁ ἔχων ὦτα ἀκούειν, ἀκουέτω ειπε {sic} δὲ [compare Lk 8.8]. Sunt tamen graeci codices, quibus hoc abest.'

[233] For examples, see above, p. 179, n. 213, and p. 181, n. 226; see also Valla, *Annotationes*, p. 876B: '"Quicunque uolunt placere in carne" [Ga 6.12]: Graece non legitur *in carne* neque tamen reprehendo interpretem, sed tantum significo non respondere uerbum uerbo quia respondere non potest.'

[234] See above, pp. 100–101, nn. 52 and 53, and Valla, *Antidotum primum*, p. 112: 'Quanquam Novum ipse {sc. Hieronymus} non transtulit, sed aliquotiens repurgavit non tam in verbis quam in sententiis; quod rursus ut opinor si revivisceret, in quibusdam depravatum vitiatumque corrigeret; quemadmodum in opere meo De collatione Novi Testamenti, quod tu opus in invidiam vocas, ostendo. Itaque ne multus sim, si quid emendo non Sacram Scripturam emendo sed illius interpretationem, neque in eam contumeliosus sum sed pius potius, nec aliud facio nisi quod melius quam prior interpres transfero. Ut mea translatio sit, si vera fuerit, appellanda sancta scriptura, non illius etsi proprie scriptura sancta sit ea, quam sancti ipsi vel Hebraice vel Graece scripserunt, nam Latinum nihil tale est … Et si proprie Scriptura Sancta sit ea que sancti ipsi vel Hebraice vel Grece

more than a translation. Yet, precisely because it is a translation, it is not always bound to agree completely with the original Greek.

Giannozzo Manetti is the only Renaissance humanist studied here to comment on the Hebrew manuscripts of the Old Testament. Generally speaking, he gives clear preference to manuscripts in the original language with regard to both the Old and the New Testament. For his translation of the Psalms, when determining their correct number and division, he opts for the Hebrew manuscripts, attributing any errors to Greek and Latin ones.[235] With regard to the New Testament, Manetti judges the Greek text to be of greater authority than the Latin version.[236]

Like Valla, Manetti thinks that translations of the Scriptures rank below the original texts.[237] The position of the Septuagint, however, is slightly different: Manetti seems to accept that it was divinely inspired, and he points out that this view was also held, for instance, by Augustine.[238] While aware of Jerome's rejection of the legend surrounding the Septuagint, he does not consider himself capable of deciding which of the two sides is correct.[239]

Giovanni Crastone, when writing about his Latin and Greek edition of the Psalms, pays no attention whatever to the Hebrew text and treats the Septuagint version as though it were the original. So, for instance, he says in the dedicatory letter that it would be too tedious to list all his emendations and simply states that he has

---

scripserunt, nam Latinum nihil tale est.' For a discussion of what *sacra scriptura* means for Valla, see Fois, *Il pensiero cristiano*, pp. 407–412.

[235] Manetti, *Apologeticus*, p. 23 (I, 49): 'De numero Psalmorum querendum restat, in quo quidem non plures nec pauciores etiam quam centumquinquaginta Psalmos in volumine *Psalterii* integro et non depravato sive hebreo sive greco sive latino contineri profitemur et dicimus. Si vero apud Grecos aut apud Latinos huiusmodi numerus forte variatus ac diversus fuisse reperiretur, certum quoddam manifestumque erratum foret.' For another example of his preference for the Hebrew, see ibid., p. 70: 'Totus hic versus superabundat, cum nihil hebraice habeatur.'

[236] See Paul Botley, *Latin Translation in the Renaissance: The Theory and Practice of Leonardo Bruni, Giannozzo Manetti and Desiderius Erasmus*, Cambridge 2004, p. 95.

[237] See ibid., p. 101.

[238] This is the opinion of his editor de Petris; see Manetti, *Apologeticus*, p. XL. Manetti quotes Augustine ibid., pp. 40–42.

[239] Ibid., pp. 36–37 (II, 27): 'Quod utrum verum fuerit an non me ignorare fateor, presertim cum Hieronymum, virum eruditissimum ac trium clarissimarum linguarum peritissimum, longe aliter sentire manifestissime videam.'

corrected 'about seventy passages according to the *graeca veritas*'.[240] Nevertheless, he quotes Augustine's comment that it is necessary for the understanding of Scripture to know both Hebrew and Greek in order to be able to consult the manuscripts in their original language, if different readings in the Latin lead to ambiguity.[241] He does not, however, attribute unquestioned validity to the Greek manuscript tradition. In one instance, he considers the possibility that the Greek codices might be wrong but says that he did not dare intervene in the Greek text. Instead, he ascribes the mistake to the Latin translators, who were confused by the similarity of θήρα (spoil, booty) and χήρα (widow). Since, however, all the Greek manuscripts have θήρα and all the Latin ones *vidua*, he leaves the decision to the reader, thereby avoiding the need to pass judgement himself.[242]

The Renaissance humanists examined here did not express any doubts about the superiority of manuscripts in the original

---

[240] Crastone, [Dedicatory letter], p. 15: 'Quod autem ad Psalterium attinet: quia longum et molestum esset omnia emendata enumerare, ea depraehendere facile est, si cum aliis exemplaribus conferantur. Circiter septuaginta loca correximus Graecam veritatem secuti.' In all likelihood, Crastone is referring to the Septuagint version of the Psalms; although not explicitly pronounced here, he mentions the Seventy in several instances in his letter.

[241] Ibid., p. 13: 'Audiant itaque theologi si qui me accusaturi sunt, quid Augustinus libro secundo praedicti voluminis [Augustine, *De doctrina christiana*, p. 42 (II, XI, 16)] praecipiat, si quid emendandum fuerit. "Contra ignota", inquit, "signa magnum remedium est linguarum cognitio. Et iccirco latinae linguae homines quos nunc erudiendos suscepimus, duabus aliis opus habent ad cognitionem scripturarum: Hebraea et Graeca: ut ad exemplaria praecedentia recurratur si quam ambiguitatem attulerit Latinorum interpretum infinita varietas."' Crastone gives no indication that he himself has any knowledge of Hebrew. Perhaps he quoted Augustine simply for the sake of adducing an authority.

[242] Crastone, [Dedicatory letter], p. 14: 'Quid si Graeca depravata essent? Omnia quotquot videre potui conveniunt. Unum duntaxat locum Psalmo centesimo primo ut inveni reliqui. *Viduam ejus* Latini ubi legunt, Graeci omnes θήραν, id est *praedam*. Exemplaria Graeca mutare ausus non sum: nec pro θήρα *viduam* interpretari potui. Sed suspicior interpretes illusos: nam inter θήραν et χήραν, id est *praedam* et *viduam*, una tantum littera, id est θ et χ, discrimen facit. Cum ergo me inter duas Symplegadas angi viderem, elegi quod nec Graeci nec Latini carperent. Qui itaque *viduam* maluerint, in Graeco χ praeponant ubi ηραν invenient. Qui *praedam* θ et in latino *praedam* ascribant.' Crastone is discussing Ps 131.15.

language.²⁴³ In contrast to their medieval counterparts, they did not discuss or even mention the possibility that Hebrew and Greek manuscripts might have been corrupted by Jews or heretics respectively. A hint that there were, nevertheless, those at the time who believed that Latin manuscripts had more authority than Greek ones is provided by Bessarion.²⁴⁴ All in all, however, the conclusion already drawn by Hamilton that the humanists started examining the reliability of Greek and Hebrew manuscripts relatively late, seems justified.²⁴⁵ None of the fifteenth-century authors discussed here dealt in a thorough and detailed way with the original texts of the Bible and their transmission – if, indeed, they took such matters in account at all.

An important point to bear in mind is that, unlike medieval textual critics, most of the humanists considered in this chapter were clearly influenced by issues which affected their views on the authority of manuscripts in different languages. Given George of Trebizond's belief that Latin translations had an authority independent of their Greek originals, it was obviously impossible for him to maintain that Greek manuscripts were superior to Latin ones. Similarly, since Bessarion was arguing in favour of a reading based on Greek manuscripts, he had to regard them as the only valid witnesses to the text of the New Testament. Manetti needed to defend his new Latin translation of the Psalms and Crastone his new edition; so, neither could ascribe a sacred status to earlier Latin translations.

There is, however, one point on which humanists and medieval textual critics were in agreement: the value of a manuscript depended on its age. Following a principle already established in late antiquity, and maintained throughout the Middle Ages, humanists preferred older manuscripts to more recent ones.

Among humanists, Lorenzo Valla says by far the most about the manuscripts he used for his collation of the New Testament. But even he supplies only scant information. It has often been pointed out that in the *Annotationes* Valla's comments on his collation of

---

²⁴³ George of Trebizond, who might have been expected to defend his preference for the Latin reading of Jn 21.22, did not comment on the question of whether Greek or Latin manuscripts were more valuable for the purposes of textual criticism of the Latin Bible; instead, he tended to regard the Latin translation as the work of the translator.

²⁴⁴ See above, p. 175, n. 197.

²⁴⁵ Hamilton, 'Humanists and the Bible', p. 102.

manuscripts are more detailed and precise than those in the *Collatio*.[246] For example, a few times he mentions the number of manuscripts he consulted, whereas in his earlier work he never indicates the exact number of manuscripts he has seen.[247] In one exceptional case he singles out for praise those who have rediscovered manuscripts, listing the number each has found as well as their provenance:

> Reddam debitam laudem ijs, qui codices inuenerunt, et si ob mirificum studium literarum antiquarum uiri laudati sunt, Cyriacus Anconitanus quinque Mediolani, et alijs circa urbibus, in quibus Augustinus diuersatus est, duos Romae Ioannes Tiburus praedicatoriae professionis ad aedem Chrisogoni et saluatoris, quos ego inspexi, mirifica et uetusta litera codices, inuenit, ut alios complures esse, uerisimile sit.[248]

---

[246] See, e.g., Camporeale, *Lorenzo Valla*, p. 285. See also Valla, *Collatio*, pp. XXX–XXXI; for a list of passages in which he refers to manuscripts, see ibid., p. XXX, n. 56 (for the *Collatio*) and p. XXXI, n. 57 (for the *Annotationes*). Perosa (ibid., p. xxx) claims that in the entire *Collatio*, Valla refers only once to Greek manuscripts; however, Valla sometimes mentions Greek readings in a general way; see, e.g., ibid., p. 18: '"Diligenter didicit" [Mt 2.7]. Non est grece *didicit* sed *exquisiuit* vel *perscrutatus est*, nec adest *diligenter* sed unum tantummodo verbum quale est *exquisiuit* sive *investigavit*, licet paulo post idem vocabulum in adverbio pro diligenter accipiat, cum inquit: "ite et interrogate diligenter de puero" [Mt 2.8]. Grece potius est: *profecti exquirite diligenter de puero*'; and ibid., p. 55: '"Hic est filius meus dilectus, in quo mihi bene complacui" [Mt 17.5]. Grece est *in quo beneplacui*.' In the *Annotationes*, he regularly provides Greek readings.

[247] See, e.g., Valla, *Annotationes*, p. 822A: 'Tres codices latinos, et totidem graecos habeo, cum haec compono, et nonnunquam alios codices consulo'; ibid., p. 823A: 'Sequitur, quod in quatuor quos inspexi codicibus non inveni latine, quod legi in quatuor graecis'; ibid., p. 842A: 'Septem graeca exemplaria legi, in quorum singulis ita scriptum est: "Ego scio eum quia ab ipso sum, et ille me misit. Quaerebant igitur eum apprehendere. " [Jn 7.29–30]'

[248] Ibid., p. 845B. This is the only time that Valla mentions the provenance of manuscripts. He is presumably referring to these same manuscripts in his invective against Poggio; see Lorenzo Valla, *Antidotum in Pogium*, IV, in his *Opera*, I, pp. 325-366, at p. 340: 'Is Cyriacus in Lombardia reperit quatuor exemplaria emendate scripta sic: *Adducunt eum a Caipha in pretorium* [compare Jn 18.28] ... Amicissimus meus ac doctissimus Ioannes Tiburtius reperit apud sanctum Chrysogonum, ubi cum magno theologo habitat Cardinali Ilerdensi, uenerandum codicem Euangeliorum, in eodem loco emendate scriptum.' As has already been pointed out by Perosa (Valla, *Collatio*, p. XXXII), however, the number of manuscripts listed here is slightly different. According to Perosa, the passage in the *Annotationes* was written after the one in the *Antidotum in Pogium*. For literature on Giovanni

I shall pay deserved praise to those who found manuscripts, even if they have [already] been praised for their outstanding contribution to ancient literature: Ciriaco of Ancona found five [manuscripts] in Milan and other nearby cities in which Augustine had spent time; Giovanni da Tivoli, a Dominican, found in the church of San Crisogono and San Salvatore in Rome two manuscripts with amazingly old writing, which I myself inspected; it is likely that there are several others [like these].

The reasons given for the different approach adopted in the *Annotationes* vary: Camporeale attributes it to Valla's more developed and wider-ranging technique and erudition,[249] while Perosa assumes that the change was the result of his exposure to the Roman milieu and the improved accessability of manuscripts there.[250] It might, of course, have been due to a combination of these reasons. Yet, Valla's comments in the *Annotationes* are still limited for the most part simply to presenting the variant readings found in different manuscripts, without providing any indication of the number of manuscripts he consulted, their provenance or date.[251] The passage quoted above, in which Valla indicates the location of the manuscripts he is referring to, is an exception both for him and for his time. It was only at the end of the fifteenth century that Angelo Poliziano formed the habit of regularly supplying information on the provenance of manuscripts.[252]

Quite frequently, in order to establish a reading in one of the Gospels, Valla drew not only on Greek and Latin manuscripts but also on parallel passages from the other Gospels, though at times he seems to have done so merely for the sake of juxtaposing them,

---

da Tivoli, see Camporeale, *Lorenzo Valla*, p. 440. Camporeale (ibid., pp. 439–440) identifies the Cardinalis Ilerdensis as Antonio de la Cerda. For Antonio de la Cerda (or Antonio de Cerdá), who became cardinal priest of San Crisogono on 16 February 1448; see also *LexMA*, II, col. 1628.

[249] Camporeale, *Lorenzo Valla*, p. 285.

[250] Valla, *Collatio*, pp. XLIX–L; Mohler (*Kardinal Bessarion*, I, p. 403) claims that neither Bessarion nor Valla had access to an extensive number of Greek or Latin manuscripts and thus to better readings. Stupperich ('Schriftauslegung', p. 230) also assumes that Valla did not have access to a great deal of Greek material.

[251] See, e.g., Valla, *Annotationes*, p. 835B: 'Quidam codices habent...'; ibid., p. 878B: 'Plerique codices graeci habent ... '

[252] See Anthony Grafton, *Joseph Scaliger: A Study in the History of Classical Scholarship*, I: *Textual Criticism and Exegesis*, Oxford 1983, pp. 28–32.

without any aim of improving the text.²⁵³ Camporeale has already noted that Valla examined the writings of Augustine, Ambrose and Jerome in order to look for traces of translations not found in the surviving Latin manuscripts.²⁵⁴ In addition to employing such parallel passages, he also analysed errors which had arisen from the context by comparing an incorrect reading to the surrounding text and explaining what had caused the mistake.²⁵⁵

As we would expect, Valla did not have a clear notion of manuscript families; however, he did classify manuscripts into groups, though without attempting to define them. So, for instance, in commenting on the word *manicabat* in Lk 21.38 'Et omnis populus manicabat ad eum in templo audire eum' ('And all the people came early in the morning to him in the temple, to hear him'), he says that he has never encountered this word before, nor is it used elsewhere in the Bible. According to Valla, instead of

---

²⁵³ Valla, *Annotationes*, p. 822A: 'Non in Matthaeo haec est interiectio sed in Marco'; Valla, *Collatio*, p. 67: 'Dixerat superius: "Et mensas nummulariorum evertit" [Mt 21.12], eisdem verbis in Marco et Luca, licet in Luca desit apud codices latinos; in Ioanne est: …'; ibid., p. 55: '"Vestimenta autem eius facta sunt alba sicut nix." [Mt 17.2] Grece est *sicuti lux*, vereorque ne *lux* sit mutatum in *nix*, presertim quia in Evangelio Marci est *nix* [Mk 9.2], neque vero absurdum est dici *lux* non minus proprie quam *nix*, cum apud Lucam legamus: "Et facta est, dum oraret, species vultus eius altera et vestitus eius refulgens" [Lk 9.29] et, ut greca vox indicat, *refulgurans*.' In the thirteenth century, Roger Bacon consulted parallel passages in the Gospels to establish correct readings; see above, p. 150, n. 139.

²⁵⁴ See Camporeale, *Lorenzo Valla*, pp. 289–290, where he cites, e.g., Valla, *Annotationes*, p. 862B: 'Magis ad uerbum transtulit Ambrosius … Ita lego apud Augustinum' and ibid., p. 837A: 'Ipse uero Hieronymus ait.' The method of using the writings of the Church Fathers to establish the correct text of the Bible was rejected, for instance, by Roger Bacon (see above, p. 149) and Gerard of Huy (see above, p. 134, n. 86).

²⁵⁵ Valla, *Collatio*, p. 111: 'Melius ii codices qui et *omnes* non habent et *pseudoprophetas* habent. Causa autem cur quidam hunc locum emendare volentes depravaverunt est quod paulo superius dicitur: "Secundum hec enim faciebant prophetis patres eorum." [Lk 6.23] Verum hec ita diversa debent esse, ut diversi sunt illi ad quos sermo fit. Hic enim Dominus ad apostolos loquitur, ibi ad amatores seculi, quorum patres prophetis quidem maledicebant, pseudoprophetis vero assentabantur'; ibid., p. 137: 'Melius ii codices, ubi legitur *sine* – ad Iudam enim dixit – , in quod depravandum inducti sunt qui locum hunc depravant per id quod subiungitur: "Pauperes enim semper habebitis" [Jn 12.8], sed hos errare greca veritas indicat; ubi illud quoque erratum est, quod non recte legitur hic locus apud nos, qui apud Grecos sic habet: *Sine eam, in diem sepulture mee* sive *funeris mei servavit illud. Pauperes enim semper habetis vobiscum, me autem non semper habetis.*'

rendering one Greek word with several Latin terms, the translator misguidedly tried to use just one Latin word. After suggesting some better translations,[256] Valla continues:

> In quibusdam exemplaribus lego: *Omnis populus conveniebat in templo audire eum*, sed hi, ut opinor, quia durum videbatur verbum illud *manicare*, quasi emendare voluerunt, verum in hoc ipso, per quod emendant, non satis significatur quod mane populus veniret sive diluculo.[257]
>
> In some manuscripts I read: 'Omnis populus conveniebat in templo audire eum.' But these, I believe, were trying, so to speak, to emend [the text], because the verb *manicare* seemed awkward; however, the word by which they emended [it] does not sufficiently denote that the people came early or at dawn.

Valla was thus aware that the manuscripts which were at his disposal fell into two groups: one which read *conveniebat* and another which read *manicabat*, the former providing a 'corrected' text. But while he separated and distinguished these two groups, he did not draw the conclusions needed to go a step further and formulate the concept of manuscript families.

In the late fifteenth century, for his bi-lingual edition of the Psalms, Giovanni Crastone named the different versions he had consulted. With reference to Ps 39.7, he says:

> Sed non *corpus*, sed *aures* habent exemplaria latina quae Hieronymi dicuntur. Psalterium vero quo Mediolanensis ecclesia utitur, *corpus* habet: nec non omnia graeca exemplaria quae ipse plurima vidi. Non est mihi consentaneum Hieronymum illum non vidisse quae ego homuntio imperitus tam facile animadverti.[258]
>
> The Latin manuscripts said to be according to Jerome have *aures* instead of *corpus*. The Psalter which the Milanese Church uses, though, has *corpus*, and so do all Greek manuscripts, many of which I myself saw. It seems odd to me that Jerome did not see what I, a humble and inexperienced man, noticed so easily.

---

[256] Ibid., pp. 125–126: '"Et omnis populus manicabat ad eum in templo audire eum." [Lk 21.38] Inauditum mihi verbum est *manicare* et quo nusquam alibi utitur interpres. Quod nunc videtur fecisse, ut pro uno greco unum verbum latinum redderet, cum satius esset per plura latina uni greco satisfacere, ut fit in Psalmo, si modo idem interpres fuit: "Deus Deus meus, ad te de luce vigilo" [Ps 62.2]. Ergo hic dicendum est *de mane surgebat* aut *de mane veniebat*.'

[257] Ibid., p. 126.

[258] Crastone, [Dedicatory letter], p. 14.

He thus distinguishes between the Milanese version and the Vulgate. Elsewhere he again presents a clear picture of these two different versions of the Psalms, now calling the Milanese version the Ambrosian Psalter, which, he claims, is in complete agreement with the Greek Psalter. He says that, according to a reliable source, the translation of six of the canticles which is very close to the Greek but not at all like his own version should be ascribed to Jerome.[259] Crastone not only takes into account other translations of the Psalms, he also consults the writings of the Church Fathers. In discussing Psalm 86, in addition to citing readings from the Greek Psalter, the Ambrosian version and Jerome's translation, he further compares it to a sermon of Augustine found in breviaries used by the Roman Curia.[260]

All in all, fifteenth-century textual critics do not seem to have made much progress in relation to the achievements of their medieval predecessors on questions concerning the transmission of the text of the Bible. In the Middle Ages, there is evidence of grouping manuscripts according to age, language and even recensions. Indeed, with regard to dating, some medieval textual critics were more detailed than their fifteenth-century counterparts, who, in general, devoted very little attention to establishing the date of a manuscript, at most asserting the standard line that older ones were to be preferred.[261] In this respect, medieval scholars were ahead of humanists. On the whole, medieval textual critics –

---

[259] Ibid., p. 15: 'Unum te, praesul memorande, ignorare nolo: psalterium, quod Ambrosianum dicitur, in paucis, imo in nullis, a Graeco discrepare. Cantica quae sex sunt omnino Graecis similia, nostris omnino dissimilia. Propterea Hieronymi ea potius dicenda est translatio, ut vir quidam fide non indignus mihi affirmavit.' For the canticles, see below, p. 266, n. 69.

[260] Ibid., p. 15: 'Quid de versiculo Psalmi octogesimi et sexti: quem translatio quam Hieronymi ferunt [Ps 86.5]: "Nunquid Sion dicet": exemplaria graeca μήτηρ, id est *mater*, legunt; et psalterium Mediolanensis ecclesiae, *mater Sion*. Quod si qui nec Graecis nec Ambrosianis codicibus credunt, legant sermonem Augustini qui recitatur iuxta breviaria curiae Romanae in solemnitate Hypopantes Domini: vel, ut vulgo dicitur, Purificationis Virginis; is enim primae lectionis matutinae initio ait: "Sic olim praedictum est: mater Sion dicet." Sed qui transtulit: venia quidem danda est μήτι, id est *numquid*: non μήτηρ, id est *mater*, videre visus est, quod vel ipsi Graecorum elementis imbuti intelligere possunt.'

[261] For medieval examples of dating manuscripts and of classifying them by date, see, e.g., above, pp. 124, 128 and 134. No attempt has as yet been made to determine whether the medieval dating of manuscripts was accurate.

especially the compilers of the *correctoria* – seem to have been more concerned with specifying which version they were discussing.[262]

With regard to accuracy, however, small steps forward can be observed. Even though Valla in his *Annotationes* mentioned the number of manuscripts he had consulted only a few times and their provenance only once, this still counts as an advance: Maniacutia, for instance, in the texts examined, never indicated how many manuscripts he consulted.

In contrast to medieval textual critics, none of the *Quattrocento* humanists examined in this study referred to the possibility that Jews or heretics had intervened in the text of their biblical manuscripts.[263] To support their position on a variety of issues, however, the majority of humanists drew on quotations from the Church Fathers, just as textual critics of the Middle Ages had done.

Oswaldus de Corda

As we have seen earlier, the Dominicans tried to impose textual uniformity on their Bibles and liturgical books.[264] They were neither the only nor the first monastic order to engage in such an undertaking: as early as the twelfth century, the Carthusian Order, which traditionally put considerable effort into correcting their books according to standardised rules, attempted to establish uniformity in their liturgical works; in 1258, this was prescribed in the Order's statutes.[265] More than thirty years earlier, in 1222,

---

[262] See, e.g., above, p. 133, n. 85.

[263] For a medieval example, see, e.g., above, p. 130 and n. 69. Medieval claims that Jews corrupted their manuscripts may be in need of closer examination: for instance, Hailperin points out that Nicholas of Lyra accused the Jews in three instances of corrupting the text of the Bible; but corrupting in these cases does not seem to mean deliberate manipulation, especially since none of the three passages (Is 9.5; Jr 23.6; Ho 9.12) was theologically sensitive; see Hailperin, 'The Hebrew Heritage', pp. 148–149.

[264] See above, pp. 137–139.

[265] Oswaldus de Corda, *Opus pacis*, ed. B. A. Egan, Turnhout 2001, p. 9*. For further information on the Carthusians' statutes regarding textual uniformity, see ibid., pp. 18*–23*. See also Gilbert Ouy, 'Le *Valdebonum* perdu et retrouvé', *Scriptorium* 42 (1988), pp. 198–203, at p. 200; and Michael G. Sargent, 'The Problem of Uniformity in Carthusian Book Production from the *Opus pacis* to the *Tertia Compilatio Statutorum*', in *New Science out of Old Books: Studies in Manuscripts and Early Printed Books in Honour of A. I. Doyle*, ed. R. Beadle and A. J. Piper, Aldershot 1995, pp. 122–141, at pp. 122 and 125.

intervention in the text of the Bible and in liturgical books was prohibited in the *Statuta Jancelini*.[266] These decisions, however, do not seem to have had the desired effect, for several writings concerning the need for textual uniformity were composed by Carthusians in the decades around 1400.[267] In this excursus I shall discuss one of these works, which displays a very different approach to the text of the Bible from those taken by textual critics of the Middle Ages and the early Renaissance.

In 1417, Oswaldus de Corda (d. 1435), then vicar of the Grande Chartreuse, composed the *Opus pacis*, a manual for his fellow brethren dealing with the copying and correction of manuscripts of liturgical works and the Bible.[268] His work is of special interest not only because it is transmitted in twelve manuscripts, including two in Oswaldus's handwriting, dating from 1417 to 1514, which attest to the popularity of the *Opus pacis*, but also because it exerted some influence beyond the Carthusian Order and inspired similar works.[269]

The most notable difference between the *Opus pacis* and the other works discussed in this study is that it is directly addressed to scribes. Oswaldus's main focus is on basic issues of orthography and

---

[266] The text of the *Statuta Jancelini* has been published as a facsimile: *The 'Statuta Jancelini' (1222) and the 'De Reformatione' of Prior Bernard (1248)*, ed. J. Hogg, vol. 2: *The MS. Grande Chartreuse 1 Stat. 23*, Salzburg 1978, pp. 28–137 (ff. 47ᵛ–102ʳ); for the passage in question, see p. 28 (f. 47ᵛ): 'Libros quoque veteris ac novi testamenti qui tam studiose emendati sunt eosve cum quibus celebrantur officia sine eiusdem {*sc. the general chapter's*} consilio nullus emendare presumat.' See also above, p. 139, n. 110.

[267] For instance, the *Valdebonum*, composed between 1378 and 1402; see Ouy, 'Le *Valdebonum*', pp. 198 and 201.

[268] For the dating and for Oswaldus's affiliation, see Oswaldus de Corda, *Opus pacis*, p. 9*. For his life, see ibid., pp. 36*–51*. The title has been interpreted in different ways by Egan (ibid., p. 58*) and Sargent ('The Problem', p. 124).

[269] Oswaldus de Corda, *Opus pacis*, pp. 10*–11*. The Bursfeld congregation, and possibly the Windesheim congregation as well, composed works which drew on the *Opus pacis*; see ibid., pp. 75*–77*. For the work's influence, see also Mary A. and Richard H. Rouse, 'Correction and Emendation of Texts in the Fifteenth Century and the Autograph of the *Opus Pacis* by "Oswaldus Anglicus"', in *Scire litteras. Forschungen zum mittelalterlichen Geistesleben*, ed. S. Krämer and M. Bernhard, Munich 1988, pp. 333–346. One of the manuscripts transmitting the *Opus pacis* (MS Bernkastel–Kues, Hospitalbibliothek 12), which also contains Hugh of St Cher's *Correctio Biblie*, formerly belonged to Nicholas of Cusa, and has mistakenly been given the number 13 by Denifle ('Die Handschriften', p. 264), as is pointed out by Egan; see Oswaldus de Corda, *Opus pacis*, p. 125*.

correct pronunciation. Although he claims that his advice is by no means binding, his work may have received official approval from the Prior of the Grande Chartreuse; and his allusions to the Carthusian statutes also lend importance to his words.[270]

What is particularly striking about Oswaldus's approach is that he never mentions the relative value of different Latin manuscripts for establishing the text of the Bible, nor does he comment on manuscript transmission in general; also, there are no references to the use of the original Hebrew or Greek for the purposes of emendation.[271] For Oswaldus's fellow brethren, the only pillar of orientation should be the corrected and approved copy of the Bible kept in the Grande Chartreuse: the Carthusians are admonished always to adhere to the corrected version in the motherhouse; and Oswaldus regularly refers to this copy and mentions the rules which it follows and which scribes are to emulate.[272] He also points out, and defends, the possibility that the Carthusian text of the Bible might differ from other versions.[273]

---

[270] Egan (Oswaldus de Corda, *Opus pacis*, p. 13*) claims that the prior of the Grande Chartreuse, Johannes, had approved of the *Opus pacis*; however, she does not give a reference, and there is only one instance in the text in which Johannes is mentioned as prior at the time of composition (ibid., p. 4): '"Valde bonum" tempore scismatis sub domno Guilhelmus est collectum, istud {*sc. Opus pacis*} autem anno extirpacionis eiusdem sub domno Iohanne nacione theutonico Cartusie priore est compilatum. Non tamen est hoc opus secundum imperium ut ita fiat, sed secundum indulgenciam, ut ita fieri uel factum esse sufficiat; ergo qua racione amplectitur a uolente cui placet, ea respui poterit a nolente cum illi displicet.' For a reference to the statutes in the *Opus pacis*, see, e.g., ibid., p. 44: 'Si autem sint aliqua mendosa uel correctione digna, non ipsi, scilicet scriptores uel lectores id faciant, nisi sicut statuta fiendum declarant.'

[271] See also ibid., p. 68*.

[272] See, e.g., ibid., p. 43: 'In omnibus supradictis correctioni librorum consulitur, non autem scribentis aut legentis arbitrium laxatur. Scribentes de nouo libros et lectores omnimodis exemplar correctum sequantur'; and ibid., p. 20: 'Similiter *his* et *he* in plurali debent scribi per simplicem uocalem, sicut in libris correctis Cartusie diligenter cauetur, non obstante aliorum usu.'

[273] Ibid., p. 6: 'Vnde non est mirandum, si aliquando ordo noster aliter habeat aliqua orthographizata, accentuata, siue secundum declinacionem et coniugacionem uariata, quam illi siue isti, ueteres scilicet siue moderni, cum et ipsi sibi plerunque dissenciant.' For accepted deviation of the Carthusian text from grammatical norms, see below, pp. 235–237.

Scribes are advised not to intervene rashly in the text, even if the same word is spelled in different ways in the same chapter.[274] They are encouraged to preserve – but not impose – local variant spellings.[275] To facilitate this task, Oswaldus provides lists of acceptable orthographical variants of biblical names and other words.[276]

Although not strictly speaking a textual critic himself, Oswaldus, like them, discusses the use of different sources of corrections and alternative spellings. First, he rejects the use of the works of the Church Fathers to emend the text of the Bible:

> Similiter nec secundum dicta doctorum biblia est corrigenda, quia ipsi sepissime allegant auctoritates taliter, qualiter nec in nostris nec in secularibus bibliis habentur, magis sequentes sensum auditoribus congruum quam uerba. Eciam sepe secuntur communem usum, sicut uel ipsi audiuerunt uel in suis bibliis inuenerunt, ubi manifeste noster textus uerius habet quantum ad hebraicam ueritatem, aut certe translaciones LXX interpretum aliquando secuti sunt.[277]

> The Bible is not to be corrected according to the sayings of the Doctors, since they themselves very often adduce authorities in such a way as exists neither in our Bibles nor in those of the secular clergy, since they follow the sense in agreement with the listener rather than the words. Also they often follow general use, either as they heard it or

---

[274] Ibid., p. 4: 'Necessarium est correctoribus, ut cum diuersa repperint, sicut aliquando fit in diuersis libris, aliquando in eodem libro, immo eciam aliquando in eodem capitulo, ut una eademque dictio sub eodem significato aliter et aliter scripta habeatur, propter causas infra expressatas, non statim ad corrigendum mittant manum, sed uelut sapientes, quid agendum sit, bene deliberent, presertim iuxta huius operis informacionem.'

[275] Ibid., p. 29: 'Similiter ubi sola linguarum diuersitas est in causa, quod aliquando uocalis pro uocali ponitur uel alia litera pro altera, ibi non est necesse corrigere secundum libros Cartusie, sed sufficit tenere modum patrie, qui plerunque certior est, inquantum talia uocabula eandem patriam concernunt, eciam in accentu'; ibid., p. 8: 'Generaliter igitur nouerint correctores, quod ubicunque eadem dictio, latina, barbara, siue hebraica, in diuersis libris et capitulis, seu eciam in eodem libro aut capitulo, propter uicium scriptorum incertum, aut propter usum inueteratum, uel propter uarietates idiomatum et dissimiles habitudines hominum secundum suas linguas aliter et aliter pronunciancium, siue alio quocunque modo, uarie inuenitur scripta, sensu tamen ac significacione propter huiusmodi uariacionem salua remanente, ibi pocius est tolerandum quam aliquid corrigendum, saltim ex necessitate. Nam talis diuersitas terminorum eciam reperitur in libris correctis.'

[276] Ibid., pp. 37–43.

[277] Ibid., p. 32.

as they found it in their Bibles, where clearly our text is more faithful in relation to the *hebraica veritas*; or others certainly at times followed the translations of the Seventy.

Reliance on the biblical quotations as found in the writings of the Fathers is thus rejected because their quotations are too loose or taken from the *septuaginta*, a version which Oswaldus does not consider to be a trustworthy source for his purposes. Instead, he prefers the text which is closer to the *hebraica veritas*. Yet even the original Hebrew is not singled out as the ultimate model to follow but rather as a rough guide, preferable to the *septuaginta*, but not above the Carthusian Bible.

Besides the writings of the Church Fathers, Oswaldus also mentions other works which should not be used to emend the text of the Bible. Concordances to the Bible are excluded because the compilers followed the version of the Bible accessible to them rather than the Carthusian version, so scribes would corrupt the Cathusian text if they relied on these works. Oswaldus also rejects the *Mammotrectus*, a fourteenth-century glossary of the Bible with accompanying texts by the Franciscan Giovanni Marchesini, noting with relief that no books in the Grande Chartreuse have as yet been corrected according to it.[278]

One glossary, however, was apparently exempt from this general condemnation: Jerome's *Interpretatio nominum hebraicorum*, which Oswaldus appears to accept as an authority for determining the

[278] Ibid., p. 33: 'Consequenter addo quod nec secundum concordancias maiores siue minores nostra corrigenda est biblia, quia qui fecerunt eas, multum studiose laborauerunt, sed ex bibliis suis posuerunt sicut inuenerunt, in quibus plura correctione digna reperiuntur. Nec secundum "Mammotrectum", de quo hucusque in Cartusia nichil correctum inuenitur.' Oswaldus's editor provides no information on the *Mammotrectus*; Baudouin van den Abeele ('The *Macrologus* of Liège: An Encyclopedic Lexicon at the Dawn of Humanism', in *Schooling and Society: The Ordering and Reordering of Knowledge in the Western Middle Ages*, ed. A. A. MacDonald and M. W. Twomey, Leuven, Paris and Dudley [MA], 2004, pp. 43–60, at p. 52, n. 37) has recently noted that there is hardly any scholarship on this work. Samuel Berger, however, has treated the transmission and the authorship at some length; see his *De glossariis et compendiis exegeticis quibusdam medii aevi sive de libris Ansileubi Papiae Hugutionis Guill. Britonis de Catholicon Mammotrecto aliis dissertatio critica*, Paris 1879, pp. 31–51. Giovanni Giacinto Sbaraglia (*Supplementum et castigatio ad scriptores trium ordinum S. Francisci*, 3 vols, Rome 1908–1936, repr. Bologna 1978, II, pp. 204–205) gives Marchesinus e Regio as the author's name. For the *concordantiae maiores* (also called *anglicanae*) and *minores*, see Ceslas Spicq, *Esquisse d'une histoire de l'exégèse latine au moyen âge*, Paris 1944, pp. 174–175.

correct spelling of Hebrew names.[279] He does not explain his decision to rely on the *Interpretatio*, though presumably it was because Jerome was the author.

Oswaldus also points out differences between liturgical works and Scripture. In contrast to Hervaeus of Bourg-Dieu in the twelfth century, he maintains that liturgical texts should not be emended to bring them into line with the Bible. In the liturgy, he writes, the biblical text has often been adapted in order to make it more easily understandable, a practice which he finds perfectly acceptable for the purpose of edification.[280]

Oswaldus's goal is much more practical than that of the other scholars investigated in this study. His readership, even though it became broader than originally intended, was meant to be Carthusian readers – and hence potential correctors – and scribes of sacred texts. The *Opus pacis* aimed to support and advance uniformity in the order's manuscripts of the liturgy and of the Bible on the basis of a *Vorlage* held in the Grande Chartreuse.[281]

---

[279] Oswaldus, *Opus pacis*, pp. 33–34: 'Et quoniam scriptores aliquando malam faciunt differenciam inter preposicionem per apposicionem a suo casu quem regit, precipue in dictionibus indeclinabilibus ubi accusatiuus uel ablatiuus ex finali terminacione non cognoscitur, inde fit ut eciam ab aliis totum aggregatum una dictio credatur, uel prima littera a casu subtracta preposicioni addatur. Vnde reor sic euenisse Iosue capitulo xi, ubi dicitur: "usque Baalgad" [Jos 11.17], et de eodem loco in sequenti capitulo: "ab Aalgad" etc. "usque ad montem" [Jos 12.7], ubi certum est primum accusatiui casus, et secundum ablatiui casus esse. Deinde sequitur in eodem capitulo iterum: *ab Aalgad*, et sic uidetur b demptum casui et additum preposicioni, quia tantum Baalgad habet *interpretacio nominum hebraicorum*, et sic de aliis.' See Jerome, *Liber interpretationis hebraicorum nominum*, ed. P. de Lagarde, in his *Opera*, I, 1, Turnhout 1959, pp. 59–161, at p. 90. It is also possible that Oswald was referring to the *Interpretationes nominum hebraicorum* which, likewise, have an entry for Baalgad, but not for Aalgad; see, e.g. MS London, British Library, Add. 39629, f. 568v for the entry Baalgad.

[280] Oswaldus, *Opus pacis*, p. 31: 'In quibus omnibus, tam apud nos quam apud seculares, plures dictiones alterantur, omittuntur, uel superadduntur propter audientium meliorem edificacionem et intellectum, que non sic sunt in biblia. In Ecclesiastico habetur: "Reple Syon inenarrabilibus uerbis tuis" [Si 36.16], sed nos in cantico legimus: *uirtutibus tuis*. Ibidem habet textus nostre biblie: "Sicut cinnamonium et aspaltum" [Si 24.20], sed in epistola, capitulo, responsorio, et antiphona, dicimus: *Sicut cinnamonium et balsamum*.' For Hervaeus's approach to emendation, see above, pp. 122–124.

[281] The *Notabilia quedam de correctione librorum*, a Carthusian text based on the *Opus pacis* from the second half of the fifteenth century, confirms that the only basis for emendation was the model from the motherhouse (Oswaldus,

Because of this clear-cut notion of what the text should look like, there was no need to discuss the value of Hebrew and Greek manuscripts or even of other Latin translations, since, as Oswaldus stresses several times, the Carthusian text might differ from others and might well be more correct.

Opus pacis, p. 34*; the text is edited ibid., pp. 84–89). *Notabilia*, p. 88: 'Nec forte in nouis bibliis essent predicta nunc scribenda. Verum in predictis duobus psalmis *sonauerunt* est emendandum, si non habeatur, et scribendum, cum ita sic ordinis nostri generalis usus; aliter pluribus simul concinentibus, illis quidem *sonauerunt*, istis autem *sonuerunt*, fieret dissonancia, nisi generaliter per capitulum auferrentur.'

Part IV:

Justifications for Interventions

Having examined the views of the textual transmission and the attitudes towards the various traditions, we will now take a closer look at two further recurring themes for justifying interventions in the biblical text. Chapter IV.1 discusses the appeals to *veritas* as an argument for emending corrupt passages. This approach, regularly found throughout the writings examined in this study, is usually contrasted – but sometimes equated – to the concept of *consuetudo*. Chapter IV.2 investigates the role of grammar for emendational purposes. While considerations regarding the application of correct grammar are less prevalent than the argument of *veritas*, they nevertheless have a remarkable story to tell that contravenes the commonly held views concerning the connection of Scripture and grammar.

IV.1 *CONSUETUDO* VERSUS *VERITAS*

There has always been a struggle, when deciding whether to intervene in the text of the Latin Bible, between emending according to *veritas*, on the one hand, and retaining the text according to *usus* or *consuetudo*, on the other. Already in some of Jerome's prefaces to biblical books, he expressed the worry that presenting a novel text, which was unfamiliar to the faithful, would clash with *consuetudo*. As early as 384, in his 'Preface to the Gospels', he noted that people, both learned and unlearned, on discovering that the text which they were used to had been changed, would become outraged and accuse him of sacrilege and forgery for daring to add, alter or correct something in the traditional translation.[1] In his letter to the Goths Sunnia and Fretela on the Psalms, written between 404 and 410, Jerome remarked that when emending the Psalms he did not want to alienate his readers with a text they had never seen before and therefore retained the old version whenever it was in conformity with the sense of the original.[2]

Like Jerome, Augustine, too, was aware of the conflict between *veritas* and *consuetudo*. In his *De baptismo*, written in 401, he strongly supported following *veritas* over adherence to *consuetudo*.[3] Yet he also understood the overwhelming power of *consuetudo*. We have already encountered the story told by Augustine in response to Jerome's new translation of Job from scratch: a bishop read a well-known passage in a new, unaccustomed version of the Bible to his congregation; this caused outrage among the faithful, who demanded a return to the old and familiar version. Augustine used

---

[1] Jerome, 'Prologus in Pentateucho', p. 3: 'Periculosum opus certe, obtrectatorum latratibus patens, qui me adserunt in Septuaginta interpretum suggillationem nova pro veteribus cudere.' For an example from his 'Preface to the Gospels', see above, p. 31, n. 7.

[2] See above, p. 131, n. 76. For the dating of the letter, see Stefan Rebenich, 'Jerome: The "Vir trilinguis" and the "Hebraica veritas"', *Vigiliae christianae* 47 (1993), pp. 50–77, at p. 64. Rebenich also provides some further bibliographical references on this letter; see ibid., p. 77, n. 111. Wilhelm Süss (*Studien zur lateinischen Bibel*, I: *Augustins Locutiones und das Problem der lateinischen Bibelsprache*, Tartu 1932, p. 18) points out that Jerome is referring to his work on the *Psalterium Gallicanum*.

[3] For the references, see below, p. 205, n. 17.

this episode to scold Jerome for not taking into consideration the power of *consuetudo*.⁴

The statements of Jerome and Augustine show that *consuetudo* or *usus* was very influential and often presented a more than sufficient reason for not changing readings in sacred texts; yet at the same time, *veritas* was regarded as a highly desirable goal. In this chapter, I shall examine how medieval and early Renaissance textual critics of the Bible approached the conflict between the two concepts.

Throughout his text-critical works, Nicolò Maniacutia regularly refers to the dichotomy between *consuetudo* or *usus* and *veritas*. The position he upholds in his theoretical considerations is consistently in favour of *veritas*. Although he was aware of and, in principle, agreed with Jerome's remark that correcting the Scriptures according to the Hebrew text would lead to the accusation of having founded a new Bible, Maniacutia, in his *Suffraganeus*, explains that he nevertheless took this liberty when correcting the Psalms,⁵ thus choosing *veritas* over *consuetudo*.

In his *Libellus*, Maniacutia notes that there are those who, supporting *consuetudo*, will say that what was good enough for our ancestors is good enough for us. Maniacutia does not accept this approach, maintaining that our ancestors would have appreciated a corrected text if only they could have been certain as to what the corruptions actually were. And if they were negligent, should their negligence force posterity to accept corruptions as the truth? Instead, he insists that incorrect readings should not be permitted to remain in texts simply on the grounds of the length of time they have been there.⁶ These examples show that, at least on a

---

⁴ See above, p. 112 and n. 19.

⁵ Maniacutia, [Preface to his *Suffraganeus Bibliothece*], p. 275: 'Quarum quidem amixcionibus vetus testamentum, quod se Ieronimus secundum hebraicum asserit transtulisse, adeo corruptum est, ut si quis vellet cuncta discutere et hebraice, id est pristine reddere puritati, nove bibliothece conditor culparetur. Quod tamen de Sepher Tellim, id est de libro Imnorum, me fateor presumpsisse.'

⁶ Maniacutia, *Libellus*, p. 121: 'Erunt fortasse qui dicant: "Sufficiat nobis quod maioribus nostris novimus suffecisse; neque enim meliores sumus quam patres nostri. Quis est hic novas condens sententias sermonibus imperitis?" Quibus respondendum est quod eos sanctos corrupta volumina non fecerunt, immo credendum est quia libenter habuissent veraces codices si certi esse super corruptionibus potuissent. Quod si negligentes fuerunt, nunquid eorum negligentia dampnum debet parere veritati? Vendicabuntne falsitates sibi in codicibus nostris locum pro temporis longitudine more eorum qui legitimum titulum non habentes in saecularibus causis praescriptionem op-

theoretical level, Maniacutia supported the right to emend the transmitted text of the Bible and rejected the hold of *consuetudo*.

Yet despite these strong words in support of *veritas* over *consuetudo*, some of Maniacutia's actual emendations reveal a drift in the opposite direction. The power of *consuetudo*, combined with a fear of appearing presumptious or offending others' beliefs, seems to have played a crucial part in his adoption of a method which entailed accepting only those readings already found in Latin manuscripts of the Bible instead of pursuing the original. In the preface to his edition of the *Psalterium Romanum*, when defending his approach to emendation, he explicitly refers to 'perpetual *consuetudo*', which, he admits, has such a hold on him that he is unable to circumvent it completely.[7] The grip of *consuetudo* on him is also confirmed by several of his comments on biblical passages. For instance, in his *Suffraganeus*, Maniacutia accepts the addition '*Egrediamur foras*' in Gn 4.8, which is not in the Hebrew original but can be found in all Latin manuscripts; the reason he gives is *usus pristinus*.[8] In his edition of the *Psalterium Romanum*, he adopts an addition to Ps 135.7 even though it is opposed to truth: 'Although it is without doubt superfluous', Maniacutia writes in the preface, 'nevertheless I was forced to integrate it since it has obtained *usus*.'[9] He states in his preface to the *Psalterium iuxta Hebraeos* that he did not want to use the Hebrew titles of the Psalms, also because he might appear presumptuous to those who, following *consuetudo*, actually prefer lies to the truth, *veritas*.[10] So,

---

ponunt an his quae dicuntur acquiescendum non erit, quia quidam homullus haec loquitur? Absit hoc a christiana doctrina et maxime ab his, qui humilitatis et discretionis spiritu vigent.'

[7] See above, p. 119, and n. 37.

[8] For the quotation, see above, p. 118, n. 33.

[9] Maniacutia, [Preface to the *Psalterium Romanum*], p. 6: '"Qui fecit luminaria magna" [Ps 135.7]: Superaddimus similiter *solus*, quod patet scriptorum uitio contigisse, nam et in ebraico non habetur. Quamquam itaque sit indubitanter superfluum, tamen quia usus optinuit, similiter facere sum coactus.'

[10] Maniacutia, [Preface to the *Psalterium iuxta Hebraeos*], p. 11: 'His inquam ambiguitatibus perturbatus nolui Hebreorum tradicionem super titulos in latinum transferre. Timui quoque his supersticiosus uideri qui solam consuetudinem pretendentes in diuersis psalmorum edicionibus nuda preferunt mendacia ueritati.'

notwithstanding his belief in the superiority of *veritas*, Maniacutia was not always able to overcome the power of *consuetudo*.[11]

Writing at roughly the same time, the Benedictine Hervaeus of Bourg-Dieu took an even more radical position than Maniacutia in his theoretical considerations. After pointing out that an incorrect text has been widely in use in the liturgy for a long time,[12] he concludes that:

> Si quis uero non euangelistam sed usum uulgate consuetudinis sequi uoluerit, non secundum euangelistam sed secundum usum pronunciet lectionem, nisi mendax esse elegerit non timens quod scriptum est, 'Os quod mentitur occidit animam' [Ws 1.11].[13]

> Anyone who wants to follow habit {*usus vulgate consuetudinis*} instead of the Evangelist, recites the lesson, not according to the Evangelist, but according to habit, except that he has decided to be mendacious, not fearing what is said in the Bible: 'the mouth that belieth, killeth the soul [Ws 1.11].'

Basing his next argument on a quotation from Augustine, probably drawn from Gratian's *Decretum*, he asserts that the worst kind of falsehood is that which is committed in religious doctrine. He drives this point home by saying that among religious falsehoods, surely one committed in the mass is the most reprehensible of all.[14]

---

[11] There are, however, also examples to the contrary; for instance, when he changed the translation of *sela* (סֶלָה) according to what he saw as fitting; see Maniacutia, [Preface to the *Psalterium iuxta Hebraeos*], p. 12: 'Pro quo scilicet "diapsalmate", quod LXX uerterunt interpretes, Simachus "in aeternum", Theodocio "in finem" transtulit. Quinta editio ipsum hebraicum habet "sela", pro quo Ieronimus ponit "semper". Igitur ubicumque in eius edicione inuenis "semper", scias in hebreo haberi "sela". Nam uerbi ambiguitatem uolens auferre, sicubi "semper" repperi quod "sela" non esset nec posset in "diapsalma" transferri, pro eo "iugiter" commutaui, quod tamen bis tantum estimo contigisse.' In all likelihood, Maniacutia derived the information in this quotation from Jerome, 'In Abacuc prophetam', p. 622 (II, iii, 3). The translation *iugiter* can also be found in Jerome's works; see Jerome, *Tractatus in librum Psalmorum*, in his *Opera homiletica*, ed. G. Morin, Turnhout 1958, pp. 3–447, at p. 44 (LXVII, 20): 'In hebraeo habet SELA, hoc est semper et iugiter.'

[12] Hervaeus, *De correctione*, p. 40: 'Nam sunt nonnulla, quae a nescio quo inuenta per audientium uel tenentium inpericiam seu negligentiam ceperunt in usu haberi longe lateque per ecclesias, quae sine dubio contraria uel dissonantia sunt ueritati.'

[13] Ibid., p. 40.

[14] Ibid., p. 42: 'Inter omnia uero mendaciorum genera, sicut Augustinus loquitur, "primum est et capitale mendacium longeque fugiendum quod fit

Holding on to *usus* in the mass, which involves mixing the devil's falsehood with the evangelical *veritas*, leads to a loss of hope for salvation, since the whole aim of the mass is to placate God, who is even more offended by a false text.[15] Consequently, he calls on all men of the Church to emend passages which deviate from *veritas*, even if this means opposing *usus*.[16]

Hervaeus also quotes other passages from Augustine – again, perhaps, taken from Gratian's *Decretum* – which support the supremacy of *veritas*;[17] and a marginal note in the manuscript of *De*

in doctrina religionis, ad quod nulla condicione quisquam debet adduci". Et cum omne mendacium quod fit in doctrina sanctae religionis tale sit, quid estimandum est de mendacio quod in missa fit?' The passage by Augustine is from *De mendacio*, in his *Opera*, V, 3, ed. J. Zycha (Corpus Scriptorum Ecclesiasticorum Latinorum, 41), Prague, Vienna and Leipzig 1900, pp. 413–466, at p. 444 (XIV, 25). This passage is also, however, quoted by Gratian, *Decretum*, col. 869 (C. XXII, qu. 2, c. 8); since Hervaeus's formulation is actually closer to the version in the *Decretum* than to Augustine's text and since there are several other passages in his work which show that he drew on the *Decretum*, it is likely that he was quoting from Gratian's text rather than directly from Augustine.

[15] Hervaeus, *De correctione*, pp. 42–43: 'Quid itaque sibi utilitatis adquirit, qui missam celebrans, mendacium quod ex diabolo est miscet euangelicae ueritati, dum pertinaciter usum sectari conatur qui in ecclesia per inpericiam plurimorum inoleuit? Quae autem spes salutis relinquitur, si unde supernus iudex placari offensus debuit, inde magis offenditur?'

[16] Ibid., p. 50: 'In irritum itaque deducenda sunt, quaecumque ueritatem quae in scripturis sanctis est uiolant, licet in usu frequentatissimo per ecclesias habeantur. Quicunque uero prelatus est ecclesiae, uigilantius oportet eum ista corrigere.'

[17] Ibid., pp. 43–44: 'Et ne quis mihi minus adquiescat, et adhuc ueterem usum neglecta ueritate sequatur, profero quid in tercio libro de Baptismo sanctus Augustinus dicat. Ait enim: "Qui contempta ueritate praesumit consuetudinem sequi, aut circa fratres inuidus est et malignus, quibus ueritas reuelatur, aut circa deum ingratus est, cuius inspiracione ecclesia eius instruitur. Nam dominus in euangelio: "Ego sum" inquit "ueritas" [Jn 14.6]. Non dixit, *Ego sum consuetudo*. Itaque, ueritate manifestata, cedat consuetudo. Reuelacione igitur facta ueritatis, cedat error ueritati ... Igitur cum Christus ueritas sit, magis ueritatem quam consuetudinem sequi debemus, quia consuetudinem racio et ueritas semper excludit" [Augustine, *De baptismo libri septem*, in his *Opera*, VII, 1, ed. M. Petschenig (Corpus Scriptorum Ecclesiasticorum Latinorum, 51), Vienna and Leipzig 1908, repr. New York and London 1963, pp. 145–375 at pp. 204; 332–333; 334; 355; 359 (III, 9, 12; VI, 35, 67; VI, 37, 71; VII, 20, 38; VII, 27, 52)]. Rursus idem Augustinus in quarto libro de Baptismo: "Frustra, inquit, quidam qui racione uincuntur, consuetudinem nobis obiciunt; quasi consuetudo maior sit ueritate, aut non id sit in spiritualibus sequendum, quod in melius fuerit a sancto spiritu reuelatum. Hoc plane uerum est, quia racio et ueritas consuetudini praeponenda sunt;

correctione provides further evidence of his decision to defend truth against *usus*: at a later date, he added a quotation from Cyprian asserting that no matter how old and how disseminated a particular *consuetudo* is, *veritas* stands above it and that *usus* which is opposed to *veritas* must be abolished – a concise summary, Hervaeus remarks, of his own position.[18]

Yet in spite of his numerous attacks on *usus* and *consuetudo*, Hervaeus – like Maniacutia – disregarded his own words about the superiority of *veritas* and accepted at least one interpolation in the text of the Bible. He defended the reading 'Erat Iosep et Maria mater Ihesu mirantes' ('Joseph and Jesus's mother Mary were wondering') instead of 'Erat pater eius et mater mirantes' ('And his father and mother were wondering'), as found in the Gospel of Luke (Lk 2.33), by observing:

> Licet euangelista non eadem uerba scripserit, nequaquam tamen falsum est, quia exponit quis sit ille pater. Et propter minus eruditos factum est, ne quis putaret Iosep carnali more patrem esse domini.[19]

---

sed cum consuetudini ueritas suffragatur, nichil oportet firmius retinere." [Ibid., p. 228 (IV, 5, 7)] Haec Augustini uerba possunt omnibus cordatis ad hoc sufficere, ut usum uel consuetudinem contra ueritatem aut iusticiam nunquam tenere vel defendere uelint.' These passages are quoted by Gratian, *Decretum*, cols 14–15 (D. 8, c. 6 and 7, respectively). Hervaeus's extensive reliance on the *Decretum* as a source for text–critical arguments deserves further investigation.

[18] Ibid., pp. 49–50: 'Unde et beatus ait Ciprianus: "Quaelibet consuetudo quantunuis uetusta, quantunuis uulgata, ueritati est omnino postponenda, et usus, qui ueritati est contrarius, abolendus." In quibus uerbis asserit breuiter cuncta quae nunc asserere nitimur, et inprobat quod inprobamus, dicentes quia consuetudini nil debetur, cui ueritas aduersatur.' This quotation, too, seems to have been taken from Gratian, *Decretum*, col. 14 (D. 8, c. 5). Morin ('Un critique', p. 49, nn. 44–45) assumes that Hervaeus probably came across this quotation after the composition of his work and thus had it added in the margin; Morin admits that he was not able to locate this quotation in the works of Cyprian and suggests that Hervaeus may have found it in Ivo of Chartres's *Decretum* ([*PL*, CLXI], Paris 1889, cols 47–1022, at col. 311C [IV, 213]). Yet Gratian's *Decretum* seems a more likely source since elsewhere Hervaeus quotes from the *Decretum*, in general, and distinction 8, in particular (see above, p. 205, n. 17). It is also possible that this passage was accidentally left out by the original scribe.

[19] Hervaeus, *De correctione*, p. 52. Long before Hervaeus, Heiric of Auxerre (d. 876) commented on the same problem; see Heiric of Auxerre, *Homiliae per circulum anni*, 3 vols, ed. R. Quadri, Turnhout 1992–1994, I, p. 132 (I, 16): 'Erant Ioseph et Maria mater Ihesu mirantes super his quae dicebantur de eo ... Cum Lucas euangelista manifeste nobis commendet quoniam dominus

Even though the Evangelist did not write these very words, it is nevertheless by no means false, for it explains who the father is. And it was done for the sake of the less learned, so that no one might think that Joseph was the father of the Lord in a carnal way.

There are relatively few statements about the role of *consuetudo* and *veritas* in the *correctoria*. Hugh of St Cher merely repeated Jerome's fear that his translation might be considered an attempt to write a new Bible and applied it to his own work, repudiating the accusation by insisting that his work was a reconstruction of the old and approved text.[20] Whether he actually managed to re-establish the faithful text is difficult to tell, given the current state of research; but, according to Denifle, he did not follow the path he had prescribed for himself, perhaps unconvinced by his own rebuttal of the possible accusations he might face.[21]

Recognising that the Latin language had changed and was still changing, Gerard of Huy opposed the correction of the text of the Latin Bible on the basis of current *usus*. Gerard quoted the pagan author Horace to show that the language of older literary works might well differ from contemporary usage. He then argued, drawing a parallel between the Bible and classical texts, that just as we do not change the text of Virgil and Ovid according to contemporary *usus*, so, too, we should not change the text of the

---

Ihesus filius solummodo uirginis fuit, nec de uiri conceptus semine, mirum ualde uidetur cur idem euangelista Ioseph hoc loco patrem saluatoris testatur fuisse; sic enim in textu euangelii habetur: "Erant", inquit, "pater eius et mater Ihesu mirantes super his quae dicebantur de illo" [Lk 2.33]. Sed consuetudinis est scripturarum ut opinionem multorum sic narret historicus quomodo eo tempore ab omnibus credebatur. Quia ergo uulgaris erat opinio quod Ioseph pater esset Christi, non solum euangelista sed et ipsa etiam mater domini Ioseph patrem illius nuncupat dicens: "Ego et pater tuus dolentes quaerebamus te" [Lk 2.48] ... Si enim hi qui alienos sibi in locum filiorum adoptant patres eorum irreprehensibiliter nuncupantur, cur non et Ioseph pater Christi sine culpa appelletur, qui etsi a procreatione illius extraneus matri tamen eius fuit nuptialiter copulatus?'

[20] Hugh of St Cher, [Preface to his *Correctio Biblie*], p. 386: '"Neque enim" ut dicit Ieronymus, "sic noua cudimus ut uetera destruamus" [Jerome, 'Prologus in libris Salomonis', p. 957], sed magis uetera statuentes quedam noua uitio scriptorum in textu de glosis et postillis inserta uel etiam per quorumdam inperitiam deprauata, non nostra sed aliorum maiorum auctoritate resecanda monstramus.' The neglect of the discussion of *veritas* in the *correctoria* might also be due to their purpose.

[21] Denifle, 'Die Handschriften', p. 295, n. 2.

Latin Bible.[22] In his *Triglossos*, he stressed the same point, this time referring to the works of Homer, Virgil and Horace.[23] Gerard thus defended *veritas* against a different kind of *usus* from that discussed by his predecessors: rather than criticising the use of long-accustomed readings – which were called, for instance, *usus pristinus* by Maniacutia – Gerard attacked the *usus* of contemporary Latin, maintaining that – just like the other type of *usus* or *consuetudo* – it would remove *veritas* from the text of the Bible. So, in agreement with his predecessors, Gerard valued *veritas* and rejected *usus*. Yet in order to establish whether he, too, like Maniacutia, Hervaeus and perhaps Hugh of St Cher before him, wavered in his adherence to this principle and at times allowed *usus* to have the upper hand, detailed research on his *correctorium* is needed, starting with a critical edition.

In his *Opus majus*, Roger Bacon provides a list of four causes which lead to the corruption of *veritas*. The second item on the list is *diuturnitas consuetudinis*, long-standing habit.[24] And even though Bacon defends Gregory the Great's exegesis of a faulty reading in the *Compendium studii philosophiae*, he does not accept that this error should be perpetuated by custom; instead, he calls for a return

[22] Gerard of Huy, [Preface to his *correctorium*], p. 308: 'Licet hic correxerim aliqua in antiquis codicibus contenta modernis inusitata: non obstat "usus, penes quem arbitrium est, et vis et norma loquendi" [Horace, *Ars poetica*, in his *Opera*, ed. D. R. Shackleton Bailey, Stuttgart 1985, pp. 310–329, at vv. 71–72], cum non corrigantur poemata poetarum vel aliorum propter usum contrarium. Nullus enim liber a quocunque autore editus, si discrepat usui postea introducto, est corrigendus secundum usum. In communi sermone scriptisque et dictaminibus vel epistolis nostris verbis uti debemus, nec propter hoc si qua nobis inusitata sunt in biblia corrigere iure possumus cum versus Virgilii vel Ovidii propter usum non emendamus.'

[23] A short extract from the work was published by Denifle, 'Die Handschriften', pp. 308–309, n. 4, ll. 6–13: 'Sed dicas: Usus aliter fert, prevalet usus. / Solvo: sermone communi cotidiano / aut dictaminibus propriis scriptis valet usus. / Scribimus et loquimur aliter quam scripsit Homerus, / Aut Maro vel Flaccus; tamen ipsa poemata sicut / Scripserunt remanent. Sic fac in bibliotheca, / ut non immutes veterum bene scripta librorum. / Usus enim factum non mutat, sed faciendum.' The chronological order of Gerard's works and the inter-relationships between them have not yet been explored.

[24] Bacon, *Opus majus*, p. 2: 'Quatuor vero sunt maxima comprehendendae veritatis offendicula, quae omnem quemcumque sapientem impediunt, et vix aliquem permittunt ad verum titulum sapientiae pervenire, videlicet fragilis et indignae auctoritatis exemplum, consuetudinis diuturnitas, vulgi sensus imperiti, et propriae ignorantiae occultatio cum ostentatione sapientiae apparentis.'

to *veritas* by consulting the original manuscripts.[25] Whether Bacon would have rigorously followed his own demand for *veritas* over *consuetudo* in the context of a large-scale work of emendation is impossible to guess. It is clear, however, that his views were in line with the general theory held by twefth- and thirteenth-century textual critics that *veritas* should always override the power of *consuetudo*.

The conflict between *consuetudo* and *veritas* produced hardly any comments in the fourteenth century. In fact, the only fourteenth-century author discussed in this study to come close to commenting on the issue was Richard FitzRalph. In his *Summa*, he has the interlocutor John mention the possibility that everything in Scripture is corrupt, amounting to a total loss of *auctoritas*.[26] When Richard takes over as speaker, he rejects John's view, insisting that although *veritas* might not be transmitted in individual manuscripts which could have been corrupted, it is by definition found in the officially approved Latin versions.[27]

In the fifteenth century, after the silence of the fourteenth century, there was a huge increase in the numbers of comments on *veritas* and *consuetudo*. Lorenzo Valla's works are the richest source. In his preface to the *Collatio*, he quotes the 'Preface to the Gospels', in which Jerome asks: when searching for *veritas*, why not go back to the Greek original and, in this way, correct the mistakes made by translators, 'correctors', or scribes?[28] And Valla did indeed rely on the original Greek for his emendations of the Bible, opposing *consuetudo* and attempting to come as close as possible to *veritas*. Yet his approach to *veritas* differed from that of his predecessors in one important respect: for Valla, *veritas*, by definition, was the exclusive preserve of the original text of the Bible; the Latin translation could do no more than imitate it. This attitude,

---

[25] See above, p. 149, n. 136.

[26] FitzRalph, *Summa*, sig. Ci^v (19, 18): 'Isto modo ostendi consequitur nichil esse securum aut certum propter hoc quod asseritur in nostra scriptura et tollitur omnino nostre scripture auctoritas. Item multa inveniuntur in translatione Ieronimi que non habent in translatione 70 interpretum.'

[27] See above, p. 64, n. 56.

[28] Valla,*Collatio*, p. 4 (quoting Jerome, 'Praefatio in Evangelio', p. 1515): '"Sin autem veritas est querenda de pluribus, cur non ad grecam originem revertentes ea que vel a vitiosis interpretibus male edita vel a presumptoribus imperitis emendata perversius vel a librariis dormitantibus aut addita sunt aut mutata corrigimus?"'

however, allowed for the emendation of the Latin Bible on the basis not only of understandability, but also of correct grammar and even good style. We can observe this approach to Latin Scripture in numerous examples from his works. For instance, although Valla was aware of the *interpres*'s customary choice of words, he did not consider it necessary to follow his usage.[29] Furthermore, he tolerated and even actively endorsed changes to the text of the Latin Bible made in order to enhance readability: he accepted, for instance, an addition which clarified a sentence in Mt 5.22 ('Whosoever is angry with his brother, shall be in danger of the judgment'), insisting on the necessity of introducing *sine causa*.[30] Similarly, supporting what he considered to be proper Latin language over *consuetudo*, he rejected neologisms and otherwise unattested grammatical forms.[31]

His refusal to accept a passage in the Latin Bible solely on the grounds of custom can be seen in two passages from the Gospels. In his discussion of Mt 21.5 in the *Collatio*, he wonders why the Latin tradition has *sedens supra asinam*, rather than the masculine *asinum* and why it is said that the Holy Spirit descended *in specie columbe* rather than *columbi*. Even though he cannot provide an explanation for the use of *asina* rather than *asinus*, he concludes that there has to be a definite reason for the use of the feminine, especially since the masculine is attested elsewhere in the Bible. In the case of the feminine plural *columbe*, a masculine form cannot be found in the Bible. Valla therefore supports the reading by stating that it also includes the male gender, as is clear from other passages

---

[29] Ibid., p. 115: '"Et si ibi fuerit filius pacis, requiescet super eum pax vestra; sin autem, ad vos revertetur" [Lk 10.6]: Quis hoc non videt hic deesse negationem, ut dicatur *sin autem non* sive *sin minus*? ... Certe grece adest negatio eritque translatio: *sin autem non* vel more interpretis *alioquin*, nam frequenter ita hec verba traducit.' Examples illustrating this approach in relation to the role of grammar for the emendation of the Latin Bible are given below, pp. 225–231.

[30] Ibid., p. 27: '"Omnis qui irascitur fratri suo" [Mt 5.22]: Deest *sine causa*'; see also Valla, *Annotationes*, p. 809A. For this passage and Valla's acceptance of additions, see also Stupperich, 'Schriftauslegung', p. 231. The original Greek does not contain Valla's addition: πᾶς ὁ ὀργιζόμενος τῷ ἀδελφῷ αὐτοῦ ἔνοχος ἔσται τῇ κρίσει; however, the word εικη is listed in the apparatus. Valla's addition might thus well constitute an attempt at bringing the Latin in line with the Greek.

[31] See below, pp. 226–227 and nn. 21–22.

in the Gospels and also from Virgil.³² In both instances, he searches for logical reasons to confirm the seemingly odd feminine forms rather than simply accepting the readings on the basis of *consuetudo*.

George of Trebizond's definition of *veritas* was the direct opposite of Valla's. Since George regarded the Vulgate as divinely inspired, the Latin text, by definition, possessed its own *veritas* in the form of Jerome's version; and the slightest change to this text – such as that from *sic* to *si* in Jn 21.22 – could be abused as an excuse for bigger changes.³³

In George's eyes, the *veritas* of the Latin New Testament was at least equal to that of the original Greek. Although some called for an emendation of Jn 21.22 according to the Greek, he maintained that the verse should not be changed, since the Latin tradition had always had the reading *sic*, which was preserved by Jerome and was

---

³² Ibid., p. 61: '"Sedens supra asinam" [Mt 21.5]: ... Sed cur potius asina quam asino, quemadmodum cur potius Spiritus Sanctus descendit in specie columbe [compare Lk 3.22] quam columbi? Sane in *asina* aliquid cause subest, nam *asinum* in Evangelio legimus [see Lk 13.15] ... *columbum* non legimus, eoque dicitur: "Cathedras vendentium columbas evertit" [Mt 21.12], et "duos pullos columbarum" [Lk 2.24], cum utique ex dimidia parte columbi essent, nec magis columbi quam palumbi. Ne Latini quidem hoc genus loquendi insuetum habent, ut Virgilius: *Gemine* venere *columbe*, quarum altera mas erat, que a dea Venere mittebantur.' See Virgil, *Aeneid*, in his *Opera*, ed. R. A. B. Mynors, 10th edn, Oxford 1990, pp. 103–422, VI, 189–190: 'Vix ea fatus erat, geminae cum forte columbae ipsa sub ora uiri caelo uenere uolantes.' The Greek reads: ἐπιβεβηκὼς ἐπὶ ὄνον. Valla does not mention that the Greek ὄνος can be both masculine and feminine (see Walter Bauer, *Griechisch–deutsches Wörterbuch zu den Schriften des Neuen Testaments und der frühchristlichen Literatur*, 6th edn, ed. B. and K. Aland, Berlin and New York 1988, col. 1163). For the use of *columbae* rather than *columbi* to denote both males and females, see also Varro, *De lingua latina*, ed. G. Goetz and F. Schoell, Leipzig 1910, p. 159 (IX, 38, 56): 'Nam et tum omnes mares et feminae dicebantur columbae, quod non erant in usu domestico quo nunc, nunc contra, propter domesticos usus quod internovimus, appellatur mas columbus, femina columba.'

³³ John Monfasani, *George of Trebizond: A Biography and a Study of his Rhetoric and Logic*, Leiden 1976, p. 94, n. 111, quoting from George's unpublished first treatise on Jn 21.22: 'Unus apex aut unum iota si ex evangelio remotum fuerit, facile, data licentia, cetera dirripientur ... Quasobres nihil, o patres, removendum, nihil addendum, nihil mutandum in evangelio Christi Catholicis est.' Of course, he still wanted the text to be purged of corruptions; see ibid., p. 94. For the divine inspiration of the Vulgate, see above, p. 73.

also found in the writings of Augustine.[34] By arguing on the basis of both the Vulgate's divine inspiration and customary use, dating to before the time of Jerome, George was apparently trying to enlist both *consuetudo* and *veritas* in support of his cause. He explicitly endorses the value of *consuetudo* in two statements found in the summary of his first treatise which he gives in the invective against Theodore Gaza. There, George insists that the form of the biblical text, as confirmed and prescribed by the Fathers, may not be changed.[35] And he concludes later on that the *consuetudo* of the habitual usage of Latin supports the reading *sic*.[36] George thus invokes two types of *consuetudo*: on the one hand, the *consuetudo* handed down by the Church Fathers; and, on the other, the linguistic *consuetudo* of the Latin language. This latter kind of *consuetudo* was also discussed by Gerard of Huy, who rejected any reasoning based on the type of contemporary usage adduced by George to back up his argument.

For George's adversary, Cardinal Bessarion, the fact that the Church Fathers also read *sic* in Jn 21.22 was of no relevance. In his opinion, their testimony was not a proof of *veritas*.[37] Nor did the Latin versions of the Bible, in contrast to the original Greek, contain *veritas*. Despite his admission that the Vulgate had been accepted by the Catholic Church, he denied that the Latin translation had the same authority as the Greek original and did not believe that it was divinely inspired.[38] He also challenged

---

[34] See above, p. 73, n. 85, and George of Trebizond, *Adversus Theodorum Gazam*, pp. 330–331 (35, 3): 'Sed graecam scripturam, unde traducta haec sunt, sequendam multi asserunt. Ego autem non sum nescius hunc locum ita lectum latine semper, etiam ante Augustini tempora fuisse, quemadmodum hodie legitur. Testis est ipse Augustinus, qui cum super evangelium Iohannis scriberet, non "si eum volo manere", sed "sic eum volo manere" saepius repetit.' For examples in which Augustine uses *sic*, see above, p. 178, n. 209.

[35] Ibid., p. 330 (35, 2): 'Primum ergo illud mihi scribendum videtur: non sunt labefactanda fundamenta, non removendi fines, non quassandi termini, qui a patribus nostris iacti, constituti firmatique sunt.'

[36] Ibid., p. 336 (35, 10): 'Illud etiam pro meo iure dico triti sermonis latini consuetudinem non *si* sed *sic* in similibus flagitare.'

[37] See above, p. 176, n. 202. For other statements that exegetical writings are not authoritative for the establishment of a text, see, e.g., Augustine, *Epistulae*, III, pp. 344–345 (148, IV, 15; quoted by Gratian, *Decretum*, col. 18 [D. 9, c. 10]).

[38] Bessarion, *In illud Evangelii.*, col. 625B: 'Quod vero rectius se haberet sermo Latinus, minime ausi sunt prosequi, stulte id a se dictum intelligentes, et contentionis potius gratia quam veritatis. Siquidem Evangelista Joannes et

George's claim that nothing could be changed in Scripture, especially in the Gospels, since this would open up the possibility of corrupting the biblical text.[39] Those who held this position thought that it was better to die than to alter the text of the Bible; and, in their eyes, anyone who corrected it could no longer be considered a Catholic.[40] Bessarion pointed out, however, that emendation of the Latin Bible was by no means unheard of: Jerome and later also the *correctoria* freely admitted to altering the Latin text.[41] Bessarion thus rejected George's claims about the value of the Latin tradition of the Bible: its *consuetudo* had no authority, and *veritas* was contained solely in the original Greek text of the New Testament.

The views on *veritas* and *consuetudo* found in the Carthusian manuals for scribes written in the fifteenth century contrast sharply with the opinions expressed by textual critics. The manuals give unconditional support to the order's *consuetudo*. In his *Opus pacis*, Oswaldus de Corda admits that habitual regional variants might be rejected by people outside the order and vice versa. Nevertheless, the Carthusian readings must be accepted: *usus* justifies deviation

Evangelium suum Graeco, non Latino sermone composuit, et ἐὰν conjunctione usus est, quae, in Latinum versa, *si* absque ulla ambiguitate significat. Interpres vero, quicunque is quidem fuerit, nec tanta Spiritus gratia, quanta Joannes illustratus fuisse existimandus est, et verbo usus est ad errorem proclivi, quippe addita *si* conjunctioni, per ignorantiam sive incuriam librariorum, *c* littera, omnis sententia subvertitur et pro conjunctione, quae dubia est, adverbium efficitur affirmandi.' Bessarion's acceptance of the official approval of the Vulgate has been discussed above, pp. 73–74. The use of the term *interpres* in this passage is very similar to Valla's, for which see above, pp. 97–99.

[39] Ibid., col. 625D: 'Asserunt, nihil in sacra Scriptura innovandum esse, praecipueque in Evangelio, ubi vel unum apicem, aut unum iota immutare nefas est. Daretur enim hoc modo facultas volentibus Scripturam sacram corrumpere, quod nullo modo est permittendum. Cum igitur apud Latinos Evangelium sic habeat, asseri aliter mutarive sine crimine non posse.'

[40] Ibid., col. 626C: 'Concludunt ergo injuriam fieri Evangelio, si quis hunc locum mutet, moriendumque potius esse quam tale aliquid tentandum; nec debere quemquam catholicum putari, qui mutandam hanc Evangelii auctoritatem existimet, censendumque eum qui id ausus fuerit, etiam pejora facturum addita ei auctoritate atque potentia.'

[41] Ibid., col. 627D: 'Hanc tantum Scripturam multo post tempore superveniens Hieronymus, egregius doctor, denuo veterem ex Hebraeo, novam e Graeco fonte traduxit; qua in re etsi multis praebuit latrandi contra se causam, multa tamen aliter quam edita a prioribus fuerant dictavit, et, ut ipse dicit, emendavit atque correxit, nec caeteras solum Scripturae partes, sed ipsa quoque Evangelia.' For his comment on the *correctoria*, see below, p. 254, n. 18.

from what others judge to be correct.[42] The same principle is applied to apparent mistakes, which are legitimised *per usum communem et consuetudinem scripturarum*.[43]

In the slightly later *Notabilia quedam de correctione librorum*, the unidentified author maintains that it is perfectly acceptable to have local deviations from the model of the Grande Chartreuse which do not contradict Carthusian *veritas*.[44] He gives various examples in which readings in accordance with the custom at that time, *ad modum nunc consuetum*, are to be preserved and not to be emended.[45]

Both authors valued the Carthusian *consuetudo* – whether found in the *Vorlage* held in the motherhouse or in the customs of various

[42] Oswaldus, *Opus pacis*, p. 5: 'Sciat eciam prudens corrector multas dictiones in nostro usu consuetas, propter diuersarum nacionum uarias habitudines et linguas uel propter scriptorum uicia aut alias undecunque sic in[s]olitas {*my correction*}, que apud antiquos uel omnino non habebantur, uel aliter scribebantur et proferebantur. Et e contrario illis consuete nobis penitus sint ignote siue minus usitate. Et multa que apud illos erant indeclinabilia secundum partes oracionis, aut defectiua, aut numero singulari uel plurali carencia, aut modis, temporibus, personis, rectis siue obliquis, aut aliis quibuslibet accidentibus, hec nostris temporibus tenent legem illis oppositam, sicut eciam e contrario. Sic eciam de accentibus et de orthographia sentiendum est.'

[43] Ibid., p. 13: 'Vnde eciam condependenter aduertendum est, plerunque partes orationis alternatim pro se inuicem, et aliquando alias pro aliis in eodem significato reperiri. Similiter reperitur numerus pro numero, casus pro casu, modus pro modo, tempus pro tempore, compositum pro simplici, etc., et e contrario, que uel per se sunt salua vel per figuras saluanda, siue eciam per usum communem et consuetudinem scripturarum, non obstantibus in contrarium regulis quorundam gramaticorum.'

[44] *Notabilia*, p. 84: 'Ex hiis que in hoc libro posita sunt et in sequentibus ponentur, satis liquet qualiter corrigendo libros in ordine nostro ab exemplaribus domus Cartusie non oporteat omnimodam seruare equalitatem, eciam saluo statuto de uno eodemque ritu mencionem faciente. Nam identitas illas potius competit similitudini ueritatis, sensus, et materie quam equalitati omnimode, alias uix unus in tot ordine haberetur aut haberi posset liber, qui per omnia libris Cartusie in litteris, sillabis, atque dictionibus latinis et barbaris in terminibus quoque transposicione ac ceteris esset equalis, eciamsi ibidem scriberetur, quia in ipsis exemplaribus nonnunquam talis diuersitas inuenitur, licet non in eodem semper loco.'

[45] Ibid., p. 88: 'Sic eciam habemus *confiderunt* in oratione Esdre [4 Esdras 8.30?], *sonauerunt* in psalmo "Deus noster refugium" [Ps 45.2], et "Deus quis similis erit tibi" *adiuuauerunt* Eccles. 24 [Si 29.4], *gemescit* 36 [Si 36.27?], et *iuuenior* capitulo ultimo [Si 51.18], tamen ista et similia, si alii libri aliarum domorum habeant ad modum nunc consuetum, scilicet *confisi sunt* pro *confiderunt* ... non oportet ea emendari, eo quod eciam hec posteriora sepius habeantur in libris et bibliis Cartusie.'

regions – to such a degree that it became their main criterion for establishing the correctness of a text. The author of the *Notabilia* even went so far as to call the Carthusian model *veritas*.

From the statements examined in this chapter, we can conclude that even though in the twelfth and thirteenth century textual critics expressed their preference for *veritas* over *consuetudo* or *usus*, the grip of custom was still so strong that it could not easily be overcome. Thus, Maniacutia, Hervaeus and perhaps Hugh of St Cher at times contravened their own bold claims to pursue *veritas* when it actually came to overturning a traditional text.

The fourteenth century, once again, occupies a special position, providing almost no comments on the question of *consuetudo* and *veritas*. This silence can be attributed to the fact that the authors examined were not concerned with textual criticism, and therefore were not confronted with the issue. In the fifteenth century, however, we find detailed discussion in the writings of Lorenzo Valla, George of Trebizond and Cardinal Bessarion. More than any of the medieval textual critics, the humanists Valla and Crastone dared to overcome the *consuetudo* of the Latin Bible in their works. Neither Valla's radical emendations of the New Testament nor Crastone's new, Greek-based Latin edition of the Psalms show any evidence of concessions to the *consuetudo* of the Latin Bible.[46] Indeed, both scholars felt free, as a matter of course, to intervene in the text of the Latin Bible.

From the statements made by textual critics and also from those found in writings for religious orders, including statutes, it is clear that the concept of *veritas* was considered to be extremely important. Modern scholars, however, have only commented on this issue in passing. Detailed studies of the notions underlying the

---

[46] Of course, a more extensive examination of their works might produce different results. Crastone's approach is clear from his aim of providing a Latin text translated more literally from the Greek Psalter, which in itself automatically precludes adherence to the *consuetudo* of Latin Scripture; an example of his advocacy of *veritas* is found in his prologue, where he praises the addressee as a *veritatis scrutator*: Crastone, [Dedicatory Letter], pp. 14–15: 'Sunt et innumera alia depravata apud omnes poene Latinos auctores item et sacros codices: quae si aliquando requiem studiis meis impetraro, quam tuis modo auspiciis spero, in animum emendare induxi; tibique talium studioso et qui omnia virtuti et musis postponas dicare, qui et unus mihi visus es dignus cui hanc novam emendationem psalterii inscriberem, tanquam veritatis scrutatori, et stomachanti ob religionis studium tot errores divina volumina invasisse.'

terms *veritas*, *usus* and *consuetudo* are required to deepen our understanding of how these principles influenced textual criticism of the Bible and other sacred texts.[47]

Judging from the number of comments on establishing uniformity in the liturgy found in the statutes of the various orders, which far outweigh those concerning the need for a uniform text of the Bible, it appears that the accuracy of liturgical books was much more of an issue than that of Scripture itself. This might have been due to the fact that liturgical texts had a communal element to them, whereas it was much less disturbing if the texts in manuscripts of the Bible used for private study and reading differed.[48]

---

[47] See, e.g., for the Carthusians: Hansjakob Becker, '"Cartusia numquam reformata quia numquam deformata": Liturgiereformen bei den Kartäusern in Vergangenheit und Gegenwart', in *Liturgiereformen*, I, pp. 325–345, at p. 331; for the Cistercians: Altermatt, '"Id quod magis authenticum..."', pp. 316–317 and 322. Rizzo (*Il lessico filologico*) does not discuss any of these terms, but she is not concerned with the textual criticism of the Bible. Statements concerning the authenticity of biblical books and their authors and the grounds on which they were accepted or rejected also deserve further research.

[48] For this assumption, see Becker, '"Cartusia numquam reformata"', pp. 343–344. For the Dominican statutes, see above, pp. 137–139; a number of comments on the Carthusian statutes are listed by Egan in her edition of Oswaldus, *Opus pacis*, pp. 28*–32*. Valla, too, ventured into the field of liturgical texts: he corrected the baptismal formula and rejected the truncation of the ending of the *Pater Noster*; see Camporeale, *Lorenzo Valla*, p. 296, and Valla, *Collatio*, p. 34: 'Cur denique tantum de oratione hac sacratissima decurtatum est? Nam ita finitur: "quia tuum est regnum et virtus et gloria in secula amen"; quam clausulam ab ea oratione, qua Dominus ipse orare nos docuit, detruncasse, ingens sane piaculum est, necessarioque quod prave sustulimus addendum.'

IV.2 THE ROLE OF GRAMMAR IN EMENDING THE BIBLE

One of the corrective measures for the text of the Latin Bible discussed by medieval textual critics was the emendation of grammatically faulty passages on the basis of the rules of Latin. The role of grammar for the emendation of the Latin Bible in the Middle Ages and early Renaissance has not so far been studied.[1] Modern scholars tend to assume that in the Middle Ages the Latin Bible was commonly regarded as exempt from the rules of grammar.[2] Yet the statements of textual critics, which up to now have been completely neglected, have an entirely different story to tell, and we can trace a clear development in their views over the course of the centuries.

It was not in itself a difficult task to correct the grammatical mistakes in the Latin Bible. The late antique grammar books, especially those of Aelius Donatus (c. 310-380), who was Jerome's teacher, and Priscian (late fifth/early sixth century), were very influential throughout the entire Middle Ages; and, together with their medieval counterparts, written, for instance, by Alexander of

---

[1] I have only been able to find a short discussion of the topic in Gillian R. Evans, *The Language and Logic of the Bible: The Earlier Middle Ages*, Cambridge 1984, pp. 85–87; but even she devotes no more than two pages to the relationship between grammar and the Latin Bible and limits her account to the grammarian Ralph of Beauvais's *Glose super Donatum*. Marie–Dominique Chenu has made some more theoretical studies of the connection between grammar and theology; see his 'Grammaire et théologie aux XIIe et XIIIe siècles', *Archives d'histoire doctrinale et littéraire du moyen âge* 10 (1935), pp. 5–28; and his *La théologie au douzième siècle*, Paris 1966, pp. 90–107, in which he devotes a chapter to grammar and theology, based on his earlier article.

[2] See, e.g., Charles Thurot, *Notices et extraits de divers manuscrits latins pour servir à l'histoire des doctrines grammaticales au moyen âge*, Paris 1874, pp. 81 and 526; Lubac (*Exégèse*, III, p. 77) refers to this view as a commonplace.

Villa Dei (1160/1170-1240/1250), were easily accessible to medieval scholars on account of their rich manuscript tradition and provided the textual critic with well-defined rules for the Latin language.[3] In theory, one could simply set out to emend the grammatically incorrect passages in a biblical manuscript with the help of a copy of an authoritative grammar book.

In reality, of course, it was not that easy, for the Latin Bible was not just any corrupt Latin text. Some medieval scholars considered it to be the Word of God; to them, the text of Latin Scripture, as transmitted, was sacred and therefore inviolable, regardless of the fact that it was a translation which had been copied and, as a result, corrupted by the hands of countless scribes.

The idea of considering the Latin translation of the Bible to be divinely inspired ultimately derived from the legend of the Septuagint. Since in Latin antiquity and also throughout the Middle Ages, the word *septuaginta* was used both for what we now call the Septuagint and for the Vetus Latina, the two versions were regarded as being in essence the same text. As a result, the notion of the divine inspiration of the Septuagint also came to include the Vetus Latina.[4] This view is expressed, for example, in the works of no less an authority than Augustine. In several instances, he writes that he regards not only the original authors of the biblical books, but also the translators of the two versions known by the name *septuaginta* as inspired. Consequently, their works were originally free of error. Yet, while granting this special status to the Septuagint and the Vetus Latina, Augustine still acknowledges that scribes made mistakes and introduced voluntary alterations into the text, which then entered the manuscript tradition.[5]

---

[3] For the popularity of Donatus's *Ars minor* throughout the Middle Ages, see Aelius Donatus, *The 'Ars Minor' of Donatus: For One Thousand Years the Leading Textbook of Grammar*, ed. and tr. W. J. Chase, Madison 1926, p. 4. For the rich transmission of Priscian's works, see Marina Passalacqua, *I codici di Prisciano*, Rome 1978. Alexander of Villa Dei's *Doctrinale*, finished in 1199, survives in at least 228 manuscripts dating from the thirteenth to the fifteenth century; see Alexander of Villa–Dei, *Das 'Doctrinale' des Alexander de Villa–Dei*, ed. D. Reichling, Berlin 1893, repr. New York 1974, p. XLIV; and p. XXXVII for the dating.

[4] For the term *septuaginta*, see above, pp. 8–13; a brief summary of the legend of the Septuagint is given above, p. 9.

[5] Augustine, *Epistolae*, p. 354 (82, I, 3): 'Ego enim fateor Caritati tuae, solis eis Scripturarum libris qui iam canonici appellantur, didici hunc timorem honoremque deferre, ut nullum eorum auctorem scribendo aliquid errasse firmissime credam. Ac si aliquid in eis offendero Litteris, quod videatur

For many influential authors, this view of the transmission of the Latin Bible soon became unacceptable. Augustine's matter-of-fact concession that the process of copying the Bible led to errors in the manuscript circulation was lost sight of. As a result, the assumption that the text of the Scriptures, however corrupt it might be in the manuscripts, was divinely inspired confronted early medieval scholars with the dilemma of having to account for grammatical mistakes which they encountered. From at least the sixth century onwards, they managed to circumvent this problem with a simple, yet at the same time all-purpose solution: they claimed that Scripture was not subject to conventional Latin grammar. For instance, in his *Moralia in Iob*, Gregory the Great refused to subject heaven-sent words to the grammatical rules of Donatus;[6] Cassiodorus insisted that deviation from the grammatical norm must not be changed, for a divinely inspired text was invulnerable to corruption and its words were reaffirmed by the fact that they were contained in many manuscripts;[7] and, in the ninth century, in his exposition of Ps 44, Paschasius Radbertus (c. 790-859), following Cassiodorus, defended the juxtaposition of a

contrarium veritati; nihil aliud, quam vel mendosum esse codicem, vel interpretem non assecutum esse quod dictum est, vel me minime intellexisse, non ambigam. Alios autem ita lego, ut quantalibet sanctitate doctrinaque praepolleant, non ideo verum putem, quia ipsi ita senserunt; sed quia mihi vel per illos auctores canonicos, vel probabili ratione, quod a vero non abhorreat, persuadere potuerunt. Nec te, mi frater, sentire aliud existimo: prorsus, inquam, non te arbitror sic legi tuos libros velle, tamquam Prophetarum, vel Apostolorum; de quorum scriptis, quod omni errore careant, dubitare nefarium est.' For a statement by Augustine supporting the authority of the *septuaginta*, see above, p. 111, n. 16.

[6] Gregory the Great, *Epistola ad Leandrum*, p. 7 (5): 'Nam sicut huius quoque epistolae tenor enuntiat, non metacismi collisionem fugio, non barbarismi confusionem deuito, situs modosque etiam et praepositionum casus seruare contemno, quia indignum uehementer existimo, ut uerba caelestis oraculi restringam sub regulis Donati. Neque enim haec ab ullis interpretibus, in scripturae sacrae auctoritate seruata sunt.'

[7] Cassiodorus, *Institutiones*, p. 44 (I, xv, 5): 'Nec illa verba tangenda sunt, quae interdum contra artem quidem humanam posita reperiuntur, sed auctoritate multorum codicum vindicantur. Corrumpi siquidem nequeunt, quae inspirante Domino dicta noscuntur.' When it comes to orthographical mistakes, however, Cassiodorus insists that one should correct the text according to Jerome's manuscripts; see ibid., p. 47 (I, xv, 11): 'Quod si tamen aliqua verba reperiuntur absurde posita, aut ex his codicibus quos beatus Hieronymus in editione septuaginta interpretum emendavit, vel quos ipse ex Hebreo transtulit, intrepide corrigenda sunt.'

preposition followed by an adverb in the phrase '*filiae regum ab intus*' [Ps 44.14] with the argument that although this kind of language was not used in profane literature, it was nevertheless proper in sacred writings.[8]

These views were perpetuated by later medieval grammarians. For instance, Ralph of Beauvais, still alive in the 1180s, makes some references to incorrect grammar in the Bible in his *Glose super Donatum*. Among other points, Ralph mentions that William of Conches (c. 1080-1154), who composed glosses on Priscian, used to respond to claims about grammatical mistakes in the Latin Bible by stating that Scripture was not subject to grammar.[9] The same conservative attitude was voiced by John of Garland (d. c. 1272). In a gloss ascribed to him in a manuscript of Alexander of Villa Dei's *Doctrinale*, he writes: 'Sacred Scripture does not want to subject itself to the rule of grammar, nor does it want to be governed by its art.'[10] And even in the late fifteenth century, we can

---

[8] Paschasius Radbertus, *Expositio in Psalmum XLIV*, ed. B. Paulus, Turnhout 1991, p. 91 (III, ll. 569–571): 'Et notandum quod ait: "Filiae regum ab intus" [Ps 44.14]. Quia ista locutio numquam in saecularibus habetur litteris sed inter propria legis divinae connumeratur eloquia.' Compare Cassiodorus, *Expositio Psalmorum*, 2 vols, ed. M. Adriaen, Turnhout 1958, I, p. 412 (XLIV, 14): 'Istam locutionem "filiae regum ab intus" inter propria legis divinae connumera, quam in communione non inuenis.' More examples of the belief that the Bible was not subject to conventional grammar, from late antiquity through the Middle Ages, can be found in Lubac, *Exégèse*, III, e.g., pp. 80, 81, 84.

[9] Ralph of Beauvais, *Glose super Donatum*, ed. C. H. Kneepkens, Nijmegen 1982, pp. 47–48: 'Participium desinens in *–ens* est tam presentis quam preteriti [im]perfecti temporis et potest coniungi uerbo cuiuslibet temporis. Magister tamen Gillelmus dicit quod non potest coniungi cum futuro. Sed opponitur de illo Psalterii "uenientes autem uenient" [Ps 125.6] et cetera. Responde[bat] quod Diuina Pagina non subiacet regulis gramatice uel quia *uenientes* est ibi nomen. Sed non adtendebat sequentem litteram "portantes manipulos suos". Si enim non esset *portantes* participium, quomodo regeret accusatiuum? Nos autem ea futuro coniungimus et aliis temporibus, ut "legens proficiam".' The text was written in the third quarter of the twelfth century; see ibid., p. XXIV. William of Conches's *Glose super Priscianum* have not yet been edited. For some information on the text, see Edouard Jeauneau, 'Deux rédactions des gloses de Guillaume de Conches sur Priscien', *Recherches de Théologie ancienne et médiévale* 27 (1960), pp. 212–247. In the passage quoted, Ralph seems critical of the view held by William of Conches. His opinion on the relationship between grammar and the Latin Bible deserves further investigation.

[10] Quoted by Thurot, 'Notices', p. 526: 'Nota quod inuenitur *murmur* in masculino genere. Unde illud "multus erat murmur in populo" [Jn 7.12].

still find scholars who accepted incorrect grammatical constructions in the Bible. The Spanish grammarian Fernando Nepote, in his *Materies* published in 1485, defends faulty gerund constructions in the Psalms with the comment that although they are not elegant, they are understandable.[11]

The legitimacy of accepting grammatical oddities, not to say mistakes, in Latin Scripture thus found continuous support from the Church Fathers to the late fifteenth century. In the mid-twelfth century, however, opposition to this widespread refusal to subject the Latin Bible to the rules of grammar was expressed by Maniacutia in his *Libellus*. He objected strongly to accepting grammatically incorrect passages. For instance, he listed three corrupt passages from the Psalms; and even though for all three verses the entire Latin manuscript tradition was in agreement he censured these errors and put the blame on the translators and scribes. What irked Maniacutia in the three verses were crass grammatical mistakes; and although he did not claim that the verses were unintelligible, he found these persistent grammatical oddities intolerable. Instead of accepting the quirks of the Latin Bible, as his predecessors had done, Maniacutia took a different approach. He defended his criticism of the passages on the ground that even though one might say that the biblical text did not have to adhere to the rules of the grammarians – a position which, generally speak-

---

Solvitur. Dicitur primo quod hoc est secundum antiquos, nec est in usu moderno. Vel aliter. Divina pagina non subiacet arti gramatice. Unde Iohannes de Gallandia: "Pagina sacra non vult se subdere legi / Grammatices, nec vult illius arte regi.'" I have not been able to locate the quotation in John of Garland's works. De Lubac, in his discussion of this quotation, (*Exégèse médiévale*, III, p. 86) regards this position as traditional. I am grateful to Anthony Lappin for pointing this out to me.

[11] Fernando Nepote, *Materies*, in *Gramáticas latinas de transición: Juan de Pastrana, Fernando Nepote*, ed. C. Codoñer, Salamanca 2000, pp. 89–147, at p. 111: 'Dicit enim propheta: "In conueniendo populos in unum" [Ps 101.23] "in conuertendo dominus captiuitatem Syon" [Ps 125.1] et "in deficiendo ex me spiritum meum" [Ps 141.4]. Et si non sit ita eleganter dictum, ut quidam dicunt, et irrationabiliter, cum sint extra condicionem actus, sufficit tamen ad confirmandam ueritatem. Poterat enim dici *populis conuenientibus in unum, domino conuertendo captiuitatem* et *spiritu in me deficiente*, quod non negamus.' The *quidam* Nepote refers to is certainly a reference to Lorenzo Valla, who discusses the same examples in his *De linguae latinae elegantia*; see below, p. 231, n. 30. The text was written early in the last third of the fifteenth century (before 1485); see *Gramáticas latinas*, p. 15.

ing, Maniacutia agreed with – nevertheless, 'no one is forced to translate corruptly'.[12]

Maniacutia's daring and self-confident attitude towards the Latin translation of Scripture differed sharply from that of his contemporaries such as William of Conches. For Maniacutia, the Latin version was not inspired and therefore was subject to corruption even in the act of translation. His belief that the biblical text did not have to adhere to the rules of grammar applied only to the original text, which he regarded as inspired. The Latin translation, on the other hand, was not an untouchable version of the Bible and must follow the rules of grammar. Because its origin was 'human' rather than divine, it contained errors of all kinds, which could and should be set right.

About a hundred years after Maniacutia, there was a further advance in the application of grammar to textual criticism of the Bible. In the preface to his *correctorium*, Gerard of Huy informs us:

> I took up not an easy task, but rather an enterprise full of nightshifts and hard work, since I, a careful investigator of the old manuscripts of the Bible and an eager examiner of the grammar of the ancients, with Priscian himself as my witness, tried as best I could to correct what was corrupt and cut back what was superfluous, relying on the faithfulness of old manuscripts and the authority of the sacred teachers.[13]

---

[12] Maniacutia, *Libellus*, p. 91: 'Tres sunt in volumine isto versus vel a translatoribus male editi vel ab antiquis notariis vitiati; nam cuncta exemplaria quae scrutatus sum in hac corruptione concordant. Primus est: "Quasi proximum quasi fratrem nostrum sic complacebam" [Ps 34.14]. Quis enim nesciat verbum *complaceo* iungi accusativo non posse? Secundus autem est: "Ascendunt montes et descendunt campi" [Ps 103.8]; de aquis nanque agitur de quibus supra dictum est: "super montes stabunt aquae, ab increpatione tua fugient, a voce tonitrui tui formidabunt" [Ps 103.6–7]. Ascendunt montes ipsae aquae, descendunt in campos. Dicendum erat: terminum posuisti eis quem non transgredientur neque convertentur operire terram sicut fecerunt in diluvio. Tertius est: "in deficiendo ex me spiritum meum" [Ps 141.4]. Vide falsitatem: gerundiva enim verborum, quae a caeteris non construuntur, construi nec ipsa solent. Dicet aliquis divinam paginam grammaticorum regulis minime subiacere; dico et ego idem. Et tamen Ieronimo docente didici quia nemo corrupte transferre cogitur.' I have not been able to locate the last sentence in the works of Jerome; Maniacutia may not be quoting, but instead summarising what he had learned from Jerome.

[13] For the Latin quotation, see above, p. 131, n. 78. An example – even though connected to orthography – of Gerard's reliance on Priscian is mentioned by Dahan ('La critique textuelle', p. 379): with regard to the spelling of Isaac /

For Gerard, it was no longer sufficient merely to announce that he wanted to follow correct grammar. What distinguishes his position from Maniacutia's is Gerard's explicit reliance on ancient grammar, as is clear from his appeal to Priscian. How – if at all – he implemented this call for correct grammar is a different matter, which would require careful evaluation of his unpublished work. His comment nevertheless shows that Gerard was in favour of subjecting the Bible to a specific set of grammatical rules.

The same trend of not relying simply on unspecified grammatical rules for the correction of the Bible, but instead grounding the corrections on a renowned ancient grammarian is even more apparent in the writings of Roger Bacon. In his *Opus minus*, written in 1267, he insists that grammar is an essential tool for the emendation of Scripture:

> Grammatica Prisciani in majori volumine maxime valet ad correctionem textus. Sed theologi non utuntur ea, nec advertunt, quia qui sunt artistae negligunt librum illum propter magnitudinem contempti, et adhaerent libro Conclusionum. Et ideo qui volunt corrigere textum mutant antiquam grammaticam, quam optime scivit Hieronymus, qui transtulit, eo quod Donatus magnus, et major Priscianus fuit ejus magister.[14]

Ysaac, Gerard points out that Priscian insisted that *y* should be used only in Greek words and not, as Gerard adds, in Hebrew and Latin ones; see Priscian, *Institutiones grammaticae*, 2 vols, ed. M. Hertz, in *Grammatici latini*, ed. H. Keil, II–III, Hildesheim 1961, I, p. 36 (I, 49): '*Y* et *z* in Graecis tantummodo ponuntur dictionibus'. Dahan does not quote the passage from Gerard.

[14] Bacon, *Opus minus*, pp. 333–334. *Liber conclusionum* may be a misprint and should perhaps read *Liber constructionum*: M. R. James (*The Ancient Libraries of Canterbury and Dover: The Catalogues of the Libraries of Christ Church Priory and St. Augustine's Abbey at Canterbury and of St. Martin's Priory at Dover*, Cambridge 1903, p. 7) lists five manuscripts in the catalogue of Christ Church library from around 1170 of Priscian's *Liber constructionum*. Margaret Gibson ('Priscian, "Institutiones grammaticae": A Handlist of Manuscripts', *Scriptorium* 26 [1972], pp. 105–124, at p. 105) points out that the last two books of the *Institutiones* also circulated under the name *De constructione* or *Priscianus minor*; it might well be, therefore, that Bacon's *Liber conclusionum* is identical to *De constructione*. Gibson (ibid., p. 105) also notes that after the Carolingian era, the *Institutiones* were hardly ever copied as a whole, but were instead divided into books I–XVI ('*Priscianus major*') and books XVII–XVIII ('*Priscianus minor*'). '*Grammatica Prisciani in majori volumine*' thus presumably means either the *Priscianus major* or the complete *Institutiones grammaticae*; an abridged version was also in circulation under the title *De nomine, pronomine et verbo*. Already Chenu ('Grammaire et

A fuller text of the *Institutiones grammaticae* of Priscian is extremely useful for the correction of the text [of the Latin Bible]. But the theologians do not use it, and they do not realise that the members of the arts faculty neglect that book because of their great contempt [for it] and instead stick to the book of Conclusions. And therefore, those who want to correct the text change the ancient grammar which Jerome, who translated [the text], knew perfectly, because the great Donatus and the even greater Priscian were his teachers.

Leaving aside the fact that Bacon is misinformed about the dates of Priscian – Jerome had been dead for almost a century when Priscian wrote his great *Institutiones grammaticae* – it is clear that he regards the writings of the ancient grammarians as absolutely vital for the reconstruction of the Latin Bible. He even goes so far as to scold the theologians of his days for trying to correct the text of Scripture without a proper knowledge of ancient grammar and thus corrupting its foundation.

Bacon, in the passage, opened a new line of thought on the role of grammar in the textual transmission of the Latin Bible: too little grammatical knowledge induced people to alter their Bible manuscripts because they were unable to grasp the intricacy of the text in front of them. Their attempts to – as they thought – rectify passages which they did not understand led to an unintended increase in corruption. Bacon provides the following example to illustrate his theory:

> Marci igitur capito octavo non dicitur esse 'qui me confessus fuerit' [Mk 8.38], sed alia litera modernis [corrupta] {*my insertion*} horribiliter propter ignorantiam antiquae grammaticae. Nam debet ibi esse 'qui me fuerit confusus', quod est verbum deponens, habens significationem hujus verbi *confundo*, sicut adhuc omnes experiunt in Scriptura haec verba *zelo zelor* in eadem significatione, unde sic solebat esse de *confundo* et *confundor*: idem enim antiquitus significabant. Sed moderni non habent hoc in usu. Et ideo abraserunt a Sacro Textu: 'Qui me confusus fuerit' et posuerunt 'Qui confessus fuerit me'.[15]

> In the eighth chapter of the Gospel of Mark [Mk 8.38], it is not meant to be '*qui me confessus fuerit*', but that is another reading, [corrupted] by modern people due to their ignorance of ancient grammar. For it should be written '*qui me fuerit confusus*', which is a deponent verb that has the same meaning as the verb '*confundo*', just as everyone discovers that in the Bible the verbs *zelo* and *zelor* have the

théologie', p. 8) remarks on the importance which Bacon attributes to grammar for theology.

[15] Bacon, *Opus minus*, p. 331.

same meaning; therefore, it used to be like that with *confundo* and *confundor*: for long ago they meant the same. But the moderns do not use it like this. And therefore they erased '*Qui me confusus fuerit*' from Holy Writ and instead inserted '*Qui confessus fuerit me*'.

To support the correct reading he has suggested, Bacon then gives quotations of Mk 8.38 from the works of Augustine, Jerome and Bede, three authoritative writers, and also compares the passage with parallel ones in the other Gospels to show that the correct version should read *qui me fuerit confusus* – easily understandable if the reader's knowledge of classical Latin grammar is sufficient to recognise that the verb is deponent. For Bacon, not only is a firm grasp of ancient grammar essential for the purpose of emendation, but too little knowledge actually facilitates the textual corruption of the Latin Bible.

The application of grammar to the emendation of the Bible reached a peak in the fifteenth century. The most outstanding example of this development, both in terms of the quantity and the quality of his remarks, is once more Lorenzo Valla. In the *Collatio* and in the *Annotationes*, Valla made extensive use of grammar as a tool to correct the Latin Bible by employing virtually every type of grammatical correction to improve the text: he corrected various syntactical features;[16] he criticised an anacoluthon;[17] and he also ventured into the finer points of the Latin language, as he had done in his *Elegantiae*, when elucidating the subtle distinctions between words of very similar meaning, for example, *sicut* and *quasi*, *tamquam* and *velut* or *natus* and *genitus*.[18] Accusing the *interpres* of

---

[16] See, e.g., Valla, *Collatio*, pp. 64–65: '"Facitis eum filium Geenne duplo quam vos" [Mt 23.15]: Non est hoc ex ratione lingue latine, cum illud *quam* desideret comparativum, quod nec grece desideratur'; for this passage, see also Valla, *Annotationes*, p. 818B; ibid., p. 851A: '"Et indignos uos iudicastis aeternae uitae" [Ac 13.46]: Quia graece genitiuus casus est, oblitus est interpres in ablatiuum mutare, quem illi non habent. *Indignus* enim *uita*, non *uitae* dicitur.' For an example of a correction of conjugation, see, e.g., ibid., p. 850B: '"Accersi Simonem qui cognominatur Petrus" [Ac 10.5]: *Accerse* dicendum fuit et hic et superius, et posterius: tertiae enim est, non quartae coniugationis.'

[17] Valla, *Collatio*, p. 101: '"Ad faciendam misericordiam cum patribus nostris, et memorari testamenti sui sancti" [Lk 1.72]: Oblitus est interpres quod per gerundium inceperat, per quod alterum quoque eiusdem periodi verbum transferre debebat.'

[18] Ibid., p. 23: '"Vidit Spiritum Dei descendentem sicut columbam de celo" [Mt 3.16]: Eodem modo apud Lucam [Lk 3.22], melius apud Marcum: "tanquam columbam" [Mk 1.10], et apud Ioannem: "quasi columbam" [Jn

violating the laws of grammar, Valla reprimanded him for not employing the proper grammatical construction for the names of cities and regions.[19] And the incorrect use of *eius* and *sui* was frequently pointed out in the *Annotationes*.[20] In addition, Valla had no qualms about censuring word forms which existed exclusively in the Latin Bible, often supporting his case with parallels from classical authors such as Juvenal and Livy.[21] For him, the classics

> 1.32], nam *sicut* non significat Spiritum Dei venis[s]e {*my insertion*} in specie columbe sed in delapsu columbe. Etenim cum dico *tu ambulas sicut camelus*, comparatio est, cum dico *ambulas tanquam* aut *quasi* aut *velut camelus*, non est comparatio, sed hic sensus: *tu ambulas quasi ipse esses camelus*. Ita Spiritus non sicut columba venit, sed quasi esset columba, siquidem *quasi, velut, tanquam* eiusdem significationis sunt, imaginem non similitudinem significantia, et multum distantia a *sicut*, quemadmodum in opere de *Elegantiis* latius ostendimus.' See Lorenzo Valla, *De linguae latinae elegantia*, ed. and tr. S. López Moreda, 2 vols, Cáceres 1999, I, pp. 256 and 258; see also the discussion of the same passage in Valla, *Annotationes*, p. 832A: '"Et descendit spiritus sanctus corporali specie sicut columba in ipsum" [Lk 3.22]: *Velut columba* dicendum fuit, non *sicut*: quia columba aliqua nunquam in Iesum descendit, sed spiritus sanctus tunc tanquam columba'; and ibid., p. 807B. For the difference between *natus* and *genitus* [Mt 1.16], see Valla, *Annotationes*, pp. 804B–805A; and Valla, *Collatio*, pp. 13–15.

[19] Ibid., p. 165: '"Apostoli et seniores et fratres iis, qui sunt Antiochie et Syrie et Cilicie fratribus ex gentibus salutem" [Ac 15.23]: Neque grammatice dicitur neque excusationem a greco capere possumus, ubi dicitur *apud Antiochiam et Syriam et Ciliciam*; at noster interpres, ut multis in locis, preter legem grammatice tribuit prepositionem nominibus urbium, ita nunc tollit nominibus regionum, ubi tolli non debet'; see also Valla, *Annotationes*, p. 851A–B.

[20] See, e.g., ibid., p. 842A: '"Dicunt autem ad eum fratres eius" [Jn 7.3] et statim post "Neque enim fratres eius credebant in eum" [Jn 7.5]: Scio superuacuum esse repetere *eius* dictum esse pro *sui*, sed frequentius noto, quod doleo me hoc crebro usu interpretis diu fuisse deceptum.' Valla composed an entire treatise on the proper use of *sui*; see his *De reciprocatione 'sui' et 'suus'*, ed. E. Sandström, Gothenburg 1998.

[21] See, e.g., Valla, *Annotationes*, p. 841B: '"Vt autem sero factum est" [Jn 6.16]: Ego dixissem *serum*, ut apud Titum Liuium "Serum erat" dici. Nam *hoc sero, huius sero* uox absurda est.' See Livy, *Ab urbe condita*, II, ed. C. F. Walters and R. S. Conway, Oxford 1951, VII, 8, 5 and Livy, *Ab urbe condita*, V, ed. A. H. McDonald, Oxford 1965, p. 171 (XXXIII, 48, 8); Valla, *Collatio*, p. 18: '"Ex te enim exiet Dux" [Mt 2.6], quod proprie dicitur *ductor*. Nescio an *exiet* reperiatur: dicimus enim *exibit*'; see also Valla, *Annotationes*, p. 806A; Valla, *Collatio*, p. 135: '"Linivit lutum super oculos eius" [Jn 9.6]: Non reperitur *linivit* sed *livit*, quod videtur sentire etiam Priscianus.' See Priscian, *Institutiones grammaticae*, I, p. 529 (X, 38): 'Sperno quoque sprevi facit et lino livi.' Valla, *Annotationes*, p. 822A: '"Et chlamydem coccineam circundederunt ei" [Mt 27.28]: Nescio cur dicatur *coccinea* potius quam

served as a guideline for the proper choice of words: even though, for example, the word *docibilis* was attested by Priscian, he refused to accept this as authoritative. The standard was set by classical writers, and Valla did not remember ever having encountered the word *docibilis* in the works of the *boni auctores*.²² The writings of classical authors constituted the authority which determined the correct usage of Latin; and this usage also applied to the Latin Bible, which, in Valla's eyes, was subject to the same set of rules and restrictions as any other Latin text. This attitude is also illustrated by other examples: discussing the gender of the word *sal* in the *Collatio*, Valla cites the rules of the grammarians, but then expresses his preference for the usage found in classical authors, whom he calls 'the most distinguished men':

> In eodem loco apud Lucam dicitur: 'Bonum est sal' [Lk 14.34], et ita in plerisque locis reperimus genere neutro, nonnunquam etiam genere masculino, ut in Iesu Sirach: 'Salem et harenam' [Si 22.18], tamen sciamus fere in usu doctissimi cuiusque auctoris esse in genere masculino, adeo ut Phocas grammaticus tantum generis masculini esse voluerit [Phocas, *Ars de nomine et verbo*, in *Grammatici latini*, ed. H. Keil, V, Hildesheim 1961, pp. 410-439, at p. 411]. Priscianus antiquos quosdam genere neutro usos ait [Priscian, *Institutiones*

---

coccina ut graece est, κοκκίνην, et latine sic dicitur, ut apud Iuvenalem: "Et coccina lena." [Juvenal, *Saturae*, ed. J. Willis, Stuttgart 1997, p. 35 (III, 283)] Et ratio postulat, quia *coccus* graece, *granum* est latine'; see also Valla, *Collatio*, p. 70.

²² Ibid., pp. 841B–842A: '"Seruum autem Domini non oportet litigare, sed mansuetum esse ad omnes, docibilem, patientem" [2 Tm 2.24]: Hunc locum transfert interpres *docibilem*; quid autem de hoc nomen intelligat, indicat e priore ad Timotheum epistola, inquiens "Pudicum, hospitalem, doctorem", [1 Tm 3.2] διδακτικόν cum quo non uidetur sentire Cyprianus, qui ait: "Docibilis autem ille est, qui est ad discendi patientiam lenis et mitis." [Cyprian, *Epistularium*, in his *Opera*, III, 2, ed. G. F. Diercks, Turnhout 1996, p. 576 (74, X, 1)] Ego hoc uocabulum, et si Priscianus ad artem refert, quia apud bonos autores non inueni, quod meminerim, inexpositum relinquo. Certe graecum Hieronymus cum hunc locum super epistola ad Timotheum tractat, ita ait "διδακτικόν, *qui possit docere*, non ut interpretatur latina simplicitas *docibilem*" [Jerome, *Dialogus adversus Pelagianos*, in his *Opera*, III: *Opera polemica*, 2, ed. C. Moreschini, Turnhout 1990, p. 29 (I, 23)].' See also Valla, *Collatio*, p. 254. Valla is probably referring to Priscian, *Institutiones grammaticae*, II, p. 219 (XVIII, 25): 'Sed *docilis* est qui facile docetur, *docibilis* qui facile discitur.' In fact, the word '*docibilis*' seems to have been used only once by a classical author, Seneca the Younger; see his *Ad Lucilium epistulae morales*, ed. O. Hense, Leipzig 1898, p. 503 (108, 12). For other examples of Valla's rejection of neologisms, see, e.g., Valla, *Annotationes*, p. 822A.

> *grammaticae*, I, p. 147 (V, 10)], quo quidam quoque recentiores utuntur, ut Macer [Macer Floridus, *De viribus herbarum*, ed. L. Choulant, Leipzig 1823, p. 31 (l. 67)] ... Ego vero, quod ad me attinet, auctoritate summorum hominum, non nisi genere masculino uti ausim.[23]

> In Luke it is written: '*Bonum est sal*' [Lk 14.34], and in many other passages we likewise find it in the neuter, sometimes also in the masculine, as in Ecclesiasticus: '*Salem et harenam*' [Si 22.18]; nevertheless, we should know that it is usually masculine in the usage of the most learned authors, to such an extent that the grammarian Phocas wanted it to be exclusively masculine. Priscian says that some ancients used it in the neuter, in which also some more recent authors use it, such as Macer ... But as far as I am concerned, I dare not use it in any other gender than the masculine, following the authority of the most distinguished men.

His argument against accepting an antiptosis found in the Gospel of John further illustrates his insistence on the exemplary status of classical authors:

> 'Et sermonem quem audistis non est meus' [Jn 14.24]: non possum adduci, ut credam interpretem eo licentiae peruenisse, ut quod in Vergilio uix toleratur, dicente: 'Urbem quam statuo uestra est' [Virgil, *Aeneid*, I, 573], ipse sibi permitteret dicere.[24]

> *Et sermonem quem audistis non est meus* [Jn 14.24]: I cannot be led to believe that the *interpres* has attained such a degree of poetic licence that he could allow himself to write what is hardly tolerated in Virgil when he writes: *Urbem quam statuo vestra est.*

---

[23] See Valla, *Collatio*, pp. 26–27. In other instances, he explained that the error was due to the adoption of the gender of the original Greek word; see, e.g., Valla, *Annotationes*, p. 838B: '"Ventres quae non genuerunt" [Lk 23.29] ... Credo interpretem deceptum, quia *uentres* graece generis est foeminini'; see also Valla, *Collatio*, p. 127.

[24] Valla, *Annotationes*, p. 844B; he continues: 'Nam illud in psalmo [Ps 117.22], quod apud Matthaeum reperitur: "Lapidem quem reprobauerunt aedificantes, hic factus est in caput angeli" [Mt 21.42] et non nihil diuersum est, et ita graece legitur, de quo genere sermonis alio in loco disputauimus. Astipulatur opinioni meae quod aliquot uetustos codices legi, in quibus scriptum est *sermo*, non *sermonem*, καὶ ὁ λόγος, ut graece habetur'; see also Valla, *Collatio*, p. 139; and Valla, *De linguae latinae elegantia*, I, p. 330: '"Sermonem quem vos audistis, non est meus": quod in Graeco, hoc est, in fonte, est *sermo*, non *sermonem*; unde interpres noster transferens maluit Latine quam grammatice loqui. Nec ignoro qualia imperiti in hoc Evangelii loco disputare soleant, profecto nequaquam sic disputari, si Graecam linguam mediocriter, Latinam perfecte tenerent. In tali sermonis genere vel idem nomen repetemus, vel accusativum in debitum casum resolvemus.'

Even though the construction found in John was attested in one of the most famous classical authors, Virgil, it was such an obscure and isolated occurrence and required the concession of such a high degree of poetic licence that Valla was not willing to permit it in the translation of the Bible.

In contrast to the *Collatio*, where there are no apologetic or explanatory comments on the role of correct grammar and of classical models, in the *Annotationes* Valla states why the Latin Bible is subject to grammatical rules and why these rules should be based on the writings of classical authors:

> Et certe cum priores fuerint autores gentiles quam fideles, siue Graeci siue Latini, nimirum multo plus obtinent autoritatis, quippe cum eos omnis posteritas, tam fidelium quam infidelium, habeat autores, et eatenus recte loquatur, quatenus ab illorum usu non discrepat. Nam consulto quidem et de industria uelle ab illis dissentire, nisi uehemens causa coegerit, insania est. Inscientem uero hoc facere inscitia, quanquam sint qui negent theologiam inseruire praeceptis artis grammaticae. At ego dico, illam debere seruire etiam cuiuslibet linguae usum, qua loquitur, nedum literatae. Nam quid stultius quam linguam, qua uteris, uelle corrumpere, et committere ne ab iis, apud quos loqueris, intelligaris. Nemo enim intelligat eum, qui proprietatem linguae non seruat, quam nemo unquam fuit qui non seruaret uolens et prudens, sed per imprudentiam labens.[25]

> Since the pagan authors were certainly earlier than the Christian ones, whether Greek or Latin, it is not surprising that they possess considerably more authority; for the whole of posterity, both believers and non-believers, has them as their models and therefore speaks correctly as long as it does not depart from their usage. Differing from them deliberately and on purpose is madness if one is not forced to do so by a compelling reason. But it is ignorance that makes the ignorant do this, even though there are those who deny that theology follows the precepts of grammar. But I say that it, too, has to obey the usage of any tongue in which it speaks, not to mention the written language. For what is more foolish than wanting to corrupt the language which you are using and making it so that you are not understood by those to whom you are speaking. For no one understands a person who fails to obey the peculiar nature of a language, which is never willingly and prudently disobeyed by anyone except out of ignorance.

Valla here confirms and defends his practice in both the *Collatio* and the *Annotationes*. The same standards apply to the translation of the Bible as to every other text, since if Latin Scripture did not

---

[25] Valla, *Annotationes*, p. 808A.

follow the precepts of grammar, it would be impossible to understand. For Valla, the Latin translation of the New Testament was a text requiring correction, and its textual tradition had no authority with regard to establishing proper Latin usage and no right to grammatical deviation from classical norms.[26]

When composing the *Elegantiae*, in which there are roughly a dozen references to the Bible, Valla already applied the same standards that he would later adopt in the *Collatio* and the *Annotationes*. In relation to the demands of grammar and style, the Latin Bible was and always remained for him a text whose language had to be judged by the same classical criteria as any other Latin text. While, in the *Elegantiae*, he takes examples from the Bible – yet another sign that he did not regard the Latin text of Scripture as essentially different from other Latin texts – in most cases he does so in order to reject and correct them: in the chapter on words finishing in *–osus*, for instance, Valla changes *foetosae* in Ps 143 to *foetuosae*;[27] and discussing the use of *sin*, he corrects the misconception that it implies a negation, illustrating the incorrect employment of the term with several passages from the Bible.[28] He also criticises the use of imprecise or improper words.[29] When

---

[26] For an explicit example of his view of the status of the Latin New Testament, see below, p. 264, n. 57.

[27] Valla, *De linguae latinae elegantia*, I, p. 136: 'Ideoque illud in Psalmo "Oves eorum foetosae" [Ps 143.13]: legendum est *foetuosae*, a *foetus*.'

[28] Ibid., I, p. 240: 'De *Sin*: ... Quorundam tamen usus est, ut dicant *sin autem* pro eo quod est *si non* quasi in *sin*, aut in *autem*, sit negatio. Mirarerque de vulgo, nisi id apud quosdam praestantis viros reperirem; quale est illud in Apocalypsi: "Sin autem venio et movebo candelabrum tuum" [Rv 2.5]. Quum praesertim paulo post dicatur: "Si quo minus, veniam" [Rv 2.16]. Ego vero in utroque dixissem *sin minus*, vel *sin aliter*. Et in Evangelio: "Si ibi fuerit filius pacis, requiescet super illum pax vestra; sin autem, ad vos revertetur." [Lk 10.6] Et alibi: "Siquidem fecerit fructum; sin autem, succides illam." [Lk 13.9] In quibus omnibus Graece negatio adest.' All three Bible passages quoted in this example were later taken up in the *Annotationes*; in the *Collatio*, which does not cover the Apocalypse, Valla mentions both passages from the Gospel of Luke.

[29] Ibid., I, p. 214: 'De *Hei, Heu, Eheu, Ue*: ... Aliquando etiam cum nominativo; ut idem Vergilius: "Heu pietas, heu prisca fides" [Virgil, *Aeneid*, VI, 878] ... Illud vero in psalmo: "Heu mihi, quia incolatus meus prolongatus est" [Ps 119.5] nescio an vitio factum sit librariorum, quale illud in Evangelio: "Ascendit in arborem sycomorum, quia inde transiturus erat" [Lk 19.4] quod scribendum est *illhac*. Et illud ad Romanos: "Tu autem cum oleaster esses, insertus es" [Rm 11.17] pro *insitus*. Et in Actis Apostolorum: "Egressi sumus foras portam iuxta flumen" [Ac 16.13] pro *extra portam*.'

commenting on the construction following gerunds, he quotes a few phrases from the Psalms as negative examples.[30] And, finally, in the *Elegantiae*, he makes his view of the Latin Bible clear by excluding it from the group of approved texts on which correct usage of Latin is based:

> Illud, quo quidam utuntur, *instruo* (quale est 'instruam te in via hac, qua gradieris' [Ps 31.8]) nobis apud idoneos auctores incompertum est.[31]

> That *instruo* (as in *instruam te in via hac, qua gradieris* [Ps 31.8]) which some people use is unknown to me in proper authors.

These examples should suffice to show that Valla took a further step in defining the grammatical standards for the establishment of the text of the Latin Bible. Like his predecessors in the thirteenth century, he regularly quoted from late antique grammarians; yet they were merely a source for a more important authority: the ancient Latin authors themselves, the *summi homines*, 'most distinguished men'.[32] For Valla, the sole criterion for Latin grammar lay in writers such as Virgil and Livy. It was their writings alone which determined the correct usage of the language, and this established usage also applied to the Latin Bible. Moreover, the Latin translation of Holy Writ was excluded from the group of approved texts on which the correct usage of Latin was based. When the Latin Bible employed words in ways that differed from the practice of the classics, Valla was in no doubt that the biblical text was wrong and in need of correction from suitable authors, *idonei auctores*, as he refers to them in the *Elegantiae*.[33]

---

[30] Ibid., I, pp. 156 and 158: 'Regunt praeterea casum more verborum participiorumque; ex quo nomina non sunt. Post se, inquam, regunt, non ante se. Nam eiusmodi locutio, qualis est: "In convertendo Dominus captivitatem Sion, facti sumus sicut consolati" [Ps 125.1] inaudita est Graeca figura decipiente, ut in aliis multis, interpretem. Graeci enim hoc loco infinitivum habent, quod vult ante se accusativum. Quod multis modis transferri poterat, vel sic: *Dum converteret Dominus captivitatem Sion*, vel sic: *Convertente Domino captivitatem Sion* et aliis, ut dixi, multis modis. Quidam imperiti aiunt casum pro casu poni, quasi Latine diceretur *si esset Dominum*; quale est illud: "In deficiendo ex me spiritum meum" [Ps 141.4]. Et alibi: "In conveniendo populos in unum, et reges, ut serviant domino" [Ps 101.23], quum, ut ostendi, gerundium non habeat ante se casum.'

[31] Ibid., II, p. 554.

[32] See above, pp. 227–228.

[33] See above, p. 231. Camporeale (*Lorenzo Valla*, p. 284) pointed out that for Valla the Latin Bible was without question subject to grammar, more

The straightforward subjection of the Latin Bible to the rules of grammar was by no means exclusive to Valla. Significantly, both George of Trebizond and Cardinal Bessarion, in their dispute over Jn 21.22, resorted to grammar to prove their points. George discussed the meaning of both ἐάν and *si* in combination with different tenses and moods to show that the traditional Latin reading *sic* expressed exactly what was intended in the original Greek.[34] In his response, Bessarion set out George's argument, including his examples, and then refuted his view not only by adducing further examples from both the Bible and Virgil, but also by referring to the opinion of the Greek and Latin grammarians, above all Priscian, on the various nuances in meaning of *si*.[35]

precisely Quintilian's grammar. A study of the influence of Quintilian on Valla's work on the New Testament would provide more detailed insight into this matter.

[34] See George of Trebizond, *Adversus Theodorum Gazam*, p. 335 (35, 10): 'Quodsi quis graeci mihi sermonis auctoritatem incutiat, sciat haec, quae de *si* particula dicta sunt, simili etiam graecae particulae ad unguem convenire. *Ean* illi subiunctivo iungunt, et affirmatio in praesenti semper includitur. Ceteris temporibus, quae derivatione diversa sunt potestate *ean* – ad futuri enim significationem praeteritum in subiunctivo transit – futuri dubitatio natura inest. Sed multi verbis inhiantes nec rem ullam intelligunt et verba quoque recte tenere non possunt. Vertat, si quis vult, exempla quae dicam, in graecum sermonem, et videbit aperte. Comedenti feria sexta carnes dicitur: "Carnes comedis hodie?" Respondet: "Si comedo, quid ad te?" aut etiam sic: "Ita comedo." Bibenti merum vinum dicitur: "Merum tu bibis vinum?" Respondet: "Si bibo, quid ad te?" aut etiam illo modo: "Sic bibo, quid ad te?" Haec si graece dicuntur, idem omnino sensus et eadem res significabitur, quae latinis habetur verbis. Non enim institutione hominum, sed natura compositionis verborum hoc fit. Quare necesse est apud omnes idem esse, de quo latius disseremus, si aut nobis per Hieremias nunc tractare propositum esset, aut breviter posset perstringi. Sed hiscant, quaeso, qui se huic veritati opponunt. Certe graecis etiam verbis utrumque: "Si comedo, quid ad te?" "Sic comedo, quid ad te?" item: "Si bibo, quid ad te?" "Sic bibo, quid ad te?" affirmationem includit.'

[35] Bessarion, *In illud Evangelii*, cols 636D–637B: 'Quod ut manifestius intelligatur, quid grammatici sentiant, dicemus, deinde quaedam ex dialectica subiungemus. Grammatici omnes tam Graeci quam Latini, et in primis Priscianus, qui non modo sequitur Graecos, sed id se facere multis in locis gloriatur, *si* conjunctionem continuativam esse aiunt; quando enim Graecum significat, eamque sicut et reliquas continuativas, cum a Graecis ab Apollonio Herodiani patre [i.e. Apollonius Dyscolus], inter causales connumeratam esse [Priscian, *Institutiones grammaticae*, II, p. 95 (XVI, 4)] ordinemque praecedentis rei ad sequentem significare, cum aliqua dubitatione essentiae rerum, vel, ut Graeci dicunt, sine significatione essentiae, "ut *Si stertit, dormit* et *Si aegrotat, pallet* et *Si febri vexatur, calet*; neque enim converso ordine in

Priscian is, in fact, the only grammarian whom Bessarion cites and from whom he probably borrowed the two quotations of Virgil, which also appear in the section of Priscian's *Institutiones* to which he refers.[36] Yet it is telling that Bessarion stressed these parallels from Virgil and endorsed the application of such examples to the text of the Latin Bible.

The fact that both George and Bessarion invoked the rules of grammar, among other arguments, to support their positions shows that grammatical correctness had gained unquestioned importance for the emendation of the Latin Bible. Furthermore, neither George nor Bessarion commented on whether or not it was appropriate to subject the Bible to the rules of grammar. They apparently regarded it as obvious that the Bible had to follow the same grammatical precepts as any other text.

Giovanni Crastone's approach differed markedly from that of the other humanists discussed here. This is because, rather than attempting to correct a Latin text of the Bible, his aim was to provide a bi-lingual Greek and Latin edition of the Psalms which would facilitate the learning of Greek.[37] Unlike Valla, Crastone was not attempting to bring his version into grammatical conformity with the Latin classics, nor was he trying to reconstruct any distinct version of the Latin Bible. Instead, as he explains, he wanted to assimilate the grammar of his Latin translation to that of the Greek text, which entailed modifying the Latin text to reflect the

---

his consequentiam sententiae servat oratio. Non enim qui dormit, omnino stertit" [ibid., p. 94 (XVI, 3)] et sic de caeteris. Non irrationabiliter eas causales esse aiunt. Et continuationis, quemadmodum et adjunctionis et effectionis, per has causa ostenditur reddi. Continuationis, ut *Si ambulat, movetur*: causa enim cur movetur, ipsa est ambulatio. Hujusmodi causales interdum pro approbativis poni commemorant, quoniam scilicet, et id quod dicimus, ita certum apertumque est, ut impossibile sit aliter opinari, tuncque duntaxat indicativo coniungi, ut apud Virgilium "Si quid usquam justitiae est" [Virgil, *Aeneid*, I, 603–604] et alibi "Di, si qua caelo est pietas" [ibid., II, 536]. Indubitatum enim et in caelo pietatem esse, et in mundo justitiae aliquid. Hinc in facilem errorem inciderunt adversarii mei, putantes quoniam *si* causalis pro approbativa posita cum indicativo conjungitur, ideo et e converso, quoties cum indicativo conjungitur, esse approbativam, quod longe est a veritate; non enim quoties indicativo conjungitur, esse approbativa potest, quamvis quoties approbativa est, indicativo jungatur.' Bessarion takes up George's examples in *In illud Evangelii*, cols 625D–626B.

[36] See Priscian, *Institutiones grammaticae*, II, p. 97 (XVI, 6).

[37] Research needs to be done to discover the actual changes which Crastone made to the Latin text.

grammatical constructions found in the original Greek. In this manner, he was hoping to come close to an *ad verbum* translation, which in turn would make it easier to understand the Greek text. He defends this approach in two ways: firstly, he cites a passage from the Latin Old Testament and another from the New Testament, each of which contains a Greek construction; and secondly, he, too, relies on Virgil, pointing out that certain elements of Greek grammar can also be found in his poems.[38]

At the same time, Crastone was not prepared to tolerate faulty grammar in the Latin translation of the Bible. He points out that a passage in the Gospel of John is grammatically incorrect and offers a better reading found in Augustine.[39] And although he explicitly says that the Bible occupies a special position, he nevertheless insists that those who claim that it is exempt from grammar should not merely be ignored but refuted.[40]

Humanist textual critics appear to have taken it for granted that the Latin Bible should obey certain grammatical rules. There were no detailed discussions of the matter; and while Valla and Crastone mentioned in passing that some held the view that the Bible was not subject to grammar, both of them strongly opposed this position. There also seems to have been general agreement that the standard for correct grammar was set by classical authors such as Virgil, who was quoted by several humanists. Although late ancient grammarians, especially Priscian, were referred to by Bessarion and

---

[38] Crastone, [Dedicatory letter], p. 16: 'Interdum tamen Graecas constructiones in sacris litteris quae prius a Graecis scriptae sunt inveniri: ut "vado piscari" [Jn 21.3], "expugna nocentes me" [Ps 34.1] et multa id genus: non inficior. Fecit hoc et Maro noster, ut in *Georgicon* secundo: "Tempus equi fumantia solvere colla" [Virgil, *Georgica*, in his *Opera*, pp. 29–101, II, 542]. Latine sane *tempus solvendi* dicendum est. Feci et ipse in hoc Psalterio: non tamen ut Graecis schematis uterer; sed ut Graece discere volentibus morem gererem verbum verbo reddidi. Quod ignorantes ad illud ineptissimum confugiunt: "Scriptura non est subiecta grammatice", quibus respondeo: "Non sua."'

[39] Crastone, [Dedicatory letter], p. 15: 'Johannis ultimo capitulo [Jn 21.18]: "Ambulabas ubi volebas." Quae ratio grammatices id permittit? At Augustinus homilia quinta in epistolam Iohannis [Augustine, *In epistolam Joannis ad Parthos tractatus X* (*PL*, XXXV), Paris 1841, cols 1977–2062, at col. 2018 (V, iii, 11)], "quo volebas" dixit. Sane hac in re non minus Hieronymus Augustino advertisset.'

[40] Crastone, [Dedicatory letter], p. 15: 'Nec omnino audiendi imo acerrime refellendi sunt theologi qui, ut illorum verbis utar, dicunt Scriptura sancta non est subiecta grammaticae. Fateor, nam praeest quia dignior, quippe quae ex Sancto Spiritu est, qui "scientiam habet vocis" [Ws 1.7], ut ait Solomon.'

Valla, they no longer had the same authority as in the thirteenth century with Bacon and Gerard: if their views disagreed with the usage of classical authors, they carried no weight.[41] Nevertheless, humanists occasionally drew on non-classical sources for their arguments: Bessarion cited examples from the Bible itself to illustrate different uses of *si*, and Crastone did the same to show that Greek grammatical constructions were already present in the Latin text.[42]

The examples and opinions discussed so far in this chapter were written down by men who dealt with textual criticism of the Bible in an increasingly specialist, highly intellectual ambience. These writers have provided us with an interesting insight into views about the application of grammar to the Latin Bible; but their outlook was far removed from the reality of the common scribe.

As a contrast, it is worth taking a look at Oswaldus de Corda's *Opus pacis*, which will give us a very different picture of the role of grammar from what we have seen in scholars such as Maniacutia, Bacon and Valla. For the copies of the Carthusian Order's books to be identical, the most essential prerequisite was that the scribes had to be reliable and faithful to the last letter and not try to emend passages which they considered grammatically incorrect. Oswaldus says of scribes:

> Deinde considerent, quod sicut diuersi fuerunt gramatici, sic eciam diuerse nonnunquam de eadem materia eorum opiniones fuere uarie, tam de ortographia quam prosodia etc. Propter quod non sic inhereant aliquorum regulis et dictis, ut uel alios errasse aut minus bene dixisse putent. Vnde accidit, quod quidam gramatici recenter de seculo uel de alia religione ad ordinem nostrum uenientes, mox ut insolita audiunt, statim hec reprehensibilia credunt, et quicquid aliter quam ipsi didicerunt reppererint, id falsitate damnant.[43]

> Then they should bear in mind that just as the grammarians were diverse, so at times also their opinions about the same matter differed, both on orthography and prosody and so forth. Because of this, they should not adhere to the rules and sayings of some in such a way that they believe that others have erred or expressed issues less well. It therefore happened that recently some grammarians from a secular background or from a different order came to our order and as soon as

---

[41] See, e.g., above, pp. 227–228, and p. 232, n. 35.
[42] See Bessarion, *In illud Evangelii*, col. 637C; for Crastone, see above, p. 234, n. 38.
[43] Oswaldus, *Opus pacis*, pp. 4–5.

they heard something unaccustomed, they immediately believed it to be reprehensible and whatever they found elsewhere differently from how they learned it, they condemned as false.

Possible criticism brought up by outsiders who were accustomed to a different textual tradition also extended to grammatical issues in Latin Scripture. Oswaldus points out that there are some passages in the Carthusian Bible which might be considered grammatically incorrect:

> Item sciant correctores, quod aliquando ordo noster aliquas in propria forma seruat dictiones antiquorum more, que non subiacent regulis gramaticalibus modernorum, sicut eas beatus Ieronimus in biblie translacione noscitur posuisse, non tamen propter hoc sunt uiciate ... Vnde in biblia Cartusie habetur ... in Ecclesiastico ... capitulo ultimo [Qo 51.18] 'cum adhuc iuuenior sum.'[44]

> The correctors should also know that at times our order preserves some readings in their peculiar form according to ancient custom, which are not subject to the grammatical rules of the moderns, as St Jerome is known to have put them in his translation of the Bible, and they are nevertheless not corrupt ... Hence, we have in the Bible of the Chartreuse ... in the last chapter of Ecclesiastes: *cum adhuc iuuenior sum*.

The grammatically incorrect form *iuuenior*, instead of *iunior*, is thus defended against the rules of grammar on the basis of age and custom. Just because it does not agree with the grammatical standards others might demand that does not mean that the Carthusian text is wrong, since it has been like this for a long time. Similarly, Oswaldus continues, there are passages where the number of a word, its case or a verb's tense contravene what one would consider correct grammar; but, nevertheless, these readings are not to be changed, since they have been approved by *consuetudo*.[45] After providing a list of passages in which the Carthusian Bibles could be considered grammatically incorrect, Oswaldus sums up by saying that even if all these and other phrases go against the rules of grammar, they should by no means be

---

[44] Ibid., pp. 6–7. Oswaldus's comment also shows that there were those who criticised the text of the Latin Bible on the basis of the rules of what was perceived as proper grammar.

[45] See above, p. 214, n. 43.

changed – for the Bible should be seen as transcending the rules of grammar.[46]

Oswaldus's opinion that the Latin Bible is not subject to grammar brings us back to the views expressed in the beginning of this chapter. The *consuetudo* of an accepted text – as, in this case, the Carthusian Bible – takes precedence over other versions and the notions of others about correct Latin.

Another important aspect which can be deduced from Oswaldus's warnings and adhortations is that scribes persistently tried to emend the text of the Bible as they saw fit. The assumption that scribes often corrected – or involuntarily corrupted – grammar in passing, without giving it too much thought, in all likelihood holds true for the entire Latin Middle Ages.[47] This might also explain why statements about the application of grammar to the emendation of the Latin Bible take up relatively little space in the works of medieval textual critics: if, despite the claims made by various influential authors that the Latin Bible was exempt from the normal rules of grammar, grammatical correction of biblical manuscripts was nonetheless frequently engaged in by scribes and readers, then justifying it might have been less of an issue.

With the exception of Oswaldus de Corda, who wrote specifically for Carthusian scribes, all the other authors examined in this study had a more scholarly readership in mind. This fact, of course, had a strong impact on the positions which they took and the possibilities which they had to express themselves. Yet compared, for example, to the copious arguments about the textual tradition and manuscript transmission of the Bible discussed earlier, the use of grammar for the correction of the Latin Bible was a

---

[46] Ibid., p. 21: 'Item in sacra scriptura inuenitur et toleratur *partibor, metibor, polibam, sancibam, munibam, molibam, odibo, deguit* et *degebo*, et Ecc. 36 [Si 36.27] in fine *gemescit*, licet contra regulas gramaticales, ubi similiter non corrigatur, nisi exemplar correctum aliter doceat in certo loco faciendum. Ait nanque Cassiodorus: "Expedit enim interdum pretermittere humanarum formulas dictionum, et diuini magis eloquii custodire mensuram [Cassiodorus, *Institutiones* p. 45 (I, xv, 7)]". Et beatus Gregorius dicit: "Indignum uehementer existimo, ut uerba celestis oraculi restringam sub regulis Donati." [see above, p. 219, n. 6]'

[47] This is confirmed by Glunz, who writes that the grammatical treatises written from the ninth century onwards probably induced scribes to intervene in the text of the Bible and make minor grammatical corrections in it, according to the rules laid out in such treatises; see Glunz, *History of the Vulgate in England*, p. 123.

relatively minor point for both medieval and early Renaissance textual critics.

Nevertheless, we can trace a clear development in the mindset of textual critics from the twelfth to the fifteenth century: the text of the Latin Bible was gradually deprived of its special status and increasingly subjected to the rules of what was considered to be proper Latin grammar. At first, in the twelfth century, Maniacutia, in his *Libellus*, insisted on correct grammar in a general way, without specifying any authorities. In the thirteenth century, late antique grammarians like Priscian and Donatus were adduced as reliable guides by Gerard of Huy and Roger Bacon. Finally, in the fifteenth century, humanists such as Lorenzo Valla and Cardinal Bessarion imposed the same grammatical rules and regulations on the Latin Bible as could be observed in the writings of classical Latin authors, with Virgil and other pagan writers regularly cited to illustrate points of grammar. For humanists, the late antique grammarians had become merely a source for classical citations and in themselves no longer carried any weight. Their medieval counterparts, however, were never mentioned as authorities, either by their contemporaries or by the humanists.

What is more, none of the textual critics ever discussed or even questioned whether grammar was an appropriate tool for the emendation of Scripture. They all agreed that it was, and that the Latin Bible should be corrected accordingly. Its status as a translation of a sacred text granted no authority of its own with regard to establishing proper Latin usage and no right to deviate from the accepted rules of grammar. At most, they briefly mentioned in passing the claim that the Latin Bible was not subject to grammar only to reject it without further ado.

Yet again, the fourteenth century proves to be an exception. None of the fourteenth-century scholars examined in this study – Henry Totting, Richard FitzRalph, Peter of Ailly – was concerned with the emendation of the Latin Bible.[48] Since they did not discuss Scripture from a text-critical viewpoint, but instead focused on more generic issues, they did not need to deal with the role of grammar.

My aim in this chapter has been to provide an insight into the views of textual critics about the application of grammar to the text of the Latin Bible. Their standpoints present us with a new

---

[48] See also below, p. 258.

perspective on medieval attitudes towards the relationship between grammar and the Latin Bible. As mentioned above, it has been common in the scholarly literature to claim that the Bible was regarded as exempt from the rules of grammar.[49] Indeed, Christine Mohrmann, in an article on the double heritage of classical and Christian Latin in the Middle Ages, goes so far as to suggest that two *auctoritates* dominated the Latin of the Middle Ages: the *auctoritas divina* of the Bible and the *auctoritas humana* of Donatus. Mohrmann also applies this division to the role of grammar.[50] Yet as we have seen in the statements of medieval textual critics of the Latin Bible, they rejected *auctoritas divina*, and called for reliance on *auctoritas humana* alone.[51]

Far more material on approaches towards the role of grammar in the Latin Bible needs to be collected from a variety of sources if we are to get a comprehensive picture of this issue – it would be worthwhile, for instance, to examine the opinions not only of grammarians but also of exegetes. Yet, as the results of this chapter show, medieval and early Renaissance perceptions of the relationship between grammar and the text of the Latin Bible were more multi-faceted than has been assumed in the past. Alongside the more frequently voiced opinion that the Latin Bible did not need to obey the rules of grammar, textual critics developed a parallel discourse and expressed their views not only about the necessity of subjecting Scripture to grammar, but also, over the course of time, about the precise set of rules which should be applied. At the same time, scribes seem to have corrected manuscripts of the Bible according to what they perceived to be proper grammar in a matter-of-fact way.[52] The correction of the text of the Latin Bible according to the rules of grammar might well have been far more common than we have previously been led to believe.[53]

---

[49] See above, p. 217, and the discussion by Lubac, *Exégèse*, III, pp. 77–98.

[50] Christine Mohrmann, 'Le dualisme de la latinité médiévale', *Revue des études latines* 29 (1951), pp. 330–348, at p. 343.

[51] For Fischer's view that the actual practice of emending the Bible according to the rules of grammar was common among Carolingian Bible editors, see above, p. 40.

[52] See, e.g., above, p. 237.

[53] For instance, Oswaldus's account of visitors criticising the corrupt grammar of the Carthusian Bible (see above, pp. 235–236) is another indication that grammatical rules were regarded as an acceptable tool for emending the biblical text.

Part V:

Conclusion

Various aspects discussed in this study either challenge common views or bring to light issues which have so far been neglected in modern scholarship. Most striking perhaps is the fact that as early as the twelfth century, biblical scholars expressed the opinion that the text of the Latin Bible they had in their manuscripts was not the Vulgate but rather an amalgamation of different versions – a position which has been confirmed for a substantial part of the transmission by the research of Bonifatius Fischer, but which has not before been credited to medieval scholars.

The waxing influence of the cult of Jerome on art, literature and religious life might well have influenced the fourteenth-century authors discussed: Peter of Ailly was a rigorous advocate of his translation of the Bible; and Henry Totting, too, defended its supremacy over other versions. Richard FitzRalph counted it among the officially approved Latin translations. In the fifteenth century, however, textual critics do not appear to have been impeded in their efforts to emend the Latin Bible by the veneration of Jerome: claims made about his divine inspiration did not spread to text-critical writings – with the exception of George of Trebizond's treatise. Nor did these scholars maintain that it was their goal to restore the Vulgate. The view of Jenkins and Preston that, in the early sixteenth century, the popularity of Jerome strengthened the status of the Vulgate does not seem to apply to fifteenth-century textual critics.[1]

The status ascribed to the Vulgate in the Middle Ages and early Renaissance constitutes another important aspect which has not been discussed in modern scholarship. Even though the Church had not officially approved of any version of the Bible, several authors claimed that it had either actively endorsed or tacitly adopted a Latin translation, usually the Vulgate. Jerome and Augustine had mentioned the general acceptance of the *septuaginta* in the Church; and these statements, together with Isidore's often quoted comment that Jerome's version was read in 'all churches' were seemingly the origin of these notions. The precise development and impact of these assumptions is in need of further investigation. Yet it is clear that it was by no means an uncommon

---

[1] Jenkins and Preston, *Biblical Scholarship*, p. 26.

assumption, found also in other authors such as Thomas Aquinas, who described the *septuaginta* as approved, and Hugh of St Victor.

Jean Gribomont has maintained that, in the Middle Ages, Jerome was so highly regarded that no one dared to criticise his translation.[2] Certainly, none of the authors examined in this study criticised him; but they did not criticise the *septuaginta* either. Anna Morisi Guerra has similarly claimed that the Church's attribution of the Vulgate to Jerome posed a problem for humanists. According to her, the idea that the text which circulated in manuscripts of the Bible was not actually Jerome's was used by Valla to resolve this dilemma.[3] This view is unfounded. Valla's position was based on his genuine conviction that the text was a corrupt amalgam of various versions of the Bible. In addition, even though many medieval and early Renaissance scholars claimed that the Vulgate had been officially endorsed, the Church did not sanction Jerome's version until the sixteenth century. Finally, the idea that the biblical text in circulation was not, in fact, Jerome's can be found several centuries earlier in the works of, for instance, Hugh of St Victor and Nicolò Maniacutia. Although in the thirteenth century the popularity and authority of Jerome's version became prominent in text-critical circles, especially in the works of Bacon and Gerard, the aim of restoring Jerome's translation was hardly ever present in the minds of medieval scholars.[4] Bacon and Gerard were, in fact, exceptions – even the great admirer of Jerome, Maniacutia, never said that it was his goal to reconstruct the Vulgate.

In Chapter III.1, we explored the opinions as to which version of Latin Scripture was contained in the manuscripts of the Bible. Not surprisingly – after all, they were concerned with the emendation of the Latin Bible for good reason – there was general agreement that the manuscripts were corrupt and contaminated; several medieval scholars regarded them as an amalgam of various translations, and some believed that it was impossible to isolate Jerome's version.[5] Some textual critics were nevertheless confident that they could distinguish between various versions of the Latin Bible. The authors of *correctoria* certainly thought that they could

---

[2] Jean Gribomont, 'Critique des lettrés et des philologues', in *La Bibbia 'Vulgata'*, pp. 137–143, at p. 139.

[3] Morisi Guerra, 'La leggenda', pp. 17–18.

[4] See Light, 'Versions', p. 74, with respect to Harding.

[5] Roger Bacon and George of Trebizond were notable exceptions.

tell apart the numerous translations, most of which they presumably knew through quotations in the works of the Church Fathers.

Concerning the textual tradition and manuscript transmission of the Bible, there seems to have been unanimous agreement on one point: older manuscripts were more authoritative than more recent ones. There was, however, no attempt to go beyond this general chronological classification. It is possible that the idea that old manuscripts were preferable was simply taken over from the Church Fathers. Original Hebrew and Greek manuscripts were also consistently held in high regard. The notion that these manuscripts, like the Latin ones, might contain scribal errors was never mentioned by Latin textual critics; nor did they ever suggest that the Greek Old Testament could have suffered corruption, as the Latin had done, in the course of its various translations. The only possibility which they considered was that the manuscripts might have been corrupted due to intentional intervention on the part of Jews or Greek heretics.[6] Although it might seem that Latin critics valued Hebrew manuscripts too highly,[7] voices were raised against this predilection for the Hebrew original: William de Mara, for instance, warned against intervening in Latin manuscripts on the basis of modern Hebrew codices; and Maniacutia and Gerard refused to introduce readings derived from the Hebrew which could not also be found in the Latin tradition.

In the fifteenth century, textual critics focused their attention, although not exclusively, on the New Testament. This shift in balance can probably be attributed to a renewed interest in Greek studies in humanist Italy, combined with the presence of Byzantine émigrés. Eugene Rice's claim that humanists did not consider correcting the Latin Bible by means of consulting the original needs modification.[8] It might hold true for the humanists he discusses. This intention, however, was not only present in the works of, for instance, Valla and Bessarion, but they also had medieval precursors

---

[6] Hans–Georg von Mutius (*Die hebräischen Bibelzitate beim englischen Scholastiker Odo: Versuch einer Revaluation*, Frankfurt a. M. 2006, at p. 156) points out that, at least in the twelfth century, other Hebrew versions, besides the Masoretic text, were in circulation and were used by Latin scholars.

[7] See, e.g., Lubac, *Exégèse*, III, p. 240; with reference to Andrew of St Victor, see Smalley, *The Study of the Bible*, p. 168.

[8] See Rice (ibid., p. 98); his position, moreover, is somewhat ambiguous: see *Saint Jerome*, pp. 94–95.

such as Maniacutia; and other textual critics regularly mentioned the value of the originals, based on statements by Jerome.

Although, in the longlasting struggle between *consuetudo* and *veritas*, textual critics of the twelfth and thirteenth centuries supported the idea of emending the text of the Latin Bible according to *veritas*, nevertheless, when push came to shove, there is evidence that they sometimes stuck to *consuetudo*. In the fifteenth century, all of the authors examined not only called for a return to *veritas*, but also seem to have carried through with their intentions more rigorously than their medieval predecessors.

In the final chapter of this study, I have argued that, contrary to the widespread belief in modern scholarship that medieval scholars were adamant that the Latin Bible was not subject to the conventional rules of grammar, textual critics believed that Scripture should be emended according to what they considered to be correct grammar – a notion which evolved from an unspecific reference by Maniacutia, to the insistence on ancient grammarians such as Priscian in the thirteenth century, and, finally, to the application of the rules observed in the writings of classical authors such as Virgil by fifteenth-century humanists.[9]

There are various related results which have emerged in this study. For instance, throughout the period examined, it was apparently perfectly acceptable to produce one's own new Latin translation of the Bible or of single books or passages. In the twelfth century, the monk Odo (d. 1120) translated from the Hebrew.[10] Ramon Martí, in the thirteenth century, provided his own translations from the original Hebrew. In the fourteenth century, Adam Easton claimed that he had rendered the entire Old Testament from Hebrew into Latin.[11] Lastly, Manetti, in the fifteenth century, was even commissioned by Pope Nicholas V to produce a new translation of the Bible. Furthermore, Crastone's method of adapting the grammatical constructions of his Latin translation of the Psalter to those found in the Greek version of the Psalms for teaching purposes highlights another interesting new development: without any attempt at justification, Crastone

---

[9] Actual emendations in manuscripts might tell a very different story: as was mentioned above, scribes seem to have been in the habit of correcting manuscripts according to rules of grammar.

[10] See Mutius, *Die hebräischen Bibelzitate*, e.g., p. 155.

[11] See MacFarlane, 'The Life and Writings', I, pp. 10–11.

significantly altered the grammatical structure of the Latin Bible for the essentially secular aim of learning Greek.

These efforts show that, at least in some circles, Latin Scripture was not treated as a static and untouchable construct, but rather as a flexible tool, and that work on the text did not require special authorisation or explanation for fear of repercussion. Moreover, we should abandon for good the notion that textual critics were, or should have been, attempting to reconstruct the Vulgate, as some modern scholars have claimed. Furthermore, equating the medieval and early Renaissance Latin Bible with the Vulgate is anachronistic.[12] Although all the textual critics examined in this study held Jerome in high regard, his translation was not usually expressly regarded as the most desirable Latin version of the Bible.[13]

Judging from the results of my research, textual critics belonged to a distinct category of scholar: their calls to subject the Latin Bible to the rules of grammar went against what most other medieval authors, and even such authoritative figures as Gregory the Great, believed. Furthermore, they wanted the text to be emended according to *veritas*, which contravened, for instance, Augustine's demand to take into account the importance of *consuetudo*, and the views of scholars like Oswaldus, who was intent on preserving the *consuetudo* of his order. Many textual critics also presented an unprejudiced view of the transmission of the Bible; and those in the fifteenth century were largely unaffected by the cult of Jerome. It should be kept in mind, however, that textual critics constituted a very small group and that their works were generally not widely diffused. Their views, consequently, do not necessarily reflect mainstream assumptions and convictions.

The fourteenth century, in many respects, occupies a special position in this study. I was not able to identify any scholars writing specifically about the emendation of the Latin Bible. Furthermore, the authors whom I discuss, convinced of the value of Jerome's version, did not critically examine the transmission of the Latin Bible. Peter of Ailly, as we have seen, must have been familiar with Bacon's opinion of the Paris Bible; yet even his scathing

---

[12] See, e.g., Denifle, 'Die Handschriften', p. 266. Vogels (*Handbuch*, p. 121) suggests that Stephen Harding's method of correcting the Latin New Testament on the basis of the Greek was the wrong approach to reconstructing Jerome's translation. But Harding's aim may have been simply to correct the Latin text of the Bible.

[13] Bacon, Gerard and George of Trebizond are exceptions to this general rule.

comments on the Latin tradition of the Bible do not seem to have instilled any doubts in Peter.[14]

The reasons for the absence of fourteenth-century discussions of these issues still need to be explored. Perhaps the immense success of the Paris Bible, combined with new claims that the Vulgate was divinely inspired, led scholars to assume that the text of the Bible which they found in their manuscripts was not in need of emendation – indeed, that to intervene would have constituted a *nefas*.

Parallels to this apparent decline in critical studies of the textual tradition of the Latin Bible can be seen in other fourteenth-century developments. For instance, there were no new Latin translations of Aristotle in this period. Charles Schmitt has identified two waves of Aristotle translations, one from 1130 to 1280, and another beginning shortly after 1400;[15] this pattern also seems to be reflected in writings concerned with the emendation of the text of the Latin Bible.[16]

I hope that my research has answered some questions and challenged some commonly held views about the Latin Bible in the Middle Ages and early Renaissance. Nevertheless, it is clear that many *desiderata* remain. First and foremost, there is a deplorable lack of critical editions: Maniacutia's *Suffraganeus*, the main texts of the *correctoria* and Valla's *Annotationes* are some examples of works in desperate need of a competent editor. The *correctoria*, in particular, urgently require further investigation. Once editions of them have been published, it should be possible to define their aim – and perhaps also their sources and influences – more clearly.[17] The three options suggested by Dahan regarding the goal of the *correctoria* need to be consolidated. His view that they might have served as an aid for scribes requires further explanation. Dahan's

---

[14] Adam Easton might prove to be an exception in the fourteenth century.

[15] Charles B. Schmitt, *Aristotle and the Renaissance*, Cambridge (Mass.) and London, 1983, p. 65.

[16] Beryl Smalley, in her study of fourteenth–century friars, does not mention any text–critical work on the Latin Bible during this period; see her *English Friars and Antiquity in the Early Fourteenth Century*, Oxford 1960.

[17] Denifle (Die Handschriften', p. 472) sees Harding's work as a forerunner of the *correctoria*. If it proves possible to show that the manuscript of the Theodulf Bible discussed above (p. 41) was in Paris during the early thirteenth century, this work might turn out to be their point of orientation, dating four hundred years earlier.

other suggestion, that they were intended to be used as tools for commentators on the Bible is more easily comprehensible. Yet even this aim, likewise, would profit of further research, given that it is not mentioned or even hinted at in the prefaces. His third suggestion that at least the Dominican *correctoria* were meant to gather together as many readings as possible, might lead us down the right track. It is conceivable that they were a product of intellectual curiosity, intended to serve as a storehouse of different translations and readings.[18] Since no text of the Bible had been authorised by the Church, the *correctoria* might have been perceived as encyclopedic collections, designed to preserve knowledge. If so, the expressions *rectus textus* and *falsi codices*, found in the *correctoria*, might have been used in the following way: a reading which was not testified in the accepted versions of the Bible or in the works of the Fathers or later authoritative commentators, such as the Venerable Bede, and was therefore considered to be corrupt, could have been designated as coming from a *falsus codex* as a *caveat* to the reader; *rectus textus* might have indicated a version approved by the order. Possibly, it was only after the genre had been devised that it was employed as a tool for scribes and commentators.

Apart from the *correctoria*, other texts also deserve more attention in order to clarify our picture of the Latin Bible, especially the as yet little explored bibles of religious orders. Similarly, there are no comparative studies of the liturgical texts. Much more material on the religious orders' texts of the Bible is, no doubt, waiting to be uncovered and would provide valuable information on their approach to Scripture. Commentaries on the Sentences might also yield interesting results, as we have seen from Henry Totting's work. While a large-scale analysis of actual emendations in manuscripts of the Bible would require a huge research team, an examination of how textual criticism influenced the interpretation of the Bible would be a more feasible project.

Much work, therefore, still remains to be done. I hope, however, that I have made a small contribution to solving the vast puzzle that was the Latin Bible in the Middle Ages and the early Renaissance.

---

[18] Glunz's discussion of this problem (*History of the Vulgate in England*, p. 185) seems to aim in the same direction.

Appendix: Biobibliographical Information

The Twelfth Century

Stephen Harding

The earliest author discussed in this study is Stephen Harding. Born in England around 1059, he became one of the founding fathers of the Cistercian Order and of the monastery Cîteaux itself. He died on 28 March 1134.[1] Having invested great effort in the production of a correct Latin manuscript of the Bible, which still survives in four volumes in the Bibliothèque municipale of Dijon, Harding described the criteria on which he had based his textual decisions in a *Monitum* inserted at the end of the first volume.[2]

Nicolò Maniacutia

Perhaps the most fascinating of medieval textual critics was Nicolò Maniacutia. He was deacon at San Lorenzo in Damaso in Rome and later entered the Cistercian monastery Tre Fontane close to Rome. He remained there during the abbacy of Bernardo Paganelli, the later Pope Eugenius III, from 1140 to 1145, and may have died at Tre Fontane around 1145.[3]

---

[1] For the life and legacy of Stephen Harding, see Jean-Baptiste van Damme, *The Three Founders of Cîteaux: Robert of Molesme – Alberic – Stephen Harding*, tr. N. Groves and C. Carr, Kalamazoo (MI) and Spencer (MA) 1998, pp. 71–128. For Harding's works, see Sharpe, *A Handlist*, pp. 623–624.

[2] See Cauwe, 'La Bible d'Étienne Harding', p. 414. Harding's *Monitum* is edited ibid., pp. 416–17. Cauwe also discusses Harding's actual methods of emendation, using Samuel as example, and provides further bibliographical references. Yolanta Załuska (*L'enluminure et le scriptorium de Cîteaux au XIIe siècle*, Cîteaux 1989, pp. 64–111) provides a detailed codicological and iconographical study of Harding's Bible, MSS Dijon, Bibliothèque municipale, 12–15. According to the colophon, the first volume (now MS 12–13) was finished in 1109; see ibid., p. 66.

[3] According to Heinrich Schmidinger ('Nicolaus Maniacutius [Maniacoria] und sein Papstgedicht', in *Patriarch im Abendland. Beiträge zur Geschichte des Papsttums, Roms und Aquileias im Mittelalter. Ausgewählte Aufsätze von Heinrich Schmidinger. Festgabe zu seinem 70. Geburtstag*, ed. H. Dopsch, H. Koller and P. F. Kramml, Salzburg 1986, pp. 47–60, at p. 58), Maniacutia entered the monastery while Paganelli was abbot there. For the year of his death, see André Wilmart, 'Nicolas Manjacoria: Cistercien à Trois-Fontaines', *Revue Bénédictine* 33 (1921), pp. 136–143, at p. 143. For a recent

Among Maniacutia's works are several treatises which touch on aspects of textual criticism, for example: a poem dealing with the orthography of the names of the popes and their chronological order;[4] a preface to his emended editions of the *Psalterium Romanum*;[5] and the *Libellus de corruptione et correptione Psalmorum et aliarum quarundam scripturarum*, a treatise entirely devoted to the correction of the Psalter, in which he collated different Latin translations and the Hebrew version of the Psalms.[6] He also composed a *vita* of St Jerome.[7]

His earliest text-critical work bears the title *Suffraganeus bibliothece*.[8] So far, only parts of the preface and the final section of the text, an introduction to the *Psalterium iuxta Hebraeos*, have been published.[9] Two manuscripts are known to transmit the text

summary of his life and further bibliographical references, see *DBI*, LXIX, pp. 30–32. There are several variant spellings of Maniacutia's name (see ibid., p. 30); I have chosen to follow the version given in the *DBI*.

[4] Edited by Heinrich Schmidinger, 'Das Papstgedicht des Nicolaus Maniacutius', in *Patriarch im Abendland*, pp. 99–109, at pp. 103–109. The full title of the poem, as given in several manuscripts, is *Versus ad incorrupta pontificum nomina conservanda, ne videlicet dicamus Eleutherius pro Eleuther et Ylarius pro Ylarus, et ad sciendum, qui sunt antiquiores*; see ibid., p. 103.

[5] The preface to the *Psalterium Romanum* has been published by Weber, 'Deux préfaces', pp. 6–7.

[6] Published by Peri, '"Correctores immo corruptores"', pp. 88–125. The *Libellus* was written while Bernardo Paganelli was abbot at Tre Fontane; see ibid., pp. 22–24. Weber ('Deux préfaces', p. 3) states that the *Libellus* contains emendations to the *Psalterium Gallicanum*. For a more detailed bibliography of Maniacutia's works, see Vittorio Peri, 'Notizia su Nicola Maniacutia, autore ecclesiastico romano del xii secolo', *Aevum* 36 (1962), pp. 534–538, at pp. 535–536.

[7] Although the author of the *vita* is not named in the manuscripts, Alberto Vaccari has ascribed it with certainty to Maniacutia; see Vaccari, 'Le antiche vite', pp. 46–47; see ibid., p. 50, for the merits of this *vita*. In *PL* XXII (cols 183–202), the text is published under the title *S. Eusebii Hieronymi incomparabilis Ecclesiae Christi doctoris, et eximiae sanctitatis viri vita ex ipsius praesertim syngrammatis, e sanctorum item Augustini, Damasi, Gregorii, Gelasii, aliorumque aliquot collecta tractatibus*.

[8] A passage in the *Libellus* supplies evidence for the earlier date of the *Suffraganeus*; see Maniacutia, *Libellus*, p. 88: 'De his satis dictum est in opusculo edito de modis quibus solent exemplaria vitiari', which has been identified as a reference to the *Suffraganeus bibliothece*; see ibid., p. 24.

[9] For an edition of the preface to the *Suffraganeus*, see Nicolò Maniacutia, [Preface to the *Suffraganeus bibliothece*], in Denifle, 'Die Handschriften', pp. 270–276. The introduction to the *Psalterium iuxta Hebraeos* has been published by Weber, 'Deux préfaces', pp. 9–14. Weber regards the

of the *Suffraganeus*: MS Brussels, Bibliothèque royale, 4031-33, written between 1460 and 1470;[10] and MS Venice, Biblioteca Marciana, Lat. Z. 289 (=1681),[11] dating from the fourteenth or the first half of the fifteenth century. With regard to the textual criticism of the Bible, the Venice manuscript provides a link between the Middle Ages and fifteenth-century Italy: in the *Quattrocento*, it belonged to Cardinal Bessarion, who quoted several times from the *Suffraganeus bibliothece* in his text-critical treatise on Jn 21.22, recommending Maniacutia's work to those who wanted to learn more about the causes of textual corruption.[12]

Hervaeus of Bourg-Dieu
The third key figure of the twelfth century was Hervaeus of Bourg-Dieu. Originating from the north-western French province of Maine, he entered the Benedictine monastery Bourg-Dieu in Déols around 1100 and remained there until his death around 1150. Nowadays little known, Hervaeus was not only a prolific exegete but also wrote a work on the emendation of the lectionary, *De correctione quarundam lectionum*.[13] Although he was not strictly

introduction to the *Psalterium iuxta Hebraeos* as a preface to an edition of the text; yet it seems more likely that it is simply a part of the *Suffraganeus bibliothece*. The text of the *Suffraganeus* is incomplete and breaks off abruptly in the introduction to the Psalms.

[10] See Martin Wittek and Thérèse Glorieux-De Gand, *Manuscrits datés conservés en Belgique*, V: *1481–1540*, Brussels 1987, pp. 119–120. The *Suffraganeus bibliothece* covers ff. 1ʳ–32ᵛ; unpublished parts of the text are quoted from this manuscript. According to J. van den Gheyn ('Nicolas Maniacoria, correcteur de la Bible', *Revue Biblique* 8 [1899], pp. 289–295, at p. 291), the Brussels manuscript dates from the beginning of the sixteenth century.

[11] The *Suffraganeus bibliothece* covers ff. 141ʳ–181ᵛ. Giuseppe Valentinelli (*Bibliotheca Manuscripta ad S. Marci Venetiarum*, IV, Venice 1871, p. 126) dates it to the fifteenth century; Vaccari ('Le antiche vite', p. 47) assumed the Venice manuscript to have been written in the fourteenth century.

[12] Bessarion, *In illud Evangelii*, col. 629A: 'Si quis de his plura desiderat testimonia et latius nosse hanc rem cupit, Nicolaum legat tituli Damasi diaconum et bibliothecae suffraganeum.' In later centuries, a misunderstanding of the phrase '*bibliothecae suffraganeum*' led to the assumption that Maniacutia was librarian of the Roman church, chosen by Pope Lucius II; see Wilmart, 'Nicolas Manjacoria', p. 136 and n. 2. Scholars of the 18th century were already aware that Bessarion knew the *Suffraganeus bibliothece*; see Denifle, 'Die Handschriften', p. 270, n. 2. For more information on Cardinal Bessarion, see below, p. 261 and n. 44.

[13] For biographical information on Hervaeus, see Lucie Doležalová, *Reception and its Varieties: Reading, Re-Writing, and Understanding, Cena Cypriani in*

speaking a textual critic of the Latin Bible, he adopted attitudes similar to those of scholars concerned with improving the text of the Bible, and his observations regularly touch on issues directly relevant to biblical textual criticism.

The Thirteenth Century

Correctoria

Probably the most remarkable examples of manuscript collation in the Middle Ages are the *correctoria*, collections of variant readings of the Bible produced by Dominicans and Franciscans in France in the thirteenth century. This new kind of systematic writing arose in the first half of the thirteenth century. The precise purpose of the *correctoria* is still under discussion (see above, pp. 136–136, for Dahan's varying interpretations). At least for the Dominican *correctoria*, seemingly the sole aim was to bring together as much material as possible by collating many different Latin versions of the Bible from manuscripts of all epochs as well as the original Hebrew and Greek.[14] The *correctoria*, none of which has been edited, are proof of an immense interest in the biblical text, especially in the mendicant milieu.[15]

> *the Middle Ages*, Trier 2007, pp. 42–44; and *LexMA*, IV, col. 2186. I have not been able to consult Benjamin Unruh, *Die Kommentare des Herveus Burgidolensis*, Heilbronn 1909. *De correctione quarundam lectionum* was published by Morin, 'Un critique', pp. 39–60. His commentaries for the most part have not yet been published; his commentaries on Isaiah and the Pauline Epistles are edited in *PL*, CLXXXI, Paris 1851, cols 18–592 (*Commentaria in Isaiam*) and 591–1692 (*Commentaria in Epistolas divi Pauli*), respectively.

[14] See Dahan, '*Sorbonne II*', p. 151. According to Denifle ('Die Handschriften', p. 295), the aim of Hugh of St Cher and several authors of marginal glosses to *correctoria* was to sift out whatever was not in the original text and to correct the Bible according to manuscripts written in the original language.

[15] See Light, 'Versions', p. 90. Mary Bateson (*Catalogue of the Library of Syon Monastery, Isleworth*, Cambridge 1898, p. 221), in her edition of the early 16th-century library catalogue of Syon monastery in Isleworth, lists Thomas Docking's *Correctiones super sacram scripturam*, now lost. Beryl Smalley ('John Russel O. F. M.', *Recherches de Théologie ancienne et médiévale* 23 [1956], pp. 277–320, at pp. 312–13) deduces from a reference by his contemporary, John Russel, to the Franciscan Docking, who was still alive in 1269, that these *Correctiones* are the same work as a biblical grammar-book attributed to Docking. The reference Russel makes is (ibid., p. 313): 'Secundum venerabilem Dokkynge debet corripi, et quod in metris producitur, hoc est propter mutam et liquidam secundum eum.' Smalley

According to Laura Light, these works circulated for the most part independently of Bible manuscripts, and there is no evidence of widespread diffusion; only a few manuscripts of each work have come down to us.[16] No detailed research has as yet been conducted on their *fortuna*. Yet traces of their use can be found in the later centuries covered in this study: already in the thirteenth century, Dominican commentators drew on the *correctoria*;[17] in the fourteenth century, Peter Olivi consulted William de Mara's *Correctorium Biblie*; and in the fifteenth, Cardinal Bessarion referred to the utility of these collations, while a manuscript of Hugh of St Cher's *Correctio Biblie* was in the possession of Nicholas of Cusa.[18] The *correctoria* also survived in the manuscript tradition of at least two Latin Bibles: the Bible of St Jacques, a Dominican Bible from the thirteenth century containing *correctoria* notes; and MS London, British Library, Add. 40006, a Paris Bible containing parts of a *correctorium*, which may be Dominican in origin.[19] It is likely

concludes that Docking's work 'must have been concerned with the correct spelling, accentuation and declension of biblical words.' Judging from the title, it also seems possible that the *Correctiones super sacram scripturam* were a *correctorium*.

[16] See Light, 'Versions', p. 90. Denifle ('Die Handschriften', pp. 264–266) lists over 30 manuscripts dating from the thirteenth to the fifteenth century, containing over a dozen different *correctoria*. The comparatively rich transmission of Hugh of St Cher's and William de Mara's *correctoria*, with more than a dozen (eleven have been identified by Denifle; for additional manuscripts of Hugh's text, see below, p. 255, n. 21) and nine manuscripts respectively, seems to be an exception.

[17] See Smalley, *The Study of the Bible*, p. 336.

[18] For Olivi, see Dahan, 'La méthode critique', p. 117. Bessarion, *In illud Evangelii*, col. 636C: 'Si igitur non impium, sed pium, imo vero piissimum fuit, Hieronymum talia emendare, addendo, subtrahendo, mutando; si posterioribus licuit, prout certe licuit, quavis causa ortos errores corrigere, ex quo tot doctorum virorum libri fluxerunt, quibus correctorium Bibliae nomen est inditum.' Denifle ('Die Handschriften', p. 265) lists two manuscripts containing *correctoria* now in the Biblioteca Marciana in Venice (MSS Venice, Biblioteca Marciana, lat. class. I, 140 and 141), but neither is mentioned by Lotte Labowsky (*Bessarion's Library and the Biblioteca Marciana. Six Early Inventories*, Rome 1979) as having formerly been part of Bessarion's collection, nor does she mention any other *correctorium* in his possession. The question of whether Bessarion actually owned a copy of a *correctorium* therefore remains open. For the manuscript owned by Nicholas of Cusa, see above, p. 192, n. 269.

[19] In the London manuscript, there are no notes on the Psalms, a trait which Dahan has associated with Dominican *correctoria*; see Dahan, '*Sorbonne II*',

that more traces of the *Nachleben* of the *correctoria* are still waiting to be unearthed.

Hugh of St Cher

At least three *correctoria* contain prefaces with text-critical comments by their compilers. The earliest of these is the *Correctio Biblie* ascribed to the Dominican Hugh of St Cher (c. 1190–1263). Hugh entered the Dominican convent of St Jacques in Paris in 1225 and on 28 May 1244 became the first Dominican cardinal. His works include a commentary on Peter Lombard's Sentences, glosses to the *Historia scholastica* of Peter Comestor, the *Postillae* and a concordance to the Bible.[20] The *Correctio Biblie*, which has not yet been precisely dated, is transmitted in more than a dozen manuscripts.[21]

Modern scholarship has become very cautious about attributing works circulating under Hugh's name to his sole authorship; instead, it is now assumed that they are the product of a group of authors or compilers, working for and with Hugh. As is the case for the *Postillae* and the concordance to the Bible ascribed to him, so, too, the attribution of the *Correctio Biblie* to Hugh alone might have to be re-evalued, pending further research into the *Correctio* itself and the role of the School of St Jacques – in fact, Gilbert Dahan has already voiced doubts about Hugh's sole authorship and instead ascribed the work to a group working under Hugh at St Jacques.[22] For the sake of simplicity and readability, I am referring

---

p. 114. For the Bible of St Jacques, see above, p. 124; for the Paris Bible, see above, pp. 42–46.

[20] For biographical information on Hugh of St Cher, see *LexMA*, V, cols 176–177. The preface to Hugh's *Correctio Biblie* has been published by Denifle ('Die Handschriften', pp. 293–294), who calls it *Correctorium A*; and, more recently, by Dahan ('La critique textuelle', pp. 386–387), whose edition I refer to. For the chronological order of the *correctoria*, see Dahan, 'Sorbonne II', pp. 113–14. For the influence of the *Correctio Biblie* on later *correctoria*, see Denifle, 'Die Handschriften', p. 544.

[21] In addition to the manuscripts listed by Denifle ('Die Handschriften', p. 264), three more have been identified by Thomas Kaeppeli and Emilio Panella, *Scriptores Ordinis Praedicatorum Medii Aevii*, 4 vols, Rome 1970–1993, II, p. 273 (no. 1986). As Dahan ('La critique textuelle', p. 368, n. 13) points out, some more manuscripts may be added from Stegmüller's *Repertorium* (IX, p. 64), who, however, mistakenly attributes Hugh's work to Guillelmus Brito.

[22] Dahan, 'Sorbonne II', p. 113. For the *Postillae*, see, e.g., Bruno Carra de Vaux, 'La constitution du corpus exégétique', in *Hugues de Saint-Cher (†*

to the author of the *Correctio Biblie* as Hugh of St Cher throughout this book.

William de Mara

Famous for his *Correctorium fratris Thomae* written before August 1279, the Franciscan William de Mara (fl. 1272-1279) compiled a *correctorium* with the title *Correctorium Biblie*. He studied theology in Paris, where he also became regent master, probably in 1274-1275. William possessed a solid knowledge of both Hebrew and Greek which he made use of in his *De Hebraeis et Graecis vocabulis glossarum Bibliae*.[23]

Gerard of Huy

No biographical data is available on Gerard of Huy, who is often claimed to have been a member of the Franciscan Order by modern scholars, though without any proof.[24] As we shall see below, he

---

1263), *bibliste et théologien*, ed. L.–J. Bataillon, G. Dahan and P.–M. Guy, Turnhout 2004, pp. 43–63, at p. 54; and, more generally, Louis–Jacques Bataillon, 'L'influence d'Hugues de Saint–Cher', in *Hugues de Saint–Cher*, pp. 497–502, at p. 497. For the concordance, see Michel Albaric, 'Hugues de Saint–Cher et les concordances bibliques latines (XIIIᵉ–XVIIIᵉ siècles)', in *Hugues de Saint–Cher*, pp. 467–479, at p. 467–468.

[23] The information in this paragraph derives mostly from John Marenbon's article on William in *ODNB*, XXXVI, pp. 624–625. For William's works and further bibliographical references, see also Sharpe, *A Handlist*, p. 787. For a discussion of the year of William's birth, see above, p. 145 and n. 128. The preface to William's *Correctorium Biblie* has been published by Denifle ('Die Handschriften', pp. 295–297); and by Dahan ('La critique textuelle', pp. 387–388), whose edition I refer to in this study. William's *correctorium* is called *correctorium D* by Denifle; on the authorship, see Denifle, 'Die Handschriften', p. 545.

[24] See, e.g., Dahan, 'La critique textuelle', p. 368; and Smalley, *The Study of the Bible*, p. 336. There is no mention of Gerard either in Luke Wadding, *Scriptores ordinis minorum*, Rome 1906, repr. Bologna 1978, or in Sbaraglia, *Supplementum*. Berger (*Quam notitiam*, p. 46) noted that no information on him was available. More recently, Anheim, Grévin and Morard ('Exégèse judéo–chrétienne', p. 110, n. 34) have said about Gerard of Huy: 'Le personnage n'est connu que par trois manuscrits qui portent son nom ... C'est uniquement par déduction qu'on en fait un franciscain disciple de Bacon.' Stegmüller (*Repertorium*, II, pp. 338–339) provides no dates and does not claim that Gerard was a member of the Franciscan Order. The preface to Gerard's *correctorium* has been edited by Denifle ('Die Handschriften', pp. 298–310), who calls it *correctorium E*; it survives in two manuscripts; see ibid., p. 265. For Denifle's identification of the author as Gerard, see ibid., p. 477.

perhaps composed his *correctorium* in the second quarter of the thirteenth century. He also wrote a work entitled *Triglossos*, in which, among other things, he discusses the Greek and Hebrew alphabets, as well as terms in both languages.[25] Like William, he, too, had a sound knowledge of the two biblical languages.[26]

Roger Bacon
The most famous proponent of textual criticism in the thirteenth century was Roger Bacon (c. 1215-1292). Born close to Ilchester in Somerset, he spent time in both Oxford and Paris. After returning to Oxford in 1247, he studied Hebrew, Arabic and Greek. Entering the Franciscan Order between 1245 and 1250, he was sent to the Paris house of the Friars Minor in 1257. Although known mostly for his scientific writings, Bacon discusses issues related to textual criticism of the Bible in several of his works: the *Opus majus*,[27] *Opus minus*, *Opus tertium* and *Compendium studii philosophiae*.[28] The first three of these works, all written at the request of Pope Clement IV, were completed before 1267; the *Compendium* is dated to 1271.[29]

[25] The text is transmitted in MS Paris, Bibliothèque de l'Arsenal, 904, ff. 25ʳ–103ʳ, where Gerard is called *frater Gerardus de Hoyo*; see ibid., f. 25ʳ; a very short extract from the introduction has been edited by Denifle, 'Die Handschriften', pp. 308–309, n. 4

[26] See Smalley, *The Study of the Bible*, pp. 336 and 338.

[27] For an account of his life, see Bacon, *Opus majus*, I, pp. xxi–xxxvi. For his knowledge of Hebrew, Greek and Arabic, see Lynn Thorndike, 'The True Roger Bacon, I', *The American Historical Review* 21 (1916), pp. 237–257, at pp. 254–256, who doubts whether Bacon's Arabic was sufficient to read scientific texts. For more information and secondary literature on Bacon, see *ODNB*, III, pp. 176–181; for a useful list of Bacon' works and their editions, see Sharpe, *A Handlist*, pp. 580–583.

[28] The last three works have all been edited in Bacon, *Opera quaedam*, pp. 3–310 (*Opus tertium*); 313–389 (*Opus minus*); 393–519 (*Compendium studii philosophiae*).

[29] See Bacon, *Opus majus*, pp. xxi and xxx; and Bacon, *Opera quaedam*, pp. xlvi and liv–lv. For information on the transmission and content of the *Opus minus*, *Opus tertium* and *Compendium studii philosophiae*, see ibid., pp. xxx–lvii. Clement IV's request and later mandate to Bacon to send him his work are discussed by Thorndike, 'The True Roger Bacon, I', pp. 240–241. Thorndike (ibid., p. 242) assumes that by the summer of 1266 the *Opus majus* was already written or at least almost finished. The *Opus tertium* was written in the same year as the *Opus minus*; see Bacon, *Opera quaedam*, p. xxxviii. There is nothing of relevance to this study in Bacon's *Compendium*

Ramon Martí

The final thirteenth-century scholar with whom I deal is the Dominican Ramon Martí (before 1220–1284).[30] He was born in Subirats, close to Barcelona, and entered the Order of Preachers some time between 1234 and 1236. In 1281 he was teaching Hebrew at Barcelona. Martí is best known for his anti-Jewish polemical writings, the *Capistrum Iudaeorum*, written in 1267, and the *Pugio fidei*, his most famous work, written in 1278.[31] In both treatises, he comments on the status of various Latin versions of the Bible.

The Fourteenth Century

The fourteenth century is somewhat unusual with regard to the issues examined in this study. I have been unable to find any works from this period which deal exclusively or to any great extent with the textual criticism of the Latin Bible.[32] Nevertheless, I have identified three authors who discuss in detail matters relevant to textual criticism, though it was not in any way their aim to emend the text of the Latin Bible.

Richard FitzRalph

Richard FitzRalph, born around 1300, hailed from the archdiocese of Armagh in Ireland.[33] He studied in Oxford and spent much of his life at the papal curia in Avignon, where he died in 1360. In 1347, he became archbishop of Armagh. During one of his stays at Avignon, he composed the dialogue *Summa de questionibus Arme-*

---

studii theologiae (Roger Bacon, *Compendium of the Study of Theology*, ed. and tr. T. S. Maloney, Leiden, New York, Copenhagen and Cologne 1988).

[30] For his life, see Martí, *Capistrum*, I, pp. 8–15.

[31] For the dating of the two works, see ibid., I, pp. 12–13.

[32] Even authors whom one might expect to have commented on the issue, such as Nicholas of Lyra, for instance in his comparison of Hebrew and Latin Scripture (*De differencia litere hebraice et nostre translacionis*, in MS Paris, BNF lat. 3359, ff. 25ra–53vb), did not make text-critical comments, but instead concentrated on exegesis. William J. Courtenay ('The Bible in the Fourteenth Century: Some Observations', *Church History* 54 [1985], pp. 176–187) deals almost exclusively with commentators and matters related to teaching at the universities of Oxford and Paris.

[33] For a detailed biography of FitzRalph, see Walsh, *A Fourteenth-Century Scholar*. See ibid., pp. 1–3, for his Irish origin and date of birth.

norum, divided into nineteen books.³⁴ Only the first ten books concern the Armenian faith. The next four deal with doctrines of the Eastern Churches in general; and the final five, which may have been added after the mid-1340s, discuss matters unrelated to the title.³⁵ The passages relevant to this study are all contained in the last of these five books. The *Summa* is dedicated to two Armenian prelates, Nerses Balientz and John Kernatzi.³⁶ In the preface, FitzRalph refers to theological discussions he had had with the two Armenians;³⁷ the dialogue's interlocutors, called Richardus and Iohannes, should therefore be identified with FitzRalph himself and, in all likelihood, John Kernatzi.

Henry Totting
The scholastic philosopher and theologian Henry Totting of Oyta was a native of Friesoythe in Eastern Frisia, where he was born around 1330. He studied at the newly founded University of Prague and was ordained a priest before 1367. After spending two years in Avignon, from 1371 to 1373, charged with heresy but later acquitted, he is next attested as a teacher at the University of Paris, from 1377 to 1381. Around 1381 he returned to Prague, before moving in 1384 to Vienna, where he taught at the university and remained until his death in 1397.³⁸

As well as various philosophical commentaries, sermons and treatises dealing with contemporary issues, Totting was the author of three works on the Sentences. One of these, the *Quaestiones super libros Sententiarum*, has survived in eleven manuscripts. Composed

---

34 For the history of the text, see Walsh, *A Fourteenth-Century Scholar*, pp. 129–181. The Armenians had asked the pope for help against the Islamic threat, but doubts about their beliefs led to hearings at Avignon not before autumn 1339: the results were compiled in 117 articles. Walsh assumes that FitzRalph was consulted to provide Latin interpretations of Armenian doctrines: see ibid., pp. 144–145.

35 See ibid., p. 148. The final preface to the *Summa* was composed after 8 July 1347; see ibid., p. 131.

36 See ibid., pp. 131–143, for information on Nerses Balientz and John Kernatzi. See FitzRalph, *Summa*, sig. aIʳ, for the dedication.

37 See ibid., sig. aiʳ: 'Cum vero super ipsis erroribus vobiscum ibidem aliquotiens contulissem meam exilitatem, devotius stimulastis, ut super questionibus vestris illud vobis scriberem quod mihi dignaretur dominus aperire.'

38 See Albert Lang, *Heinrich Totting von Oyta: Ein Beitrag zur Entstehungsgeschichte der ersten deutschen Universitäten und zur Problemgeschichte der Spätscholastik*, Münster i. W. 1937, pp. 6–43.

shortly after 1378, it consists of thirteen *quaestiones*, the second of which, entitled *Quaestio de Sacra Scriptura*, concerns the transmission of the Bible and the status of the Vulgate.[39]

Peter of Ailly
During Henry Totting's time at Paris, Peter of Ailly (1351-1420) read the Sentences there, becoming a doctor of theology in 1380,[40] and later holding the post of chancellor of the university. In 1395 he became bishop of Le Puy and, two years later, of Cambrai. In 1411 he was made cardinal and participated in the Council of Constance (1414-1418).[41]

Peter wrote two treatises which are relevant to this study. In 1378, he composed his *Epistola ad novos hebraeos* in order to refute accusations that the text of the Vulgate diverged considerably from the original. His *Apologeticus* was written as a complement to the *Epistola*.[42]

The Fifteenth Century

Cardinal Bessarion and George of Trebizond
Only a handful of fifteenth-century humanists wrote at any length about textual criticism of the Latin Bible.[43] The most influential of

---

[39] For a summary of his works and their diffusion, see Lang, *Heinrich Totting*, pp. 43–137. For the dating, see ibid., pp. 66–68. In his earlier edition of the work, Lang dates it to between 1385 and 1388; see Totting, *Quaestio*, p. 6. Frank Rosenthal ('Heinrich von Oyta and Biblical Criticism in the Fourteenth Century', *Speculum* 25 [1950], pp. 178–83) gives a brief summary of Totting's life and of the content of the *Quaestio*; he does not deal with textual criticism of the Bible.

[40] See Lang, *Heinrich Totting*, p. 30.

[41] See Louis Salembier, *Le Cardinal Pierre d'Ailly: Chancelier de l'Université de Paris, Évêque du Puy et Cambrai, 1350–1420*, Tourcoing 1932 (pp. 90–112 for his time as chancellor of the university; pp. 113–152 for his period as bishop of Le Puy and Cambrai; pp. 264–87 for the Council of Constance).

[42] For the dating, see Salembier, *Petrus ab Alliaco*, p. XIV. The relationship between the two works is discussed ibid., p. 304. Both works are partly edited in Tschackert, *Peter von Ailli*, pp. [7]–[12] (*Epistola ad novos Hebraeos*) and pp. [50]–[51] (*Apologeticus*); other passages are quoted by Salembier.

[43] I shall not take into consideration the discussions at the Council of Ferrara and Florence concerning the addition of the *Filioque* to the Creed. Although at first glance this question might seem related to textual criticism, in fact, the issues discussed were mainly theological. For an account of the *Filioque* question, see Joseph Gill, *The Council of Florence*, Cambridge 1959, pp. 147–69. For a short overview of fifteenth-century approaches to the text of the

these scholars at the time was Cardinal Bessarion (1403-1472), on account of his powerful position in the papal curia, the circle of humanist scholars gathered around him and his library.[44] In the early 1450s, Bessarion and George of Trebizond, two Byzantine émigré humanists, found themselves on opposite sides of a contentious issue. George of Trebizond, who came to Italy from Greece as early as 1412, had composed a treatise dedicated to Pietro da Monte on the question of whether the Latin translation of Jn 21.22 (ἐὰν αὐτὸν θέλω μένειν ἕως ἔρχομαι, τί πρὸς σέ;) should read '*si* eum volo manere donec venio quid ad te' or '*sic* eum volo manere donec venio quid ad te'. Large parts of this work, which has not yet been published, are also included in George's invective against Theodore Gaza, written in the autumn of 1453 or the winter of 1453/1454.[45] Bessarion responded with a treatise on the same topic, possibly composed in 1455,[46] to which George wrote a reply entitled *In expositionem illius textus evangelii 'Sic volo eum manere, etc' et quod S. Joannes Evangelista nondum sit mortuus ad Sixtum IV pontificem maximum*. George insisted that the verse should read '*sic* eum volo manere', following the Latin tradition; Cardinal Bessarion, however, claimed that, in accordance with the

Latin Bible, see Salvatore Garofalo, 'Gli umanisti italiani del secolo XV e la Bibbia', *Biblica* 27 (1946), pp. 338–375.

[44] For the group of scholars centred on Bessarion, which developed during the papacy of Eugenius IV, see Mohler, *Kardinal Bessarion*, I, pp. 252 and 326; on his library, see Labowsky, *Bessarion's Library*, especially pp. 5–23, and Mohler, *Kardinal Bessarion*, I, pp. 408–415. Bessarion came to Italy from Greece to attend the Council of Ferrara; for more information and literature on Bessarion, see *DBI*, IX, pp. 686–696.

[45] See George of Trebizond, *Adversus Theodorum Gazam*, p. 330 (35, 1): 'Hanc enim inter summae dignitatis viros aut certo summae proximos contentionem fuisse nuper audivi ... Ea igitur ipsa repetam, quae mihi ad praestantem patrem Petrum de Monte, Brixiensem episcopum, conscripta sunt.' For the dating, see ibid., p. 275. Monfasani (*George of Trebizond*, pp. 90–102) gives a summary of the discussion between George and Bessarion, focusing on the theological aspects of the issue. He also notes (ibid., p. 92, n. 102) that George's first treatise was rediscovered in MS Parma, Biblioteca palatina, 28, ff. 17–25, by Paul Oskar Kristeller, *Iter Italicum. A Finding List of Uncatalogued or Incompletely Catalogued Humanistic Manuscripts of the Renaissance in Italian and Other Libraries*, II: *Italy. Orvieto to Volterra. Vatican City*, London and Leiden 1967, p. 44: 'Georgius Trapezuntius, letter to Petr. de Monte ep. Brixiensis, on a passage of the Gospel.' For a recent account of George's life, see *DBI*, LV, pp. 373–382.

[46] Bessarion, *In illud Evangelii*. For the dating, see Mohler, *Kardinal Bessarion*, I, p. 400.

Greek original, the text should read 'si eum volo manere', translating the crucial word ἐάν literally as si.

Lorenzo Valla
In the long term the most important biblical scholar of the fifteenth century was Lorenzo Valla (1407-1457).⁴⁷ Famous for his *Elegantiae*, the first draft of which was finished in or before 1441,⁴⁸ he also composed two treatises which dealt exclusively with the improvement of the Latin text of the New Testament: the *Collatio Novi Testamenti*⁴⁹ and the *Annotationes in Novum Testamentum*.⁵⁰

By early 1443, Valla's first treatise on the New Testament, the *Collatio*, was already written or at least drafted, as can be established from a few allusions to it in his other works.⁵¹ Valla worked on the

---

47 The literature on Valla is vast. To cite only the most important monographs: Girolamo Mancini, *Vita di Lorenzo Valla*, Florence 1891; Fois, *Il pensiero cristiano*; di Napoli, *Lorenzo Valla*; Camporeale, *Lorenzo Valla*.

48 For the dating, see Valla, *De linguae latinae elegantia*, I, p. 24. Camporeale (*Lorenzo Valla*, p. 106) assumes a slightly earlier date, around 1438 to 1439.

49 The *Collatio* survives in two 15ᵗʰ-century manuscripts, both probably written in Naples in 1477 (MS Paris, BNF, nouv. acq. lat. 502) and 1478 (MS Valencia, Biblioteca de la Catedral, 170); see Valla, *Collatio*, pp. XI–XVII, for a description of the manuscripts. Both Anna Morisi ('A proposito di due redazioni della *Collatio Novi Testamenti* di Lorenzo Valla', *Bullettino dell'Istituto storico italiano per il medio evo e archivio muratoriano* 78 [1967], pp. 345–375, at p. 351) and Perosa (Valla, *Collatio*, p. XXIV) mention the absence of notes on the letter to Philemon and the Apocalypse in the *Collatio*; while Morisi assumes that the treatise is a finished work, Perosa is more careful and considers it likely that Valla did not complete the autograph.

50 Valla, *Annotationes*, in his *Opera*, I, pp. 803–895. The only manuscript known to have survived is MS Brussels, Bibliothèque royale, 4031–33, which also contains Maniacutia's *Suffraganeus*. Erasmus, who rediscovered the manuscript in 1504, brought out the first edition of the *Annotationes*, printed in April 1505; see Valla, *Collatio*, p. IX and XI. An abridged version of the work, possibly rooted in a *reportatio*, containing the annotations to the Gospels of Mark, Matthew and John, and Acts is preserved in Archivio privato Bichi Ruspoli, Siena, b. 122; see Riccardo Fubini, 'Una sconosciuta testimonianza manoscritta delle *Annotationes in Novum Testamentum* del Valla', in *Lorenzo Valla e l'umanesimo italiano. Atti del convegno internazionale di studi umanistici (Parma, 18–19 ottobre 1984)*, ed. O. Besomi and M. Regoliosi, Padua 1986, pp. 179–196, at pp. 179–180 and 191–192.

51 See, e.g., Lorenzo Valla, *In errores Antonii Raudensis adnotationes*, in his *Opera*, I, pp. 390–438, at p. 413: 'Nam de usu euangeliorum hoc loco non attinet dicere, cum plura disseramus in libris super nouum testamentum.' For a dating of his *Adnotationes in Raudensem* to 1442, see Camporeale, *Lorenzo Valla*, pp. 355–56. Perosa lists all the passages in the *Adnotationes in*

second treatise, the *Annotationes*, up to his death in 1457;[52] it was never finished.[53] He had started on the project after moving in 1448 from Naples to Rome. Here, he encountered a milieu which was more interested in scriptural studies and also came into contact with Bessarion and Nicholas of Cusa; he also gained access to a larger number of Latin and Greek Bible manuscripts.[54] His *Annotationes*, in fact, reveal the influence of Bessarion, at least in the discussion of Jn 21.22.[55]

Raudensem which relate to the *Collatio*; see Valla, *Collatio*, pp. XXXVIII–XXXIX. Cesare Vasoli ('Nuove prospettive su Lorenzo Valla', *Nuova rivista storica* 57 [1973], pp. 448–458, at p. 452) dates the *Collatio* to 1443. Camporeale (*Lorenzo Valla*, p. 357) placed the final version of the *Collatio* in spring 1443; according to him (ibid., pp. 353–354), this dating is confirmed in a letter written by Valla to Aurispa on 31 December 1443 (Lorenzo Valla, *Epistole*, ed. O. Besomi and M. Regoliosi, Padua 1984, p. 252: 'Feram ad te ... libros octo *De collatione Novi Testamenti*'). Some scholars believe the *Collatio* was begun as early as 1434; see Fois, *Il pensiero cristiano*, p. 414, who assumes that in this period Valla examined Bible manuscripts brought to Italy by Ciriaco of Ancona. The same opinion is held by Anna Morisi ('La filologia neotestamentaria di Lorenzo Valla', *Nuova rivista storica* 48 [1964], pp. 35–49, at p. 35) who thinks that Valla commenced his work on the New Testament in 1433–1434. Perosa (Valla, *Collatio*, p. XXXII and n. 60) expresses doubt about this early date for a meeting between Ciriaco and Valla.

[52] Vasoli ('Nuove prospettive', p. 452) says that Valla worked on the *Annotationes* in the years 1453–57.

[53] See Botley, *Latin Translation*, p. 89, n. 126.

[54] See Valla, *Collatio*, pp. XLIX–L.

[55] Mohler (*Kardinal Bessarion*, I, p. 334) assumed a connection between the writing of the *Annotationes* and Bessarion's circle, but claimed wrongly that Bessarion's treatise on Jn 21.22 gave Valla the incentive to compose his *Annotationes*; see ibid. p. 403, and Ludwig Mohler, 'Kardinal Bessarions kritische Untersuchung der Vulgatastelle: "Sic eum volo manere, quid ad te?"', *Römische Quartalschrift für christliche Altertumskunde und für Kirchengeschichte* 41 (1933), pp. 189–206, at p. 189; in this article, Mohler also published the original Greek version of Bessarion's treatise; see ibid., pp. 190–206. Mohler dates Bessarion's Latin treatise to 1455 (see above, p. 261); but Valla had already mentioned Bessarion's contribution to his work in one of his invectives against Poggio Bracciolini; see Valla, *Antidotum in Pogium*, p. 340: 'Habet {sc. *Cardinalis Nicenus, i.e. Bessarion*} in opere meo partem: quippe qui illud, cuius supra feci mentionem: "sic eum uolo manere, quid ad te?" quod ego non animaduerterem, ut adderem admonuit.' The last book of his *Antidotum in Pogium* was written before the appearance of Bessarion's treatise: Wesseling (Valla, *Antidotum primum*, p. 36) dates it to March or April 1453.

Valla's two treatises are different redactions of the same work.[56] Many of the improvements he suggested deal solely with aspects of style or translation; and he himself seems to regard his emendations of the Latin Bible as building blocks for a new translation.[57] He probably never published either of his treatises on the Bible. A letter written to Giovanni Tortelli on 1 January 1447 supports this view: Valla laments the loss of the only manuscript of the *Collatio*.[58] Paul Botley plausibly deduces from this that it was still a work in progress, but that Valla was nevertheless willing to lend the draft to those who were interested in it.[59] Another indication that neither of the treatises ever came to publication is the meagre manuscript tradition.[60] At least Valla had not yet published the works by 1452, as he makes clear in his *Antidotum primum in Pogium* (1452). His formulation in this passage, *nondum ... publicaverim*, suggests, however, that he was planning to do so.[61]

[56] See Morisi, 'A proposito', p. 351, for approximate percentages of the lemmata found both in the *Collatio* and the *Annotationes*. She (ibid., pp. 371–372) mistakenly believes, however, that the *Collatio* was written after the *Annotationes*, assuming that it might have represented an intermediate stage. Perosa (Valla, *Collatio*, p. IX) and Wesseling (Valla, *Antidotum primum*, p. 24) consider the treatises to be two redactions of the same work, a view which I share. For a comparison of the two works, see Valla, *Collatio*, pp. XXIII–XXXVII.

[57] See Valla, *Antidotum primum*, p. 112: 'Itaque, ne multus sim, siquid emendo non Scripturam Sacram emendo, sed illius interpretationem, neque in eam contumeliosus sum, sed pius potius, nec aliud facio nisi quod melius quam prior interpres transfero, ut mea translatio si vera fuerit sit appellanda Sancta Scriptura, non illius.' For Valla's use of the term *interpres*, see above, pp. 97–99.

[58] Valla, *Epistole*, pp. 305–306: 'Ego vero et *Elegantias* et *Raudens[ianas]* et libros super *Novum Testamentum*, cum diversis hominibus commodassem, istic, culpa Ambrosii amisi, qui repetere neg[lexit] ... Itaque tribus quasi vulneribus confossus sum, quorum [duo] altius penetrant: nam *Raudensianas* librosque *Novi Testamenti* nusquam alibi habeo.' The editors identify Ambrosius with Ambrogio Dardanoni; see ibid., p. 293.

[59] Botley, *Latin Translation*, p. 88. For an example of Valla lending the text to others, see also his letter to Marino Tomacello from 23 March 1454 (Valla, *Epistole*, p. 386): 'Cui {*sc*. Antonello} ... dicas ut proemium meum super *Collationem Novi Testamenti* ad me mittat, magnopere enim illud desidero.' The reference is to Antonello Petrucci (see ibid., p. 371), who prepared the text of the *Collatio* in MS Paris, BNF, nouv. acq. lat. 502; see Valla, *Collatio*, p. XIV.

[60] As suggested by Botley, *Latin Translation*, p. 93.

[61] Valla, *Antidotum primum*, p. 118: 'Aut *edidit* accipis pro *condidit*, quod barbarum est, aut plane mentiris, cum nondum illud {*sc. the annotations*}

Giannozzo Manetti

Around 1449, Pope Nicholas V commissioned Giannozzo Manetti (1396-1459), the first humanist to devote himself seriously to the study of Hebrew,[62] to produce a new Latin translation of the Bible.[63] Whether Valla's work on the New Testament had any influence on Giannozzo Manetti's translation of the Bible is still a matter of debate. Although it seems likely that the two humanists crossed paths, it remains unclear whether Manetti had any knowledge of Valla's treatises.[64]

In 1454–55, Manetti produced a new version of the Psalms, the only book of the Old Testament which he managed to translate.[65] In response to the criticism he received for this translation, he wrote the *Apologeticus*, in which, among other issues, he expressed his views on the various paths of transmission of the Bible.[66]

Giovanni Crastone

Giovanni Crastone was born in the second decade of the fifteenth century close to Piacenza and died in or not much after 1497 in Milan.[67] Like Manetti, Crastone also produced a new Latin version of the Psalms. In contrast to his predecessor, however, he published a bi-lingual edition, with the Latin translation facing the Greek. Since the Psalter was often used to teach Greek, Crastone, whose

---

publicaverim nec tu unquam inspexeris, in quo tamen ais a me reprehendi Hieronymum.'

[62] De Petris (Manetti, *Apologeticus*, p. XIII) states that Manetti started learning Hebrew in 1442; see also Charles Trinkaus, *In Our Image and Likeness: Humanity and Divinity in Italian Humanist Thought*, 2 vols, London 1970, II, p. 581; Trinkaus considers it possible that Manetti began his Hebrew studies around 1435. For Manetti, see also the article on him in *DBI*, LXVIII, pp. 613–617.

[63] See Manetti, *Apologeticus*, p. XVI; and Botley, *Latin Translation*, p. 89. Manetti was the first translator to produce a Latin version of the New Testament from the Greek original in the humanist period; see Manetti, *Apologeticus*, p. V.

[64] See the detailed discussion in Botley, *Latin Translation*, pp. 87–95.

[65] Trinkaus, *In Our Image*, II, p. 582. For the dating, see Manetti, *Apologeticus*, p. XVI.

[66] See ibid., p. XVI. Both the *Apologeticus* and the translation of the Psalms are dedicated to Alfonso the Magnanimous; see Trinkaus, *In Our Image*, II, p. 582.

[67] For this and more information, see *DBI*, XXX, pp. 578–580.

aim it was to facilitate the learning of Greek, adapted the Latin version to the Greek.[68] In the prefatory letter to his edition, printed on 20 September 1481 in Milan, Crastone comments on the transmission of the Latin Bible.[69]

---

[68] On the use of the Psalter for learning to read in medieval and Renaissance Italy, see Robert Black, *Humanism and Education in Medieval and Renaissance Italy. Tradition and Innovation in Latin Schools from the Twelfth to the Fifteenth Century*, Cambridge 2001, pp. 35–36 and 366; for its application to the teaching of Greek, see Paul Botley, *Learning Greek in Western Europe, 1369–1529: Grammars, Lexica and Classroom Texts*, Philadelphia 2010, pp. 75–76. Crastone might also have chosen this form because it was requested by his publisher. So far, no research has been conducted on the changes Crastone introduced to the Latin text.

[69] Crastone, [Dedicatory letter], pp. 13–16. In the incunable, (Giovanni Crastone, [Bi-lingual edition of the Psalms], Milan 1481, sig. x5ʳ–z6ʳ – the copy I have consulted is London, British Library, shelfmark IB.26564), the Psalms are followed by the apocryphal Psalm 151 and a collection of canticles, commonly added to the Psalms in the Septuagint, also both in Latin and in Greek.

BIBLIOGRAPHY

Manuscripts

Brussels, Bibliothèque royale, 4031-33 (= *B*; ff. 1^r–32^v: Nicolò Maniacutia, *Suffraganeus bibliothece*).
London, British Library, Add. 17737 ('Floreffe Bible').
London, British Library, Add. 39629 (Paris Bible).
London, British Library, Add. 40006 (Paris Bible).
London, British Library, Egerton 839 (Ps.-Augustine, *De magnificentiis beati Hieronymi*, ff. 159ra-162va).
Paris, Bibliothèque de l'Arsenal, 904 (ff. 25^r-103^r: Gerard of Huy, *Triglossos*).
Paris, Bibliothèque de l'Arsenal, 94 (Hugh of St Cher, *Correctio Biblie*).
Paris, BNF, lat. 17 (Paris Bible).
Paris, BNF, lat. 3218 (ff. 137^r-161^r: Hugh of St Cher, *Correctio Biblie*).
Paris, BNF, lat. 3359, (ff. 25ra-53vb: Nicholas of Lyra, *De differencia litere hebraice et nostre translacionis*).
Venice, Biblioteca Marciana, Lat. Z. 289 (=1681) (ff. 141^r-181^v: Nicolò Maniacutia, *Suffraganeus bibliothece*).

Primary Sources and Secondary Literature

Acta capitulorum generalium Ordinis Praedicatorum, I: *Ab anno 1220 usque ad annum 1303*, ed. B. M. Reichert, Rome 1898.
Albaric, Michel, 'Hugues de Saint-Cher et les concordances bibliques latines (XIIIe-XVIIIe siècles)', in *Hugues de Saint-Cher*, pp. 467-479.
Alexander of Villa-Dei, *Das 'Doctrinale' des Alexander de Villa-Dei*, ed. D. Reichling, Berlin 1893, repr. New York 1974.
Altermatt, Alberich Martin, '"Id quod magis authenticum...": Die Liturgiereform der ersten Zisterzienser', in *Liturgiereformen*, I, pp. 304-324.
Ambrose, *Expositio Evangelii secundum Lucam*, ed. M. Adriaen, in his *Opera*, IV, Turnhout 1957, pp. 1-400.
– *Expositio Psalmi CXVIII*, in his *Opera*, V, ed. M. Petschenig, Vienna and Leipzig 1913, repr. New York and London 1962.

Analecta hymnica medii aevi, LII, ed. C. Blume, Leipzig 1909, repr. New York and London 1961.

Andrew of St Victor, *Expositio super heptateuchum*, ed. C. Lohr and R. Berndt, Turnhout 1986.

Anheim, Étienne, Grévin, Benoît and Morard, Martin, 'Exégèse judéo-chrétienne, magie et linguistique: un recueil de *notes* inédites attribuées à Roger Bacon', *Archives d'histoire doctrinale et littéraire du moyen âge* 68 (2001), pp. 95-154.

[Aristeas], *Aristeas to Philocrates (Letter of Aristeas)*, ed. and tr. M. Hadas, New York [1951].

Augustine, *Contra adversarium legis et prophetarum*, in his *Opera*, XV, 3, ed. K.-D. Daur, Turnhout 1985, pp. 35–131.

– *Contra epistulam quam uocant fundamenti*, in his *Opera*, VI, 1, ed. J. Zycha (Corpus Scriptorum Ecclesiasticorum Latinorum, 25), Prague, Vienna and Leipzig 1891, pp. 193-248.

– *Contra Faustum*, in his *Opera*, VI, 1, ed. J. Zycha (Corpus Scriptorum Ecclesiasticorum Latinorum, 25), Prague, Vienna and Leipzig 1891, pp. 251-797.

– *De baptismo libri septem*, in his *Opera*, VII, 1, ed. M. Petschenig (Corpus Scriptorum Ecclesiasticorum Latinorum, 51), Vienna and Leipzig 1908, repr. New York and London 1963, pp. 145-375.

– *De civitate Dei*, in his *Opera*, XIV, ed. B. Dombaert and A. Kalb (Corpus Christianorum. Series Latina, 47), Turnhout 1955.

– *De consensu evangelistarum*, in his *Opera*, III, 4, ed. F. Weihrich (Corpus Scriptorum Ecclesiasticorum Latinorum, 43), Vienna and Leipzig 1904.

– *De doctrina christiana*, in his *Opera*, IV, 1, ed. J. Martin (Corpus Christianorum. Series Latina, 32), Turnhout 1962, pp. 1-167.

– *De mendacio*, in his *Opera*, V, 3, ed. J. Zycha (Corpus Scriptorum Ecclesiasticorum Latinorum, 41), Prague, Vienna and Leipzig 1900, pp. 413-466.

– *De vera religione*, in his *Opera*, VI, 5, ed. W. Green (Corpus Scriptorum Ecclesiasticorum Latinorum, 77), Vienna 1961.

– *Enarrationes in Psalmos*, in his *Opera*, X, 1-3, ed. E. Dekkers and J. Fraipont (Corpus Christianorum. Series Latina, 38-40), Turnhout 1956.

– *Epistulae*, in his *Opera*, II, 1-5, ed. A. Goldbacher (Corpus Scriptorum Ecclesiasticorum Latinorum, 34; 44; 57; 58), Prague, Vienna and Leipzig 1895-1923.

– *In Iohannis evangelium tractatus CXXIV*, in his *Opera*, VIII, ed. R. Willems (Corpus Christianorum. Series Latina, 36), Turnhout 1964.
– *In epistolam Joannis ad Parthos tractatus X* (*PL*, XXXV), Paris 1841, cols 1977-2062.
– *Sermones* (*PL*, XXXVIII), Paris 1865.
Aux origines de la liturgie dominicaine: le manuscrit Santa Sabina XIV L 1, ed. L. E. Boyle and P.-M. Gy, Paris and Rome 2004.
Bacon, Roger, *Compendium of the Study of Theology*, ed. and tr. T. S. Maloney, Leiden, New York, Copenhagen and Cologne 1988.
– *Compendium studii philosophiae*, in his *Opera quaedam*, pp. 393-519.
– *Opera quaedam hactenus inedita*, ed. J. S. Brewer, London 1859.
– *Opus majus*, ed. J. H. Bridges, 2 vols, Oxford 1897.
– *Opus minus*, in his *Opera quaedam*, pp. 313-389.
– *Opus tertium*, in his *Opera quaedam*, pp. 3-310.
Bataillon, Louis-Jacques, 'L'influence d'Hugues de Saint-Cher', in *Hugues de Saint-Cher*, pp. 497-502.
Bateson, Mary, *Catalogue of the Library of Syon Monastery, Isleworth*, Cambridge 1898.
Bauer, Erika, 'Hieronymus-Briefe', in *Die deutsche Literatur des Mittelalters: Verfasserlexikon*, ed. K. Ruh et al., III, Berlin and New York 1981, cols 1233-1238.
Bauer, Walter, *Griechisch-deutsches Wörterbuch zu den Schriften des Neuen Testaments und der frühchristlichen Literatur*, 6th edn, ed. B. and K. Aland, Berlin and New York 1988.
Becker, Hansjakob, '"Cartusia numquam reformata quia numquam deformata": Liturgiereformen bei den Kartäusern in Vergangenheit und Gegenwart', in *Liturgiereformen*, I, pp. 325-345.
Bede, The Venerable, *Homeliarum Evangelii libri II*, in his *Opera*, III-IV, ed. D. Hurst, Turnhout 1955.
– *In Marci evangelium expositio*, in his *Opera*, II, 3, ed. D. Hurst, Turnhout 1960, pp. 431-648.
– *Retractatio in Actus apostolorum*, in *Expositio Actuum apostolorum et Retractatio*, ed. M. L. W. Laistner, Cambridge (Mass.) 1939, pp. 93-146.
Bentley, Jerry H., *Humanists and Holy Writ. New Testament Scholarship in the Renaissance*, Princeton 1983.

Berger, Samuel, *De glossariis et compendiis exegeticis quibusdam medii aevi sive de libris Ansileubi Papiae Hugutionis Guill. Britonis de Catholicon Mammotrecto aliis dissertatio critica*, Paris 1879.
– *Histoire de la Vulgate pendant les premiers siècles du moyen âge*, Nancy 1893.
– *Les préfaces jointes aux livres de la Bible dans les manuscrits de la Vulgate*, Paris 1902.
– *Quam notitiam linguae hebraicae habuerint Christiani Medii Aevi temporibus in Gallia*, Paris, 1893.
Bernard of Clairvaux, *Sermo de festivitatibus sancti Stephani, sancti Ioannis et sanctorum Innocentium*, in his *Opera*, IV: *Sermones*, I, ed. J. Leclercq and H. Rochais, Rome 1966, pp. pp. 270-273.
Bessarion, Cardinal, *In illud Evangelii secundum Joannem:* ἐὰν αὐτὸν θέλω μένειν ἕως ἔρχομαι τί πρὸς σέ; *Si eum volo manere donec veniam, quid ad te?* (*Patrologia Graeca*, ed. J.-P. Migne, CLXI), Paris 1866, cols 623-640.
Bezner, Frank, 'Lorenzo Valla (1407-1457)', in *Lateinische Lehrer Europas: Fünfzehn Portraits von Varro bis Erasmus von Rotterdam*, ed. W. Ax, Cologne, Weimar and Vienna 2005, pp. 353-389.
La Bibbia del XIII secolo. Storia del testo, storia dell'esegesi. Convegno della Società Internazionale per lo Studio del Medioevo Latino (SISMEL). Firenze, 1-2 giugno 2001, ed. G. Cremascoli and F. Santi, Florence 2004.
La Bibbia 'Vulgata' dalle origini ai nostri giorni. Atti del simposio internazionale in onore di Sisto V, Grottammare, 29-31 agosto 1985, ed. T. Stramare, Rome and Vatican City 1987.
Biblia sacra iuxta vulgatam versionem, ed. R. Weber et al., 4th edn, Stuttgart 1994.
Black, Robert, *Humanism and Education in Medieval and Renaissance Italy. Tradition and Innovation in Latin Schools from the Twelfth to the Fifteenth Century*, Cambridge 2001.
Bogaert, Pierre-Maurice, 'Bulletin de la Bible latine', VIII, *Revue Bénédictine* 118 (2008), pp. 148-170.
– 'La Bible latine des origines au moyen âge: aperçu historique, état des questions', *Revue théologique de Louvain* 19 (1988), pp. 137-159 and 276-314.
– 'Les bibles d'Augustin', in *Saint Augustin et la Bible. Actes du colloque de l'université Paul Verlaine-Metz (7-8 Avril 2005)*, ed. G. Nauroy and M.-A. Vannier, Berne 2008, pp. 17-36.

Botley, Paul, *Latin Translation in the Renaissance: The Theory and Practice of Leonardo Bruni, Giannozzo Manetti and Desiderius Erasmus*, Cambridge 2004.
– *Learning Greek in Western Europe, 1369-1529: Grammars, Lexica and Classroom Texts*, Philadelphia 2010.
Brown, Francis, Driver, Samuel R., and Briggs, Charles A., *A Hebrew and English Lexicon of the Old Testament*, Oxford 1907, repr. 1972.
Burke, David G., 'The First Versions: the Septuagint, the Targums, and the Latin', in *A History of Bible Translation*, ed. P. A. Noss, Rome 2007, pp. 59-80.
Cabrol, Fernand, *Les livres de la liturgie latine*, [Paris] 1930.
Calo, Pietro, *Miracula sancti Dominici mandato magistri Berengarii collecta. Petri Calo legendae sancti Dominici*, ed. S. Tugwell, Rome 1997.
The Cambridge History of the Bible, II: *The West from the Fathers to the Reformation*, ed. G. W. H. Lampe, Cambridge 1969.
Camporeale, Salvatore I., *Lorenzo Valla: umanesimo e teologia*, Florence 1972.
Canones et decreta sacrosancti oecumenici Concilii Tridentini sub Paulo III. Iulio III. et Pio IV. pontificibus maximis: cum patrum subscriptionibus, Leipzig 1887.
Carra de Vaux, Bruno, 'La constitution du corpus exégétique', in *Hugues de Saint-Cher*, pp. 43-63.
Cassiodorus, *Expositio Psalmorum*, 2 vols, ed. M. Adriaen, Turnhout 1958.
– *Institutiones*, ed. R. A. B. Mynors, Oxford 1937.
Cauwe, Matthieu, 'La Bible d'Étienne Harding: principes de critique textuelle mis en œuvre aux livres de Samuel', *Revue Bénédictine* 103 (1993), pp. 414-444.
Cavallera, Ferdinand, *Saint Jérôme: sa vie et son oeuvre*, 2 vols, Louvain and Paris 1922.
Chartularium Universitatis Parisiensis, 4 vols, ed. H. Denifle, Paris 1889-1897, repr. Brussels 1964.
Chenu, Marie-Dominique, 'Grammaire et théologie aux XIIe et XIIIe siècles', *Archives d'histoire doctrinale et littéraire du moyen âge* 10 (1935), pp. 5-28.
– *La théologie au douzième siècle*, Paris 1966.
Courtenay, William J., 'The Bible in the Fourteenth Century: Some Observations', *Church History* 54 (1985), pp. 176-187.

Crastone, Giovanni, [Bi-lingual edition of the Psalms], Milan 1481 (copy used: London, British Library, shelfmark IB.26564).
– [Dedicatory letter to Ludovico Donato, Bishop of Bergamo, of his bi-lingual edition of the Psalms], in *Praefationes et epistolae editionibus princibus auctorum veterum praepositae*, ed. B. Botfield, Cambridge 1861, pp. 13-16.
Cyprian, *Epistularium*, in his *Opera*, III, 2, ed. G. F. Diercks, Turnhout 1996.
Dahan, Gilbert, 'La connaissance de l'hébreu dans les correctoires de la Bible du XIIIe siècle: notes préliminaires', *Revue théologique de Louvain* 23 (1992), pp. 178-190.
– 'La connaissance du grec dans les correctoires de la Bible du XIIIe siècle', in *Du copiste au collectionneur: Mélanges d'histoire des textes et des bibliothèques en l'honneur d'André Vernet*, ed. D. Nebbiai-dalla Guardia and J.-F. Genest, Turnhout 1998, pp. 89-109.
– 'La critique textuelle dans les correctoires de la Bible du XIIIe siècle', in *Langages et philosophie: hommage à Jean Jolivet*, ed. A. de Libera, A. Elamrani-Jamal, A. Galonnier, Paris 1997, pp. 365-392.
– 'La méthode critique dans l'étude de la Bible (XIIe-XIIIe siècles)', in *La méthode critique au moyen âge*, ed. M. Chazan and G. Dahan, Turnhout 2006, pp. 103-128.
– '*Sorbonne II*. Un correctoire biblique de la seconde moitié du XIIIe siècle', in *La Bibbia del XIII secolo*, pp. 113-153
– *L'exégèse chrétienne de la Bible en Occident médiéval: XIIe-XIVe siècle*, Paris 1999.
– *Les intellectuels chrétiens et les juifs au moyen âge*, Paris 1990.
Denifle, Heinrich, 'Die Handschriften der Bibel-Correctorien des 13. Jahrhunderts', *Archiv für Literatur- und Kirchengeschichte des Mittelalters* 4 (1888), pp. 263-311 and 471-601.
d'Esneval, Amaury, 'Le perfectionnement d'un instrument de travail au début du XIIe siècle: les trois glossaires bibliques d'Étienne Langton', in *Culture et travail intellectuel dans l'occident médiéval. Bilan des 'Colloques d'humanisme médiéval' [1960–1980] fondés par le R.P. Hubert, O.P.*, ed. G. Hasenohr and J. Longère, Paris 1981, pp. 163–175.
di Napoli, Giovanni, *Lorenzo Valla: filosofia e religione nell'umanesimo italiano*, Rome 1971.
Dizionario biografico degli italiani, Rome 1960- (= *DBI*).

Doležalová, Lucie, *Reception and its Varieties: Reading, Re-Writing, and Understanding Cena Cypriani in the Middle Ages*, Trier 2007.
Donatus, Aelius, *The 'Ars Minor' of Donatus: For One Thousand Years the Leading Textbook of Grammar*, ed. and tr. W. J. Chase, Madison 1926.
du Cange, Charles du Fresne, *Glossarium mediae et infimae latinitatis*, [no place] 1883-1887, 10 vols in 5, repr. Graz 1954.
Duchet-Suchaux, Monique, and Lefèvre, Yves, 'Les noms de la Bible', in *Le Moyen Age*, pp. 13-23.
Durand, William, *Rationale divinorum officiorum*, 3 vols, ed. A. Davril and T. M. Thibodeau, Turnhout 1995-2000.
Easton, Adam, *Defensorium ecclesiastice potestatis*, in MacFarlane, 'The Life and Writings of Adam Easton, O. S. B.', II, pp. 38-246.
Ederle, Guglielmo, *Dizionario cronologico bio-bibliografico dei vescovi di Verona. Cenni sulla Chiesa veronese*, Verona 1965.
Eissfeldt, Otto, *Einleitung in das Alte Testament*, 3rd edn, Tübingen 1964.
Elliott, J. K., 'The Translations of the New Testament into Latin: The Old Latin and the Vulgate', in *Aufstieg und Niedergang der römischen Welt. Geschichte und Kultur Roms im Spiegel der neueren Forschung*, II, 26, 1, ed. W. Haase, Berlin and New York 1992, pp. 198-245.
Encyclopaedia judaica, 16 vols, Jerusalem 1971-2.
Epistolae Karolini Aevi, II, (*Monumenta Germaniae Historica, Epistolae* IV) ed. E. Dümmler, Berlin 1895, repr. Munich 1978.
Evans, Gillian R., *The Language and Logic of the Bible: The Earlier Middle Ages*, Cambridge 1984.
The Evolution of the Carthusian Statutes from the 'Consuetudines Guigonis' to the 'Tertia Compilatio', 6 vols, ed. J. Hogg, Salzburg 1989-1992.
Fischer, Bonifatius, 'Bibelausgaben des frühen Mittelalters', in *La Bibbia nell'alto medioevo: 26 aprile – 2 maggio 1962*, Spoleto 1963, pp. 519-600.
– 'Bibeltext und Bibelreform unter Karl dem Großen', in *Karl der Große: Lebenswerk und Nachleben*, II: *Das geistige Leben*, ed. B. Bischoff, Düsseldorf 1965, pp. 156-216.
– 'Der Vulgata-Text des Neuen Testaments', in his *Beiträge zur Geschichte der lateinischen Bibeltexte*, Freiburg i. Br., 1986, pp. 51-73.

- 'Zur Überlieferung altlateinischer Bibeltexte im Mittelalter', *Nederlands Archief voor Kerkgeschiedenis* 56 (1975), pp. 19-34.
- *Die Alkuin-Bibel*, Freiburg i. Br. 1957.

FitzRalph, Richard, *Summa ... in Questionibus Armenorum*, ed. J. Sudoris, [Paris] 1512. (copy used: London, British Library, shelfmark 4373.k.1)

Fois, Mario, *Il pensiero cristiano di Lorenzo Valla nel quadro storico-culturale del suo ambiente*, Rome 1969.

Frede, Hermann Josef, 'Bibelzitate bei Kirchenvätern. Beobachtungen bei der Herausgabe der *Vetus Latina*', in *La Bible et les Pères. Colloque de Strasbourg (1er-3 octobre 1969)*, Paris 1971, pp. 79-96.

Freudenberger, Theobald, *Augustinus Steuchus aus Gubbio, Augustinerchorherr und päpstlicher Bibliothekar (1497-1548) und sein literarisches Lebenswerk*, Münster i. W. 1935.

Fubini, Riccardo, 'Una sconosciuta testimonianza manoscritta delle *Annotationes in Novum Testamentum* del Valla', in *Lorenzo Valla e l'umanesimo italiano. Atti del convegno internazionale di studi umanistici (Parma, 18-19 ottobre 1984)*, ed. O. Besomi and M. Regoliosi, Padua 1986, pp. 179-196.

Fürst, Alfons, *Hieronymus: Askese und Wissenschaft in der Spätantike*, Freiburg i. Br. 2003.

Garofalo, Salvatore, 'Gli umanisti italiani del secolo XV e la Bibbia', *Biblica* 27 (1946), pp. 338-375.

Gasquet, Francis Aidan, 'Roger Bacon and the Latin Vulgate', in *Roger Bacon: Essays Contributed by Various Writers on the Occasion of the Commemoration of the Seventh Centenary of His Birth*, ed. A. G. Little, Oxford 1914, pp. 89-99.

George of Trebizond, *Adversus Theodorum Gazam in perversionem Problematum Aristotelis*, in Ludwig Mohler, *Kardinal Bessarion als Theologe, Humanist und Staatsmann. Funde und Forschungen*, III: *Aus Bessarions Gelehrtenkreis. Abhandlungen, Reden, Briefe von Bessarion, Theodoros Gazes, Michael Apostolios, Andronikos Kallistos, Georgios Trapezuntios, Niccolò Perotti, Niccolò Capranica*, ed. L. Mohler, Paderborn 1942, repr. Aalen and Paderborn 1967, pp. 277-342.
- *In expositionem illius textus evangelii 'Sic volo eum manere, etc' et quod S. Joannes Evangelista nondum sit mortuus ad Sixtum IV pontificem maximum* (*Patrologia Graeca*, ed. J.-P. Migne, CLXI), Paris 1866, cols 867-882.

Gerard of Huy, [Preface to his *correctorium*], ed. Denifle, 'Die Handschriften', pp. 298-310.
Gibson, Margaret, *The Bible in the Latin West*, Notre Dame and London 1993.
– 'Priscian, "Institutiones grammaticae": A Handlist of Manuscripts', *Scriptorium* 26 (1972), pp. 105-124
Gill, Joseph, *The Council of Florence*, Cambridge 1959.
Glunz, Hans, *Britannien und Bibeltext: Der Vulgatatext der Evangelien in seinem Verhältnis zur irisch-angelsächsichen Kultur des Frühmittelalters*, Leipzig 1930.
– *History of the Vulgate in England from Alcuin to Roger Bacon: Being an Inquiry into the Text of Some English Manuscripts of the Vulgate Gospels*, Cambridge 1933.
Graf, Georg, *Geschichte der christlichen arabischen Literatur*, 5 vols, Vatican City 1944-1953.
Grafton, Anthony, and Williams, Megan, *Christianity and the Transformation of the Book: Origen, Eusebius, and the Library of Caesarea*, Cambridge (Mass.) and London 2006.
Grafton, Anthony, *Joseph Scaliger: A Study in the History of Classical Scholarship*, I: *Textual Criticism and Exegesis*, Oxford 1983.
Gramáticas latinas de transición: Juan de Pastrana, Fernando Nepote, ed. C. Codoñer, Salamanca 2000.
Gratian, *Decretum Magistri Gratiani*, in *Corpus iuris canonici*, I, ed. E. Friedberg, Graz 1959.
Graves, Michael, *Jerome's Hebrew Philology: A Study Based on his Commentary on Jeremiah*, Leiden 2007.
Gray, Hanna H., 'Valla's *Encomium of St. Thomas Aquinas* and the Humanist Conception of Christian Antiquity', in *Essays in History and Literature Presented by Fellows of the Newberry Library to Stanley Pargellis*, ed. H. Bluhm, Chicago 1965, pp. 37-51.
Gregory the Great, *Epistola ad Leandrum*, in his *Moralia in Iob*, I, pp. 1-7.
– *Moralia in Iob*, ed. M. Adriaen, 3 vols, Turnhout 1979-1985.
Gribomont, Jean, 'Aux origines de la Vulgate', in *La Bibbia 'Vulgata'*, pp. 11-20.
– 'Critique des lettrés et des philologues', in *La Bibbia 'Vulgata'*, pp. 137-143.
Hailperin, Herman, 'The Hebrew Heritage of Mediaeval Christian Biblical Scholarship', *Historia judaica* 5 (1943), pp. 133-154.

Hamilton, Alastair, 'Humanists and the Bible', in *The Cambridge Companion to Renaissance Humanism*, ed. J. Kraye, Cambridge 1996, pp. 100-117.
Hamm, Berndt, 'Hieronymus-Begeisterung und Augustinismus vor der Reformation. Beobachtungen zur Beziehung zwischen Humanismus und Frömmigkeitstheologie (am Beispiel Nürnbergs)', in *Augustine, the Harvest, and Theology (1300-1650): Essays Dedicated to Heiko Augustinus Oberman in Honor of his Sixtieth Birthday*, ed. K. Hagen, Leiden, New York, Copenhagen and Cologne 1990, pp. 127-235.
Harding, Stephen, *Monitum*, in Cauwe, 'La Bible d'Étienne Harding', pp. 416-417.
Heiric of Auxerre, *Homiliae per circulum anni*, 3 vols, ed. R. Quadri, Turnhout 1992-1994.
Hervaeus of Bourg-Dieu, *Commentaria in Epistolas divi Pauli* (*PL*, CLXXXI), Paris 1851, cols 591-1692.
– *Commentaria in Isaiam* (*PL*, CLXXXI), Paris 1851, cols 18-592.
– *De correctione quarundam lectionum*, ed. Morin, 'Un critique', pp. 39-60.
Highfield, J. R. L., 'The Jeronimites in Spain, their Patrons and Success, 1373-1516', *The Journal of Ecclesiastical History* 34 (1983), pp. 513-533.
Hody, Humphrey, *De bibliorum textibus originalibus versionibus Graecis et Latina Vulgata libri IV*, Oxford 1705.
The Holy Bible. Translated from the Latin Vulgate, London 2003.
Horace, *Ars poetica*, in his *Opera*, ed. D. R. Shackleton Bailey, Stuttgart 1985, pp. 310-329.
Houghton, Hugh, *Augustine's Text of St John*, Oxford 2008.
Hrabanus Maurus, *Expositio super Jeremiam prophetam* (*PL*, CXI), Paris 1852, cols 793-1272.
Hugues de Saint-Cher († 1263), bibliste et théologien, ed. L.-J. Bataillon, G. Dahan and P.-M. Guy, Turnhout 2004.
Hugh of St Cher, *Correctio Biblie*, MSS Paris, Bibliothèque de l'Arsenal, 94; and Paris, BNF, lat. 3218, ff. 137^r-161^r.
– [Preface to his *Correctio Biblie*], ed. Dahan, 'La critique textuelle', pp. 386-387.
Hugh of St Victor, *De scripturis et scriptoribus sacris* (*PL*, CLXXV), Paris 1879, cols 9-28.
– *Didascalicon de studio legendi. A Critical Text*, ed. C. H. Buttimer, Washington D. C. 1939.

Hulley, Karl Kelchner, 'Principles of Textual Criticism Known to Jerome', *Harvard Studies in Classical Philology* 55 (1944), pp. 87-109.
Hümpfner, Tiburtius, 'Die Bibel des hl. Stephan Harding', *Cistercienser-Chronik* 29 (1917), pp. 73-81.
Isidore of Seville, *De ecclesiasticis officiis*, ed. C. M. Lawson, Turnhout 1989.
– *Etymologiae*, ed. W. M. Lindsay, 2 vols, Oxford 1911, repr. 1962.
Ivo of Chartres, *Decretum* (*PL*, CLXI), Paris 1889, cols 47-1022.
James, M. R., *The Ancient Libraries of Canterbury and Dover: The Catalogues of the Libraries of Christ Church Priory and St. Augustine's Abbey at Canterbury and of St. Martin's Priory at Dover*, Cambridge 1903.
Jeauneau, Édouard, 'Deux rédactions des gloses de Guillaume de Conches sur Priscien', *Recherches de Théologie ancienne et médiévale* 27 (1960), pp. 212-247.
Jedin, Hubert, *Geschichte des Konzils von Trient*, II: *Die erste Trienter Tagungsperiode 1545/7*, Freiburg i. Br. 1957.
Jellicoe, Sidney, *The Septuagint and Modern Study*, Oxford 1968.
Jenkins, Allan K., and Preston, Patrick, *Biblical Scholarship and the Church: A Sixteenth-Century Crisis of Authority*, Aldershot 2007.
Jerome, *Commentarii in Epistulam Pauli Apostoli ad Galatas*, ed. G. Raspanti, Turnhout 2006.
– *Commentarii in Esaiam*, 2 vols, in his *Opera*, I: *Opera exegetica*, 2, ed. M. Adriaen, Turnhout 1963.
– *Commentarii in prophetas minores*, 2 vols, in his *Opera*, I: *Opera exegetica*, 6, ed. M. Adriaen, Turnhout 1969-1970.
– *Commentarius in Ecclesiasten*, ed. M. Adriaen, in his *Opera*, I: *Opera exegetica*, I, Turnhout 1959, pp. 249-361.
– and Gennadius, *De viris inlustribus*, ed. C. A. Bernoulli, Freiburg i. Br. and Leipzig 1895, repr. Frankfurt a. M. 1968.
– *De viris inlustribus*, ed. W. Herding, Leipzig 1879.
– *Dialogus adversus Pelagianos*, in his *Opera*, III: *Opera polemica*, 2, ed. C. Moreschini, Turnhout 1990.
– *Die Chronik des Hieronymus. Hieronymi Chronicon*, in Eusebius, *Werke*, VII, ed. R. Helm, Berlin 1956.
– *Epistulae*, 4 vols, ed. I. Hilberg and M. Kamptner, 2nd edn, Vienna 1996.
– *Hebraicae quaestiones in libro Geneseos*, ed. P. de Lagarde, in his *Opera*, I: *Opera exegetica* 1, Turnhout 1959, pp. 1-56.

- 'In Abacuc Prophetam', in his *Commentarii in prophetas minores*, II, pp. 579-654.
- 'In Ionam prophetam', in his *Commentarii in prophetas minores*, I, pp. 377-419.
- 'In Michaeam prophetam', in his *Commentarii in prophetas minores*, I, pp. 421-524.
- *Liber interpretationis hebraicorum nominum*, ed. P. de Lagarde, in his *Opera*, I: *Opera exegetica*, 1, Turnhout 1959, pp. 59-161.
- 'Praefatio in Evangelio', in *Biblia sacra*, pp. 1515-1516.
- 'Praefatio in libro Psalmorum', in *Biblia sacra*, p. 767.
- 'Prologus in Danihele propheta', in *Biblia sacra*, pp. 1341-1342
- 'Prologus in libro Iob', in *Biblia sacra*, pp. 731-732.
- 'Prologus in libro Regum', in *Biblia sacra*, pp. 364-366.
- 'Prologus in Pentateucho', in *Biblia sacra*, pp. 3-4
- 'Prologus Iudith', in *Biblia sacra*, p. 691.
- 'Prologus Tobiae', in *Biblia sacra*, p. 676.
- *Tractatus in librum Psalmorum*, in his *Opera*, II: *Opera homiletica*, ed. G. Morin, Turnhout 1958, pp. 3-447.

The Jerusalem Bible, ed. A. Jones, London 1966.

[John of Neumarkt], *Schriften Johanns von Neumarkt*, II, ed. J. Klapper, Berlin 1932.

Josephus, *Antiquitates*, ed. F. Blatt, *The Latin Josephus*, I: *Introduction and Text. The Antiquities: Book I-V*, Aarhus 1958.

Jungblut, Renate, *Hieronymus: Darstellung und Verehrung eines Kirchenvaters*, Bamberg 1967.

Juvenal, *Saturae*, ed. J. Willis, Stuttgart and Leipzig 1997.

Kaeppeli, Thomas, and Panella, Emilio, *Scriptores Ordinis Praedicatorum Medii Aevii*, 4 vols, Rome 1970-1993.

Kaulen, Franz, *Geschichte der Vulgata*, Mainz 1868.

Kelly, John Norman Davidson, *Jerome: His Life, Writings and Controversies*, London 1975.

Ker, Neil Ripley, *Medieval Manuscripts in British Libraries*, I: *London*, Oxford 1969.

Klapper, Joseph, 'Aus der Frühzeit des Humanismus. Dichtungen zu Ehren des hl. Hieronymus', in *Bausteine. Festschrift Max Koch zum 70. Geburtstage dargebracht*, ed. E. Boehlich and H. Heckel, Wroclaw 1926, pp. 255-281.

- *Johann von Neumarkt: Bischof und Hofkanzler. Religiöse Frührenaissance in Böhmen zur Zeit Kaiser Karls IV.*, Leipzig 1964.

Klauser, Theodor, *A Short History of the Western Liturgy*, London, New York and Toronto, 1969.
Kristeller, Paul Oskar, *Iter Italicum. A Finding List of Uncatalogued or Incompletely Catalogued Humanistic Manuscripts of the Renaissance in Italian and Other Libraries*, II: *Italy. Orvieto to Volterra.* Vatican City, London and Leiden 1967.
Labowsky, Lotte, *Bessarion's Library and the Biblioteca Marciana. Six Early Inventories*, Rome 1979.
Lang, Albert, *Heinrich Totting von Oyta: Ein Beitrag zur Entstehungsgeschichte der ersten deutschen Universitäten und zur Problemgeschichte der Spätscholastik*, Münster i. W. 1937.
Lexikon des Mittelalters, 9 vols and *Registerband*, Munich 1980-1999 (= *LexMA*).
Libru di lu transitu et vita di misser sanctu Iheronimu, ed. C. di Girolamo, Palermo 1982.
Light, Laura, 'French Bibles c. 1200-30: A New Look at the Origin of the Paris Bible', in *The Early Medieval Bible. Its Production, Decoration and Use*, ed. R. Gameson, Cambridge 1994, pp. 155-176.
– 'The New Thirteenth-Century Bible and the Challenge of Heresy', *Viator* 18 (1987), pp. 275-288.
– 'Versions et révisions du texte biblique', in *Le Moyen Age et la Bible*, pp. 55-93.
Linde, J. Cornelia, '"Augustine" versus Jerome: Commentaries on Gratian's *Decretum*, D. 9, c.6, from Paucapalea to Juan de Torquemada', *Tijdschrift voor Rechtsgeschiedenis* 77 (2009), pp. 367-384.
Liturgiereformen. Historische Studien zu einem bleibenden Grundzug des christlichen Gottesdienstes, I: *Biblische Modelle und Liturgiereformen von der Frühzeit bis zur Aufklärung*, ed. M. Klöckener and B. Kranemann, Münster i. W. 2002.
Livy, *Ab urbe condita*, II, ed. C. F. Walters and R. S. Conway, Oxford 1951.
– *Ab urbe condita*, V, ed. A. H. McDonald, Oxford 1965.
Lobrichon, Guy, 'Les éditions de la Bible latine dans les universités du XIIIe siècle', in *La Bibbia del XIII secolo*, pp. 15-34.
– 'Les traductions médiévales de la Bible dans l'Occident latin', in *Biblia. Les Bibles en latin au temps des Réformes*, ed. M.-C. Gomez-Géraud, Paris 2008, pp. 19-36.
– *La Bible au moyen âge*, Paris 2003.

Loewe, Raphael, 'The Medieval History of the Latin Vulgate', in *The Cambridge History of the Bible*, II, pp. 102-154.

Lubac, Henri de, *Exégèse médiévale: Les quatre sens de l'Écriture*, 4 vols, [Paris] 1959-1964.

Macer Floridus, *De viribus herbarum*, ed. L. Choulant, Leipzig 1823.

MacFarlane, Leslie John, 'The Life and Writings of Adam Easton, O. S. B.', unpublished PhD thesis, 2 vols, University of London 1955.

Mancini, Girolamo, *Vita di Lorenzo Valla*, Florence 1891.

Manetti, Giannozzo, *Apologeticus*, ed. A. de Petris, Rome 1981.

Maniacutia, Nicolò, [Preface to his *Suffraganeus bibliothece*], in Denifle, 'Die Handschriften', pp. 270-276.

– [Preface to the *Psalterium iuxta Hebraeos*], ed. Weber, 'Deux préfaces', pp. 9-14.

– [Preface to the *Psalterium Romanum*], ed. Weber, 'Deux préfaces', pp. 6-7.

– *Libellus de corruptione et correptione Psalmorum et aliarum quarundam scripturarum*, ed. Peri, '"Correctores"', pp. 88-125.

– *Suffraganeus bibliothece*, in MS Brussels, Bibliothèque royale, 4031-33, ff. 1^r–32^v.

– *Versus ad incorrupta pontificum nomina conservanda, ne videlicet dicamus Eleutherius pro Eleuther et Ylarius pro Ylarus, et ad sciendum, qui sunt antiquiores*, ed. Schmidinger, 'Das Papstgedicht', pp. 103-109.

[Maniacutia, Nicolò], *S. Eusebii Hieronymi incomparabilis Ecclesiae Christi doctoris, et eximiae sanctitatis viri vita ex ipsius praesertim syngrammatis, e sanctorum item Augustini, Damasi, Gregorii, Gelasii, aliorumque aliquot collecta tractatibus* (*PL*, XXII), Paris 1854, cols 183-202.

March, Josep M., 'En Ramon Martí y la seva "Explanatio simboli Apostolorum"', *Anuari de l'Institut d'Estudis Catalans* 2 (1908), pp. 443-496.

Martí, Ramon, *Capistrum Iudeorum*, 2 vols, ed. A. Robles Sierra, Würzburg 1990-1993.

– *Explanatio simboli Apostolorum*, ed. March, 'En Ramon Martí', pp. 450-496.

– *Pugio fidei adversus Mauros et Judaeos*, Leipzig 1687, repr. Farnborough 1967.

Martin, J. P. P., 'Le texte parisien de la Vulgate latine' [I] *Le Muséon* 8 (1889), pp. 444-466.

- 'Le texte parisien de la Vulgate latine' [II], *Le Muséon* 9 (1890), pp. 55-70 and 301-316.
- 'La Vulgate latine au treizième siècle, d'après Roger Bacon', *Le Muséon* 7 (1888), pp. 88-107; pp. 169-196; pp. 278-291; pp. 381-393.

McManamon, John M., 'Pier Paolo Vergerio (the Elder) and the Beginnings of the Humanist Cult of Jerome', *The Catholic Historical Review* 71 (1985), pp. 353-371.

Meiss, Millard, 'Scholarship and Penitence in the Early Renaissance: The Image of St. Jerome', *Pantheon* 32 (1974), pp. 134-140.

Modona, Leonello, *Catalogo dei codici ebraici della biblioteca della R. Università di Bologna*, in *Cataloghi dei codici orientali di alcune biblioteche d'Italia*, IV, Florence 1889, pp. 323-372.

Mohler, Ludwig, 'Kardinal Bessarions kritische Untersuchung der Vulgatastelle: "Sic eum volo manere, quid ad te?"', *Römische Quartalschrift für christliche Altertumskunde und für Kirchengeschichte* 41 (1933), pp. 189-206.

- *Kardinal Bessarion als Theologe, Humanist und Staatsmann. Funde und Forschungen*, 3 vols, Paderborn 1923-1942.

Mohrmann, Christine, 'Le dualisme de la latinité médiévale', *Revue des études latines* 29 (1951), pp. 330-348.

Monfasani, John, *George of Trebizond: A Biography and a Study of his Rhetoric and Logic*, Leiden 1976.

Montfaucon, Bernard de, *Diarium Italicum sive monumentorum veterum, bibliothecarum, musaeorum, et c. notitiae singulares in Itinerario Italico collectae*, Paris 1702.

Morin, Germain, 'Un critique en liturgie au XIIe siècle. Le traité inédit d'Hervé de Bourgdieu *De correctione quarundam lectionum*', *Revue Bénédictine* 24 (1907), pp. 36-61.

Morisi Guerra, Anna, 'La leggenda di San Girolamo: temi e problemi tra Umanesimo e Controriforma', *Clio* 23 (1987), pp. 5-33.

Morisi, Anna, 'A proposito di due redazioni della *Collatio Novi Testamenti* di Lorenzo Valla', *Bullettino dell'Istituto storico italiano per il medio evo e archivio muratoriano* 78 (1967), pp. 345-375.

- 'La filologia neotestamentaria di Lorenzo Valla', *Nuova rivista storica* 48 (1964), pp. 35-49.

Le Moyen Age et la Bible, ed. P. Riché and G. Lobrichon, Paris 1984.

Müller, Sascha, *Richard Simon (1638-1712): Exeget, Theologe, Philosoph und Historiker. Eine Biographie*, Würzburg [2005].

Mutius, Hans-Georg von, *Die hebräischen Bibelzitate beim englischen Scholastiker Odo: Versuch einer Revaluation*, Frankfurt a. M. and Oxford 2006.

Nepote, Fernando, *Materies*, in *Gramáticas latinas*, pp. 89-147.

Nogarola, Isotta, *In beati Hieronymi laudem oratio*, in her *Opera quae supersunt omnia*, ed. A. Apponyi and E. Abel, 2 vols, Vienna and Budapest 1886, II, pp. 276-289.

Notabilia quedam de correctione librorum, in Oswaldus de Corda, *Opus pacis*, pp. 84-89.

Novum Testamentum Graece, ed. E. Nestle et al., 27th edn, Stuttgart 2004.

Olin, John C., 'Erasmus and Saint Jerome', *Thought* 54 (1979), pp. 313-321.

Oswaldus de Corda, *Opus pacis*, ed. B. A. Egan, Turnhout 2001.

Ouy, Gilbert, 'Le *Valdebonum* perdu et retrouvé', *Scriptorium* 42 (1988), pp. 198-203.

Oxford Dictionary of National Biography. From the Earliest Time to the Year 2000, 61 vols, ed. H. C. G. Matthew and B. Harrison, Oxford 2004 (= *ODNB*).

Pantin, William A., 'The *Defensorium* of Adam Easton', *The English Historical Review* 51 (1936), pp. 675-680.

Paschasius Radbertus, *Expositio in Psalmum XLIV*, ed. B. Paulus, Turnhout 1991.

Passalacqua, Marina, *I codici di Prisciano*, Rome 1978.

Patriarch im Abendland. Beiträge zur Geschichten des Papsttums, Roms und Aquileias im Mittelalter. Ausgewählte Aufsätze von Heinrich Schmidinger. Festgabe zu seinem 70. Geburtstag, ed. H. Dopsch, H. Koller and P. F. Kramml, Salzburg 1986.

Peri, Vittorio, '"Correctores immo corruptores". Un saggio di critica testuale nella Roma del XII secolo', *Italia medioevale e umanistica* 20 (1977), pp. 19-125.

– 'Notizia su Nicola Maniacutia, autore ecclesiastico romano del xii secolo', *Aevum* 36 (1962), pp. 534-538.

Peter Comestor, *Scolastica historia: Liber Genesis*, ed. A. Sylwan, Turnhout 2005.

Peter Lombard, *In epistolam ad Romanos* (*PL*, CXCI), Paris 1880, cols 1297-1534.

Peter of Ailly, *Apologeticus*, ed. Tschackert, *Peter von Ailli*, pp. [50]-[51].

– *Epistola ad novos Hebraeos*, ed. Tschackert, *Peter von Ailli*, pp. [7]-[12].
Petitmengin, Pierre, 'Les plus anciens manuscrits de la Bible latine', in *Le monde latin antique et la Bible*, ed. J. Fontaine and C. Pietri, Paris 1985, pp. 89-127.
Petrarch, *De otio religioso*, in his *Opere latine*, 2 vols, ed. A. Bufano, Turin 1975, I, pp. 568-809.
– *Le familiari*, I, 1, ed. and tr. U. Dotti, Urbino 1974.
Phocas, *Ars de nomine et verbo*, in *Grammatici latini*, V, ed. H. Keil, Hildesheim 1961, pp. 410-439.
Poggio Bracciolini, *Invectivae in L. Vallam*, in his *Opera omnia*, 4 vols, Basel 1538, repr. Turin 1964-1969, I, pp. 188-251.
Poncelet, Albert, 'Le légendier de Pierre Calo', *Analecta Bollandiana* 29 (1910), pp. 5-116.
Pope, Marvin H., *Job*, 3rd edn, Garden City 1973.
Priscian, *Institutiones grammaticae*, 2 vols, ed. M. Hertz, in *Grammatici latini*, II-III, Hildesheim 1961.
Ps.-Augustine, *De magnificentiis beati Hieronymi* (*PL*, XXII), Paris 1854, cols 281-289.
Ps.-Cyril of Jerusalem, *De miraculis Hieronymi* (*PL*, XXII), Paris 1854, cols 289-326.
Ps.-Eusebius of Cremona, *De morte Hieronymi* (*PL*, XXII), Paris 1854, cols 239-282.
Quentin, Henri, *Mémoire sur l'établissement du texte de la Vulgate*, I: *Octateuque*, Rome and Paris 1922.
Ralph of Beauvais, *Glose super Donatum*, ed. C. H. Kneepkens, Nijmegen 1982.
Rebenich, Stefan, 'Jerome: The "Vir trilinguis" and the "Hebraica veritas"', *Vigiliae christianae* 47 (1993), pp. 50-77.
Resnick, Irven M., 'The Falsification of Scripture and Medieval Christian and Jewish Polemics', *Medieval Encounters* 2 (1996), pp. 344-380.
Rice, Eugene F., *Saint Jerome in the Renaissance*, Baltimore and London 1985.
Rizzo, Silvia, *Il lessico filologico degli umanisti*, Rome 1973.
Rosenthal, Frank, 'Heinrich von Oyta and Biblical Criticism in the Fourteenth Century', *Speculum* 25 (1950), pp. 178-183.
Rouse, Mary A. and Richard H., 'Correction and Emendation of Texts in the Fifteenth Century and the Autograph of the *Opus Pacis* by "Oswaldus Anglicus"', in *Scire litteras. Forschungen zum*

mittelalterlichen Geistesleben, ed. S. Krämer and M. Bernhard, Munich 1988, pp. 333-346.

Rufinus, *Die 'Summa Decretorum' des Magister Rufinus*, ed. H. Singer, Paderborn 1902.

Rufinus of Aquileia, *Apologia contra Hieronymum*, in his *Opera*, ed. M. Simonetti, Turnhout 1961, pp. 37-123.

Rupert of Deutz, *De sancta trinitate et operibus eius*, ed. H. Haacke, 4 vols, Turnhout 1971-1972.

Salembier, Louis, *Le Cardinal Pierre d'Ailly: Chancelier de l'Université de Paris, Évêque du Puy et Cambrai, 1350-1420*, Tourcoing 1932.

– *Petrus ab Alliaco*, Lille 1886.

Salutati, Coluccio, *De fato et fortuna*, 2, 6, ed. Rizzo, *Il lessico filologico*, pp. 342-344.

Sargent, Michael G., 'The Problem of Uniformity in Carthusian Book Production from the *Opus pacis* to the *Tertia Compilatio Statutorum*', in *New Science out of Old Books: Studies in Manuscripts and Early Printed Books in Honour of A. I. Doyle*, ed. R. Beadle and A. J. Piper, Aldershot 1995, pp. 122-141.

Sbaraglia, Giovanni Giacinto, *Supplementum et castigatio ad scriptores trium ordinum S. Francisci*, 3 vols, Rome 1908-1936, repr. Bologna 1978.

Schmidinger, Heinrich, 'Das Papstgedicht des Nicolaus Maniacutius', in *Patriarch im Abendland*, pp. 99-109.

– 'Nicolaus Maniacutius (Maniacoria) und sein Papstgedicht', in *Patriarch im Abendland*, pp. 47-60.

Schmitt, Charles B., *Aristotle and the Renaissance*, Cambridge (Mass.) and London 1983.

Schneider, Heinrich, *Der Text der Gutenbergbibel zu ihrem 500jährigen Jubiläum untersucht*, Bonn 1954.

Sedulius Scotus, *Collectaneum in Apostolum*, I: *In epistolam ad Romanos*, ed. H. J. Frede and H. Stanjek, Freiburg i. Br. 1996.

Seneca the Younger, *Ad Lucilium epistulae morales*, ed. O. Hense, Leipzig 1898.

Septuaginta: id est Vetus Testamentum graece iuxta LXX interpretes, 2 vols, ed. A. Rahlfs, 3rd edn, Stuttgart 1949.

Sharpe, Richard, *A Handlist of the Latin Writers of Great Britain and Ireland Before 1540*, Turnhout 1997.

Simon, Richard, *Histoire critique des principaux commentateurs du Nouveau Testament...*, Rotterdam 1693.

– *Histoire critique des versions du Nouveau Testament...*, Rotterdam 1690.
– *Histoire critique du Vieux Testament. Suivi de Lettre sur l'inspiration*, ed. P. Gibert, Paris 2008.
Smalley, Beryl, *English Friars and Antiquity in the Early Fourteenth Century*, Oxford 1960.
– 'John Russel O. F. M.', *Recherches de Théologie ancienne et médiévale* 23 (1956), pp. 277-320.
– *The Study of the Bible in the Middle Ages*, Oxford 1941, 3rd edition Oxford 1983, repr. Oxford 1984.
Spicq, Ceslas, *Esquisse d'une histoire de l'exégèse latine au moyen âge*, Paris 1944.
The 'Statuta Jancelini' (1222) and the 'De Reformatione' of Prior Bernard (1248), ed. J. Hogg, vol. 2: *The MS. Grande Chartreuse 1 Stat. 23*, Salzburg 1978.
Stegmüller, Friedrich, *Repertorium biblicum medii aevi*, 11 vols, Madrid 1940-1980.
Stummer, Friedrich, *Einführung in die lateinische Bibel: Ein Handbuch für Vorlesungen und Selbstunterricht*, Paderborn 1928.
Stupperich, Robert, 'Schriftauslegung und Textkritik bei Laurentius Valla', in *Text – Wort – Glaube: Studien zur Überlieferung, Interpretation und Autorisierung biblischer Texte. Kurt Aland gewidmet*, ed. M. Brecht, Berlin and New York 1980, pp. 220-233.
Süss, Wilhelm, *Studien zur lateinischen Bibel*, I: *Augustins Locutiones und das Problem der lateinischen Bibelsprache*, Tartu 1932.
Sutcliffe, E. F., 'Jerome', in *The Cambridge History of the Bible*, II, pp. 80-101.
– 'The Name "Vulgate"', *Biblica* 29 (1948), pp. 345-352.
Swete, Henry Barclay, *An Introduction to the Old Testament in Greek*, Cambridge 1900.
Tertullian, *Adversus Marcionem*, ed. E. Kroymann, in his *Opera*, I, Turnhout 1954, pp. 441-726.
Thomas Aquinas, *Catena aurea in quatuor evangelia*, 2 vols, Turin 1925.
– *Summa theologiae*, II, ed. B. de Rubeis, C.-R. Billuart and X. Faucher, Turin 1950.
Thorndike, Lynn, 'The True Roger Bacon, I', *The American Historical Review* 21 (1916), pp. 237-257.

Thurot, Charles, *Notices et extraits de divers manuscrits latins pour servir à l'histoire des doctrines grammaticales au moyen âge*, Paris 1874.
Totting of Oyta, Henry, *Quaestio de Sacra Scriptura*, ed. A. Lang, Münster i. W. 1932.
Translatio corporis S. Hieronymi (*PL*, XXII), Paris 1854, cols 237-240.
Trinkaus, Charles, *In Our Image and Likeness: Humanity and Divinity in Italian Humanist Thought*, 2 vols, London 1970.
Tschackert, Paul, *Peter von Ailli (Petrus de Alliaco). Zur Geschichte des grossen abendländischen Schisma und der Reformconcilien von Pisa und Constanz*, Gotha 1877.
Unruh, Benjamin, *Die Kommentare des Herveus Burgidolensis*, Heilbronn 1909.
Unterkircher, Franz, *Die datierten Handschriften der Österreichischen Nationalbibliothek von 1401 bis 1450*, in *Katalog der datierten Handschriften in lateinischer Schrift in Österreich*, II, 2 vols, Vienna 1971.
Uttenweiler, Justinus, 'Zur Stellung des hl. Hieronymus im Mittelalter', *Benediktinische Monatschrift* 2 (1920), pp. 522-541.
Vaccari, Alberto, 'I salteri di s. Girolamo e di s. Agostino', in his *Scritti*, I, pp. 207-255.
– 'Le antiche vite di s. Girolamo', in his *Scritti*, II, pp. 31-51.
– *Scritti di erudizione e di filologia*, 2 vols, Rome 1952-1958.
Valentinelli, Giuseppe, *Bibliotheca Manuscripta ad S. Marci Venetiarum*, IV, Venice 1871.
Valla, Lorenzo, *Annotationes in Novum Testamentum*, in his *Opera*, I, pp. 803-895.
– *Antidotum in Pogium*, IV, in his *Opera*, I, pp. 325-366.
– *Antidotum primum. La prima apologia contro Poggio Bracciolini*, ed. A. Wesseling, Assen and Amsterdam 1978.
– *Collatio Novi Testamenti*, ed. A. Perosa, Florence 1970.
– *De linguae latinae elegantia*, ed. and tr. S. López Moreda, 2 vols, Cáceres 1999.
– *De reciprocatione 'sui' et 'suus'*, ed. E. Sandström, Gothenburg 1998.
– *Epistole*, ed. O. Besomi and M. Regoliosi, Padua 1984.
– *In errores Antonii Raudensis adnotationes*, in his *Opera*, I, pp. 390-438.
– *Opera omnia*, I, Basel 1540, reprint Turin 1962.

Van Damme, Jean-Baptiste, *The Three Founders of Cîteaux: Robert of Molesme – Alberic – Stephen Harding*, tr. N. Groves and C. Carr, Kalamazoo (MI) and Spencer (MA) 1998, pp. 71-128.
van den Abeele, Baudouin, 'The *Macrologus* of Liège: An Encyclopedic Lexicon at the Dawn of Humanism', in *Schooling and Society: The Ordering and Reordering of Knowledge in the Western Middle Ages*, ed. A. A. MacDonald and M. W. Twomey, Leuven, Paris and Dudley (MA), 2004, pp. 43-60.
van den Gheyn, J., 'Nicolas Maniacoria, correcteur de la Bible', *Revue Biblique* 8 (1899), pp. 289-295.
Vanek, Klara, *'Ars corrigendi' in der frühen Neuzeit: Studien zur Geschichte der Textkritik*, Berlin 2007.
Varro, *De lingua latina*, ed. G. Goetz and F. Schoell, Leipzig 1910.
Vasoli, Cesare, 'Nuove prospettive su Lorenzo Valla', *Nuova rivista storica* 57 (1973), pp. 448-458.
Vergerio, Pier Paolo (the Elder), *Epistolario*, ed. L. Smith, Rome 1934.
– *Pierpaolo Vergerio the Elder and Saint Jerome: An Edition and Translation of 'Sermones pro Sancto Hieronymo'*, ed. and tr. J. M. McManamon, Tempe 1999.
Vernet, André, *La Bible au moyen âge: Bibliographie*, Paris 1989.
Virgil, *Aeneid*, in his *Opera*, pp. 103-422.
– *Georgica*, in his *Opera*, pp. 29-101.
– *Opera*, ed. R. A. B. Mynors, 10th edn, Oxford 1990.
Vogels, Heinrich Joseph, *Handbuch der neutestamentlichen Textkritik*, Münster i. W. 1923.
Wadding, Luke, *Scriptores ordinis minorum*, Rome 1906, repr. Bologna 1978.
Walsh, Katherine, *A Fourteenth-Century Scholar and Primate: Richard FitzRalph in Oxford, Avignon and Armagh*, Oxford 1981.
Wasserstein, Abraham and David J., *The Legend of the Septuagint: From Classical Antiquity to Today*, Cambridge 2006.
Weber, Robert, 'Deux préfaces au psautier dues à Nicolas Maniacoria', *Revue Bénédictine* 68 (1953), pp. 3-17.
William de Mara, [Preface to his *Correctorium Biblie*], ed. Dahan, 'La critique textuelle', pp. 387-388.
Wilmart, André, 'Nicolas Manjacoria: Cistercien à Trois-Fontaines', *Revue Bénédictine* 33 (1921), pp. 136-143.
Witte, Julius, *Zur Geschichte der Vulgata*, Hanover 1876.

Wittek, Martin, and Glorieux-De Gand, Thérèse, *Manuscrits datés conservés en Belgique*, V: *1481-1540*, Brussels 1987.

Załuska, Yolanta, *L'enluminure et le scriptorium de Cîteaux au XIIe siècle*, Cîteaux 1989.

Zetzel, James E. G., *Latin Textual Criticism in Antiquity*, New York 1981.

תורה נביאים וכתובים: *Biblia Hebraica Stuttgartensia*, ed. K. Elliger et al., 5th edn, Stuttgart 2007.

INDEX OF BIBLICAL REFERENCES

OLD TESTAMENT

Genesis

1.4	120 n40
2.5	63 n52
2.7	29 n1
2.8	24 n49
2.12	120 n39
4.8	118 n33; 203
8.6–7	87 n17
8.7	148 n135
36.24	126 n59
37.28	142

Exodus

5	130 n69

Deuteronomy

27.20	148 n135
27.26	107 n55
32.39	162 and 163 n168

Joshua

11.17	196 n279
12.7	196 n279
19.48	130 n70

2 Kings

5.23	21 n38

Nehemiah

8.1–4	164 n170

4 Esdras

8.30	214 n45

Psalms
31.8	231
34.1	234 n38
34.10	106 n2
34.14	222 n12
39.7	189
41.3	143 n118
44.14	220
45.2	214 n45
45.11	134 n86
62.2	189 n256
86.5	190 n260
101.23	221 n11; 231 n30
103.6–7	222 n12
103.8	222 n12
117.22	228 n24
119.5	230 n29
125.1	221 n11; 231 n30
125.6	220 n9
131.15	184 n242
135.7	203
141.4	221 n11; 222 n12; 231 n30
143.13	230 n27

Proverbs
9.4–5	138

Ecclesiastes
51.18	236

Wisdom
1.7	234 n40
1.11	204

Ecclesiasticus

22.18	227
24.20	196 n280
29.4	214 n45
36.16	196 n280
36.27	214 n45; 237 n46
51.18	214 n45

Isaiah
9.5	191 n263
19.15	92 n27
19.17	92 n27

Jeremiah
23.6	191 n263

Daniel
3.23	82 n5
3.90	82 n5
7.26	82 n5
12	82 n5
12.12	82 n5

Hosea
9.12	191 n263

Jonah
4.6	10

Micah
5.2	108; 109 n10

NEW TESTAMENT

Matthew
1.16	225 n18
2.6	109 n10; 226 n21
2.7	186 n246
2.8	186 n246
3.16	225 n18
5.22	210
10.33	150 n139
13.24-30	172 n192
17.2	188 n253
17.5	186 n246
21.5	210; 211 n32
21.12	188 n253; 211 n32
21.30	180 n217
21.42	228 n24
23.15	225 n16
27.28	226 n21

Mark
1.10	225 n18
5.1	181 n222
7.37	181 n224
8.38	149 n137; 224; 225
9.2	188 n253
16.15	154 n149

Luke
1.4	180 n221
1.72	225 n17
2.24	211 n32
2.33	206; 206 n19
2.48	207 n19
3.22	211 n32; 225 n18
3.34-36	16 n25
6.23	188 n255
8.8	182 n232
9.26	150 n139
9.29	188 n253
10.6	210 n29; 230 n28
12.21-22	182 n232

INDEX OF BIBLICAL REFERENCES

12.35	124 n48
13.9	230 n28
13.15	211 n32
14.34	227
16.2	100
19.4	230 n29
21.38	188
23.29	228 n23

John
1.32	225 n18
6.16	226 n21
7.3	226 n20
7.5	226 n20
7.12	220 n10
7.29-30	186 n247
9.6	226 n21
10.11	123 n47
10.14	123 n47
12.8	188 n255
14.6	205 n17
14.24	228
18.28	186 n248
21.3	181 n224; 234 n38
21.10	181 n224
21.18	234 n39
21.25	172
21.22	see the Index entry *John, Gospel of: 21.22*

Acts
1.17	179 n214
7.14	24 n49
10.5	225 n16
13.46	225 n16
14.1-5	171 n190
15.13-14	181 n223
15.23	226 n19
16.13	230 n29

Romans
3.10   15 n24
11.17   230 n29

1 Corinthians
2.9   98 n46
9.6   166
13.3   108
15.10   180 n218

Galatians
3.3   181 n226
4.24   29 n1
6.2   97
6.12   182 n233

Philippians
1.26   99 n48

1 Thessalonians
2.13   179 n213

1 Timothy
3.2   227 n22

2 Timothy
2.24   227 n22

1 Peter
1.13   180 n215
3.19   180 n215

3 John
4   180 n220

Jude
1.14-15   166

Revelation
2.5	230 n28
2.16	230 n28
10.11	178 n207
22.18-19	165 n172

INDEX OF MANUSCRIPTS

BERNKASTEL–KUES
Hospitalbibliothek
12   192 n269

BRUSSELS
Bibliothèque royale
4031-33   252; 262 n50

DIJON
Bibliothèque municipale
12-15   250 n2
114   139 n110

LONDON
British Library
Add. 17737   82 n5
Add. 39629   173 n194; 196 n279
Add. 40006   173 n194; 254
Egerton 839   50 n7

MADRID
Biblioteca Nacional de España
Vitr. 13-1 (Tol. 2-1)   41 n11

PARIS
Bibliothèque de l'Arsenal
94   19 n33; 138 n104
904   257 n25

BNF
lat. 17   126 n59
lat. 3218   19 n33; 138 n104
lat. 3359   258 n32
lat. 9380   41 n11; 45
lat. 15554   124
nouv. acq. lat. 502   262 n49; 264 n59

PARMA
Biblioteca palatine
28   261 n45

VALENCIA
Biblioteca de la Catedral
170   262 n49

VENICE
Biblioteca Marciana
Lat. Z. 289 (=1681)   252
Lat. class. I, 140   254 n18
Lat. class. I, 141   254 n18

VIENNA
Österreichische Nationalbibliothek
1217   138 n106

INDEX

Page numbers in italics indicate that the entry is found in a footnote only on that particular page. Scholars active after 1600 are not listed. For particular passages of the Bible, see the Index of Biblical References. Because of the vast number of references to Jerome, only the most important ones are given in this index. For the same reason, there are no entries for Latin and Vulgate.

Aaz apprehendens. See
   Interpretationes nominum
   hebraicorum
Abraham Ibn Ezra, 53
acceptability of preparing new
   translations, 246–47
Acts of the Apostles, 37, *262*
additions, 45, 47, 65, 68, 106, 120,
   135, 165, 170, 177, *210*
age of manuscripts (criterion), 109,
   115, 130, 132, 134, 151, 179,
   181, 185, 245
Alcuin, 41, 46
   edition of the Bible, *31*, 39–41,
      44, 45, 47, 128, 135
Alexander of Villa Dei, 218, 220
Alfonso the Magnanimous, *265*
amalgamation. *See* conflation of
   different versions
Ambrose, 71, 99, *178*, 188
Ambrosian Psalter. *See* Psalms:
   Milanese Psalter
anacoluthon, 225
Andrew of St Victor, 24, 62, *245*
antiptosis, 228
antiqui (and equivalents), *21*, *25*,
   45, 64, 70, 88, *91*, *92*, *94*, 124,
   127, 128, *130*, *131*, *132*, 133,
   135, *142*, *147*, *148*, 150, *161*,
   162, *172*, 208
Antonio de la Cerda, *187*
Apocalypse, 37, 165, *178*, 230, *262*

Apollonius Dyscolus, *232*
Aquila, 9, 11, 18, *19*, *65*, 86, *100*,
   102
Arabic, *50*, 52, 53, *106*, 142, 151,
   257
Aramaic, 53
Aristeas, Letter of, 8, *109*, 111
Aristotle, 248
Armagh, 258, 259
Armenian faith, 259
Augustine, 9–29 *passim*, 34, *36*, 50,
   54, 58, 67–87 *passim*, *98*, 99,
   101, 105, 109–16, *119*, 131–
   34, 146, 147, 148, 149, 156,
   170, 171, *172*, 175–90 *passim*,
   204, 205, 212, 225, 234, 243
   on corruption caused by
      copying, 218, 219
   on the importance of Church
      recognition, 74
   on the importance of *consuetudo*,
      112, 116, 202, 247
   on the importance of the source
      languages, 114, 152, 156,
      177
   on the special status of the
      septuaginta, 67, 81, 111, 115,
      171
   on the superiority of old
      manuscripts, 115, 129, 131,
      132

preference for greater number of
manuscripts, 115
Ps.-Augustine, 50
rejects the idea that the Jews
have corrupted their texts,
113
Avignon, 258, 259
Aymeric of Piacenza, *164*
Bacon, Roger, 11, *15*, 17–20, 24,
25, 26, 42, 45, 46, 61–63, 68,
70, 74, 75, 76, 87–95, 100,
101–4, *129*, *136*, 138–53, *169*,
188, 208, 209, 223–25, 235,
238, 244, 247, 257
applies methods used in
correctoria, 143
criticism of *correctoria*, 140–41
dismisses *septuaginta*, 147–48
idea that Jerome had translated
the Bible twic, 91
idea that Jerome had translated
the Bible twice, 93
on the standing of the Vulgate,
63
plan for the restoration of the
Latin Bible, 151–53
possibly influenced by Gerard of
Huy, 143–44
praises a *homo sapientissimus*,
144–46
rejects corrections based on
works of Church Fathers,
149
rejects idea of *simplex* and
composita, 88, 90
uses Eusebius's *canones* for
emendation, 150
Balientz, Nerses. See Nerses
Balientz
Barcelona, 258
Baruch, Book of, 32, *37*, *41*, 44
Bede (the Venerable), 23, *43*, *85*,
92, *149*, *178*, 225, 249
Benedictines, 158, 204, 252
Bernard of Clairvaux, *178*

Bessarion, 12, 76, 101, 103, 136,
169, 175–77, 179, 185, *187*,
212, 215, 234, 238, 245, 252,
254, 261–62, 263
rejects value of the Latin Bible,
74, 75, 213
use of grammar, 232–33
Bethlehem, 31
Bible of St Jacques. *See*
Dominicans: Bible of St Jacques
Bologna, 52, *56*, 137, 162, 164
Bonavia da Lucca, Niccolò, 55
Bourg-Dieu, 252
Bracciolini, Poggio, 72, 98, 100,
103, 182, *264*
Bursfeld congregation, *192*
Calo, Pietro, 51
Cambrai, 260
canon, *32*, 53, 69
Hebrew canon, 32, 37
canones. *See* Eusebius
canticles, 190, 266
Carthusians, *48*, *139*, 191–97, 213,
216, 235–37
text of the Bible, 196, 193–97,
236, 239
veritas and *consuetudo*, 214
Cassiodorus, 35, 39, *92*, *109*, 219,
237
chapter division, 42, 43
Charlemagne, 39, 40, 58, 128
Church Fathers, 12, 13, 17, 20, *29*,
34, 36, 47, 49, 53, 55, 56, 87–
90, 92, 105, 115, 119, 123,
126, 127, 131–35, *136*, 143,
149, 150, 176–79, *188*, 190,
191, 194, 195, 212, 221, 245
Greek, 177
value of their works for
reconstructing the text of the
Bible, 149
Cicero, *109*
Ciriaco of Ancona, 186, 187, *263*
Cistercians, 9, *48*, 59, 60, 116,
122, *139*, *216*, 250
Cîteaux, 250

Clement IV (pope), 152, 153, 257
collation, 30, 41, 45, 105, 115,
    120, 125–31, 135, 142–43,
    143, 150, 153, 154, *158*, 162,
    185, 251, 253, 254
  criteria suggested by Augustine,
    115
  of biblical commentaries, 128
  of biblical passages from the
    works of the Church Fathers,
    131, *133*, 135
  of Greek, 109, 129, 131, 135,
    182
  of Hebrew, 41, 106, 117, 128,
    129, 131, 135, 251
communis, 21, 22, 23, 125, *130*
  editio, 15
  littera, 21, 23, *95*, 125, 127,
    129, 130
  translatio, 22, 23, 64, 95
Conclusions, book of. *See De
  constructione*
concordance to the Bible, 195, 255
  concordantiae maiores, *195*
  concordantiae minores, *195*
conflation of different versions, 33,
  34, 48, 59, 70, 83, 87, 104,
  243, 244
consuetudo, 5, *26*, *31*, *83*, 112, *119*,
  131, 199–216, 236, 237, 246,
  247, *See also usus*
  as a criterion for establishing the
    correct text, 213–15
  different types, 212
contamination, 48, 70, 83, 87, 90,
  94, 244, *See also* conflation of
  different versions
Conversini, Giovanni, 55
correctiones Senonenses. *See*
  Dominicans:*correctiones
  Senonenses*
correctoria, 4, *13*, 16, 20–25 *passim*,
  42, 44, 45, *47*, 124–39, 191,
  207, 208, 213, 222, 244, 248,
  249, 253–57
  and Roger Bacon, 140–46

  purpose, 136
  Sorbonne II, 22, 23, 124, 125,
    127, 130, *133*, *135*, *136*, 138
  terminology used to designate
    versions of the Bible, 124–28
corruption, 3, 12, 31, 32, 45–47,
  60, 66, 70, 71, 82, 83, *89*, 93–
  104 *passim*, 113, 118, *125*, 129,
  131, 140–74 *passim*, 195, 202,
  208, 209, 213, 219–25 *passim*,
  244, 245, 249, 252
  by exegetes, 83
  by heretics, 171, 185, 245
  by Jews, 107, 113, 115, 118,
    119, 122, 130, 131, 153,
    156, 160, 168, 171, 185,
    191, 245
  by scribes, *15*, 31, 33, 42, 47,
    64, 70, 83, 90, 91, 94, 99,
    101, 102, 104, 114, 161,
    177, 195, 209, 218, 221,
    237, 239, 245
councils, *35*, 67, 69, *96*, 123, 161,
  170
  authority of, 123
  Council of Constance, 260
  Council of Ferrara and Florence,
    261
  Council of Ferrara and Florence,
    261
  Council of Trent, 6, 13, *34*, 74
  Fourth Council of Toledo
    (633), *36*
  Second Council of Seville (619),
    36
Crastone, Giovanni, 26, 74, 76, *85*,
  102, 103, 183, *184*, 185, 189,
  190, 215, 235, 246, 266
  use of grammar, 233–34
Creed, 157, *261*
Cyprian, 12, 206, *227*
Cyril of Jerusalem (ps.), 50
Damasus I (pope), 30, 31, 34, 37,
  38, 71, 72
Daniel, Book of, *16*, 52, 53, 82,
  83, *86*, 93, *128*

Dardanoni, Ambrogio, *264*
Dati, Agostino, 55
De constructione, 223
decline of critical studies, 248
Déols, 252
deutero-canonical books, *37*
divine inspiration, 53, 59, *63*, 65, 69, 73, 75, 76, 101, 109, 111, 114, *164*, 169, 170, 183, 211, 212, 218, 219, 222, 243, 248
Docking, Thomas, *253*
Dominic (Saint), *51*
Dominicans, 19, *48*, 50, 85, 124, 125, 128, 129, 135, 137–44, 162, 164, 187, 191, *216*, 249, 253, 254, 255, 258
    Bible of St Jacques, 125, 137, 254, 255
    convent of St Jacques, 125, 255
    correctiones Senonenses, 126, 137, 138, 139
    General Chapter of 1236, *126*, 137, 138
    General Chapter of 1251, *137*
    General Chapter of 1256, 137
    General Chapter of 1257, *139*
    General Chapter of 1258, *139*
    General Chapter of 1259, *139*
    General Chapters, 141
Donato, Ludovico (Bishop of Bergamo), *74*
Donatus, 217, 219, 223, 224, 238, 239
Durand, William, 25
Easton, Adam, 158, 174, 246, *248*
Ecclesiasticus, 32, *37*, *128*, *196*, 228
Eleazar, 67, 84, 170
emendation, 3–5, 31, 39, 46, 74, 75, 81, 96, 100, 101, 103, *114*, 119, 123, 124, 131, 140, *144*, 149, 150, 160, 161, 177–215, 217, 223, 225, 233, 235, 237–49, 264
    by Alcuin, 40
    by Jerome, 8, 31, 37, 73, *106*, *131*, *219*, *254*
    by means of parallel passages, 109
    of liturgical texts, 122, *140*, *192*, 252
England, *29*, *32*, *47*, 250
Enoch, 165
Erasmus of Rotterdam, *262*
Eugenius III (pope), 250, *See also* Paganelli, Bernardo
Eugenius IV (pope), *261*
Eusebius of Caesarea, *87*, 150
    canones, 150
Eusebius of Cremona (ps.), 50, 53
Eustochium, *33*
exegesis, 4, *120*, 136, 208, *258*
    as tool for detemining the correct text, 179
    as tool for determining the correct text, *169*, 176, *212*
    may lead to corruption, 83
exemplar vulgatum, 21, 142, 146
Ezra, 162, 163
Ezra, Book of, *53*
Filioque, 261
FitzRalph, Richard, *18*, 21, 22, 23, 64, 74, 95, 96, 104, *125*, *130*, 159–70, 174, 175, 209, 238, 243, 258–59
    authority of Church council, 161
    on three translations, 22, 64, 95
    translatio communis, 64, 95
    use of reason, 160–61
Five Books of Moses. See Pentateuch
France, 36, 127, 253
Franciscans, 129, 135, 140, *142*, 144, 195, 253, 256, 257
Franciscus Thebaldus, 56
Fretela, *15*, 201
Friesoythe, 259
Frisia, 259

George of Trebizond, *53*, 73, 101, *103*, *176*, 177–79, 179, *185*, 215, *244*, *247*, 261–62
  attributes separate authority to translation, 177, 185
  claims that the Vulgate was divinely inspired, 73, 75, 243
  on *consuetudo* and *veritas*, 211–13
  use of grammar, 232–33
Gerard of Huy, 12, *15*, 16–18, 20, 25, *45*, 61–63, 76, 85, 86, 103, 126, 131–36, 140, 144, 143–46, *151*, *188*, 207, 208, 212, 222, 223, 235, 238, 244, 245, *247*, 256–57
  possible influence on Roger Bacon, 143–44
  rules out existence of a third translation, 86
Germany, 49, *51*
Giovanni d'Andrea, 52–54, 56, 57, *76*
Giovanni da Tivoli, 186, 187
Gisla (Charlemagne's sister), 40
Gospels, 30, 31, 34, 37, 38, *40*, 74, 98, 109, 122, 150, 155, 172, 174, 187, 210, 213, 225
graeca veritas, 7, 23–26, 26, 30, *71*, *73*, 162, 179, *180*, 184, *188*
grammar, 5, 40, *144*, *149*, *152*, 200, 210, 237, **217–40**, 246, 247
  Bible not subject to grammar, 218–21
  standard set by classical authors, 226–29
Grande Chartreuse, 192, 193, 195, 196, 214, 236
Gratian, *108*, *156*, 171, 204, 205, *206*, 212
Greece, 261
Greek
  Church, 20, 111, 112
  manuscripts, 71, 107, 108, 109, 113, 114, 126, 132, 133, 136, 151, 160, 168, 171, 172, 175, 177, 179, 180, 182, 183, 184, 185, 187, 189, 197, 245, 263
  New Testament, 25, 26, 36, 72, 96, 101, 104, 105, 129, 176, 181–83, 193, 209, 211, 212, *247*, 253, 262
  translation of Old Testament, 245
  translation of the Old Testament, 8–10, 12, 16, 18, 81, *82*, 90, 100, 101, 110, 111, 113, 115, 119, 126, 148, 162, 168, 190, 246
Gregory the Great, *20*, 35, *59*, 86, *129*, 148, 149, 208, 219, 247
Guarino Veronese, 55
Guillelmus Brito, *255*
Gutenberg, Johannes, *42*
Hagiographa, *33*
Harding, Stephen, *13*, 23, 59, 60, 75, 116, 117, 121, 122, 128, *244*, *247*, *248*, 250
hebraica veritas, 7, 11, 23–26, 68, *69*, *83*, *84*, *101*, *108*, *117*, *119*, *122*, *133*, 162, *165*, 194, 195
Hebrew
  manuscript allegedly written by Ezra, 162, 163
  manuscripts, 106, 107, 115–22 *passim*, 126–33 *passim*, 133, 151, 153, 156, 157, 160, 168, 171, 183–85, 197, 245
  manuscripts owned by Christians, 168
  original, 23–26, *33*, 65, 67, 68, *83*, 91, 105–7, 110, 113, 114, 118, 119, 122, 129, 131, 136, 148, 156, 170, 182, 183, 193, 195, 202, 203, 246, 253
  predilection for, 245
  superiority of, 107
Hebrew Bible, *37*, 63, *69*, 157, *163*
Heiric of Auxerre, *206*

heretics, *65*, *66*, *92*, 171–73, 185, 191, 245
Hermas, *32*
Hervaeus of Bourg–Dieu, 13, 26, 60, 61, 76, 108, 122, 123, 129, 196, 204, 205, 204–6, 206, 208, 215, 252–53
Hexapla, *9*, 12, 15, *31*, 102
Hilary, 12, 71, 99
Holy See, 35, 61, 89, 129, *146*
Holy Spirit, 53, 65, 66, 67, 73, *109*, *164*, *167*, *170*, 174, *175*, *205*, 210, *213*, *234*
Homer, 208
Horace, 207, 208
Hrabanus Maurus, 41, 45, *92*, *128*, *134*
Hugh of St Cher, 19, 20, 21, *26*, 45, 75, 85, 103, 124, *126*, 128, 129, 135–39, *151*, *192*, 207, 208, 215, *253*, 254, 255–56
  authorship of works attributed to him, 255–56
Hugh of St Victor, 18, 19, 18–20, 59, 60, 74, 83, 84, 87, 244
Iberian peninsula, 35
Ilchester, 257
Interpretationes nominum hebraicorum, 43, *196*
Ireland, 258
Isaac (orthography of), *222*
Isidore of Seville, *18*, 20, 35, 39, 58, 61, 62, 63, 65, *66*, 67, 81, 85, 89, 90, *92*, 93, 148, 151, 243
Itala, *36*
Italy, 34, 36, 49, 52, 56, 57, 245, 252, 261, *263*, *266*
Ivo of Chartres, *206*
Jacobus de Colonna (bishop of Lombez), *54*
Jerome
  attitudes towards Jerome and the Vulgate, 57–77
  claims to have translated the entire Bible, 36
  depiction in the visual arts, 56
  family background as reason for his authority, 65
  forged letters about, 51
  involvement in the *Gallicanum*, 101–2, 103
  knowledge of various languages, 50
  on *consuetudo*, 201
  on the Jews' alleged corruption of manuscripts, 107
  on the *septuaginta*, 109–11
  on the value of Hebrew manuscripts, 106, 107, 129, 152
  on the value of old manuscripts, 109
  rejects emendation based on parallel passages, 108–9
  stages of his work on the biblical text, 30–32
  translated the Bible twice according to Bacon, 93, 95, 144
  veneration of, 49–57, 57, 243
Jeronimites, 56
Jews, 8, 10, 67, *84*, 159, 160, 168, 173
  consultation of, 112, 116, 117, 120, 122
  converted, *42*, *163*
  reasons for allegedly willful corruption, 156
  rivalry with Christians, 155
  said to have willfully corrupted their texts, 107, 113, 115, 118, 119, 130, 153, 155–56, 160, 164, 168, 171–72, 185, 191, 245
  would not willfully corrupt their texts, 155, 157
Job, Book of, *19*, *31*, 53, 65, 106, 112, 148, 149, 201
  translated from Arabic, 52
Johannes (prior of the Grande Chartreuse), *193*

John Cassian, 34
John Kernatzi, 259
John of Garland, 220
John of Neumarkt, 51
John, Gospel of, 172, 175, 228, 234, *262*
   21.22, 12, 73, 175, 176, 178, *185*, 211, 212, 232, 252, 261, 263
Josephus, 9, 10, 67, 88, 89, 142
Jude, Epistle of, 165, 167
Judith, Book of, 32, 36, 37
Justin Martyr, 9
Juvenal, *227*
Kernatzi, John. *See* John Kernatzi
Kings, Books of, *33*, 117, *121*
Lanfranc of Bec, *46*
Le Puy, 260
Leander of Seville, 35
Libru di lu transitu et vita di misser sanctu Iheronimu, 51
liturgical texts, 61, 88, 122, 123, 137, 139, 191, 192, 196, 216, 249
   breviary, *31*, 190
   lectionary, 60, 122, 123, 252
liturgy, 5, 14, *32*, 34, 88, 89, 196, 204, 216
Livy, 231
Lucius II (pope), *252*
Luke, Gospel of, 123, *150*, *188*, 206, 228, *230*
Maccabees, Books of, 32, *37*, *128*
Macer Floridus, 228
Mammotrectus, 195
Manetti, Giannozzo, 76, 101, 102, 103, 183, 185, 246, 265
Maniacutia, Nicolò, 9, 10, 16, 24, 25, *48*, 49, 75, 76, 87, 122, *133*, 191, 203, 204, 206, 208, 223, 235, 244–46, 248, 250–52, *262*
   approach to Hebrew manuscripts, 118–20, 122
   on *consuetudo* and *veritas*, 202–4, 215
   on grammar, 221–22, 238
   on the status and survival of Jerome's rendering, 59–60
   on the transmission of the Latin Bible, 81–84
   rejects quantity as a criterion, 120–21
Marchesini, Giovanni, 195
Marchesinus e Regio, *195*
Mark, Gospel of, 224, *262*
Martí, Ramon, *18*, 153–58, 158, 258
   arguments against corrupt transmission, 155
   claims that Jews had corrupted their texts, 155–56
   on the status of the Vulgate, 63
   provides his own translation from the Hebrew, 156, 246
   transmission in different languages preserves correct sense, 153–54
Masoretic text, *245*
Matthew, Gospel of, *150*, *262*
Methusaleh, 113
Metz, 36
Milan, 187, 266
moderni, 88, 124, *132*, *133*, 135, 150, *156*, *172*, *193*, *208*, 224, 236
Naples, *262*, 263
Natali, Pietro de', 51
neologisms, 210, 227
Nepote, Fernando, 221
   criticism of Lorenzo Valla, *221*
Nerses Balientz, 259
Netherlands, 49
New Testament, 10, 12, 23, 26, 36, *37*, 52, 72, 96–98, 101, *134*, *150*, 154, 155, *160*, 167, 172–85, 211, 213, 215, 230, *232*, 234, 245, *247*, 262–65
   doubts concerning Jerome's contribution, 96, 99, 104
   increased interest in, 245

minor role in medieval discussions, 105
multitude of translators, 100
Nicholas of Cusa, *192*, 254, 263
Nicholas of Lyra, *191*, *258*
Nicholas V (pope), 246, 265
Nogarola, Isotta, 55
Notabilia quedam de correctione librorum, *196*, 214, 215
Old Latin. *See* Vetus Latina
Old Testament, 8–10, 12, 23, 31, 32, *38*, 59, *93*, 100, 105–7, *110*, 111, 133, 147, 148, 156, *160*, 162, 165, 167, 174, 183, 234, 246, 265
   books translated by Jerome, 37
   cannot be corrupt, 155
   criticism of Jerome's translation, 113
   focus of medieval scholars, 105
   not entirely translated by the Seventy translators, 10, 81
   not translated entirely by Jerome, 85
   translated entirely by the Seventy translators, 9
omissions, 65, 68, 105, 119, 120, 135, 165, 166, 170, *196*
Origen, *9*, 15, *19*, *31*, 102, *170*
original language (authority of), 106, 108, 114, 117, 118, 122, 129, *133*, 136, *152*, 156, 168, 183, 184, 185, *253*
orthography, 5, 35, 40, 192, 194, *214*, *219*, *222*, 235, 251
   local variants, 194
   of Hebrew names, 196
Oswaldus de Corda, 191–97, 213, *239*, 247
   on grammar, 235–37
Ovid, 207
Oxford, 257, 258
Paganelli, Bernardo, 250, *251*, *See also* Eugenius III (pope)
Pammachius, 110
pandects, 33, 40, *41*
parallel passages, 108, 150, 163, 167, 187, 225
Paris, 45, *124*, 125, 137, 138, *248*, 255, 256, 257, 260
   University of, 43, *58*, *258*, 259, 260
Paris Bible, 21–22, 36, 42–46, 46, 47, 58, 70, 91–93, 95, 121, 124–25, 143, 150, *168*, *169*, *173*, 247, 248, 254
   Bacon's account of the origin, 42
   identifying features, 43
   medieval appellations, 127, 130
   status of, 132, 135, 140, 146–47
   text of, 46
Paschasius Radbertus, 219
Pater Noster, *216*
Paul of Middleburg, 85
Paula, *33*
Pentateuch, 8, 9, 10, 16, 81, 147, 148, 155, *163*
   Samaritan, *107*
Peter Comestor, 18–20, 255
Peter Lombard, *172*
   Sentences, 249, 255, 260
Peter of Ailly, *53*, 74, 76, *96*, 159, 174, 175, 238, 247, 260
   criticism of Roger Bacon, 68
   exalts the Vulgate, 67–70, 75, 76, 243
Peter Olivi, 254
Petrarch, *54*, *76*, *134*
Petrucci, Antonello, *264*
Philemon, Epistle to, *262*
Phocas, 227
Piacenza, 266
Pietro da Monte, 261
Poliziano, Angelo, 187
Prague, 259
   University of, 259
prefaces to books of the Bible, *31*, 43, 53, 81, *173*, 201
   role in establishing the translator, 84, 85, 95, 102, 103

INDEX 307

Priscian, 217, 220, 222–24, 227, 228, 232, 234, 238, 246
pronunciation, 193
provenance of manuscripts, 186, 187, 191
Proverbs, Book of, 44, *85*
Ps.-Augustine. *See* Augustine: Ps.-Augustine
Psalms, 25, 26, 30–32, *37*, 61, 74, 90–93, 98, 101, 102, 103, 119, *142*, 183, 185, 189, 190, 201, 202, 203, 215, 221, 231, 233, 246, 251, *255*, 265, 266
  Milanese Psalter, 189, 190
  Psalterium Gallicanum, 24, 31, 37, *62*, 90, 91, 103, 101–4, *201*
  Psalterium iuxta Hebraeos, 25, 32, 83, 90, 100, 101, 120, 203, 251
  Psalterium Romanum, 24, 30, 59, 83, 119, 203
Ptolemy II, 8–10, *109*, *111*, *114*, 166, *169*, *171*
punctuation, 40, 137
quantity of text (criterion), 116, 120–21, 121
  in the Paris Bible, 45
quinta, 18, 19, *20*, 86, *204*
Quintilian, *232*
Ralph of Beauvais, *217*, 220
reason (criterion), 160–61, *227*
rectus textus, 125, 249
Reformation, 6
Remigius of Auxerre, *42*, *43*
rivalry of faiths
  ensures correct transmission, 155
Romagna, *50*
Rome, 35, 37, *50*, *99*, 181, 187, 250, 263
Rotrud (Charlemagne's daughter), 40
Rufinus (decretist), *171*
Rufinus of Aquileia, *13*, 37
Rupert of Deutz, *16*, 24

Russel, John, *253*
S. Eufemia (monastery), *57*
Salutati, Coluccio, *144*
Salzburg, 36
San Crisogono (church), 187
San Lorenzo in Damaso (church), 250
San Salvatore (church), 187
Santo dei Pellegrini, *55*
scribes, 3, 39, *99*, 120, *125*, 136, *141*, 192, 193, 194, 196, 213, 235, 237, *246*, 248, *See* also Corruption:by scribes
sedes apostolica. *See* Holy See
Sedulius Scotus, *15*, 36
sela, 204
Seneca the Younger, *227*
sense, original, 153, 154, 161, 169
  and textual diversity, 165–67
septima, 86
Septuagint, 7–15, *17*, 18, 19, 26, 30, *33*, *34*, 82, *93*, 101, 106, 107, 109–14, 115, 126, *132*, *134*, 148, *160*, *163*, 171, 183, 218, *266*
septuaginta, 7, *24*, 25, *33*, *45*, 59, *62*, *63*, 64, 74, 75, 76, *84*, 86, 87, 90–95, *100*, *102*, 103, 105, *107*, *109*, 126, *132*, *133*, 134, *143*, 153, 156, 157, 162, 170, 171, 194, 195, *201*, *204*, *209*, 218, *219*, 243, 244
  divine inspiration of, 53, 75
  does not have a special status, 147, 148
  medieval use of the term, 8–13
  omnipresence of, 58, 82, 86
  preferred by Augustine, 67
  status according to Jerome and Augustine, 110–16
  superior to the Vulgate, 72, 81
  terminological relationship with *vulgata*, 14–22
  textual differences from the Vulgate, 165, 166

used by Church Fathers for their commentaries, *135*
sexta, *19*, 86, *100*
Somerset, 257
Spain, *32*, 36, 56, 57
St Jacques. *See* Dominicans
St Martin of Tours (monastery), 39
Statuta Jancelini, 192
Steuco, Agostino, 85
style, 174, 180, 210, 230, 264
Subirats, 258
Sunnia, *15*, 201
Symmachus, 9, 18, *65*, 86, *204*
syntax, 225
Talmud, 156
Teobaldo (bishop of Verona), *56*
Tertullian, 29
Theodore Gaza, 73, 178, 212, 261
Theodotion, 9, 11, *16*, 18, *65*, 82, 86, 93, *100*, *204*
Theodulf of Orleans, *32*, 39, *40*, 41, 44–46, 121, 128, 135, *147*, *248*
Thomas Aquinas, *76*, *178*, 244
tikkun soferim, 156
Tobit, Book of, 32, 36, 37
Toletanus, 41
Tomacello, Marino, *264*
Torah, *8*, *164*
Tortelli, Giovanni, 264
Totting, Henry, 18, *63*, 64–67, 75, 76, *96*, *108*, 170–75, 238, 243, 249, 259–60
Tours, 39, 40
Translatio corporis S. Hieronymi, 50
Tre Fontane (monastery), 250, *251*
uniformity (textual), *41*
    attempt at creating, 191, 196
    call for, *139*, 216
    lack of, 192
    lack of, 29, *46*, 47, 84
Urban VI (pope), *158*
usus, 201–8, 213, 215, 216, *See also* consuetudo
Valdebonum, *192*, *193*

Valla, Lorenzo, 26, 76, 95, 101, 104, 181, 183, 187–89, 191, 211, *213*, 215, *216*, *221*, 232, 233, 234, 235, 238, 244, 245, 248, 262–65, 265
    attitude towards Church Fathers, 72–73, 99
    authority of Greek manuscripts, 179, 180–81, 182
    critique of Jerome's 'Preface to the Gospels', 38, 71–72, 77
    disputes Jerome's translatorship of the entire NT, 104
    on *consuetudo* and *veritas*, 209–11
    on Latin manuscripts, 181
    on provenance of manuscripts, 185–87
    on the authority of Greek manuscripts, 179–81
    on the multitude of translations, 100–101
    on the status of the Latin Bible, 182–83
    on the Vulgate, 96–97
    on transmission, 99–100
    role of *interpres*, 97–99
    use of grammar, 225–31
    use of grammar for emendation of the Latin Bible, 225–31
vatis, 66, 67, *109*
Veneto, 50
Vergerio, Pier Paolo (the Elder), 54, 55
veritas, 5, 26, *31*, *70*, 73, *92*, 97, 114, *118*, *121*, 132, *141*, 147, *149*, *152*, *153*, *155*, *157*, 162, *166*, *167*, *169*, 173, 174, *176*, 199–216, *219*, 246, 247
Vetus Latina, 8–15, *19*, *22*, 29, 30, 32–37, 37, 44, 47, 48, 81, 87, 88, 92, 102, 106, 108–12, 116, *126*, 132, *134*, 148, 168, 218
Vienna
    University of, 259

INDEX 309

Virgil, 207, 211, 228, 229, *230*, 231–34, 238, 246
vulgata, 7, *8*, 9, 10, 13–20, 23, *86*, *87*, 90, *92*, *93*
   difference between *vulgata* and *vulgatus/-um*, 21
William de Mara, 21, 23, *24*, 75, 127–35, 143–46, *151*, 245, 254, 256, 257

William of Conches, 220, 222
Windesheim congregation, *192*
Wisdom, Book of, 32, *37*, *128*
Xenophon, *109*
κοινή, 15, 20
תקון סופרים. See tikkun soferim

www.ingramcontent.com/pod-product-compliance
Lightning Source LLC
Chambersburg PA
CBHW030523230426
43665CB00010B/737